Peter Wallensteen

UNDERSTANDING CONFLICT RESOLUTION

FOURTH EDITION

Los Angeles | London | New Delhi
Singapore | Washington DC | Boston

Los Angeles | London | New Delhi
Singapore | Washington DC

SAGE Publications Ltd
1 Oliver's Yard
55 City Road
London EC1Y 1SP

SAGE Publications Inc.
2455 Teller Road
Thousand Oaks, California 91320

SAGE Publications India Pvt Ltd
B 1/I 1 Mohan Cooperative Industrial Area
Mathura Road
New Delhi 110 044

SAGE Publications Asia-Pacific Pte Ltd
3 Church Street
#10-04 Samsung Hub
Singapore 049483

Editor: Natalie Aguilera
Assistant editor: James Piper
Production editor: Katie Forsythe
Copyeditor: Clare Weaver
Indexer: W.D. Farrington
Marketing manager: Sally Ransom
Cover design: Francis Kenney
Typeset by: C&M Digitals (P) Ltd, Chennai, India
Printed and bound by CPI Group (UK) Ltd,
Croydon, CR0 4YY

Library of Congress Control Number: 2014952242

British Library Cataloguing in Publication data

A catalogue record for this book is available from
the British Library

MIX
Paper from
responsible sources
FSC
www.fsc.org   FSC® C013604

ISBN 978-1-4739-0210-7
ISBN 978-1-4739-0211-4 (pbk)

UNDERSTANDING CONFLICT RESOLUTION

SAGE was founded in 1965 by Sara Miller McCune to support the dissemination of usable knowledge by publishing innovative and high-quality research and teaching content. Today, we publish more than 750 journals, including those of more than 300 learned societies, more than 800 new books per year, and a growing range of library products including archives, data, case studies, reports, conference highlights, and video. SAGE remains majority-owned by our founder, and after Sara's lifetime will become owned by a charitable trust that secures our continued independence.

Los Angeles | London | Washington DC | New Delhi | Singapore

To Lena

TABLE OF CONTENTS

TABLE OF CONTENTS

TABLE OF CONTENTS

LIST OF FIGURES

LIST OF TABLES

ABOUT THE AUTHOR

Peter Wallensteen is Senior Professor of Peace and Conflict Research at Uppsala University, Uppsala, Sweden, since 2012. He held the Dag Hammarskjöld Chair of Peace and Conflict Research, Uppsala University (1985–2012). He is also the Richard G. Starmann, Senior Research Professor of Peace Studies at the Kroc Institute for International Peace Studies, University of Notre Dame, Indiana, USA (since 2006). He directs the Uppsala Conflict Data Program (UCDP) and the Special Program on International Targeted Sanctions (SPITS). His *Understanding Conflict Resolution: War, Peace and the Global System* (Sage, earlier edition, available also in an Arabic translation) is used in teaching around the world. His book *Peace Research: Theory and Practice* (Routledge 2011) demonstrates his range of research interests and has recently been translated into Chinese. Recently he also edited together with Ambassador Anders Bjurner *Regional Organizations and Peacemaking: Challengers to the UN?* (Routledge 2015). In 2010, he and Isak Svensson published *The Go-Between* (United States Institute of Peace Press), a study of mediation efforts by the renowned Swedish diplomat Jan Eliasson. Wallensteen has published widely on conflict trends, conflict resolution, mediation, prevention, sanctions and the United Nations.

PREFACE TO 4TH EDITION

The world of conflict resolution is constantly changing. The surprising Arab Spring of 2011 initially seemed promising but unleashed an unforeseen series of events, affecting the Middle East, adjacent regions and major power relations. Similarly, the ambition to peacefully incorporate Ukraine into the EU orbit set in motion dynamics that led to a war in the country and concerns for all of Russia's neighbours. The 4th edition takes up these issues, but also highlights achievements in peace processes.

The first two parts of the book retain the structure from previous editions, of course, updated as far as possible and until mid-2014. The third part of the book has been somewhat reorganized to incorporate more on regional organizations (Chapter 9) and enlarging the tools available for international conflict resolution: Chapter 10 deals with negative, coercive instruments (sanctions, peacekeeping, peace enforcement) and Chapter 11 takes up positive, peaceful ones (prevention, mediation, disarmament, peacebuilding). Finally, Chapter 12 discusses present challenges and new resources, ranging from geopolitics to gender equality.

It is my hope that the 4th edition makes clear the continued relevance of conflict resolution in seemingly turbulent times. I wish to thank all the team members of the Uppsala Conflict Data Program (UCDP), Uppsala University, for their continued good work and for support in working on this particular addition. The Kroc Institute's Peace Accords Matrix, University of Notre Dame, has become an important source on peace agreements and been valuable for this edition.

Also for this edition, my good friend Bill Montross has taken his time to react in most helpful ways to this manuscript. Finally, let me record that this edition would not have been possible without the continuous support from my wife Lena. It is dedicated to her.

Peter Wallensteen
Uppsala, Sweden and Notre Dame, USA
September 2014

LIST OF ABBREVIATIONS

ABM	Anti-Ballistic Missiles Treaty
AKP	Justice and Development Party (Turkey)
AKUF	Causes of War project, Hamburg
ALBA	European Support operation in Albania
AMISOM	African Union Mission to Somalia
ANC	African National Congress (South Africa)
AQIM	Al-Qaida in the Maghreb
ARTEMIS	European Union Force in the Democratic Republic of Congo
ASEAN	Association of South East Asian Nations
ATT	Arms Trade Treaty
AU	African Union
BATNA	Best Alternative To Negotiated Agreement
CIS	Commonwealth of Independent States
COPAZ	National Commission for the Consolidation of Peace, El Salvador
COW	Correlates of War Project
CSCE	Conference for Security and Cooperation in Europe
DDR	Disarmament, Demobilization and Reintegration of ex-combatants
DRC	Democratic Republic of Congo
ECOWAS	Economic Community for West African States
EPLF	Eritrean People's Liberation Front
EPRDF	Ethiopia Peoples Revolutionary Democratic Front
EU	European Union
FMLN	Farabundo Marti Front for National Liberation, El Salvador
GCC	Gulf Cooperation Council
IAEA	International Atomic Energy Agency
ICC	International Criminal Court
ICFY	International Conference on Former Yugoslavia
ICJ	International Court of Justice
IGAD	Inter-Governmental Agency for Development
INF	Intermediate Nuclear Force
IRA	Irish Republican Army, Provisional, Northern Ireland
ISAF	International security assistance force (Afghanistan)

LIST OF ABBREVIATIONS

ISIS	Islamic State of Iraq and Syria
KFOR	Kosovo Force (NATO-led UN operation)
KLA	Kosovo Liberation Army, UCK
LRA	Lord's Resistance Army, Uganda
LTTE	Liberation Tigers of Tamil Eelam
MINURCA	UN Mission in the Central African Republic
MINUSMA	United Nations Multidimensional Integrated Stabilization Mission in Mali
MONUCSCO	UN Stabilization Mission in DRC
NAM	Non-Aligned Movement
NATO	North Atlantic Treaty Organisation
NGO	Non-governmental organisation
NPA	New People's Army, of the Communist Party of the Philippines
NPT	Non-Proliferation Treaty
OAS	Organisation of American States
OAU	Organisation of African Unity
OECD	Organisation for Economic Cooperation and Development
OHR	Office of the High Representative, Bosnia-Herzegovina
OIC	Organisation for Islamic Cooperation
ONUCA	United Nations Observer Group in Central America
OPCW	Organisation on the Prohibition of Chemical Weapons
OSCE	Organisation for Security and Cooperation in Europe
PAM	Peace Accords Matrix, University of Notre Dame
PIF	Pacific Islands Forum
PKK	Kurdistan Workers' Party, Turkey
PLO	Palestinian Liberation Organisation
PNG	Papua New Guinea
PRIO	Peace Research Institute, Oslo
R2P	Responsibility to Protect
SAARC	South Asian Association for Regional Cooperation
SADC	Southern African Development Community
SDLP	Social Democratic and Liberal Party, Northern Ireland
SIPRI	Stockholm International Peace Research Institute
SSR	Security Sector Reform
SWAPO	South West African People's Organisation
UCDP	Uppsala Conflict Data Program, Uppsala University
UCK	Kosovo Liberation Army, KLA
UK	United Kingdom of Great Britain and Northern Ireland
UN	United Nations
UNHCHR	UN High Commissioner for Human Rights
UNHCR	UN High Commissioner for Refugees
UNITA	National Union for the Total Independence of Angola
UNMOVIC	United Nations Monitoring, Verification and Inspection Commission, Iraq

LIST OF ABBREVIATIONS

UNPREDEP   United Nations Preventive Deployment Force, Macedonia
UNSCOM   United Nations Special Commission, Iraq
UNTSO   United Nations Truce Supervision Organization, Middle East
US, USA   United States of America
WTO   World Trade Organization

PART ONE
THE PROBLEM AND
HOW TO APPROACH IT

1

UNDERSTANDING CONFLICT RESOLUTION

1.1 Peacemaking as a New Experience

Since the Cold War ended there have been more peace agreements than in any period after the termination of the Second World War. Many of these accords curtailed violence successfully and transformed conflicts into more constructive relations between states, peoples and groups. Others failed utterly and remained signatures on paper with no effect in the lives of human beings exposed to the dangers of warfare. There is, consequently, a need to understand conflict resolution in a new way. It is not enough for the outside world to ask for negotiations and contacts between warring parties. There is also a need to suggest what the parties should discuss, how they may agree, how agreements can be turned into reality and, not least, how settlements can be made durable and freeing new generations from repeating bitter war experiences. It is, furthermore, important to ask what can be learned for effective conflict prevention, allowing for just aspirations to develop without systematic and deliberate violence.

In the early 1990s knowledge in conflict resolution for war conditions was limited. There was considerable insight in negotiations in domestic political affairs and in the art of deal-making. Understanding was generated from societies and conditions, which involved little violence and war. It referred to situations of shared values and norms, where few cultural borders were transgressed. However, conflict resolution takes on an entirely different dimension when parties have been trying to kill each other. In the management of conflict between employers and employees there is the threat of strikes and lockouts. This is not the same as when negotiators, their families, relatives, friends and colleagues have been under armed attack by the other side. Involving issues of life and death, war is a qualitatively different form of conflict. Negotiation and peacemaking in ending wars can learn from other experiences but face unique problems. The issues at hand – the incompatibilities – are central to such an analysis and are likely to concern major questions of society and its direction. Also crucial are the ways to end the fighting. This has to be done without inviting a repetition of war. It also has to meet standards of justice and, at the same time, provide physical security for the opposing sides. There is a need to compensate for sufferings that cannot be compensated or redressed. Norms of human relations have been violently broken, leaving the difficult task of finding sufficiently shared grounds on which to build a new relationship. There is the requirement that the opposing sides be equally committed to viewing an agreement as *theirs*, and to taking responsibility for implementing it under conditions which may be novel to the society. Thus, there are reasons for analysts to believe that peacemaking after war is a losing proposition. Still, it takes place and it seems to be working. How this is possible is what this book is all about.

Only in the early 1990s did the world start seriously to attend to peacemaking after war. During the Cold War, negotiations and agreements on issues that involved the use of weapons were few and limited. There was a peace agreement on Indochina in 1954, but, like its successor in 1973, it was quickly undermined. There were also settlements between India and Pakistan after the 1965 and 1971 wars, achieving a reduction in tension, but not an end to the incompatibility. The emphasis in the major power confrontation of the time, the Cold War, was victory, not compromise. The ideological components and the historical record made the Cold War an existential battle. It was waged between right and wrong, democracy and dictatorship, capitalism and socialism, liberation and imperialism. Compromise was seen as morally questionable. The same attitude was reflected in other disputes of the period, whether related to the Cold War or not.

There were reasons for this aversion to negotiated resolution. The memory of the flawed and failed agreement at Munich in September 1938 haunted some of the actors. At that time, the democratic countries (Britain and France) agreed with a totalitarian one (Nazi Germany) on the dissolution, rather than the protection, of a small, democratic country, Czechoslovakia. Even so, Hitler chose not to honour the agreement. It became part of a rapid series of developments towards major war. To Western leaders it showed the futility of compromising with dictatorships. Appeasement became a synonym for negotiations. The Soviet leadership may have drawn similar conclusions from its deal with Nazi Germany in August 1939, the agreement that made the Second World War inevitable. Although it aimed at preventing a war between the two – by dividing influence in Eastern Europe and the Baltic region – Germany attacked the Soviet Union less than two years later. Thus, both sides in the Cold War that followed the joint defeat of Nazi Germany could agree on the dangers of making peace with an opponent. For both, the conclusion was that lasting peace required solid victory. Consequently, there were few agreements on political issues in armed conflicts in the decades that followed.

It is, then, remarkable to find that negotiations were still possible in a particular sphere: arms control and disarmament. There were agreements banning nuclear weapons tests, restricting the production of missiles, and even eliminating whole categories of weaponry. These negotiations aimed to reduce the risk of inadvertent war between the major powers, without settling their fundamental incompatibilities. This was an effort at conflict management, making sure the relationships between the major powers would not unintentionally get out of hand. In spite of this, the Cold War continually led to new crises. Basic distrust and confrontation, though contained from becoming nuclear conflict, guided the leaderships. All other types of conflict were allowed: wars were waged by proxy, in secret, as interventions. The danger of local conflicts escalating into nuclear war was an element of most serious analysis. An important Cold War lesson is that the reduction of weaponry has limited value in conflict resolution. After all, the 'political' issues involved in forming the conflict are primary, and weapons are used to pursue such interests. Conflict management can help to reduce the dangers of crisis, creating some confidence and lessening (potential or actual) suffering. Conflict resolution is more ambitious as it tries to affect the basic issues, the incompatibilities that direct the conflicting parties. This book is devoted to this difficult and delicate material.

1.2 Peace Research and Conflict Resolution

Conflict resolution is approached on the basis of the insights generated in contemporary peace research. This means drawing conclusions from the study of causes of war, issues of disarmament and arms control, and conflict dynamics. This involves quantitative and qualitative studies. Although conflict resolution in armed conflict has been part of the peace research agenda, it has yet to develop a consistent set of research-based propositions. The methodological approach taken by many scholars today is comparative. History-oriented methods have dominated. Systematic quantitative research has begun to emerge. The basis for this book is, consequently, not a consolidated set of insights about which strategies work or why agreements endure. Rather, it brings together plausible understandings which, it is hoped, help to highlight policy dilemmas and stimulate more study.

Peace research, like any other field of inquiry that deals with societal affairs, is, of course, coloured by major historical changes and events. Peace research, with its ambition to understand the causes of violence and to find ways to reduce/remove violence, has been sensitive to such changes. Sometimes they have constituted challenges to the existing research paradigms, thus leading to new fields of inquiry. At other times, the historical developments have confirmed the importance of the existing agenda. Either way, the dialogue with realities remains a constant feature. As can be seen from Table 1.1, peace research has developed agendas resting on the traumatic experiences of the past century, but also from hopeful developments that are integral to the flow of events (Wallensteen 2011a, 2011b).

Table 1.1 identifies 18 major themes that have served to enlarge the agenda of what was originally a limited topic. Peace research arose as a field devoted to understanding the causes of war by systematic analyses of the historical experiences of war. Pioneering studies integrated many dimensions, notably the works of Pitirim A.

Sorokin (1937) and Quincy Wright (1942). The causes of war remain, to this day, fundamental questions for peace research. The solution to the problem of the origins of war has since then been enlarged to involve a vast array of analytical questions. Table 1.1 indicates how such issues have come to take a central role.

Table 1.1   Traumas and hopes forming the agenda of peace research

Event		Understanding of event	Peace research topics
First World War	Trauma	Loss of crisis control, 1914	History, causes of war
League of Nations	Hope	Aggression, need for rules	International law
Second World War	Trauma	Again, lost control	Strategic study v. peace research
Hiroshima	Trauma	Science used for war	Disarmament, arms control
Gandhi in India	Hope	Use of non-violent means	History, cases of non-violence
United Nations	Hope	International cooperation	International organization
Holocaust	Trauma	Genocide, ethnic violence	Human and collective rights
Cold War	Trauma	Danger of polarization, escalation	Conflict theory, gaming
European Unity	Hope	Overcoming enmity	Integration and democracy theory
Vietnam War	Trauma	Dependence, imperialism	Structural violence
Dissidence	Hope	Popular moves for democracy	NGOs, popular attitudes
Détente	Hope	Confidence-building	Cooperation, common themes
Environmental threats	Trauma	Hope or cause of conflict	Scarcity, conflict and cooperation
Bosnia	Trauma	Ethnic identities as element	Ethnic security dilemmas
Peacemaking	Hope	Ending of wars	Conflict resolution and peacebuilding
Emancipation	Hope	Gender and peace	Gender as variable/ paradigm
September 11, 2001	Trauma	Terrorism	Pre-emption v. human security
Arab Spring	Hope/ Trauma	Popular revolts met with repression	Non-violence, social media

There are almost equal numbers of traumatic, negative experiences, and hopes, creative events that point to new possibilities. The *traumas* are connected with human suffering on a large scale affecting many, also outside the scene of action. The same is true for the *hopes*, which are not only isolated events, but also developments that have drawn global attention. The common feature of traumas and hopes is that they challenge conventional wisdom and, thus, result in breaks in trends, or even paradigm shifts. The traumas suggest limits to established thinking that clearly have to be overcome, and where research can play a role in the process. The hopes suggest that reality offers many surprises. Some of them stem from theoretical thoughts of 'utopian' character, which unexpectedly take material forms. This closeness of reality to research is a feature of social science in general but, in peace research, a culture of openness and willingness to challenge one's assumptions has been particularly central.

Certainly, none of the topics mentioned in Table 1.1 is exclusive to peace research. In spite of a vigorous development, peace research *per se* continues to be organizationally distinct and a financially limited field of the full study of war and peace, international relations, foreign policy, sociology, economics, international law, etc. Many of the topics mentioned as subjects for peace research are administratively and intellectually embraced in other disciplines. The debate during the Cold War, positing strategic studies against peace research, subsided, but re-emerged in revised forms following September 11, 2001. More comprehensive concepts of security are common on both sides, and their shared understanding has increased to the point where there is today little necessity to draw a sharp line. If there is one, however, it has to do with the close connection to political decision-making in leading countries and views of the use of force. The calculated use of violence remains, as a strategy, alien to peace research. The idea is instead to search, as far as is possible, for 'peace with peaceful means' (Galtung 1996). War-fighting strategies are not likely to be developed at peace research institutions. Even so, the ideas of an international responsibility to protect populations exposed to the risk of genocide or ethnic persecution are debated in peace research institutions, but without the formulation of practical strategies for such operations. This fits, however, with the broader concern of human security as a means of reducing the risk of future terrorism.

Conflict resolution, as Table 1.1 makes clear, is a more recent concept. It certainly has roots, as evidenced by the reference to international law, conflict theory, cooperation and integration. During the 1990s it has taken on a new, more significant and central meaning. Systematic study is found only from the middle of the 1980s, and the literature has grown in recent years. There certainly are – as will be seen throughout this book – mixed experiences in the field. Collecting such lessons, systematizing and making them explicit, is a way to move forward. This book aims at understanding when peace agreements are likely to become durable settlements. This requires an analysis of different types of conflict. Agreements, it will be argued, are particularly dependent on the central issues of contention, the incompatibilities. Furthermore, emphasis will be given to the significance of the ways agreements are derived, as the processes themselves can explain some of the agreements, but also are important for assessing their durability. In addition, it is important to observe the interconnections between conflicts in the same region and the role of the international community. The analysis builds on the conflict resolution agreements concluded after the Cold War but also draws on general theories of conflict, negotiation and mediation. It is a book reporting on a record, in a way which hopefully will stimulate practice as well as research in the field.

1.3 Defining Conflict Resolution

Before we can proceed further, there is a need to establish a preliminary definition of conflict resolution. The definition will be discussed in more detail in Chapter 2. The distinction between conflict management and conflict resolution has already been introduced. We have also mentioned the recent phenomenon of peace agreements. They are an integral part of conflict resolution. Without some form of agreement among the conflicting parties, it is hard to talk about conflict resolution. However, an agreement, even if implemented, may not be sufficient to establish a durable peace. Peace requires more than a deal among the parties. The peace accord is, however, a necessary step to a lasting arrangement. Thus, we can preliminarily define conflict resolution as a situation *where the conflicting parties enter into an agreement that solves their central incompatibilities, accept each other's continued existence as parties and cease all violent action against each other*. This means, of course, that conflict resolution is something that necessarily comes 'after' conflict. It means that we first need to have concepts and tools for the analysis of conflict. This is what conflict theory is all about. Conflict resolution in the context of conflict theory is the theme of Chapter 2.

Let us scrutinize key elements in this definition. The *agreement* is normally a formal understanding, a document signed under more or less solemn conditions. However, there can be more informal, implicit understandings worked out between the parties. Such agreements may exist in secret documents, for instance, a crucial promise made as a precondition for the formal arrangements, or as deals about which the parties have been more or less explicit. Many cases are likely to see as much dispute around such informal understandings as over the formalized documents. Furthermore, such informal pacts require considerable trust between the parties. They are not likely without a formal arrangement. Thus, the agreed document is important for any peace process.

The definition talks about the parties accepting *each other's continued existence as parties*. This is an important element as it distinguishes a peace accord from agreed capitulation. An agreement of capitulation is the strongest consent to victory and defeat. It means that one side lays down its weapons, dissolves its organization, departs from the disputed territory and, in short, ceases to be an actor of influence and significance. An example is a withdrawal agreement. This is an arrangement where one side agrees to remove its troops from an area of dispute and where this is the only matter the agreement regulates. The withdrawing party is not likely, however, to see it as a matter of capitulation, although the essence of the agreement is to end that party's participation in the conflict. An example is the Soviet withdrawal from Afghanistan that was agreed in 1988 and implemented by 1989. It ended the dominant role of the Soviet Union in internal Afghan affairs. Another example is the resignation of a party leader from the government, where he/she also leaves the country. This was the case with the departure of Charles Taylor from Liberia in 2003, thus ending a civil war and opening a chance for long-term peacebuilding in the war-torn country. Lately, there have also been victories without agreements or acts of capitulation. The USA declared the defeat of Iraq to be 'one victory in a war on terror', on May 1, 2003. The government of Sri Lanka won over the Tamil Tigers in May 2009, without a formal consent (i.e., capitulation) from the losing party. The Gaddafi regime in Libya ended with the death of the leader in 2011.

However, the conflict resolution agreements of interest here are more complex. They refer to documents in which the fighting parties accept each other also as parties in future dealings with one another. It means that nobody wins all that there is to win, but no one loses all that there is to lose. Such arrangements are more difficult to maintain, no doubt, but they are more frequent than perhaps recognized at first. Of course, the word 'accept' in the definition does not imply that the parties agree to everything or that they 'like' each other. It only means that they accept the other as much as they need for the agreement to be implemented by the opposing sides.

The formulation that the parties *cease all violent action against each other* is most important. Many times it is part of the same treaty but it can be done as a separate undertaking. Often the cessation of violence is made public at about the same time as the peace agreement is concluded. To the public at large, it means that the war ends and the dangers of being killed are reduced. Sometimes, however, cease-fire agreements can precede the actual conclusion of the agreement regulating the incompatibilities between the parties. There is debate whether cease-fires should precede, be simultaneous with, or come after the more political agreements. There are a number of truce agreements that have lasted a long time, without resulting in peace accords. The armistice lines drawn in 1949 separating Israel from its Arab neighbours were used in the agreements with Egypt 30 years later. The same territorial divisions are relevant for a final agreement between Israel and Palestine. The lines have now existed for more than 65 years. The separation lines between Korea's two states in 1953 will soon reach a similarly venerable age. Perhaps an agreement will be achieved earlier on Cyprus, where the territorial divisions that are the references for today's discussions date from the war in 1974. The line separating Georgia from South Ossetia today dates to the cease-fire of 1992. Cease-fire agreements, in other words, are closer to conflict management, a way of freezing a military status quo, and do not necessarily result in peace efforts. It is safe to conclude that a peace agreement, solving the central incompatibilities between the parties, which does not include a simultaneous undertaking to cease fighting, is not likely to be credible. Thus, the agreements included as conflict resolution measures are those which both solve incompatibilities and end fighting.

1.4 Limits of Conflict Resolution

Conflict resolution is not necessarily identical with peace. There is considerable overlap, however, as most notions of peace are based on the *absence or ending of war*. A conflict, we have just made clear, is not resolved if it does not include an end to armed struggle. At the same time, it is not sufficient that it *only* contains the ending

9

of fighting. Conflict resolution is more than the limited definition of peace. It is more than the absence of war. The parties are agreeing to respect each other and prepare for living together with one another. However, there are broader under-standings of what peace is, such as the presence of cooperation, justice and integra-tion. Conflict resolution may or may not include such larger values. It will depend on the situation. The preferred definition does not, a priori, include such elements. The definition is dependent on what the parties want or can agree to include. Conflict resolution may, or may not, contain broader aspects.

In the worst of circumstances, a peace agreement may negate widely held values. The accords studied here have been concluded between parties with arms. They are militarily stronger than other parties in their societies. Thus, there is a danger that the agreed form of conflict resolution will contain *privileges for the armed par-ties*, at the expense of other interests in the society. There are many examples of this, even where persons who have been responsible for considerable destruction take up government positions, thus becoming legal powerholders. Such develop-ments create fear in parts of society. From a conflict resolution perspective, it is necessary to warn against such arrangements. They may contain the seeds of renewed conflict or initiate entirely new conflict dynamics. The deal, from the population's point of view, is that granting privileges will stop a war. The hope may be that these privileges can be challenged by a stronger civil society once the war is over. The conditions of peace may require new types of leadership, and thus, the hope may be borne out. A minimum conclusion is to ensure that the peace agreement does not prevent such developments; a better position is that it actually encourages it.

A question that has gained increased importance is the issue of *crimes* committed during a war, as part of the fighting or under the protection of the war. The interna-tional war crimes tribunal was set up in 1993 for the conflict in former Yugoslavia, followed by a similar tribunal for Rwanda a year later. By the summer of 1998 a fully-fledged International Criminal Court (ICC) was created through an interna-tional treaty. With enough ratifications by 2004, the ICC became operational (although the USA chose to remain outside and initially tried to reduce its interna-tional reach). The ICC is a dramatic new development. After the Second World War, war crime tribunals were set up for the responsible actors in Germany and Japan. They were not permanent institutions and war crimes were seldom pursued interna-tionally in the following decades. The only consistent effort taken up by some coun-tries and some non-governmental organizations was to bring to trial those involved in the Holocaust. The Cold War precluded an international consensus on the pursuit of war crimes.

Thus, only after the Cold War could a shared understanding again develop on war crimes, necessary procedures and punishments. Nevertheless, there are recent peace agreements which include different forms of amnesty to leaders and decision-makers. Amnesty has been seen as necessary by negotiators for any agreement at all to be concluded. Leaders could, in other words, protect themselves from legal procedures, the opposing sides and the legitimate anger of their own populations. Developments during the 1990s make such agreements increasingly unlikely. They are not easily accepted internationally. In that sense, conflict resolution today has become more demanding than it was immediately after the Cold War. The first indictment from the ICC concerned the leader of a rebellion in Uganda, at the same time making further negotiations for an end to the civil war more complicated. Thus, the effects of the focus on war crimes can be discussed. Some argue that it threatens to prolong conflict, as parties fearing to be brought to trial have little incentive to make agreements which endanger their own means of control. Others argue that it deters parties from getting into war in the first place, as the ICC increases the likelihood that war crimes will be legally pursued, thus, in the long run, preventing new wars.

Finally, we should also note that conflict resolution is not the same as complete *disarmament*. The agreement may allow the parties to retain a certain arsenal. It is likely, however, that this will be lower than what has been put to use in the war itself. The parties may, nevertheless, maintain that they need special protection. Clearly, the higher the level of protection required and agreed, the more likely it is that this creates renewed insecurity in a society. Thus, it is probable that peace agreements will only be durable if they result in some disarmament, as well as changes in all security sectors towards transparency, integrity and a professionalism that includes human rights. Particularly, disarming and demobilization need to be coupled with reintegration and rehabilitation of soldiers, not the least child soldiers. In recent years, such disarmament, demobilization and reintegration (DDR) programmes have become central efforts in peacebuilding following the ending of wars.

There are also other aspects of peace. Conflict resolution finds itself at a bridge between a very narrow concept of peace (no war) and a very broad one (justice). By leaving conflict resolution as a concept defined by the parties, it may become difficult to compare one situation to another. However, the fact is that there are increasingly established norms for the content of internationally acceptable peace agreements. International law has set some standards for conflict resolution between states. The end of the Cold War has also led to signposts for the settlement of internal conflicts: principles of democracy, human rights, criminal justice, reconciliation and economic cooperation are part of this. In this sense, an international understanding of conflict resolution is developing. It contributes to pushing the concept further in the direction of justice, or what could be termed quality peace, not simply cessation of violence.

1.5 Outlining this Book

The existing peace agreements are important inputs in this work. The analysis, however, has to start with the phenomenon that precedes any peace agreement and may eventually replace it: conflict. It requires some tools for understanding the extent of armed conflict and types of outcome. This is covered in Chapter 2, which gives information on patterns of conflict and peacemaking. Then we will go into the theoretical underpinnings, to review some of the elements of contemporary conflict theory that are relevant for peacemaking (Chapter 3). From this, we proceed to the necessary instruments for basic conflict analysis. This is done in Chapter 4, which presents three types of prevalent conflict, the trichotomy of conflict, which requires different types of agreement. This completes Part One. In Part Two, the peace agreements since the end of the Cold War, as well as previous experiences, are married to this structure to show how the distinctions serve to highlight features for durable agreements (Chapters 5, 6 and 7). Part Three examines particularly complex issues in conflict analysis. These relate to the linkages between different conflicts into conflict complexes, within regions, with or without major power involvement (Chapter 8). In Chapter 9, the roles of the United Nations and regional organizations in conflict resolution are assessed. Chapters 10 and 11 focus on tools used in peacemaking and, finally, in Chapter 12, the new challenges to conflict resolution are discussed.

Further Readings

Go to the *Understanding Conflict Resolution* web page at https://study.sagepub.com/wallensteen4e for free access to journal articles listed.

On the Concept of Peace

Journal of Peace Research 1964. 'An Editorial', *Journal of Peace Research*, 1 (1): 1–4.
This is a classical text that made the dichotomy of negative and positive peace well known to the research community. Although not signed it is commonly agreed that it was written by the editor of the Journal, Johan Galtung, the founder and first editor of the Journal.

Galtung, J. 1969. 'Violence, Peace and Peace Research', *Journal of Peace Research*, 6 (3): 167–91.
In this article Galtung elaborates on the meaning of positive peace by introducing a new concept, 'structural violence', largely in response to a critique of peace research as being too focused on 'direct violence', i.e. wars, conflicts and violence. The concept of structural violence has since then been used in peace research but also in other disciplines.

Höglund, K. and Söderberg Kovacs, M. 2010. 'Beyond the Absence of War: The Diversity of Peace in Post-Settlement Societies', *Review of International Studies*, 36 (2): 367–90.
These two authors return to the issue of positive peace by elaborating on a set of other possible notions of peace. It was part of a new discussion on 'peace',

in particular in relation to the conditions after a protracted war. What kind of peace is to be built?

Regan, P.M. 2014. 'Bringing Peace Back in: Presidential address to the Peace Science Society', 2013. *Conflict Management and Peace Science*, 31 (4): 345–356.
In the continued discussion on positive peace, Regan, as president of the Peace Science Society, poses the challenge to the research community to put 'peace' in the forefront of research, thus making scholarly sense of 'positive peace'. He also demonstrates that the dichotomy of negative and positive peace was used already in the 1950s, thus giving it a history.

Peace and Peace Research

Wallensteen, P. 2011a. 'The Origins of Contemporary Peace Research', in K. Höglund and M. Öberg (eds), *Understanding Peace Research*. London: Routledge. pp. 14–32.
Wallensteen, P. 2011b. *Peace Research: Theory and Practice*. London: Routledge. pp. 4–20.
These two publications elaborate on the effect the choice of peace concept has on the forming of a research agenda. The first one shows how 'traumas' and 'hopes' have formed the present agenda. The second one shows that 'peace' is researchable, gives the arguments for its pursuit within universities as an autonomous activity, and discusses ethical aspects of research results.

The Philosophical Underpinnings of Peace Research

Organized peace research is, of course, not the originator of a discussion on 'peace'. Through time, this has been an important concern by many writers. Three important texts are the following:

Kant, I. 1795. *Perpetual Peace: A Philosophical Sketch.*
The renowned philosopher outlines his approach to a lasting international peace arrangement emphasizing matters such as republican rule, international federations and arms control. These visionary ideas were widely read during the 1800s. It influenced the formation of international organizations in the 1900s and sparked a modern research approach, referred to as the Kantian Peace.

Machiavelli, N. 1532. *The Prince.*
This text from the sixteenth century was published after the death of Machiavelli. It gives advice to the political leader who wants to retain power in turbulent times. It is a classical reading for a 'realist' approach emphasizing the importance of power. It has also sparked an ongoing discussion on moral and power.

(Continued)

(Continued)

More, T. 1516. *Utopia*.

The work on *Utopia* is contemporary to Machiavelli and can be seen as a critique of the power struggles that went on in Europe at the time. It does so by outlining a vision of a different society, 'Utopia'. The concept is firmly entrenched in European thinking, and has also led to new derivations, such as 'dystopia' as a negative vision on a future society.

2

ARMED CONFLICTS AND PEACE AGREEMENTS

2.1 The Concept of Conflict

A strong statement is that conflicts *are* solvable. This is not necessarily an idealistic or optimistic position. As this book will show, it is a realistic proposition. Most actors in conflicts will find themselves in need of negotiations at one time or another. Even if a conflict results in war and destruction, there may have been other options and alternative paths for the conflict. There are frequent statements on the inevitability of conflict, violence and war. Indeed, finding solutions may often be difficult. This may arise not only out of political constraints, but can also be due to a lack of insight or imagination. There are also views of the desirability and even necessity of violence and war. Unbearable conditions or overwhelming threats may make such opinions understandable. Too often, however, the results of war negate the very hope for a better future that may initially have motivated the war. Few wars follow the paths anticipated by the actors. Short wars may avoid such pitfalls, but who is to guarantee that a war will be short? Many wars have started from this premise. Afterwards, it will be asked: were all avenues used to find a peaceful solution prior to the initiation of war? Only after this can be convincingly proven do the arguments of inevitability and desirability approach validity. The determined search for a solution is not only a moral question; it is also a rational one. This is the sole way in which a free society will be prepared to accept the strains of war. Indeed, if conflicts are exposed to such early challenges, solutions may actually be found, even in unexpected situations. Thus, conflicts are solvable and there are many and varied experiences of such solutions.

If conflicts *are* solvable is it also true that conflicts – sooner or later – *will be* solved? Clearly, once a conflict has developed into a war the options are fewer. At that moment, the primary actors will pursue victory rather than a joint solution. The victory of one side over the other is, then, a possible outcome, even to the point of the other's capitulation, dissolution or disappearance as an actor. The record shows that this is what happens in some conflicts, but by no means all. Conflicts will come to an end at some point. Whether that ending is a solution, a victory or a stalemate has to be scrutinized. To this should be added the question of whether the conflict is likely again to be armed and violent.

Victory is the outcome preferred by most actors. If achieved, it may solve parts of an issue, but often not the entire problem at hand. The victory of the allied countries over Nazi Germany is a case in point. After the failure of the agreement reached in Munich in 1938, it was no longer possible for the Western powers to consider negotiations with Adolf Hitler and the Nazi regime. The end of the Second World War meant the implementation of the demand for unconditional surrender and the elimination of the Nazis as an actor. This was as clear-cut a victory as can be. It did not, however, mean the end of Germany. The issue of Germany's position in the international system still had to be settled. Conflict among the victors arose over this question. It became one of the few core issues in the Cold War. A solution developed as new leaders emerged in West Germany. They were democratically inclined, conscientiously building on pre-1933 democratic traditions and new ideas from the Western powers. A reintegration of Germany into the international system took place, ultimately even allowing for its reunification in 1990, but only 45 years after the end of the Second World War. It was only possible with a new Germany, willing to admit its responsibility for the past and able to accommodate to the present. If the Second World War had been a question solely of Germany's role in the international system, there was a route through peaceful dialogue and development. A solution within a democratic framework among democratic countries was found. It could have been found before the Nazis took power. For any country, there are, in other words, always alternatives to a war strategy for achieving goals. Regimes, however, may deliberately narrow their options and construct situations where the choice becomes defeat or victory. Nazi Germany chose such a path.

Conflict precedes conflict resolution. There is considerable analysis of the origin and the pursuit of conflict. Machiavelli and Clausewitz are important writers in one Western tradition of conflict analysis. Adam Smith and Karl Marx offered competition and class analysis as other tools for understanding. In classical Chinese discourse Sun Tzu is a central writer, as is Kautilya in India or Ibn Khaldun in the Arab world. Military-strategic thinking has become universally shared, and there is often, among military officers, a surprising degree of common understanding across battle lines. Also, the analysis of societal contradiction has such cross-cultural traits, Smith and Marx being influential in different quarters across the globe. The same, however, is not true for conflict resolution thinking. It is a novel topic. It is less developed and less coherent. Thus, it is important to introduce the ideas of modern thinkers. It is also necessary to relate them to trends of social science thinking.

'Conflict' has many meanings in everyday life. To some it refers to *behaviour* or *action*. There is conflict when a trade union goes on strike or an employer locks out its employees. It is also conflict when two states are at war with one another, and where battlefield events determine their relations. The actions constitute the conflict. If this were all, however, it would mean that a conflict ends once this behaviour ends. Few would agree to this. A cease-fire is not the end of a conflict, only an end to violence. Even the ending of non-violent forms of actions may only indicate an interlude in the conflict. Violent and/or non-violent actions may resume at a later stage. There may still be dissatisfaction. Obviously, conflict is more than the behaviour of the parties.

A closer look indicates that the parties in an industrial dispute will not cease their actions until there is some movement on the issues which sparked the dispute. The 'issue' refers to the incompatible positions taken by the parties, motivating their actions. This, then, is a deeper understanding of what a conflict is. It contains a severe disagreement between at least two sides, where their demands cannot be met by the same resources at the same time. This is an *incompatibility*. Positions are incompatible. There is some form of scarcity. If there is an abundance of resources, the demands from the various sides may easily be met and the incompatibility can be solved. If there are limited resources, however, problems will arise. The easy solutions are no longer available and more ingenious ways have to be found. How this can be done will be discussed later. For the time being, it is sufficient to note that when the parties adjust their demands so that there is no longer scarcity, the conflict disappears. The incompatible demands have been handled. Incompatibility appears to be a key to the existence of conflict. If there are no actions, but it is possible for an outsider to point to incompatibilities, there is a latent conflict. Manifest conflict requires both action and incompatibility.

This is still not enough to get an initial understanding of the concept of conflict. We need to include the actors as well. Many would say that trade unions are created by employees to deal with an existing incompatibility from a stronger position, which may result in conflict. This is why they have a membership. Members expect to be protected even to the point where a manifest conflict becomes a distinct possibility. This means that there is tension built into the relationship between the employer and the employees. 'Conflict' does exist, even if there are no actions taken or demands formulated. The conflict is internal to the system. Similar descriptions can be found for the interstate system. It is argued that sovereign states are inevitably locked into conflict with one another. States are continuously preparing to defend themselves from possible attack in order to protect their own survival. Such preparations only confirm to others that there are real dangers, thus they do the same. These are the dynamics of the well-known security dilemma (Herz 1950; Waltz 1959, 1979). This perspective suggests that the existence of one state is a danger to any other state. As long as there is unpredictability in the system, there will be fear and, thus, conflict. For our purposes it means that *actors* or *parties* are fundamental for conflict to exist. If the actors are formed, and if they make an analysis where their needs for survival are in conflict with others, then there is conflict built into the system. The history of the actors, the actors' understanding of their own role and their resources are important elements in conflict analysis. From this we can conclude that conflict consists of three components: incompatibility, action and actors. Combining them, we arrive at a complete definition of a conflict as *a social situation in which a minimum of two actors (parties) strive to acquire at the same moment in time an available set of scarce resources.* This definition brings together essential elements from a number of commonly used definitions. It includes the actors or 'parties' in the definition which, as we have just seen, is basic. In many definitions the actor is left as a separate item. However, the preceding arguments make clear that it is integral to the analysis and to the definition.

The word 'strive' in the defining sentence requires a comment. It is a vague term, but the point is that when the parties are acting, they are doing something (however minimal) to acquire the resources. 'Strive' may even include warfare. It covers a wide range of activities.

An additional phrase needs some reflection. It is said that the parties are striving to acquire the resources 'at the same moment in time'. This is sometimes overlooked in definitions and may, again, be self-evident. If one actor is satisfied with having its demands met a year from now, other actors may be able to meet their goals today. There is no conflict today. Perhaps the first actor will worry for the future – will there be anything left? – but if the party believes it has guarantees, the incompatibility is gone. It is clearly a different matter when the demands are geared to the same moment in time. It is conventional wisdom that only one person can be prime minister at a time and that only one country can have formal jurisdiction over a particular piece of territory at a time. These resources are regarded as indivisible, for the time being. If this is what the parties believe, then this is their reality. In actual life there are solutions even to such problems, for example, the creation of posts as first and second prime minister (as in Cambodia in the 1990s); president and prime minister; or finding forms of shared rule for a territory. Such solutions emerge only if the parties perceive an incompatibility to be divisible. Time, as we notice every day, is scarce but still has this quality of divisibility, something that our calendars make clear. Schedules may dissolve incompatibilities.

The notion of an 'available set of scarce resources' should not be taken to include only economic matters. The term 'resources' covers all kinds of positions that are of interest to an actor. To be a prime minister, to control a particular piece of territory, to be able to propagate a particular idea in the media can all be covered by the notion of 'available resources'. This definition demands that something is desired which is scarce, be it positions of power, attractive land, or access to airwaves. Such resources can sometimes be estimated in money, square metres or other measures, but often they are intangible. For examples, demands for recognition, acceptance of responsibility for destructive actions or psychological retribution, exemplify intangible values. They are still highly important. They may involve admissions that have implications for an actor's standing nationally or internationally, but only indirectly relate to material resources. Thus, there are incompatibilities relating to matters of justice, moral norms and guilt.

Hopefully, with the conflict concept clarified, we move to the most difficult of all conflicts: wars. They are different from all other conflicts in that they are irreversible actions. Wars involve the taking of territory, the eviction of inhabitants, the death of soldiers and civilians, the destruction of property, resources and the environment, and the disruption of people's mental, physical, economic and cultural development. War is among the most destructive phenomena that one human group can inflict on another. In the same category of extreme conflict we can also locate systematic repression, totalitarianism and genocide. These are actions initiated by human beings. These are matters that can be ended and remedied by humans, but not undone. They become strong and conscious elements in the history of peoples, groups and individuals. Let us first look more closely at the exact meaning of war and then proceed to study recent trends in armed conflict and war.

2.2 Identifying Armed Conflict

Three Projects

A commonly asked question is whether conflict and war have become more frequent and are more destructive today than they used to be. It is a question about quantity, where it is assumed that conflicts are easily comparable. The question is asked to reach an understanding of where the world is headed, as a whole, for a particular region or for a particular phenomenon (for example, arms production). It is often a question about the future, not only about history. At the same time, there are those who resent having 'their' conflict compared to other situations. Each conflict is unique and has its own characteristics. There are qualities which make them different. The question of frequency makes little sense to those who are parties in conflict. Why should they worry, it is bad enough with one conflict, they would say.

Both perspectives are valid. The projects that exist within the peace research community all aim at understanding why conflicts occur or how they can be terminated. Their answers to the questions of frequency of wars are actually by-products of other ambitions. The questions are nevertheless important and contribute to the development of deeper answers. If there are general patterns recurring over a large number of different conflicts, it suggests something that can possibly explain why wars begin. By implication, it may yield ideas for improving the situation. Certain factors can be singled out for closer analysis. Questions of frequency interest the media and the public for other reasons. Today, it is frequently asked if there is a difference between the post-Cold War years and the Cold War period, or before/after September 11, 2001, or the onset of the Arab Spring. Changes in the international system or in domestic policies, associated with the ending of this confrontation, may explain our present predicament. There are many other candidates for possible causation, however, and the impact of each may be difficult to disentangle. In the analysis, many factors are mentioned, such as bipolarity, the deterrent effect of nuclear weapons, the changed roles of international organizations, democratization, the spread of free market mechanisms, changes in media access, concern for human rights, the growth of civil society, etc. Comparisons across time can illustrate a number of effects. However, they do not necessarily prove them. To be scientific, evidence, cases and periods have to be selected with rigour and there have to be many observations. For the purpose of this book, it is important to have a general idea of the frequency and severity of armed conflicts in the world. It helps to set the topics of conflict resolution in perspective. Thus, let us review some ongoing efforts.

Armed conflict patterns are mapped continuously by several projects. This book uses the work of the Uppsala Conflict Data Program, based at the Department of Peace and Conflict Research, Uppsala University, in Sweden. Data are published by the department in the annual publication *States in Armed Conflict.* Information is also available through the yearbooks of the Stockholm International Peace Research Institute (SIPRI) (for conflicts in the last ten years); the *Journal of Peace Research* (JPR); from the International Peace Research Institute, Oslo (PRIO) (all armed conflicts, backdated to 1946); the *Human Security Report* (from the Simon Fraser University); and, most fully, through accessing the Uppsala Conflict Data Program itself and its database (www.ucdp.uu.se).

Second, there is the project on wars and armed conflict by the Causes of War project at the University of Hamburg (AKUF, from its name in German), mapping the global record of local wars since 1945 (Gantzel and Schwinghammer 2000), but less known internationally. The third enduring project is the Correlates of War project (known as COW), originating at the University of Michigan, Ann Arbor, Michigan, carrying information on wars since 1816. This information is normally available in the form of datasets, sometimes also in printed publications (Sarkees and Wayman 2010). It has found a wide usage in research projects and the findings have been systematized (Geller and Singer 1998; Vasquez 2012).

There are additional important projects that aim to highlight the present dilemmas of war and violence. Among these is the Minorities at Risk project, University of Maryland, College Park, Maryland, focusing on a subset of conflict: those involving ethnic minorities around the world. It contains data for minority groups which have been involved in some form of conflict since 1945. From this has also developed a biannual report on peace and conflict, most recently 2014 (Backer et al. 2014). Crisis behaviour between states can also be used to discuss questions of frequency (Brecher 1993, most recent update 2010). A number of researchers have their own systematic collections of conflict-related information which are reported in international journals (Bercovitch 1996; Carment 1993; Fearon and Laitin 2003; Gibler 2012; Goldstein 1992; Holsti 1991; Levy 1983; Licklider 1995; Luard 1986; Morton and Starr 2001; Tillema 1989). For overviews see Eck (2005) and Forsberg et al. (2012).

The first three projects stand out, however, as the most consistent specifically addressing armed conflicts of all categories, whether between or within states. They contain additional information which is useful for theorizing on the war phenomenon. Two are oriented towards understanding the causes of conflict (the Hamburg and Michigan projects) and one deals specifically with conflict resolution (the Uppsala project). What, then, do they tell us about trends in armed conflict and war?

The question is simple but requires an understanding of key definitions before an answer can be given. The definitions of conflict and war guide the types of information any project will collect. Potentially, conflict data projects can show different global tendencies, depending on what categories of conflict they focus on. The comparability, in other words, can be limited. Furthermore, there are several criteria that have to be met for a conflict dataset to be reliable. First, it must have a definition that is sufficiently general to go beyond what is important only to a particular period in history. The definitions in these projects meet these criteria: they do not vary with time or with the phenomena studied. The projects may still be relevant for other concerns as well. For example, although ethnic conflict is not used as a category in these three projects, it is possible to retrieve information from them which is relevant for the study of ethnic conflict. They have separate categories of internal war. In this way, the projects cover a wider range of conflict than does, for instance, the Minorities at Risk project.

Second, there has to be a definition that captures conflict between as well as within states. It means that it has to tap the general issue of violence, cutting across particular legal categories. This allows for an understanding of war beyond the category of interstate events. Clearly, data on interstate conflicts are more easily compiled. What two states do to one another that might lead to war is of interest to the surrounding community as well. Thus, such disputes will have more attention. Conflicts inside a state, however, are not as likely to immediately affect neighbours, thus threatening to make the international recording of such conflicts more sporadic. A full study might require intimate knowledge of all countries in the world. Thus, it still has to be the ambition to include *all* conflicts. This is a third criterion, which is necessary if changes in armed conflict over time are to be discussed meaningfully. Fourth, the definitions have to be precise, so as to guide data collection (operationalization) and delimit a particular conflict in time and space (beginning, ending) from other conflicts. Finally, the data must be open to scrutiny by other researchers.

The Michigan and Hamburg Projects

The Michigan project is the oldest and serves as a reference point for many projects. It was initiated in the middle of the 1960s by J. David Singer and Melvin Small and is still maintained, something which is an achievement in itself. It has now turned into an inter-university cooperation programme and is physically located at Pennsylvania State University. Since 2012, Professor Zeev Maoz, University of California, Davis, is the Director. It contains data on wars since 1816 and its record is constantly updated. A major review has been undertaken during the 2000s, resulting in more coherent lists of wars (Sarkees and Wayman 2010).

Basic to COW is the delineation of an international system consisting of states. Thus, wars are conflicts between states where at least two are members of the international system. In addition, there are extra-systemic conflicts ('extra-state wars') between one system member and another entity (such as colonial and liberation wars). Furthermore, there are intra-state conflicts where most of the military action takes place within a state that is a member of the system ('intra-state wars'). Innovatively, COW has now also included a category of wars between non-state actors ('non-state wars'). For all conflicts there is the requirement of 1,000 battle-related fatalities. COW also now has included the parties' motives for engaging in war, thus borrowing a feature from the Uppsala Conflict Data Program; however, it is only applied to the category of intra-state wars. For the period 1816–2007, COW reports 95 interstate wars, 163 extra-state wars, 335 intra-state wars and 62 non-state wars (Sarkees and Wayman 2010: 75–7, 193–7, 337–46, 485–7). It therefore identifies a total of 655 wars for the period, meaning an average of more than three wars of some kind starting somewhere in the world every year. War, in other words, is shown to be a pervasive and global phenomenon.

The Hamburg project was initiated by Istvan Kende in Budapest. It was later modified and developed at the University of Hamburg, through the efforts of Klaus Jürgen Gantzel. Its results are different. Its definition does not require that a party be a member in the international system for a conflict to be included. The AKUF project, however, has the criterion that a state should be the actor on one side in a conflict. The actors should have, at a minimum, central command and practical control over the fighting. It is also stipulated that there has to be a measure of continuity in battle. There is no requirement for a particular number of deaths, which is an important consideration in the Michigan project (and in the Uppsala project). The Hamburg project, in fact, regards this criterion as a questionable indicator for practical, theoretical and ethical reasons. It is argued that information on deaths is unreliable and that there is no reason to include only those who have died from battle, but not those who have suffered from other consequences of the war (Gantzel and Meyer-Stamer 1986: 4–5; Jung et al. 1996: 52). Instead, the 'continuity' in the struggle is decisive for inclusion of a particular conflict. This criterion, of course, results in a problem of judging continuity in a reliable way.

These criteria mean that AKUF covers a broader set of cases than COW. The project has data on all wars since 1945. For the period to 2007, the project reported in 2010 on 238 wars. On average this gives almost four new wars per year. The effect of the definitions can be seen more clearly by comparing the years where the projects overlap and where the state is an actor in the conflict. For the same period, COW reports 38 interstate wars, 23 extra-state wars and 118 intra-state wars, a total of 179 wars. It gives an average of close to three new wars per year. The two projects clearly overlap, but still AKUF reports more activity. It could mean that the projects do not include the same major conflicts, although this should not have such a strong impact, as the number is limited. More likely is that many armed conflicts are below the threshold of 1,000 battle-related deaths. As would be expected, a considerable number of conflicts with lower intensity levels are not covered by COW.

In its studies of a separate category of conflicts, militarized interstate disputes, COW has accumulated information, which corrects for this effect. This category, which is also of great theoretical significance, covers relations between states. It includes more confined events, such as military interventions, limited wars and threats of war. Together with the war data, this gives a more comprehensive picture for relations between states. There is no record, however, in the COW project of militarized disputes *within* states. For both projects, internal or civil conflicts take up a large percentage of all events recorded. To develop a definition that parallels militarized interstate disputes for intra-state conditions is a cumbersome task. A very large number of episodes would have to be scrutinized for possible inclusion. It would, needless to say, be difficult to make a global comparison, as unbiased information is harder to obtain the more limited the episodes are. For example, threats to use force in internal affairs may involve military as well as police forces. Such threats can also be issued by opposition groups with limited credibility and representativity. Thus, drawing the lines of inclusion will require additional distinctions.

It is, however, possible to do by relying on data on human rights violations or other indicators of repression.

Both AKUF and COW are oriented to searching for the origins of violent conflict. The difference in approach is partly a reflection of distinct theoretical concerns. COW focuses on understanding interstate conflict, and particularly aims at questioning or modifying so-called realist thinking. This means it is designed to understand factors such as the balance of power, military capabilities, interdependence and other variables of importance for the working of the international system. There is, deliberately, no coherent theoretical perspective guiding the project. Instead, there is a conscious methodological approach. Reality, as expressed in the data, will speak for itself. It shows how the world actually functions: Correlations are important, thus the name of the project. This is an empirical approach, where theory development will build on what has been proven to be repeated and verified ways in which states really behave. Theoretical assumptions that are common in realist thinking are tested against observable patterns of conduct. An advantage with this open approach is that it also makes COW data useful for other purposes. The concepts and their operationalizations are explicit and simple, constructed to reflect world developments over close to 200 years. COW's information has been used for very different investigations. For example, there is research on whether arms races lead to war (this can be studied by using the militarized disputes and comparing them to the war data, with the original work done by Michael Wallace in 1979 and Paul Diehl in 1983). The data are also used for analysis of the hypothesis on peace among democratic states, resulting in the much debated democratic peace proposition (a large number of articles is devoted to this puzzle, the early phases of which were crystallized in work by Bruce Russett in 1993 (see also Russett and Oneal 2001). They have also been used in discussions on a possible decline of conflicts and violence globally (Pinker 2011; Gleditsch et al. 2013).

The Hamburg project departs from a fairly coherent theoretical approach. It relates the onset of war to the development of capitalist societies, and sees conflict as a result of the new forms of production, monetarization of the economy and the resulting dissolution of traditional forms of social integration. The large number of conflicts in the Third World fits with this relationship. As the project reports that there is an increasing frequency of conflicts since 1945, researchers also conclude that 'the contradictions in world society are increasing'. In an interesting twist, relevant here, the authors point out that even a phenomenon such as 'ethnic' conflict is a result of processes in 'which all social mechanisms that previously allowed us to live together are destroyed' (Jung et al. 1996: 52–61). In other words, conflict resolution instruments are being eliminated and this makes armed conflict more frequent. The issue of such social breakdown has lately captured considerable attention, with the term 'state failure' as a central concept (Zartman 1995b; more on this in Section 6.5 below).

This perspective points to the difference between the two projects. The Correlates of War project departs from the notion of a system that consists of a larger number of independent states. It is a system that does not have central institutions and lacks means to maintain or enforce decisions for all. Thus, it is a picture of an uncoordinated world that is the point of departure. In this world, states maintain some predictability through their actions. When war breaks out, it is not the result of an international society breaking down, as there is no assumption about such a society in the first place. The problem is found in the strategies for survival used by different states. War is a result of failed choices, but also the conditions which make it difficult for states to pursue other options. In some writings inspired by the project, the importance of norms comes forth as an important conclusion, based on the experiences that peace nevertheless exists in the system (Vasquez 2012). An implication may eventually be the need for constructing an organized international order.

The Hamburg project, on the contrary, departs from an understanding of an international system that is fairly integrated, almost having a purpose of its own, which is to promote market economy and democracy. It is a highly hierarchical world, centred on the strongest actors in the system, the Western countries. These actors are also influenced by the strength of the system. They are all capitalist, market-oriented and expansive, furthering a system of asymmetrical linkages. This international system penetrates into all parts of the world, creating instability and pushing aside traditional forms of social relations. There is an asymmetry between stronger actors that benefit from this development, and weaker actors that risk becoming marginalized. The project has a critical attitude to the basis of the existing international system. In this way, the disagreement on whether fatalities should be used as a criterion has a deeper meaning. The Hamburg project could argue as follows: If one side is vastly superior, it can win an armed conflict within a short period of time, and thus the casualties will be limited. It is still a military operation for purposes that might be the same as those found in more protracted and devastating conflicts. From the point of view of causes of war, in other words, the magnitude may not be so significant. For the Michigan project, with its elaborate measurements of battle-related deaths per month, only very large confrontations are interesting. The extent of destruction makes them more important. They suggest inadequacies in balance-of-power thinking and deterrence strategies. Such realist theories are developed exactly to prevent major disasters. If these still occur, the project can show this, and take a critical attitude to this particular aspect of the international system and its interpreters. The two projects contrast on important points of departure, their epistemology. This affects their definitions for data collection and interpretation of the resulting data. Thus, both projects are needed and valuable. Together they highlight different sides of the contemporary global system.

2.3 Trends in Armed Conflicts

The Uppsala Conflict Data Program (UCDP)

The Uppsala Conflict Data Program (UCDP) uses the concept of 'armed conflict' and focuses on conflict resolution. Like AKUF, it reports annually on ongoing conflicts and has much current information. Its definitions and understandings of conflict put it somewhere between the Michigan and Hamburg projects. From the beginning it treated all conflicts in an identical way, as did the Hamburg project and as COW now does, whether they take place between or within states. The same definition applies to both situations. For UCDP, this means that the distinction between an international system and an intra-state system is not of primary importance. What counts is the use of violence. The conflicts included are those that have at least one state or government as a party. This is also the case for the other two projects.

It covers conflicts from a threshold level of 25 battle-related deaths in a conflict in a year. This is an easily identifiable criterion and requires less evaluation by the researchers than, for example, the continuity criterion used in the Hamburg project. It also means that there is a way of discussing intensity in conflict, as is done in the Michigan project. There are two thresholds (25 and 1,000 battle-related deaths, respectively), resulting in two categories of intensity: 'minor armed conflicts', conflicts with more than 25 deaths but fewer than 1,000 for the year; and 'wars', conflicts with more than 1,000 battle-related deaths in one year. The casualties are significant in a study of conflict resolution. The more destruction, the more difficult will be peacemaking, reconstruction and the creation of a new post-war relationship. These distinctions are also relevant from a conflict prevention perspective. It is a common belief that a conflict in its early phase can be brought to an end most successfully. Thus, conflicts with lower levels of casualties may reflect preventive efforts, not just superiority. It becomes important to understand which conflicts remain on a low level and which ones do not. The criteria make this possible.

The Uppsala project adds an element which was not originally found in either COW or in AKUF, and it is introduced for theoretical as well as practical reasons. It requires that the conflict should have an issue, an incompatibility. This is derived from the theoretical considerations that guide this book. In the definition of conflict given in Section 2.1, this is an important element and it is, as a consequence, reflected in the data collection. The two other projects are satisfied once they have identified the actors and the actions. Still, there is an implicit understanding that only political violence is included. The Uppsala project handles this openly by requiring that there be an explicit issue of contention, defined in political terms. In this way, a clear line is drawn between political and non-political violence.

The project includes as armed conflicts only those events that concern control over government or control over territory. These are in turn defined as two exclusive categories. Control over government means that the issue is who should rule a particular state, and that demands for change include the change of rulers. The incumbents are not likely to abide by such a demand easily. Thus, an incompatibility exists. This means that interventions from abroad to remove a leadership in a country are recorded as armed conflicts (for instance, the United States intervening in Panama in 1989 or occupying Iraq in 2003). So are rebellions against a government by internal forces (for instance, the uprising against the Mobutu regime in Zaire in 1997 or against the successor Kabila regime a year later, or the ongoing civil war in Syria pitting numerous rebel groups against the Assad regime). Control over territory means that demands by one state for territory in another state, even the occupation of another state, is included. So are rebellions inside a state to achieve autonomy, independence or the joining of a particular territory to the neighbouring state. This has an international dimension (for instance, Iraq's claim on Kuwait, occupying the country in 1990 and being forced out by 1991) as well as an intra-state one (Kosovo Albanians aspiring to leave the Federal Republic of Yugoslavia, 1997–98, or uprisings by different Kurdish actors at different times against states such as Turkey, Syria, Iran and Iraq).

There are theoretical reasons for bringing incompatibility into the conflict definition. Conflict theory suggests that parties act for particular purposes. Thus, they need initially to be taken at face value. In other analyses such purposes are regarded as secondary. The Correlates of War project in Michigan originally focused on armed behaviour, the war. It aims at understanding what triggers this particular type of behaviour. The project design focuses on structural conditions as potential explanations, such as balance of power and other elements in the international system. At first it did not include the party's own perception of why the conflict is there. In the latest version, however, such a distinction is made for intra-state wars, where the project now separates conflicts for control of the central government from conflicts over local or regional interests (Sarkees and Wayman 2010: 339). The terminology is close to the one used in the Uppsala project for two decades. Thus, the Hamburg project is nearer the original COW definition in this regard and its perspective is equally structural (notably, capitalism or globalization) as are those of COW (the international system). However, if the focus is shifted to conflict resolution, as is the case for the Uppsala project, the parties' intentions become more important. Conflict exists, the parties will say, because there are particular grievances and, thus, the conflict cannot end until such concerns are resolved, ended or at least attended to. With its categories, the Uppsala project attempts to capture such explicitly stated grievances. This approach receives interesting support from other studies, pointing to the importance of territory, for example, by Holsti (1991), Vasquez (1993, 1995) and most recently by Gibler (2012). The Uppsala project aims at connecting its data to the development of conflict theory, in particular, theories of conflict resolution.

There is also a practical consideration, alluded to in the Hamburg project (Jung et al. 1996: 51), that a line has to be drawn between political violence and sheer banditry, mutinies and other forms of collective violence. There are cases where drug dealers clearly are behind the assassination of presidential candidates. Colombia had such an experience in the 1990s. However, the purpose is seldom for the assassin and his/her bosses to take control of the government. The aim is rather to prevent actors from taking power, if they might affect the government's policy on drug trade (changes in laws, operations and effectiveness of the policy). This type of violence is different, as it reflects criminal concerns. Such matters require police strategies, not peace research. There are delicate borderlines to observe, however. It is known that regular armed services, grey-zone paramilitary groups as well as many so-called liberation movements sustain themselves through the drug trade or other smuggling operations. There are also warlords who draw a thin line between politics and commerce.

The UCDP has expanded considerably and now operates an Internet-based database, that is available free of charge, for all armed conflicts since 1975 (www.ucdp.uu.se). It also cooperates with other institutions: with the International Peace Research Institute, Oslo (PRIO), the definitions have been applied back to 1946, a dataset that is available on the UCDP website; and with the Human Security Project at Simon Fraser University, Vancouver, Canada, additional aspects are studied, such as conflicts between non-state actors and one-sided violence against unorganized populations (for example, genocide and ethnic cleansing). Thus, the types of political violence included in UCDP go beyond those reported by AKUF. As mentioned, COW has introduced a category of non-state war. For the period since 1946, there are ten such wars according to COW. It should be noted that the UCDP category of non-state conflict contains 361 conflicts for the period 1989–2008, of which 14 had more than 1,000 battle-related deaths for a year (Pettersson 2010). For non-state conflict, the inclusion threshold of 1,000 deaths may be particularly problematic. In this volume, however, the focus is on the armed conflicts where the state is one party.

Patterns of Armed Conflict

The number of armed conflicts for the period 1989–2013 with the Uppsala definition is 144 (Themnér and Wallensteen 2014). For the 25-year period, this means that the average number of new conflicts per year is close to six, a higher ratio than reported in the two other projects. Adding information on non-state conflicts and actors involved in one-sided violence, we see that politically motivated violence is considerably higher (Pettersson and Themnér 2010). For the longer period 1946–2007, COW reports 179 wars, AKUF 238 conflicts and UCDP 254 armed conflicts. Figure 2.1 shows the trends in armed conflict for the entire period of 1946–2013 using UCDP definitions.

Given the discussion on wars, the bottom area of Figure 2.1 is most interesting to follow. The trends are not linear. During the Cold War period there was a constant increase in overall conflict frequency. The number of wars parallels what is reported by the Correlates of War for these years. By the middle of the 1990s, the total numbers as well as the numbers of wars declined somewhat. Several wars were brought to a halt or settled by peace agreements. However, there are continuous variations and it seems difficult to consistently stay below the level of 30 armed conflicts or five wars.

This pattern is even more pronounced when studying different regions. Europe, which for a large part of the Cold War saw little manifest armed conflict, was the first region to experience a sharp rise in conflicts. These were associated with the break-up of the Soviet and Yugoslav unions. The numbers went from two armed conflicts in 1989 to nine by 1993. By 1997 they were down to zero, only to see two conflicts in 1998 (Northern Ireland and Kosovo) and three in 1999 (Kosovo, Dagestan and Chechnya). Since then, minor conflicts have been recorded in Macedonia, Georgia and Chechnya. The conflicts in Georgia and Chechnya had heavy Russian involvement. To this, the conflict over Ukraine has been added, recorded as an armed conflict only in 2014, more remarkable but not unexpected. UCDP records a war between the Soviet Union and Ukrainian forces in 1946. Indeed, there were many references to those events also in the 2014 situation. Soviet media portrayed the Ukrainian forces as fascist as Ukrainian nationalists did benefit from the German invasion from 1941 onwards. For the Ukrainian side, Russia's and Russian separatist actions remind of Soviet-style behaviour. To many, President Putin's project on a Eurasian Union had traits of Russian restoration.

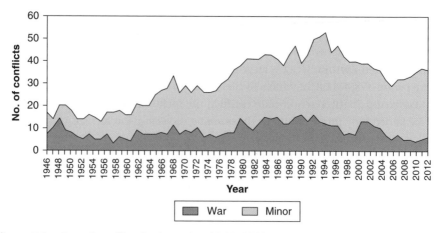

Figure 2.1 Armed conflicts by intensity, 1946–2013

For Africa, there is another pattern. By the middle of the 1990s, this continent appeared to be a beneficiary of the end of the Cold War. Wars on the continent that had been sustained by the Cold War, as well as by South African polarization, were ending. This could be observed for the Horn of Africa and Southern Africa. West Africa and the Sudan seemed to be the only conflict areas left. From 12 armed conflicts in 1989 and 17 in 1991, the numbers were down to 10 in 1995, only to be back up to 15–16 for 1998–2002. New wars were experienced in the Horn of Africa (Eritrea v. Ethiopia) and, most challenging, in Central Africa, connecting conflicts over a vast, highly populated and resource-rich region. Conflicts in this area became increasingly difficult to disentangle. A regional conflict complex was created, initially centred on the Hutu–Tutsi conflict which, by way of refugee flows, guerrilla movements and interventions, came to engulf a number of states.[1] Similarly, regionally related wars took place in Western Africa. There were also, however, concerted efforts to deal with the violence which, by 2004–05, began to pay off. The war in the Democratic Republic of Congo tapered off, although Rwandan troops were battling Hutu groups in the territory. The protracted war in Sudan ended in a peace agreement in 2005, resulting in only 7 remaining. However, the tide turned and by 2013 the numbers of conflicts were again 13. The initially peaceful division of Sudan in 2011 was soon followed by conflicts between the two states, as well as within them. By 2013, the Central African Republic and Mali had been drawn into serious armed conflicts and Mozambique saw renewed fighting between the parties to the 1992 peace agreement.

In comparison to the dramatic shifts in Europe and Africa, other regions show a repetitive pattern of conflict. The Gulf War of 1990–91 saw a continuation in the US-led intervention in 2003, resulting in a civil war in Iraq. By 2010, US combat forces were withdrawn. The Arab Spring of 2011 resulted in battles between the government and the democratic opposition in Libya and then in Syria. By 2014, both countries were still in turmoil, and the civil war in Syria was the most devastating one in a long time. The conflict also spilled into Iraq, through a spin-off grouping from al-Qaida, mostly known as ISIS, the Islamic State of Iraq and Syria, but obviously having larger ambitions. This was seen in its proclamation of a Caliphate in 2014, challenging the existing border arrangements in the region.

To this should be added the situation in South Asia, where the India-Pakistan peace process stalled. However, there was still no sustained direct violence between the two. The long war in Sri Lanka ended with government victory in 2009. The situation in Afghanistan became increasingly complicated, drawing in Pakistan as well as a host of allies to the United States and the Karzai government. The Obama administration prioritized this conflict, acting under the lingering impact of the attacks on September 11, 2001. The al-Qaida leader, Osama bin-Laden, was located and killed in Pakistan in 2011. Nonetheless, the fighting against the Taliban in Afghanistan as well as in Pakistan remained intense.

In the Americas, Colombia was the major battlefield, while Mexico saw a dramatic escalation of drug-related violence, much of which UCDP categorized as non-state violence. However, a peace process got under way in Colombia with facilitation by Cuba and Norway, and had by 2014 made considerable headway.

The same could be said for the situation in Southeast Asia: The protracted conflict in the Philippines over Mindanao was in a constructive peace process with considerable achievements in 2013 and 2014. The possibilities of solving many ethnic conflicts in Myanmar (or Burma) appeared to improve with increasing democratization of the country. However, in neighbouring Thailand the trend was the reverse: a military take-over and no progress in dealing with the conflict in South Thailand.

For the world as a whole, the total number of armed conflicts is staggering. Despite great efforts at conflict resolution, it appears that, for each conflict solved between parties with international efforts, a new one emerges, often pursued by splinter groups, requiring the same mix of improvisation and standard operating procedures by the international community. This repeated experience of inadequacy should fuel the interest in preventive conflict management as well as post-conflict peacebuilding. Also, it shows the need to search for the underlying causes in order to find remedies that combine conflict prevention with social change and popular participation. In a longer perspective, however, none of the armed conflicts initiated in the 1990s has been as devastating as some of the older conflicts. The protracted war in Afghanistan, which began in 1978, has more than 1 million battle-related deaths. The 1980s also witnessed the Iran–Iraq War with 1.2 million deaths. The Vietnam War or, more appropriately, the Second Indochina War, ended in 1975, with possibly 2 million deaths. The Nigerian Civil War in the 1960s was a disaster, with 1 million deaths. The Korean War in the 1950s reportedly led to 2 million deaths. The civil war in the 1940s in China, ending with the Communist Party taking control, saw 1 million battle-related deaths (Singer 1991; Small and Singer 1982). The war scenarios since the Cold War are equally serious. Still, it might be suggested that there is greater agreement on the goal to reduce human suffering. There are examples of humanitarian support even in the midst of war, in Bosnia, for instance. Principles containing a responsibility to protect exposed populations have gained adherence. There is also a willingness from the outside community to act earlier in a serious conflict to prevent it from becoming more destructive. This means that the reported reduction in battle deaths and risks of death in armed conflict since 1946 – surprising as it might be to the normal consumer of daily news – is plausible (Lacina and Gleditsch 2005; Lacina et al. 2006).

This notwithstanding, there are marked fluctuations in battle-related deaths in the post-Cold War period, where the war in Syria since 2011 clearly is one of the most devastating in the past 25 years (Themnér and Wallensteen 2014).

2.4 Outcomes of Armed Conflict

The concept of conflict resolution was given a preliminary definition in Chapter 1. It will be further refined in Chapter 3. Having delineated armed conflict and war, peacemaking is easier to portray. It is something done by the warring parties, expressed in the form of an agreement, implemented by first ending the fighting and then followed through in all other respects. The value of agreements has been challenged. It is, however, not easy to end a war and start a process of forging a post-war order without having some shared awareness of what the new arrangement should look like. An agreement expresses such a joint understanding. It may not include everything that needs settlement, and there are likely to develop different interpretations of what has been concluded. Still, an agreement provides a basis for a new relationship. It is not easy to make accords after a war, even when the parties have been allies, as was the case of the USA, Britain and the Soviet Union during the Second World War. Even before the war ended, the allies had serious disagreements on the post-war world, although they had made agreements (one was concluded in Yalta, Crimea, in February 1945, but soon gave rise to disputes). If victors cannot agree among themselves, it is probably even more difficult for enemies to develop a shared document on the future of their interaction. A peace agreement, in other words, is a particular result in a process that began before the agreement was signed and continues after the ink has dried.

The Uppsala program is collecting data on peace agreements and the information is available in its database for the period after 1975. It makes possible closer scrutiny of frequencies of different types of war ending. The date shows, for the period 1989–2013, a total of 144 armed conflicts, where 111 actually had been terminated by the end of 2013, that is, three-quarters of the total. This supports the statement in Section 2.1 that conflicts and wars actually do end.

However, a peace agreement may not be the ending of a conflict. Agreements may not be implemented, or only implemented by some actors or in some respects. This means that conflict may continue. The same is true for victory and other outcomes. Thus, the information on peace agreements needs to be complemented with data on conflict terminations, that is, situations where there has been no fighting for a period of time, often set to be for one year. This will give us a fuller picture of the intricacy of conflict. For instance, such terminations may be due to a victory or to a peace agreement, but could also be the result of other arrangements (cease-fires, unilateral withdrawals, etc.).

Table 2.1 shows that the number of conflicts terminated through victories are more than double the number of peace agreements, but even so more than half of all conflicts end in other ways (cease-fires and other outcomes, which includes unilateral withdrawal, for instance). Furthermore, peace agreements fail earlier than victories, but in the long run the recurrence of armed conflict is somewhat less frequent. In fact, the failure rates are much higher for cease-fires and other outcomes, both in the short run and in the longer perspective. It is also so that victory outcomes are often seen in short conflicts. Kreutz (2010: 246) observes that: 'parties often manage to quickly defeat their opponents through military superiority in the beginning of a conflict. If neither party is able to do so, the conflict is more likely to be settled through a negotiated process.' In fact, Table 2.1 demonstrates that peace agreements and cease-fires are almost as common as victories, and both are examples of negotiated arrangements.

The variety of possible outcomes displayed in Table 2.1 is probably not what the initiators have normally planned for. The preference is for durable victory within a reasonably short period. Many conflicts are deeply entrenched, have witnessed broken negotiations, failed cease-fire arrangements, and abandoned peace agreements. They are probably increasingly difficult to settle. For many initiators, however, what was originally planned may no longer be possible to accomplish.

Table 2.1 Duration and types of conflict termination, 1946–2009

	No. of conflict terminations	Conflicts recurring within 3 years (%)	Conflicts recurring at all during the period (%)
Peace agreement	59	14	36
Victory	125	12	42
Cease-fire	55	18	47
Other outcomes	176	36	61
Total	415	23	50

Note: There are a total of 415 terminated conflict episodes in 244 armed conflicts that took place in this period, that is, fighting ceased for at least one year. The endings have been coded according to four categories. Status by end of 2009.

Source: Kreutz (2010); UCDP Conflict Termination Dataset v (2010–1), www.ucdp.uu.se

One of the most protracted conflicts has been that in Afghanistan. The war began as an attempt by a communist party to reform the feudal society, change the land distribution and give women a stronger standing. After 20 years of war with many special features – Soviet invasion, US support to opposition movements and involvement from a host of neighbouring and Middle Eastern countries – the communist party was eliminated and many of its leaders brutally murdered. The conflict was then pursued along traditional divisions, and the dominating group until November 2001 (the Taliban) was unusually Islamic and anti-women. The conflict dynamics have become entirely different from what the originators had anticipated. The rule of the Taliban was effectively ended by December 2001, when a local and international alliance led by the United States, escalated the war in order to rout the al-Qaida organization based in the country. Resistance linked to the Taliban regrouped and returned, however, and, since 2010, the conflict is one of the wars recorded in the world.

Victory is difficult to achieve. It does occur, however. The most obvious example is the US intervention in Panama, capturing the 'strongman' of the leadership, General Noriega, bringing him to trial in Florida, convicting him for drug-trade offences and putting him in a US prison until 2010 when he was extradited to France for further trials. In 2011 he was sent back to Panama, where he is to serve the remainder of his sentence. The Gulf War is also a victory: Iraqi forces had to withdraw and Kuwait was restored as a sovereign country. In 1997 a rebellion against the incumbent regime in Zaire ended with victory. The war lasted eight months. The new regime faced another rebellion less than nine months later. A peace agreement concluded in July 1999, and signed in September the same year, was meant to end the war, without accomplishing this by the end of 2000. Since then Congo has been the scene of many armed actors and stability is still illusive. The US victory over the regime in Iraq in 2003 seemed swift. The statue of Saddam Hussein was brought down on April 9, 2003, and major combat was declared to be over by May 1. The continued fighting illustrates the difficulty of sustaining victory. By 2010, 4,400 US fighters had been killed in an internal war which was 'won' more than seven years earlier. By the end of the year US combat forces were withdrawn, but conflict continued. In 2014, ISIS, known for brutality, religious zeal and fighting ability, even seized control over Iraq's second largest city, Mosul, prompting renewed US military engagement, years after the mission was supposedly accomplished.

Such dynamics of victory, defeat and protracted conflict are known from history. The large number of peace agreements is a most novel aspect, and part of the experience since the Cold War. A recent review of conflict terminations shows that peace agreements have become more common since 1990 (27 compared to 12 for the 1946–89 period) and more common than victories (Kreutz 2010). Also, 46 conflicts had a total of 139 such agreements and that violence remained ended for at least five years following 78 of these agreements (Högbladh 2006).

Furthermore, some agreements outlined processes towards a solution (Israel v. Palestine since 1993) where other parties nevertheless pursued a violent ending. There are even cases of a complete settlement concluded between the main parties, where other actors took up or continued armed struggle nevertheless (Mindanao in 1996, and possibly again in 2014). Of course, there are also agreements that have been functioning for a period of time but then have been undermined by the parties. This is true for the settlements for Angola in 1991 and 1994, Chechnya in 1996, Sierra Leone 1996 and 1999 and Sudan where the peace agreement resulted in state separation in 2011 and renewed conflict. However, all peace agreement failures do not have to result in renewed war. Côte d'Ivoire saw a series of failed agreements from 2003 to 2010, but no renewed fighting in that period (Wallensteen et al. 2011). A short armed conflict erupted in March–April 2011, but no armed conflict has been recorded since then.

The record of successful peacemaking is as varied as can be expected from the difficulties of ending long-lasting wars. Still, the ambition to do so with the help of negotiation and agreement makes the period since the end of the Cold War an interesting object of study. The developments of the post-Cold War period can legitimately be compared to the very few peace agreements ending wars that were concluded during the entirety of the Cold War. There were cease-fire agreements, no doubt, but very few peace agreements. As we noted in Chapter 1, some of the cease-fire lines drawn during the Cold War still constitute the main territorial divisions in many conflicts. To cases such as Palestine, Korea and Cyprus we can add the territorial division between India and Pakistan in Kashmir in 1949 that ended their first war. New wars in the area in 1965 and 1971 led to a return to the previous cease-fire lines. The conflict remains unresolved.

Among the few comprehensive peace agreements concluded during the Cold War, the Geneva peace agreement for Indochina in 1954 was effectively undermined within two years. The war between Malaysia and Indonesia, which began in 1963, was concluded through a peace pact in 1966, and the conflict has not resumed. A short war in 1963 between Algeria and Morocco found a mediated agreement the same year. An agreement in 1972 to end the war in the Sudan was shattered in 1983 and war returned. The Camp David agreement between Israel and Egypt in 1979 has stood the test of time. For the 45 years of Cold War, the peace agreements are few, probably 12 by the latest account (Kreutz 2010; Licklider 1995; Mason and Fett 1996; Stedman 1991). This is not a particularly striking record at peacemaking. It contrasts the many arms control agreements made, where one source lists 27 international accords from 1963 to 1991 (Goldstein 1992). This makes the large number of peace agreements during the turbulent period since 1989 unique, valuable and worth a closer analysis.

Since 1989, peace agreements have been concluded in all regions of the world. This means that peacemaking has a global meaning. Without peacemaking efforts the number of wars would probably have increased significantly. The agreements may have been concluded between parties too exhausted to find resources to win the wars, but sometimes they are also not capable of concluding agreements on their own. The Dayton Agreement on Bosnia-Herzegovina may fit into this category, as the warring parties only accepted the deal under strong international pressure. Thus, we will proceed to the theme of conflict resolution by departing from the peace agreements concluded or implemented since 1989. With this in mind, it is now necessary to turn to a more theoretical discussion on conflict theory and its implications for conflict resolution. This is done in Chapter 3.

Further Readings

Go to the *Understanding Conflict Resolution* web page at https://study.sagepub.com/wallensteen4e for free access to journal articles listed.

Conflict Data Projects

The text mentions several projects that deal with the collection of systematic data and that have been influential for the presently important projects. They are

(Continued)

(Continued)

valuable to study, to see the development of definition, methods of data collection and ways of presenting information. The work presented in *Understanding Conflict Resolution* departs largely from the Uppsala Conflict Data Program. It can be reached at www.ucdp.uu.se. For the history of this project see Wallensteen, P. 2011. *Peace Research: Theory and Practice*. London: Routledge. pp. 105–24.

AKUF, Working Group on the Causes of War, University of Hamburg, www.wiso.uni-hamburg.de/en/fachbereiche/sozialwissenschaften/forschung/akuf/akuf/

This is a project that originated in Budapest, Hungary, and now continues from the University of Hamburg, Germany, mostly publishing in the German language for a German public.

The Correlates of War homepage: www.correlatesofwar.org/

This is the site of the seminal project that also stimulated quantitative studies in international relations research globally. It was initially led by J. David Singer at the University of Michigan, Ann Arbor, MI, USA.

Singer, J.D. 1972. 'The Correlates of War Project', *World Politics*, 24: 243–70.

Introduced the early phases of this project, presents the underlying ideas as well as the hopes for the project.

Backer, D., Huth, P. and Wilkenfeld, J. 2014. *Peace and Conflict 2014*. Herndon, VA: Paradigm Publishers.

This is a recent publication emanating from the studies of conflict at the University of Maryland in the US, and where the original foundations go back to the project on Minorities at Risk, led by Ted R. Gurr and associates.

Wright, Q. 1942. *A Study of War*. Chicago: University of Chicago Press.

Many of these projects explicitly refer to the work of Quincy Wright, and the original study with its many observations and data collections still remains interesting to read. There is also a later, abbreviated version of this work.

Comparing Conflict Data Collections

Dixon, J. 2009. 'What Causes Civil Wars? Integrating Quantitative Research Findings', *International Studies Review*, 11 (4): 707–35.

This work compares the sources used by different researchers for the study of civil wars and also assesses agreed findings.

Eck, K. 2005. A Beginner's Guide to Conflict Data. Finding the Right Dataset, Uppsala, Sweden: UCDP Papers No 1. www.pcr.uu.se/research/ucdp/publications/ucdp_papers/

Eck's overview provides a quick introduction to all the data collections that were known at the time. It still remains a useful guide.

Forsberg, E., Duursma, A. and Grant, L. 2012. *Theoretical and Empirical Considerations in the Study of Ethnicity and Conflict.* Uppsala: Uppsala University, UCDP Paper No 8. Download at www.pcr.uu.se/digitalAssets/66/66310_1paper8.pdf
This work is based on a conference drawing together a number of the leading data collection projects focusing specifically on ethnic conflict.

Trends in Armed Conflict

The issue of whether wars and violence is in decline has given rise to a number of discussions. It was, in particular, stimulated by the best-selling work of Steven Pinker:

Pinker, S. 2011. *The Better Angels of our Nature.* New York: Viking.

Gleditsch, N.P., Pinker, S., Thayer, B.A., Levy, J.S. and Thompson, W.R. 2013. 'The Forum: The Decline of War', *International Studies Review*, 15: 396–419.
In a forum for discussion, the issues of a trend towards a reduction in numbers and fatalities of conflicts were debated at the annual convention of the International Studies Association 2012. Some of the interventions were brought together in this volume, which thus gives an update on the discussions as they stood in the early 2010s.

The issue of trends has also been discussed by authorities affiliated with the Uppsala Conflict Data Program. An important contribution is the one by Joakim Kreutz in 2010. The annual update of the armed conflict record is published in *Journal of Peace Research*, giving the observers a basis for making their own conclusions:

Kreutz, J. 2010. 'How and When Armed Conflicts End: Introducing the UCDP Conflict Termination Dataset', *Journal of Peace Research*, 47 (2): 243–50.

Themnér, L. and Wallensteen, P. 2014. 'Armed Conflicts 1946–2013', *Journal of Peace Research*, 51 (4): 541–54.

Interpretations of Conflict Information

Of course, data are still open to interpretation. The facts provided by the data project create a framework for understanding, but may also lead to a quest for

(Continued)

(Continued)

different ways of collecting information. Two significant contributions are provided by Ann Tickner and John A. Vasquez:

Tickner, A. 1997. 'You Just Don't Understand: Troubled Engagements Between Feminists and IR Theorists', *International Studies Quarterly*, 41 (4): 611–32.
Vasquez, J.A. (ed.) 2012. *What Do We Know about War?* (2nd edn). Lanham, MD: Rowman and Littlefield Publishers.

Note

1 The genocide in Rwanda in 1994 is separated from armed conflict in the Uppsala Conflict Data Program. It is located in a category of one-sided violence as it is directed against unorganized civilians by a state or a non-state actor.

3

APPROACHING CONFLICT RESOLUTION

3.1 The Evolution of Conflict Analysis

During the Cold War, conflict analysis was developed largely to handle the understanding of the East–West conflict. It used tools such as system analysis and game theory. Game theory could illustrate the dangers inherent in a prisoner's dilemma game, but it could also be used to sharpen strategic thinking. To some, conflict theory could also be used for conflict resolution studies (Kriesberg 1997). Pertinent questions were how it was possible that three major powers (the USA, Britain and the Soviet Union), which had been united in the greatest war ever fought on this planet, only a couple of years later found themselves in a mortal conflagration. How could allies become deadly enemies so quickly? There were ready-made answers drawn from 'realist' power calculations, but there were also fears and misunderstandings arising from closed decision-making. The threats of the nuclear confrontation and the global reach of the Cold War made it urgent to understand the dynamics of conflict. The focus was on escalation and polarization, and how to manage and contain the violence built into such processes.

The simultaneous and surprising experience of the integration of the two former enemies, Germany and France, illustrated the potential of reversing dynamics. It showed that it was possible to move from being enemies to allies, in a relationship that was closer than traditional alliances of convenience. Again this took place in a short period of time. Thus, it was necessary to develop conflict analysis as well as integration studies. Considerable work was done in the 1950s and 1960s.

Soon, the perspectives began to deepen. Conflicts in the global South not only reflected the dynamics of polarization and integration; there were other forces at play as well. The leading power, the United States, saw intense, even armed, internal disputes in the 1960s and 1970s with riots and militant parties. The analysis had to focus on grievances that could drive conflicts. Scholars saw a role in contributing to a process of solving conflicts, in forms which the academics were used to (workshops and seminars). Towards the end of the 1980s and in the 1990s, the experience of settlement of local conflicts, as well as the ending of the Cold War, again strengthened the interest in conflict resolution. September 11, 2001, may have led to a return of strategic analysis, at least in conflicts relating to terrorism. However, many pointed to the needs for social change and conflict resolution for dealing also with such conflicts, particularly in a longer perspective. The surprising Arab Spring of 2011 again changed the perspectives and pointed to the importance of local dynamics, the possibilities of non-violent change, popular participation but also the dangers of repression and terror. The divergent origins have resulted in different approaches which all need to be understood. To this task we devote this chapter.

The different modes of analysis are brought together under three headings. There are approaches which emphasize: (1) conflict dynamics; (2) needs-based conflict origins; and (3) rational, strategic calculations. These constitute distinct forms of analysis. However, they do intersect and many writers use them interchangeably. They are presented with reference to the work of particular researchers, but should not necessarily be seen as coherent 'schools of thought' or as the exclusive approach of a particular writer. They are tools which are needed for any researcher, something that will be made clear in the synthesizing section of this chapter.

3.2 Focusing on Conflict Dynamics

A classic understanding of conflict sees it as a dynamic phenomenon: one actor is reacting to what another actor is doing, which leads to further action. Quickly, the stakes in the conflict escalate. One sequence of events follows another, and it is difficult to decipher which party is more responsible for what happens. In popular understanding, it is expressed as 'it takes two to conflict'. There are many observations which evoke this theme, notably the prevalence of mirror images, that parties and issues are seeing the conflict in the same way, only reversing the picture. There are also dynamics pushing the actors in conflicts into two camps (polarization), creating commanding leadership (centralization), and forming institutions with particular responsibilities and little insight (secrecy and protection). The conflict takes on a life of its own, engulfing the actors and, seemingly irresistibly, pushing them into ever increasing conflict. The idea of conflict as a social phenomenon moving by itself is powerful. It is invoked when parties say that they have no alternatives. The dynamics of the conflict have removed all other possible actions, and are said to give a party no choice but to continue to react at increasing levels of threat and violence.

For the analysis of such dynamics, some tools have been developed. Game theory is a way of illustrating how parties act within the confines set up by the game itself. If the parties follow the rules, the outcomes are predictable. But it also raises the possibility that actors can change the dynamics by making particular moves or even breaking some of the 'rules' that the conflict has generated. Such an analysis was developed in the 1960s for the polarized East–West conflict, suggesting credible de-escalating steps that could lead to positive responses. The idea was that if one actor begins to act on its own, the other(s) may follow, and thus the dynamics change direction. Some of these ideas were used for the US–Soviet relations in early periods of *détente* (Etzioni 1967; Osgood 1962).

In a slightly more complicated version, the conflict triangle – introduced by Johan Galtung in the 1960s – provides a helpful analytical tool (Galtung 1969a, 1996; Mitchell 1981; Wiberg 1976/1990). It suggests that a conflict moves among the triangle's three corners, where corner A refers to conflict attitudes, B to conflict behaviour and C to the conflict or contradiction itself (the incompatibility). A conflict sequence can begin in any of these corners. In later writings, Galtung gives somewhat more emphasis to C as a more frequent – or even logical – starting point. The dynamics are still most important, however, even expressed in conflicts having life-cycles. From this it follows that the resolution of conflict, conflict transformation, is a 'never-ending process'. A solution 'in the sense of a steady-state, durable formation is at best a temporary goal'. The conflict is transformed, for instance, through transcendence (where the goals are met fully for the conflict parties), compromise (goals are met less than fully for the sides) and withdrawals (goals are given up) (Galtung 1996: 72, 81–90, 96).

Although structural features, such as frustration and structural violence, are mentioned in this approach, dynamics are more central. The dynamics can be affected and steered in ways that make conflict creative. This is achieved by the parties themselves or with contributions from outsiders, intervening in a benign way. In Galtung's version of conflict dynamics, finding agreements through diplomatic means is less important, but not excluded. In fact, his examples point to the importance of procedures for changing conflict dynamics. Ingenious conference arrangements can help make complexity more manageable, as exemplified by the Law of the Sea Conference in Caracas in 1974 and the Helsinki process for *détente* in the East–West conflict in Europe, initiated in 1972 (Galtung 1996: 92–3). Such examples might be surprising as these conferences did not involve a solution to the substance of the conflicts, but only provided a reasonable process through which the issues could be handled. It points out, however, that negotiations are ways in which conflicts can be transformed. Finding a mutually acceptable process may be a necessary precursor to a solution.

In the end, Galtung concedes, agreements on substance are also needed. They may be informal, as in the examples of how children divide an orange and spouses solve a dispute over vacation plans, or formal, as is the case when ending a multilateral conference (the Convention on the Law of the Sea, the Helsinki Final Act). Transcendence means finding an agreement on who divides the orange and chooses among the parts, or finding a place where one family member can climb in the mountains and another remain on the beach (one place is clearly Taormina, Sicily; others might be found in California and New Zealand!). Accords concluded in such disputes do not need to be written into a document, as there is considerable confidence and integration among the parties. But Galtung's third example, the creation of a confederation between Israel and Palestine (Galtung 1996: 98), is unthinkable without negotiations and a signed agreement, constitution or other mutually understood arrangements. This illustrates that conflict resolution after war cannot be thought of in the same way as solving conflicts between parties with a high level of mutual trust. It is not without reason that wars tend to end with documents, signatures and ceremonies. It is a way for the parties to make sure that the other side is committed to the process and to the agreement. An agreement may help to transform the conflict from a destructive, divisive experience to a constructive, shared endeavour.

The work by Galtung has here been used as an example of the dynamic perspective on conflict analysis. There is a considerable body of thinking along similar lines (Kriesberg 1992; Mitchell 1981; Pruitt and Rubin 1986; Wiberg 1976/1990). It represents an early perspective in the development of conflict analysis and parallels game theory advances (Axelrod 1984; Rapoport 1960). It remains rich in its emphasis on the changing and powerful dynamics of conflict. Without insight into such dynamics, conflict analysis misses an important aspect. Central is the understanding of how difficult it is to break the dynamics. Conflict resolution is about changing the direction of the flow of events, so that escalation is turned into de-escalation and polarization into positive interaction.

Particularly fruitful is Galtung's depiction of incompatibility as central to the dynamics of conflict. A way to do an incompatibility analysis is reproduced in Figure 3.1, which shows two actors, A and B, with contradictory goals. What the dispute is about is not significant. It could concern a piece of territory, a sum of money, an attractive government post, or other scarce valuables. If A gets 100 per cent of the available resources, there is nothing left for B, and vice versa. If either one wins, the situation finds itself at point A or point B, respectively, meaning complete victory for one actor and complete defeat for the other. It is an outcome an actor is not likely to abide by easily and voluntarily. Anything beyond these points may, however, be more acceptable and possible. Along the diagonal there are positions at which the parties may meet. C marks a classical point, where the parties divide the resources 50–50, equally much (or little) for each side. The parties may also agree on going to point E, none of them takes anything, but instead the valuables are handed over to actor C, also an agreed solution. In a more sinister scenario, C may enter the conflict and take the valuables from the fighting parties – an opportunistic move by an outsider. The resources may also have been destroyed during the fighting. In the space to the left and below the diagonal in Figure 3.1, there are many outcomes. Different forms of compromise may be found here. To the right and above the line, however, there are other complications. This is where Galtung's ideas lead: transcendence. The hope is to find points of type D, where both parties can get what they want at the same time (again, the example of Taormina, Sicily!). The mathematical formulation is, of course, impossible. There cannot be 200 per cent of something, but this space indicates the challenge of finding solutions beyond established rules and thinking. Creativity is needed for transcendence. Political battle often stifles innovation and reduces the options perceived by the actors. Sometimes, the strains of the effort may result in imaginative actions. In all, Figure 3.1 is a useful device to describe an incompatibility. It will be used later in this book.

The dynamic approach to conflict analysis points to the significance of *establishing a dialogue* between the parties. This is where, for instance, finding a conference format is important. It requires that the parties can participate, but together with others who can serve as practical go-betweens and add issues which may unlock positions. It also points to the importance of *confidence-building measures*, not only in the military field,

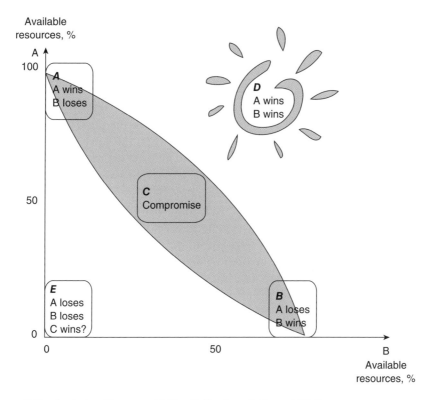

Figure 3.1 Analysis of incompatibility (following Galtung 1996)

but also in social, cultural, economic and other areas, as they can be instrumental in changing the dynamics of a conflict. Conferences and confidence-building are mostly multilateral, and in this approach the injection of mediators and facilitators is important. Third parties take a particular role in such settings.

An original idea is the one of *conflict resolution mechanisms*. This refers to the creation of independent procedures in which the parties can have confidence. These are formal or informal arrangements to which they can agree to hand over their conflict, whose solution they can accept and which can define the termination of a conflict (Coser 1967; Galtung 1965; Schelling 1960). Such mechanisms exist in internal affairs, for instance, courts, democratic procedures, and elections called to solve a parliamentary stalemate. They are scarce in international relations, where court systems are weak and political fora easily become arenas of dispute, rather than frameworks for handling conflicts. In internal affairs, the possibilities of appeal are important, creating opportunities to review what has been done on lower levels. As part of a future conflict resolution mechanism this can also be a useful device in the international system.

Finally, it follows from this perspective that *parties with non-violent methods* are potentially efficient in changing the dynamics. This gives a role to peace movements, but also to other groups, non-governmental organizations (NGOs) and civil society at large (including academic institutions) that work for conciliation and understanding across divides. Such parties can even be involved in conflicts and take sides, but they pursue their goals with peaceful means, not with violence.

They constitute an alternative approach for a community wishing to achieve change, but not convinced that violence is an appropriate action. For instance, in Western Europe, social democratic ways of impacting capitalist systems seem to have achieved more welfare, enjoyed stronger support in the public and lasted longer than did the bitterly competing communist parties. This particular divide focused on the possibility of peaceful versus violent change. Similarly, the non-violent party representing the Nationalist community in Northern Ireland (SDLP) for a long time drew a larger share of the Catholic vote than the party closer to the IRA (Sinn Fein). These non-violent actors may be important in bridging the dynamics, giving space for alternative actions and, thus, be central in a transition from war to peace.

Still, this perspective is weak in its understanding of why conflicts start. Is it reasonable to assume that conflicts really begin with conflict attitudes, or are such attitudes a result of previous behaviour and pre-existing incompatibilities? Can there be a more complex background that also has to be part of the analysis? What if the parties who often are modelled to be of equal strength are, in fact, highly unequal? These are critical challenges to conflict theory. This gives reason for considering alternative approaches.

3.3 Focusing on Basic Needs

A classic writer in social conflict theory is Lewis A. Coser. His book, *The Functions of Social Conflict* (1956), contains a series of statements on how conflicts can contribute positively to the functioning of society. There are also dysfunctional effects, but by devoting his work entirely to the functions, the book stimulated research, influencing all three perspectives that are presented here. Coser's work cannot be easily categorized. His functional approach indicates a dynamic perspective on conflict. It is noteworthy that he has very little to say on the ending of conflict, for instance. However, his definition of what he calls 'realistic conflicts' points in a different direction. These are conflicts 'which arise from frustration of specific demands ... and ... are directed at the presumed frustrating object' (1956: 49). Thus they are instrumental actions, not just a form of tension release, or 'anger' (Fry and Björkqvist 1997: 27–8).

In a later work, Coser analysed the 1965 Watts riots in Los Angeles, California, demonstrating empirically what this approach would mean. What happened in Watts, he says, 'was an effort of an active minority ... to announce their unwillingness to continue accepting indignity and frustration without fighting back. In particular, they were communicating their desperation through violent acts since no other channels of communication seemed open to them' (1967: 103). Thus, Coser argues that the conflicts as well as the violent actions stem from not being accepted in society, a matter of dignity, political access and power. The rioters struck, in particular, against those who had treated members of their ethnic community in a condescending way. Coser points to a remedy: access to the political system. He writes that 'only where there exist open channels of political communication through which all groups can articulate their demands, are the chances high that the political exercise of violence can be successfully minimized' (1967: 106). This means that violent conflict can be terminated by satisfying needs for access.

Furthermore, this has to be maintained over time. The solution, in other words, is likely to be found in building new institutions, whether formal or informal.

In his work on 'protracted social conflict' 20 years later, Edward Azar outlined ideas for explaining the duration of conflicts and the repeated failure of conflict resolution. He was concerned, for instance, with the civil war in Lebanon which, by the time of writing, had raged for more than a decade. This and other protracted conflicts dealt with such needs as security, identity, recognition and participation, factors which are identical to those that Coser singled out (Azar and Burton 1986: 29). These contributions by Coser and Azar result in a different approach to conflict resolution. If the basis of a conflict is the denial of particular needs, then the resolution process must identify those needs and include ways of answering them. Negotiations have a tendency to give advantages to elites, and if agreements 'do not touch upon the underlying issues in the conflict [agreements] do not last'. Instead, Azar finds, conflict resolution requires decentralized structures and ways in which psychological, economic and relational needs can be satisfied (Azar and Burton 1986: 30–9).

This thinking is part of a materialist theoretical tradition and constitutes a significant element in class analysis. But Marxist theorists seldom have come to an understanding of conflict resolution. On the contrary, much Marxist thinking is based on the idea of continuous conflict, ending only with the defeat of the oppressive system – at this time, capitalism. Negotiation and compromise were not part of the political formula, or of the academic study. Only in the reformist, social democratic version, as we have just seen, was conflict within capitalism manageable. Another root of the idea of conflict stemming from frustration is the approach of analysing revolution as emerging from unsatisfied needs. Theories of deprivation have been given thoughtful consideration in a number of works and been exposed to empirical tests (Davies 1971; Gurr 1970). The results are mixed. In his elaborate treatment of relative deprivation, Ted R. Gurr found support for 'relative deprivation' as a systematic way for conflicts to become violent. In his later work on ethnic groups, Gurr reports factors that were associated with escalation into violent conflict, most notably the negative effects of the removal of autonomy for a particular group. It often becomes an important reason for the group to revolt (Gurr 1993). This observation is linked to Coser's reflections on dignity and political access. The removal of channels of influence may spark violence. Thus, the creation of such channels can be important in terminating violence and making non-armed conflict a constructive part of the political process.

These theorists refer to concepts such as frustration and deprivation. What they provide is an analysis of social frustration. Basic needs are not met in a particular society; instead they are out of reach for a group, which thus becomes frustrated. The conflict originates in or feeds on this frustration. It comes close to classical studies on frustration as resulting in aggression, and aggression as stemming from frustration (Dollard et al. 1939), which has given rise to considerable debate and revision. For instance, it has been asked if aggression is the only way to direct frustration, and whether there are other possible explanations for frustration and conflict behaviour (Fry and Björkqvist 1997: 26–32).

The sequence is captured in James C. Davies' figure on revolution, as shown in Figure 3.2. It shows pointedly how a gap emerges and when the difference between expectations and frustration becomes obvious. As the figure is constructed, expectations are always higher than what is accomplished. A certain difference is, therefore, manageable. The achievements are seen as the lower line in the figure. When the gap becomes too large, however, it is likely to be unacceptable. This may happen, for instance, if the economy ceases to grow after a period of sustained growth. The actual achievement becomes considerably lower than was expected and thus discontent rises. This, it has been argued, leads to a revolution of rising expectations. Interestingly, Davies finds in his study that this pattern fits with the economic performance of several countries before a revolution breaks out. However, this does not settle the issue. For instance, a question is whether or not the same experience has occurred in a number of other countries, but without revolution. Frustration, as described by Davies, may be theoretically interesting, but does it hold up empirically? Gurr's initial study (1970) did not result in strong correlations, but his work focusing on what we may call political frustration (1993) suggests intriguing relationships.

The model in Figure 3.2 is confined to internal, or intra-state, situations. Revolutions are directed at the leaders in the same society. How can frustration result in international conflict? John W. Burton, who has written extensively on conflict resolution, suggests there is a 'spillover' effect. Conflicts, 'especially at the international level', he says, 'are a spillover of some internal institutional or personal problem'. These are ways in which leaders 'divert attention' (Burton 1996: 41). Thus, internal conflict may arise from a group's reaction to discrimination, and the resulting disturbances are diverted by the government into international conflict. This is a popular theory. Theoretically,

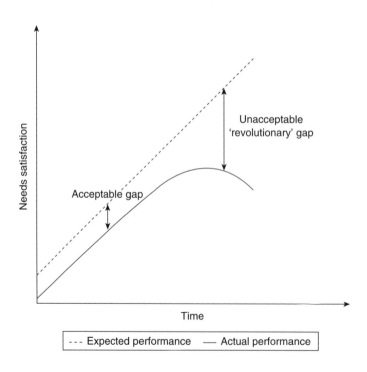

Figure 3.2 Satisfaction of needs and revolution (following Davies 1971)

however, there are a number of other ways in which frustration can be diverted or covered, for instance, in the Roman slogan of 'Bread and Circus', meaning that basic economic necessities were met and that spectacular shows were arranged to give the populations interests other than politics. Today this may be seen in the form of food price subsidies and Olympic Games. There is also the possibility that leaders actually attempt to solve the grievance. As Heldt points out, adding an international problem to an internal one will actually risk making the leader's position even more precarious. Thus, the diversion hypothesis needs to specify how a certain type of frustration may lead to an attack on another group, or even another state. Empirically, the evidence for a systematic spillover effect is not strong (Heldt 1996). It continues to be an attractive idea, however, and thus has an impact on conflict resolution strategies. As we saw in the conflict dynamics perspective, ending of conflict is not necessarily part of the approach; conflicts are transformed, not eliminated. Similarly, we may ask, is it at all possible to meet all the needs that humans and human groups may have? If not, then conflict resolution becomes but a way of managing conflict, possibly channelling it, but not ending it. Alternatively, we may ask if there are some needs that are possible to meet, and if so, are these the ones which are important to handle in order to reduce the amount of violent conflict in the world? The researchers using this approach still owe us answers to such questions.

There are distinct conflict resolution techniques that follow from this, no matter what the origins of the conflict. One is the *problem-solving workshop,* which, according to Burton, was first used in the middle of the 1960s for the Confrontation Crisis and involved representatives from Indonesia, Malaysia and Singapore (Azar and Burton 1986: 46–7; Burton 1987). The three governments nominated participants to a workshop in London. The meeting lasted ten days and was controlled by a group of scholars. With this, a tradition of workshops was initiated. There is now a broad array of different approaches (Broome 1997; Doob 1970; Fisher 1983; Kelman and Cohen 1976; Mitchell and Banks 1996) and assessments of their importance (Fisher 1997). It has been argued that they can contribute to changes in political culture between the opposing sides. Assessing effects is difficult as the impact can be 'outweighed by other forces' and thus special evaluation methods have to be developed (Kelman 2008).

The original purpose of the workshop was to go beyond the parties' stated positions and reach the underlying needs (Rouhana 1995). Theoretically, such an analysis should not necessarily assume that all parties are equally responsible for a conflict. In practice, the workshops have included the opposing sides, trying to make them understand each other's needs. Thus, the approach becomes quite symmetric (Rouhana 1995). If one side were defined as the more aggressive, as analysis of conflict causes might suggest, workshops would actually be designed to work with only one side.

However, the problem-solving workshops cannot, by themselves, lead to the solutions. It is more likely that they set an agenda and, thus, inform the parties on the needs of the other side. They will be able to act on a more complete understanding of each other's preferences. Still, needs may not be met in a society, due to a lack of resources or the way scarce resources are managed. Thus, *equitable economic policies* become central, as a way of preventing future conflicts as well as handling acute crises within a society. Although this is easily said, there may be unexpected effects.

It may, for instance, result in serious conflict with other actors who fear to lose their positions. Solutions to the frustrations of one actor can lead to fears and frustrations of others. There are also arguments against economic equality. Discrepancies are said to be the way in which economies develop. Certain differences in income and wealth are important as they give incentives to work hard (Olson 1971). However, with the same logic, too large and growing differences would create a revolutionary potential and that is, of course, the starting point for Marxist analysis. It is expressed in Figure 3.2 above. It is reasonable to assume that a society, in order to sustain itself, needs to distribute economic resources relatively equitably to all citizens. This may be equally true whether the economy as a whole is growing or declining.

This, then, relates to conflict inside one society. Does it also translate into an international community, where a few countries are very wealthy and many are very poor? Certainly, resentment exists, and forms of terrorism build on this fact. The logic of the argument would not halt at the border of states. It does not require spillover arguments either, as frustration emerges once the differences and injustices are seen. In today's world they are apparent. But, a sceptic could ask, is this manageable through a problem-solving workshop? Also, is a global policy for a fair economy feasible?

Such considerations make Coser's ideas of *open channels* interesting. The most important would be to have access, thus giving hope for a positive change. The argument speaks in favour of democratization, but also for a democracy to be efficient in delivering desired change. The same logic follows from Gurr's conclusion on autonomy. The democratic system would make it possible for grievances to be heard. It gives a chance to all groups, perhaps more than any other system. This would also be true for the international system as a whole, if frustrated needs of relevance can be channelled through legitimate procedures. This requires radical change of the world, combining conflict resolution with a quest for development and dignity.

A final point: aggression has victims and perpetrators. When needs and grievances are seen by actors to coincide with ethnic, linguistic, religious, cultural or historical lines, they add elements which make a situation even more explosive. In many riots, it is not the distant leaders who feel the direct impact of rage, but those who are closest to the mobs, be they shop owners, the weak, poor, women or children. They have to face the destruction, as was the case in Watts and repeated elsewhere, for instance, in Indonesia in 1998 (targeting property of the Chinese population, but also the Suharto family) or France in the autumn of 2005 (in areas dominated by immigrant populations). The dynamics of the conflict may be reflected in the targeted groups. Examples are Kosovo in 1999 (first targeting Albanians, then Serbs, Romas), East Timor in 1999 (first pro-independence groups, later leaving pro-Indonesia groups in fear) and Iraq since 2003 (first American troops, then Westerners, Iraqi police recruits, later Shiites, then Sunnis and mosques whether Shiite or Sunni, and, most recently, Christians). The aggressive group, the perpetrators, needs a closer analysis, not only the societal relationship. One may ask: why did this group think that atrocities against another group would improve its lot? Were there alternative thoughts? Are there outside incentives for pursuing these actions? Who is actually participating in actions? There are many and legitimate questions asked about this form of mobilization of popular energy and why it takes a particular direction. Such questions, furthermore, lead to ideas about the possibility of *non-aggressive reactions* for more constructive uses of accumulated energy. In most revolutionary situations, there are groups that share the sentiments of the militants, but find other courses of action to be more effective. Internal debates on the appropriate course of action within a particular group are important. The outside world can impact on this debate in ways which may favour conflict resolution.

With the needs-based approach, it is the difficulty of meeting an individual party's need that is the origin of the conflict and the key to its solution. The analysis aims at locating unmet needs. It may then be more important to work with one particular actor than another, although different sides are represented. In an asymmetric situation, it is a matter of conveying to the dominant group the perspective of the dominated, but also to clarify to the dominated constraints on the dominating side. In the conflict dynamics approach, it is basic that the actors are treated in a similar, symmetric fashion, as all have some responsibility for the conflict and, thus, also for the solution of the conflict. The two perspectives contrast with each other, but they do not necessarily exclude each other. Let us see if this is also true for the third perspective on conflict resolution.

3.4 Focusing on Rational Calculations

The perspectives we have presented so far see actors, incompatibilities and actions as stemming from the circumstances in which actors find themselves. The actors individually or as a system of actors have to handle conditions that drive them apart. The third perspective assumes that actors have their own rationality, form their own judgements, make decisions, pursue strategies and, thus, initiate the chain of events that lead to war. The reversal of this, that is, ending wars and reaching agreements, has to be seen in the same light. There is a need for actors to make calculations that can terminate a conflict, but at the same time, ending war is not the actor's only interest. A good presentation of this thinking is found in the many publications of I. William Zartman, but many have worked in similar directions (Fisher and Ury 1981; Stedman 1991).

The idea that wars rise from a rational calculation is, of course, not novel. It is part of established realist and neorealist thinking about the origins of wars. The new twist is to see the ending of wars in such terms. Paul Pillar did pioneering work (1983). The ideas of Zartman have brought the approach further, without leading to the construction of formal models and illustrative diagrams. Zartman outlined such ideas before the end of the Cold War, and continues to adhere to them (Zartman 1989, 1995a; Zartman and Berman 1982; Zartman and Rasmussen 1997; Zartman and de Soto 2010). The literature of the type presented by *Getting to Yes* (Fisher and Ury 1981) rests less on explicit calculation, but still applies a rationalist perspective. The purpose is to understand the real interests of the parties, and thus look beyond their stated positions. Roger Fisher and William Ury introduced a set of notions which were primarily geared to negotiations in general, although the authors were clearly thinking of their utility for armed conflicts and war. In later work, Charles W. Kegley and Gregory A. Raymond state that such calculations have to include moral arguments, to provide a basis for justice in ending war and increasing the chances of durable settlements (Kegley and Raymond 1999). The rational approach, which focuses on the ending of war, appears fruitful and politically relevant. Its main assertions need a closer inspection.

It is assumed that the parties, which may be states, groups or movements, initiate wars to win them. This means that the parties, or at least the initiator, make internal calculations showing that the benefits outweigh the losses when escalating a conflict to a violent confrontation. Such calculations may look different for the opposing sides, but, in principle, the variables and their values are the same. One side makes a calculation for starting the violence, the other for defending itself against the attack. As time passes and nobody wins, the initial calculations are affected and have to be revised. The potential benefits from victory are reduced as the costs increase. The fact that so much time, energy, resources and human life have been invested – destroyed – makes it difficult not to continue, until the final moment of victory is reached. Otherwise the investment would be lost and the suffering meaningless. The parties, in Zartman's analysis, look towards the future. If that does not include a reasonably early chance of victory, but instead suggests a continued stalemate, perhaps even a catastrophe for the fighting sides, then there are elements of a 'ripe moment' for resolution. In Zartman's illuminating words, the conflict offers nothing but a 'flat, unpleasant terrain stretching into the future' (Zartman 1989: 268).

If the parties find this stalemate to be painful, what Zartman calls a 'hurting stalemate', it may lead them to strategic rethinking. There may be a chance for peace. Not necessarily, however. If none of the sides is comfortable with the present and can see no way forward to win the dispute – perhaps only fearing more destruction, without breakthrough – this is likely to be a moment requiring a change of action. At this point the parties might agree on a cease-fire, to reduce the pain, have a chance of recuperation, even getting an opportunity for buying new weapons. It could be time for a pause, perhaps calculated on what is needed before a new offensive. It is a limited strategic rethinking, where the goals are maintained. A cease-fire, in other words, may slow down the move towards a settlement, and instead prolong the fighting. This is an important dilemma in conflict termination. Many have strong opinions on this, but there is little empirical study on the merits of cease-fires for conflict resolution. However, the hurting stalemate can also be turned into, as Zartman has termed it, an 'enticing opportunity'. It can be used for a move forward to settlement, not simply freezing the present situation, the status quo. Here enters another of Zartman's concepts, the need for 'finding the formula'. There must be a way out for the parties, the weaker as well as the stronger. This line of argument gives an important role to outside powers. They can point out that there is a stalemate, and a danger of catastrophe in the near future – 'precipice' in Zartman's words – and they can suggest alternatives for settling the conflict (Ohlson 2011; Zartman 1989).

The calculations that go into the decision-making of the warring parties are, by necessity, complex. Let us attempt to project the situation for two sides at different times in a conflict. In the first stage, the dominant side, A, expects to be able to prevail by defeating the other side, B, and keep control over the resources in dispute, be it governmental power, territory, or something else. Actor B at this time expects considerable sacrifice, as B knows it is challenging a dominant actor, threatening to change the status quo, to achieve an improved standing in the long run. Thus, the expectations are different. Side A may be less psychologically prepared to manage a sustained battle than is B, for whom this has been a plan for a longer period of time. In terms of casualties, for instance, B may be prepared to accept more pain than A.[1] At a certain moment in time, however, the equation changes. The war has become longer than planned. A has had to invest more and all of A's other policies are affected. The gains from the conflict are decreasing, the costs are mounting. For B, the expectation of victory in a reasonably short period of time was not fulfilled. The status quo, the challenger learns, is more entrenched than expected. Victory and associated gains are postponed into the future. The balance between benefits and costs of war may not break evenly. This is one of the appropriate moments for ending the war, a ripe moment. Neither side is winning within the time framework it had expected nor with the resources it had at its disposal. The prognoses are gloomy for both sides. A stalemate exists in the minds of the leaders. If it is reflected on the battlefield, in the form of trenches and unbreakable defensive lines, there is a stalemate in the war, and it might be the right opportunity for interjecting ideas of conflict resolution. It may come, for instance, right after one side has tried and failed to break the military stalemate with an offensive. In more recent studies, the developments on the battlefield are seen as information to the parties about the strength and resources of the opponent, as well as the parties' ability to win. The longer the conflict continues the more willing the parties seem to be to accept offers of mediation (Greig and Regan 2008).

However, the same information can pull the equation in a different direction. It may be argued that one side, be it A or B, has now used so much of its resources that the effect of making a 'final' offensive is only a marginal additional cost, and the gains from such an offensive could be so much greater. Some of the losses could be regained. Failed negotiations, Zartman observes, mean that at least one party 'saw the cost of concessions as being greater than the cost of continuing conflict' (Zartman 1995a: 33). The calculations become increasingly geared to marginal utilities. With a particular, measured, military or political move, A might be able to strengthen its position, so that A will not have to make this particular concession. In a negotiation, in other words, a party may have alternative actions that rest outside the realm of the talks. The term used by Fisher and Ury for this is BATNA, the 'best alternative to negotiated agreement'.[2] In the same way, of course, there might be a 'best alternative' to continued warfare. There are always choices. Each of them carries different costs and benefits. At a certain point, however, terminating the war becomes rational to the warring parties, and an agreed ending can be reached.

The rational calculations are difficult to see from the outside, the information is kept private and not willingly revealed to the other side. At a certain moment in time, it may be possible to argue rationally for a continuation of war as well as a search for peace. This makes it difficult at a particular time to determine, with any certainty, that there *is* a ripe moment. This approach attempts to specify something that goes further than we have seen in either the dynamic or the needs-based approaches. It tries to specify *when* a conflict can be brought to an agreed ending. Neither dynamic approaches nor needs-based analysis can readily point to shifts in the conflict that would signify when and how it can be ended or transformed. The rational calculations are also closer to the practical policy-makers, who see themselves as capable of forming policies and moulding the future. In the previous approaches, such actors are more likely to be regarded as objects of circumstance rather than subjects of will and power.

The policy prescriptions that follow from the rational approach are many. More than the other two approaches, *the outside world* has an active role, particularly when we are concerned with conflicts in smaller countries. It seems legitimate to influence the parties in the direction of conflict management and resolution. Outsiders may be *influencing the calculation* rather than the dynamics or the needs. The calculus for conflict and conflict resolution can be affected, for instance, *by rewards and punishment*. Assistance to one or both sides may be a credible promise made by the outside world. This can be done on condition that the primary parties end the war. It is likely that reconstruction programmes interest the fighting sides. There can also be sanctions for not going into negotiations or for not compromising. This can come in the form of reductions in aid, loss of preferential treatment in trade, a ban on investments, etc. These are measures contributing to the economic constraints for parties already burdened by the war effort. Such steps are generally seen to be legitimate for achieving conflict resolution. It points to the significance of major powers in forcing parties to the negotiation table (Greig and Regan 2008). However, there is some evidence that ongoing wars can be affected by the imposition of monitored UN arms embargoes, making warring actors more interested in negotiations (Fruchart et al. 2007; Strandow 2006).

Even more controversial is whether rewards and punishment can or should be *administered by military means*, in the form of direct military attacks on one party, aiming at tipping the military balance in favour of the other. NATO's bombings in Bosnia in 1995 and in Yugoslavia during the Kosovo crisis in 1999 are in this category. Did they achieve what had been planned? What is the balance of pain inflicted and pain relieved, for instance? Such actions raise legal issues and ethical questions, not only instrumental ones. Also, the decisions to use military arsenals are not taken lightly by the outsiders. They are likely to be available only for some few conflicts, of particular interest to particular outsiders, thus, often involving additional reasons for action not necessarily related only to conflict resolution.

The fact that the outside world can have a strong impact on conflicts involving smaller countries raises an increasingly important question: *who are the parties that should settle a particular conflict?* In line with the dynamic perspective, as many actors as possible should be involved. There is a preference for a broad agenda and liberal rules of invitation. In the needs-based approach, the opposite is favoured. The workshops should be held far from the scene, have little media access, and concentrate on a limited number of parties, who act as representatives, not as individuals. For an approach building on rational calculations, however, the answer is simply that those who count should be in. There is, in Zartman's writing, a repeated observation that not all parties need to be involved in a peace deal. It may be desirable to have as many as possible included, but it is not always necessary. Another calculation can be made: which parties are needed to make an agreement durable? Some parties may create difficulties, and their interests may be better left for later.

In the dynamic approach, the incorporation of as many actors as possible is important. It is not only seen to be more democratic, it is said also to be more fruitful, as there are more issues and there is a larger potential for trade-offs. The outcomes, too, will be more innovative.

From a rational calculation perspective, larger meetings and intensive dialogue can appear as a waste of resources and time. The urgency of solving a conflict, using the ripe moment, may be lost. In the rational calculation perspective, *timing* is very important. Opportunities should be seized, particularly in a situation where a war is ongoing. This requires swift action, often by a few, determined actors. The dynamic and needs-based approaches see conflict resolution as a process and, thus, do not advocate rapid action and political manoeuvring. Ripe moments may come and go. This is not the way conflicts will ever be solved, they would argue.

The question of urgency and timing leads to an observation of which Stedman has given the most elaborate formulation – the issue of *spoilers* and how to handle them (Stedman 1997, 1998). It is not possible to work on the goodwill of the parties, Stedman argues. Experience since the Cold War shows that much violence comes *after* peace agreements are made, not before. There are actors who are dissatisfied with the deal. He gives examples from Rwanda (where the genocide in 1994 was unleashed after the peace agreement was concluded and aimed partly at preventing its implementation). More recently, East Timor could be added. Among Stedman's many observations is that the custodians of the peace agreement have to be united and determined to implement the accords as expeditiously and as unchanged as possible. This is also supported in a comparative study (Höglund 2008). It minimizes the space open to the spoilers and serves to deter them from attacking the agreement. Determined spoilers might quickly exploit even minor disagreements among the custodians. There are also ripe moments for the destruction of peace. The rational calculation approach helps to locate such situations.

The most difficult problem identified by Stedman is whether potential or actual spoilers should be included from the outset in the peace process, as follows from the dynamic approach, or excluded, as the rational calculations approach would often prefer. In the first case, urgency may be lost. Time and energy have to be spent on integrating the recalcitrant party into the process and the outcome would still be uncertain. In the second case, the hope may be that a speedy agreement and its effective implementation may change the local situation in such a way as to erode the support for the spoilers. The first approach, in contrast, may run the risk of legitimizing the spoiler and make the process hostage to spoiler tactics. The second approach, in turn, may rest on the power of the custodians and their ability to marginalize the spoilers. Most likely, the sum of these arguments is in favour of not excluding the (potential or actual) spoilers, but trying to develop a second channel for such groups. Many of them are not likely to participate – as witnessed by the actions of militant unionists and republicans in the Northern Ireland negotiations, sections of Hamas in Palestine and settlers in Israel – but, in the long run, peacebuilding cannot be accomplished without having such parties involved in the process. In fact, they may have strong followings and in democratic processes achieve parliamentary leading or tipping positions (as has happened in all three cases mentioned).

Spoilers have a capacity to undermine or slow down a peace process by their ability to pressure the custodians on 'their' side. In a democratic framework, peacemakers and spoilers are probably competing for support from the same population, and thus mistakes or problems in implementation will be turned against the custodians and against the peace process. In fact, this makes the management of implementation central to the durability of peace agreements (Stedman et al. 2002). However, this does not exclude the possibility that settlements including only some of the warring rebels can still be lasting. It will be determined by the signatories' commitment when they enter the deal (Nilsson 2008). In Burundi, some of the parties entered into the agreement in 2003 and other rebel groups joined in so that by the end of 2008 all warring actors were part of the agreement. The first and partial agreement became a step in an increasingly inclusive peace process.

In the preceding sections we have looked at three perspectives which seemingly contradict each other. They all generate tools for analysis which are important for a complete understanding of ending wars through conflict resolution. In the next section, a synthesis of these approaches is suggested.

3.5 Synthesizing Conflict Resolution

The three approaches yield distinct perspectives of conflict. They carry different understandings of why conflicts emerge, have a particular dynamic and find a distinct resolution. However, one can also see them as complementary. They point to different aspects of the conflict phenomenon. For actors and analysts concerned with conflict resolution, it is an advantage to be accustomed to many approaches rather than only one. These considerations suggest that they can be integrated into one scheme for conflict analysis. Such an attempt will be made here and the utility of this will, hopefully, become apparent when we draw practical conclusions for research and policy.

Refining the Definition

The definition needs to be specified. Chapter 1 offered a preliminary definition of conflict resolution. In the review just completed, additional terms have been introduced, such as conflict transformation and conflict management. It becomes necessary to distinguish conflict resolution from these terms. Also, the examination has pointed to a discrepancy between conflicts with and without arms. As the former is our interest, the definition of conflict resolution has to take this into account. These and further considerations, soon to be spelled out, result in the following definition of conflict resolution: it is a *social situation where the armed conflicting parties in a (voluntary) agreement resolve to live peacefully with – and/or dissolve – their basic incompatibilities and henceforth cease to use arms against one another.* This means that the conflict is transformed from violent to non-violent behaviour *by the parties themselves*, not by somebody else, for instance, an outsider or third party. The first test of conflict resolution is that arms are no longer used. This means that a cease-fire and a process of demilitarization are initiated according to agreed plans. To the general public this is *the* sign that the situation has actually changed. Then comes the implementation of the agreement's basic issues, which should follow soon. A second test is that the parties do not resort to violence or to the threat of violence in this phase.

The definition stipulates that the parties enter into agreement. This means that the primary parties take responsibility for the accords, and commit themselves to their implementation and legitimation. In this way, the agreement will have considerable chance of surviving when encountering challenges, as it no doubt will. There are additional arguments for emphasizing the role of the parties in conflict resolution. They are the ones who know the conflict most intimately. Obviously, they were there from the beginning, they have raised the resources and mobilized the people for conflict. This makes them the actors who most legitimately can decide when the conflict is over. All other actors, such as splinter groups, dissidents or civilian groups, will have less authority in this process than the leaders who actually formulated the initial goals for the struggle. Thus, there are reasons for involving these very leaders in any peace process, and for the outsiders to expect that parties initiating conflict are also capable of ending it.

Of course, this leads us into a question of who a *party* actually is. When those who started the war are still leading actors, the identification of responsible parties is easy. Even if the same individuals who started the war are no longer around to sign the peace, there is a continuity that new leaderships take on when assuming power. They build legitimacy on leading a party that has been an actor in the same conflict over a long period of time. They also have to take responsibility for actions that this very party pursued before the incumbent leadership came to power. Recognition of atrocities as well as issues of compensation can be part of the agreement, and builds on this continuity of responsibility. Clearly, the problem is easier to handle when we refer to a state, as it has its laws, decision-making machinery and rules of succession. For popular movements, liberation organizations and many religious communities, continuity is more difficult to establish. Rules of succession are less stable or sometimes non-existent. Splits and mergers change the picture. Thus, there needs to be a careful analysis of each case to determine who actually is a party and who are its leaders.

A delicate situation is the one in which one side does not regard the other as a legitimate party and, consequently, does not want to enter into an agreement with that party. This takes many forms. States may not recognize each other and, thus, have no diplomatic relations (as was the case between the Federal Republic of Yugoslavia and the Republic of Bosnia-Herzegovina, although they were negotiating with one another at Dayton in 1995). There could be a de facto recognition, of course, but agreements require a de jure arrangement. In the case of an intra-state conflict, governments are reluctant to extend recognition to an armed opposition movement. It regards itself, as we shall see in Chapter 4, as the sole legitimate user of violence. Thus, an agreement with an armed opponent can, in extreme cases, mean the recognition of the indefinite existence of two armies in the same state (as was the outcome of the Dayton negotiations). It can also be that the government regards the opponents as terrorists or bandits and, thus, not on an equal footing. In the case of Mozambique, the Frelimo government faced a South Africa-supported insurgency, Renamo, which it described as 'bandits'. Steven Chan and Moisés Venancio write in favour of recognition of Renamo. The argument is not a legal one but one of commitment: 'people do not fight and risk death as they had no fear, they do not kill as if they had no moral agency at all; they do not do this for a decade for the sake of it, or because they are puppets only' (Chan and Venancio 1998: xiii). Even such movements, in other words, have to be taken seriously. In this book, we include all parties that have armed forces under their control, have a central command and explicitly pursue political goals as parties or actors (these two words are used interchangeably).

There are other elements in the definition that require scrutiny, notably the notion of *a (voluntary) agreement*. How voluntary is an agreement likely to be? The parties have been fighting a war, perhaps over years, and their ambitions have been to win. Thus, accepting something less than this may appear to the parties to be a bitter pill to swallow. This use of force is, however, a part of customary war dynamics. If one party applies force, the fact that the opposite side does the same should not come as a surprise. The force of the opposing side is part of the equation.

More interesting is the pressure from the outside world, notably *secondary parties*. These are actors who do not directly commit their own troops or other regular military resources to the conflict, but still take sides and (openly or not) support a particular primary party. Secondary parties can be extremely important to a primary party, both militarily (providing bases, routes for arms deliveries) and psychologically (making clear to the party that it is 'not alone'). They may also have their own agenda and, thus, use their leverage on the primary parties, if they so wish. If secondary parties on either side agree on how the conflict should be ended, they may very well be in a position to impose this on the parties. This is what many primary parties suspect and fear. They may nervously watch summit meetings between major powers, who may be their main suppliers of weapons. The highly concentrated world trade in major arms gives the five permanent members of the UN Security Council considerable leverage in many conflict situations, if they would act jointly. In this way, a local conflict may in fact become part of a global conflagration, something which was constantly happening during the Cold War. A relatively minor issue, from the point of view of the populations in the major countries, may escalate into a nuclear confrontation (Nincic 1985). A close relationship to outside actors may be necessary but can also be risky for a primary party. Thus, it is noteworthy that agreements made under external pressure tend to be more short-lived than others (Nordquist 1992). The ending of the war 'prematurely' may be blamed on the outsider. Outside pressure may be a good tactic to get support for an agreement at one stage, but when that constraint disappears, the settlement may no longer hold. Thus, agreements with a reasonable amount of voluntary involvement by the parties themselves are likely to last longer.

Conflict resolution here is focused on an *agreement*. It is, as indicated in Section 3.2, difficult to imagine that parties in a war would end their armed conflict and live side by side without some minimum form of understanding. It can be specified in an agreement, highly formalized as a treaty. It may also take other forms. But some arrangement is needed for this to be conflict resolution. It specifies commitments made by the parties, for all to see. The agreement, furthermore, marks the end point of the armed phase of the conflict and the beginning of something new. However, it does not mean that entering an agreement is the same as ending a peace process. Agreement is only one element in a larger process. Concepts such as conflict transformation and peacebuilding bring us into a wider array of concerns. They are all important for the durability of the settlement and for the creation of new, 'normal' conditions. In addition, the focus on agreement distinguishes conflict resolution from conflict management, which often works on implicit, even secret, understandings, or simply ways of 'handling' a problem. Conflict management typically focuses on the armed aspect of the conflict: bringing the fighting to an end, limiting the spread of the conflict and, thus, containing it. Such action may even be regarded as successful. The interest for a particular conflict may disappear. Conflict resolution is more ambitious, as it expects the parties to face jointly their incompatibility and find a way to live with or dissolve it. The significance of entering into an agreement illustrates how 'conflict resolution' differs from other concepts.

One element in the definition requiring further analysis remains – the incompatibility. By studying this, we are also able to isolate a set of resolution methods to be studied more closely in the rest of this book.

Transcending Incompatibility: Seven Mechanisms

The phrase *live with – and/or dissolve – the incompatibility* requires close attention. In the overview of thinking on conflict resolution, different ideas were indicated. These need to be brought together in a more systematic fashion, which can be done by focusing on the incompatibility. The concept of incompatibility is defined as the inability to meet the demands of two or more parties at the same time with the available resources. Giving a certain resource to A will mean that B will not receive its desired share. Resources, of course, may be something less tangible than land, capital, natural resources, military positions or political posts. They can also be the desire to obtain recognition, respect, restitution or restoration (which the party may feel entitled to, due to its historical role or experience of historical injustice). It can concern meeting a historical mission (which in reality is close to the question of recognition or redress of a historical grievance). There is also the question of security, which takes on such significance that it sometimes is not just a means to other goals but a goal in itself.

How can parties with such incompatible positions ever be able to arrive at the stipulation in the definition: live with – and/or dissolve – the incompatibility? As we have noted, there has been a record number of peace agreements since the end of the Cold War. Parties who have been involved in deadly struggles have found ways to live with one another. Their partnership may not be easy but is, by the parties themselves, defined as preferable to the struggle that preceded it. The solutions may sometimes dissolve the incompatibility, which means finding an arrangement that no longer makes this issue a salient one. It disappears. It may, in a way, mean that a party gives up some of its ambitions. For instance, the (white) Nationalist Party agreed to dismantle apartheid in South Africa. But the Party remained a political party (until its demise for other reasons) and the white population stayed in the country, safeguarded by the state in an equal way, like other citizens. The political rules have been changed with the enfranchising of the majority of the population. In other situations, the parties agree to disagree, but agree to a framework for disagreement. Thus, they are committing themselves to live peacefully with the incompatibility. This frequently means resorting to democratic forms of politics. In these cases, they have not dissolved the disagreement over, for example, land ownership, but created safe channels to the political process for all sides. There is a set of rules through which the conflict can continue, but without use of arms. How can this be done, theoretically and in practice? Here we will attempt to answer the question theoretically, throughout the book we will discuss it empirically.

In theory, there are seven distinct ways in which the parties can live with or dissolve their incompatibility. These are mechanisms, procedures or forms of transcendence that can be derived from Figure 3.1.

First, a party may change its goals, that is, *shift its priorities*. It is rare that a party will completely change its basic positions, but it can display a shift in what it gives highest priority to. This may open ways in which the other side can reciprocate. Leadership changes are particularly pertinent in this respect. With such changes, new possibilities are created. It does not mean that conflict resolution has to wait for a revolution. Leadership is often recruited from a limited segment of the population, and continuity remains important. Still, new leaders think differently and, thus, new leadership matters. There are also other changes that can take place. Changes in the surrounding world may be important, leading to shifts in strategic priorities. Among major powers, the rise of a new power or the fall of an old one may be such a condition. For less powerful actors, changes in major power relations have many implications. Shifts between *détente* and confrontation can be important for conflict resolution, as was clearly seen at the end of the Cold War. Economic crises can change priorities. The costs of pursuing a war may drain important resources and, thus, the chances of a peace dividend may seem more attractive. However, the possibility for such changes should not be overestimated and it would be outright dangerous for a party to hinge a negotiation policy on expectations of change in a particular direction. New leaders may be weaker, major power relations may change for the worse, economic crises may induce less interest in compromise, etc. But it is important for the parties continuously to probe the other side, to find out if there are shifts in priority.

The second way is a classical one: the parties stick to their goals but find a point at which resources can be *divided*. This is point C in Figure 3.1. It is sometimes seen as the essence of compromise, but it is only one form of compromise. It may mean that both sides change priority. However, it is done in such a way that the change by side A is coupled to a change by side B. To meet halfway, at some point which has a symbolic value, is easier for the parties. Then, it is also possible for them to defend the deal to other decision-makers and to the general public. It may appear reasonable and be in accordance with values in the society. If the incompatibility concerns territory, this may mean drawing a border approximately half the distance between the two demands. It makes sense, but only so long as the areas are not inhabited by people who will have their own interests, or if the area contains resources that also should be part of the deal. Compromise is most readily made with monetary resources. Negotiations between employers and employees have a long history of finding optimal points at which to draw the dividing line between the two sides. In many such situations, it is important for the parties to get some resources, rather than nothing. With power positions this may be more difficult, but even so there are ways in which power can be divided, for instance, along the lines of central–regional divisions or along functions (presidency, prime minister, speaker, supreme court, important committees, etc.). As mentioned, there are examples of two prime ministers in the same cabinet (Cambodia). Rotation of the office of Prime Minister was used for a time in Israel, each party getting an equal number of years – an interesting time-sharing arrangement. This is institutionalized in Switzerland, with its annual shifting of presidency.

A third way is *horse-trading*, where one side has all of its demands met on one issue, while the other has all of its goals met on another issue. It means using two separate incompatibility diagrams (Figure 3.1), one for each issue, where each party gets 100 per cent. This can also be described as a compromise, but works in a different way from the division we just described. In horse-trading over territory, the idea would be that A takes area 1 and B takes area 2, although both of them have had demands on areas 1 and 2. Instead of making a complicated division, an entire piece of territory is taken over by one or the other. Again, as we noted before, this assumes that there are no particular features to the territory, or that such features somehow are equal for both (for instance, oil in both). In a contest over political power positions, A may support B in some matters and receive corresponding support from B in others, meaning A and B abandon previous views and together form what is sometimes referred to as 'national pacts' or 'historical compromises'.

A fourth way is *shared control*. In this case the parties decide to rule together over the disputed resource. This comes close to outcome D indicated in Figure 3.1. A territory can be shared by being ruled as a condominium, where decisions require the consent of both parties. An economic resource can be operated by a joint company and a formula devised for investment and profit sharing. A country can be run by a coalition government, a frequent phenomenon in most parliamentary democracies. Shared control may require some degree of trust; it may also be a temporary arrangement for a transition period. Power-sharing arrangements also exemplify this. This is where all parties are represented in government according to a formula agreed upon beforehand (for each 5 per cent of the national vote a party gets one seat in the cabinet, for instance). Even if agreed to only for a predetermined period, it can mean that a conflict is successfully transcended and that, at the end of the period, the conflict situation is very different from what it was at the beginning. This can also be applied to international regimes setting up rules for using water in shared rivers. In international affairs, such arrangements may mean the beginning of regional integration; in internal affairs they can be contributions to the integration of a fragmented society.

A fifth way is to *leave control to somebody else*, which means externalizing control, so that the warring parties agree not to rule the resources themselves. This is outcome E in Figure 3.1. The primary parties agree, or accept, that a third actor takes control. Such solutions have gained prominence in the discussions on international conflicts during the 1990s. The notion of protectorates has returned to serious discussions. There are recent examples of independent countries having had their sovereignty strongly circumscribed. Bosnia-Herzegovina is one case with its complex constitution. In 1999, one part of a sovereign country was placed under international protection, Kosovo, in the south of the Federal Republic of Yugoslavia. In the case of Kosovo, it meant that neither the Yugoslav authorities nor the Kosovo Albanian representatives ran the area, but instead authority resided with the UN, for the following nine years. In these cases, the parties accepted the set-up, but only after considerable warfare (the Bosnian War and NATO's actions in 1995, the Kosovo wars and the aerial bombardments of Yugoslavia in 1999). Similarly, East Timor was under UN administration 1999–2002, neither a part of Indonesia nor an independent country. It was more a trusteeship than a protectorate.

Obviously, there are other, less dramatic, ways of handing control to third parties. Economic resources can be given as concessions to private companies. The cabinet can be taken over by parliamentary minorities or experts in order to detach the official administration from major political divides in the country. The latter can be important, particularly at times of elections. Bangladesh has such a stipulation in its constitution.

Sixth, there is the possibility of resorting to *conflict resolution mechanisms*, notably arbitration or other legal procedures that the parties can accept. It means finding a procedure that can resolve the conflict according to some of the previously mentioned five ways, with the added quality that it is done through a process outside the parties' immediate control. The legal mechanism builds on the idea of neutrality, distance and resort to precedents and history. Among conflict resolution mechanisms we would also include holding new elections and arranging a referendum, which means leaving the issue to a concerned but still non-predetermined audience. For this to be a legitimate way of ending a conflict, the conflicting parties should have a fair chance to present their views. Studies show that if parties believe that they have been given a fair chance, they are more likely to accept defeat (Tyler 2000). A number of border disputes have been resolved with the use of arbitration. A remarkable case is the drawing of the border between Iraq and Kuwait after the Gulf War, settled according to an exchange of documents between the two parties, but under the authorization of the UN Security Council. The democratic system solves some disputes by resorting to new elections or referenda. Territorial issues can also be resolved this way, by giving a voice to the population itself. That was part of the agreement ending the internal conflict between North and South Sudan, through a successful referendum on independence in January 2011.

Seventh, issues can be *left to later* or even to oblivion. By appointing a commission, parties can gain time, and when the commission reports, political conditions and popular attitudes may have changed. Some issues may gain from being delayed, as their significance may pale or their symbolic character may be reduced. This is an argument for not solving all questions at the same time. But it requires that there be a second chance to bring them up. In fact, the second chance is important for a loser to accept defeat or enter into a compromise. If there is a credible way in which one can return to the issue later or run in a new election, then the agreement is more acceptable. The party does not argue that the issue is given less priority, only that its time is not yet ripe. In the case of the first mechanism, in contrast, there is a significant change of position and the party does not return to its previous view.

3.6 Identifying Key Elements in Conflict Analysis

Living with or dissolving the incompatibility is a central element in conflict analysis. This is learned from the dynamic approach to conflict presented in Section 3.2 as well as from the rational calculation approach given in Section 3.4, for instance, in differentiating between positions and interests and getting into the calculations of the parties. The focus on the needs of parties, as given in Section 3.3, brings with it a close look at the parties themselves, their needs, perceptions and the history behind the conflict. These are elements that are also important for an analysis of rational calculations. There is a relationship between conflict behaviour and changing positions, as indicated in terms such as action–reaction, and carefully, rationally calibrated moves. In all, the three approaches have many shared features. They are, as a consequence, all useful. They illustrate different elements in the conflict process and how it can be turned into a peace process. Figure 3.3 describes this and suggests a shared framework for the analysis.

The dynamics of conflict are illustrated by the arrows in Figure 3.3. There are no convincing arguments for assuming that a conflict always starts in one corner. It is more fruitful to assume that connections exist and are more fluid. The different boxes require some closer description. First, in the box on conflict formation is located the creation of parties, which we have stipulated to be an integral part of conflict analysis. Some parties are formed deliberately to make conflicts; others may be there for other purposes. When a party is formed, it begins by making itself known, developing its identity and giving itself a role in the conflict to which it adheres. The history, recruitment and financing of a party are important to understand, as well as its internal decision-making. If there are needs in the society on which its actions purport to be based, then, of course, those needs have to be focused. To this also belongs whether a party really represents the needs of a larger share of the population.

Second, obviously, an analysis of the incompatibility is necessary. What are the conflicting interests, what is the relationship between interests, positions and needs of the actor or of the population it claims to represent? The actors are likely to have an internal priority in terms of issues. Some are more basic than others. It is important for the analyst to have an idea of such hierarchies. Third, there are the actions. Conflicts are fuelled by destructive actions, actions aimed at reducing the influence of the other side, and enhancing the influence of its own side. Hence, this box in Figure 3.3 not only involves actual warfare, but also the making of alliances, finding friends and locating financiers, as well as preventing the opponent from doing the same. These are seen, by the parties, as integral elements of their struggle. The conflict strategies are important elements in the analysis.

In Figure 3.3, however, a statement of great consequence is made. It is argued, in line with the dynamic approach, that behaviour can be changed, and that such a change is strategic in making a conflict take a different direction. That is described as constructive action. These are actions that aim at bridging the gap to the other side. Included are measures such as confidence-building, but also unilateral actions. The now classical example is the visit by Egypt's President Sadat to Jerusalem in 1977. It was an unexpected action. It was not clear how the Israeli government would receive it. With the support of the Carter administration in the USA, it helped to change the dynamics in the Middle East conflict. Such measures are rare, and risky, but ways out of many recent wars have contained unilateral and constructive moves. Thus, the behaviour of the opposing sides is the element in the conflict that the parties themselves watch most closely. They will ask, for instance, if a positive

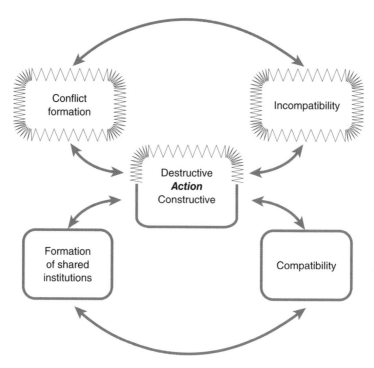

Figure 3.3 Synthesizing concepts in conflict analysis

announcement is followed by positive steps. If not, the former is regarded as propaganda and the latter as the reality. The proof of 'good intentions' is 'good actions'.

Once there is a shift in behaviour, perhaps by separating the parties in a cease-fire through traditional peacekeeping, the lower half of Figure 3.3 comes into operation. A dynamic development may follow and build momentum. The parties may start to search for compatible positions (shared needs or a formula meeting the interests of the primary parties) and, when they find them, there will also be attempts to create new structures through which these can be expressed. This can be simple negotiation fora (multilateral conferences) but also transitory forms of government or even entirely new permanent bodies (the European Union (EU) could be regarded as a way of ending the earlier Franco-German conflict, although it is more often described as a measure to prevent a future one). The detection of compatibilities and the formation of new organizations mean that dynamics are created which may generate more constructive action. Thus, Figure 3.3 describes two processes, a process of conflict formation and escalation in the upper half of the figure and one of peacebuilding and shared interests in the lower half.

The utility of Figure 3.3 can be demonstrated with the phenomenon of spoilers and spoiler management introduced by Stedman. It can now be located theoretically. Spoilers are those actors who have no interest in the conflict process shifting from the higher to the lower level in Figure 3.3. If there is a peace agreement, as postulated by Stedman, then a spoiler aims to prevent the dynamics in the lower level from spinning further. This runs counter to interests held by particular groups. Thus, violent action can be used to attempt to shift the conflict back into the upper level (Höglund 2008). If successful, peace moves are spoiled, for the time being. When a conflict is locked in the upper part of Figure 3.3, most actors are spoilers as long as they all pursue destructive action. Thus, it makes sense to link, as Stedman does, the spoiler phenomenon to a peace agreement or at least a fairly entrenched peace process. In a way, a spoiler is a party still living in the dynamics of the upper level, preferring to be there at least as long as its interests are not met. This also illustrates the importance for the custodians to make clear that the situation has changed and decisively moved into the lower level of Figure 3.3. The custodians have to show in action that they are committed to preventing the conflict from sliding back to the dynamics of the upper level.[3]

The fact that behaviour is the point combining the two dynamics makes clear its dual nature. It may promote one or the other development, but it is also the juncture at which conflict dynamics can change from one loop to the other and back again. It means that conflicts are not unilinear, for instance, moving from frustration to conflict to resolution. Instead, they develop through twists and turns, with changes in behaviour, positions and parties, new frustrations and new calculations all affecting the dynamics. It means that conflicts are not simply escalating and de-escalating, or that they are easily predicted and calculated. They are all of these simultaneously and that is the reality with which the analysts have to cope.

In Chapter 4 we will give some additional building blocks for conflict analysis, thus completing Part One and preparing for a closer look at basic as well as complex realities in conflict resolution.

Further Readings

Go to the *Understanding Conflict Resolution* web page at https://study.sagepub.com/wallensteen4e for free access to journal articles listed.

Conflict Dynamics

It is not easy to categorize literature, as many authors use all the approaches mentioned. However, there may be more elements of a certain approach in some:

Bercovitch, J. (ed.) 1996. *Resolving International Conflicts: The Theory and Practice of Mediation.* Boulder, Colorado: Lynne Rienner.
In this work, Jacob Bercovitch brings together a number of contributions on mediation, illustrating the many ways in which third parties can act in different types of conflicts. The focus is on international conflicts.

Staub, E. 1989. *The Roots of Evil: The Origins of Genocide and Other Group Violence.* New York: Cambridge University Press.
Ervin Staub is an insightful analyst of genocide. In this work he describes the origins of such one-sided violence in four cases demonstrating both the dynamics between perpetrators and victims and the role of the bystanders.

(Continued)

(Continued)

Basic Needs

Azar, E. and Burton, J. 1986. *International Conflict Resolution: Theory and Practice*. Boulder, Colorado: Lynne Rienner.
Burton, J. 1990. *Conflict: Resolution and Provention*. London: Macmillan.
These two books outline the framework of basic needs and how it relates to conflict resolution as well as conflict prevention. Burton argues for early action, and promoting the term 'provention'.

Berdal, M. and Malone, D.M. 2000. *Greed and Grievance. Economic Agendas in Civil Wars*. Colorado: Lynne Rienner.
Collier, P., Elliott, V.L., Hegre, H., Hoeffler, A., Reynal-Querol, M. and Sambanis, N. 2003. *Breaking the Conflict Trap. Civil War and Development Policy*. Washington, D.C.: The World Bank.

In a series of case studies and with the help of statistical analysis these two books specify the economic factors that may lead to civil war. The 'greed' of actors was seen to be more important than 'grievances' felt by marginalized groups. The debate has continued and is summarized in the following works:

Ballentine, K. and Sherman, J. 2003. *The political economy of armed conflict: beyond greed and grievance*, New York: International Peace Academy.
Wallensteen, P. 2014. 'Theoretical Developments in Understanding the Origins of Civil War', in E. Newman and K. DeRouen, Jr. (eds) *Routledge Handbook of Civil Wars*, Routledge, Chapter 2, pp 13-27.

Rational Calculations

Zartman, I.W. (ed.) 1995a. *Elusive Peace. Negotiating an End to Civil Wars*. Washington, D.C.: The Brookings Institution.
Here I. William Zartman brings together a number of contributions demonstrating the possibilities of ending civil wars at particular moments in time.

Notes

1 It is possible that B plans for a surprise attack, which would be swift and, thus, A would be the one who will be prepared for a longer confrontation. A and B simply shift places in the description given in the text.
2 This notion, Daniel Druckman has pointed out, emanates from Thibaut and Kelley, who introduced the comparison level for alternatives (1959: 21–3).
3 Obviously, this can result in the simultaneous pursuit of both upper and lower level conflict dynamics, for instance, punishing spoilers according to the upper level dynamics, while rewarding actors working according to the lower-level dynamics. Indeed, there is even an interplay between the two: acting tough on spoilers may enhance the gains for actors adhering to the peace process. Targeted sanctions may be used this way.

4

ANALYSING CONFLICT RESOLUTION

4.1 Basic and Complex Levels of Analysis

In the preceding chapters, we developed a general understanding of the concept of conflict. This is a necessary initial step in conflict analysis. Here, our task is to approach conflicts where arms are used and the role this gives to conflict resolution. Armed conflict is one category of the general phenomenon of social conflict. It has some distinct features. It normally grows out of non-armed conflict, in the sequences illustrated in Figure 3.3, but involves not just a shift in behaviour. It has other aspects associated with the three concepts of parties, incompatibility and action. First, there is a particular role for the state as soon as a conflict becomes armed. The reasons for this are explained in Section 4.2. There are also armed, as well as unarmed, non-state actors in many armed conflicts, and, for a fuller analysis, it is necessary to include them. The conflict analyst not only faces traditional conflict material of states fighting wars among themselves, but also the analytically less well-developed circumstances of intra-state conflicts. This will also be pursued in this chapter. Second, an additional building block is the incompatibility, where the analysis concentrates on two types that are particularly frequently associated with armed conflict. These are incompatibilities dealing with political power (here termed incompatibility over government) and those dealing with control over land (here described as incompatibility over territory). Third, when a conflict shifts from nonarmed to predominantly armed conflict behaviour, this may involve a shift of parties and of issues. This makes the task of conflict resolution more cumbersome. It becomes not only a matter of ending violence. It also means affecting relationships between the parties as well as their incompatibilities. Together, these distinctions result in three types of conflict, a trichotomy of conflict. They are the basic units of conflict analysis. Part Two of this book, that is Chapters 5, 6 and 7, is devoted entirely to an analysis of the resolution of such conflicts. There is also a more complex level. Conflicts are often connected to one another, where parties may have alliances or, in fact, be the same across borders or social divides. Incompatibilities may form components in regional or global confrontations. This has to be taken into account. In addition, there is frequent involvement from outside actors, which has to be considered in a complex, comprehensive analysis. The complex level is pursued in Part Three where the five chapters provide tools for an understanding of the full reality in which conflicts arise.

4.2 The Role of the State

Actors in Conflict

The definitions of conflict and conflict resolution have so far not offered much about who the parties are. In Chapter 3 we have only specified them as 'actors' or 'parties', giving them some general characteristics. However, the definitions used for collecting war statistics in the Michigan and Uppsala programmes described in Chapter 2 limit armed conflict to a considerably smaller cluster of social interactions (although there is also now an increasing interest in non-state violence). They concentrate on conflicts that have a state as one of the parties. The examples used in much of the theorizing on conflict resolution indicate similar restrictions for the selection of cases. The practice of researchers is more restrained than their theories would necessarily require.

In fact, the study of conflict resolution is a merger of two different strands of thought. Conflict theory has the objective of creating a general understanding of conflict. For example, it takes note of apparent parallels between person-to-person conflicts and state-to-state relations. Thus, it is tempting to search for general understandings. No doubt, interesting lessons can be drawn, building on an intimate knowledge of particular cases and their specific dynamics. The other strand is the causes of war studies, which aim to find general patterns for wars throughout history, ideally by including all wars and empirically discovering similarities. Thus, it requires general definitions across time and space in order to arrive at data consisting of comparable phenomena. The value increases with larger numbers and longer time-spans. The state is such a 'stable' actor, providing for comparability, for example between the end of the Napoleonic Wars (that is, since 1816) or following the Westphalian Peace (that is, since 1648). The merger of these two strands into studies of general conflict resolution theory runs into empirical difficulties. For instance, the cases analysed may be insightful, but how typical are they for the general phenomenon? Can a state be compared to a person, a social group or a social institution? Similarly, data collected for causes of war studies often are not necessarily well designed for conflict theory purposes. Ending of conflicts has seldom been part of the understanding, except when searching for a termination date, for instance. Merging these two strands requires particular efforts.

The Uppsala Conflict Data Program is specifically devoted to conflict resolution. Even so, it initially restricted itself to the types of conflict that the causes of war studies include. The agenda has now been enlarged to also make possible the study of conflicts between non-state actors, and actions of one-sided violence. The solution to such conflicts will gradually enter the agenda and enlarge our understanding of conflict resolution in the coming years.

The study of person-to-person relations in state-to-state conflicts, notably the personal relationships between leaders, would be a valuable point of convergence. For example, the rapport between the very conservative Republican US President Ronald Reagan and the Soviet Secretary-General of the Communist Party, Mikhail Gorbachev, from their first meeting in 1985, appears to have had a profound impact on world developments. A similar understanding between US President George W. Bush and Russian President Vladimir Putin in the early 2000s, however, did not last. By 2014, also the relations between US President Barack Obama and Putin were cold. Of course, they met as state leaders, and this is likely to have affected their personal relations as well. From whatever angle we would like to approach the question of conflict resolution in armed conflict, an analysis of the state is unavoidable.

The Special Roles of the State

There are theoretically valid reasons for having the state as a main actor in the analysis of armed conflict and its resolution. The state is, according to most political science definitions, the only legitimate user of physical violence in a society (Weber 1964: 154–6). Thus, it is almost, by definition, involved whenever there is an armed conflict in society. The control of violence is not the only distinguishing feature, however. There are also fiscal, territorial and ideological monopolies. The concurrent exercise of these four monopolies provides the state with coherence internally and independence internationally. This requires some further elaboration.

The state has a fiscal monopoly, being the only unit that can collect taxes and tariffs, where the inhabitants have to pay a certain sum of money in return for services whose delivery and quality they cannot immediately inspect and where choice is limited. The fiscal monopoly is unique and distinct from the monopoly that can be exercised by a corporation on a market or a trade union in recruiting members in a company, for instance. A central state may hand over its rights and obligations to others, for example, to states in a federation, to local communities or even to other units. But this authority derives from the right of the state to collect tax revenue. In the writings of economic historians, the state's fiscal monopoly is seen as particularly important for the state's emergence and growth, compared to other organizational units (Tilly 1990).

The state is the sole legitimate authority within its territory, and is expected by other actors, notably neighbouring states, to maintain that authority. The border is not only a line of territorial separation, but also the geographical space where one legitimate authority is replaced by another. A central governmental task is to uphold authority all the way to the border. However, in an increasingly interdependent world of cross-border transactions, it is in the interest of governments on either side of the border that there also be control on the other side. Otherwise border areas may become bases for non-legitimate actors, such as criminal gangs, drug traders or guerrilla groups directed against one or both governments. The border is no longer only the exposed front line of defence against an unknown or hostile actor on the other side. Borders are increasingly matters of shared interest. In another interesting development, humanitarian concerns change the agenda of the state inside its area of authority, as the state is seen as the guarantor of exposed groups or even a guardian of human rights. One state's failure to pursue this may expose it to international sanctions from other states. Indeed, the 2005 World Summit meeting in New York endorsed the principle that in such cases there is even an international responsibility to protect exposed populations. Protection of civilians has become a reason for international involvement affecting actions of the United Nations.

In addition to these elements, it is also evident that the state, notably through its control over the educational system, is the originator of an official view of what the state is all about. There is an ideological function. For each state, the government's interpretation of what the role is of a particular state is likely to be highly influential. It determines the range of debate that is acceptable within the state, but it may at the same time restrict the options available to the political leadership. It cannot act easily beyond established parameters of customary conduct. Thus, the state determines and expresses the way in which a society describes its history, pursues its values and reproduces the myths that exist for legitimizing its existence. This is an ideological leadership, which is a monopoly in non-democratic states and a more subtle hegemony in many open societies.

All these roles may make the state an actor in conflict as well as an object of conflict. That the state is an actor is obvious. This is the way policy is made, and the instruments available to the state are used (administration, police, military forces, tax collection, etc.). That the state is an object of conflict is also clear. For example, the access to tax revenue makes it valuable to control the state. It makes the state a resource-rich actor, and is probably perceived to be more so, the poorer a country is. The state may sometimes be the sole provider of wealth in a society. The control over violence indicates that there is a powerful military and police apparatus, with its own interests but also attractive to control. This invites group competition for entry into power. The ideological function means that the state machinery can be used to transmit perspectives and legitimize values directing the society at large. This can be an instrument that groups may value to control. One by one, or taken together, the four functions of a state's monopoly or near-monopoly on force, fiscal resources, territorial control and ideological leadership, make the state an asset for those pursuing particular perspectives, be they of left, right, religious, secular, democratic, nationalistic or other orientations.

The one who controls the state acts in its name, and can use the state's legal systems for its own purposes. The state, as a consequence, is a unique actor and cannot be compared to a political party, a guerrilla movement or a business corporation. These may all have resources of different sorts, but will not have the legitimacy that follows with the state. There is a limit, however. If the state is not capable of performing some of these functions, its strength as an actor diminishes, and so does its value as an object. This is the essence of the phenomenon of warlord politics that can be observed in different parts of the world (Duffield 1998; Reno 1998). The phenomenon of state failure – known throughout the history of the state – has received particular attention since the 1990s. This is a matter that affects conflict dynamics and conflict resolution. Thus, we will have to return to it in Parts Two and Three. However, it raises important theoretical and normative issues that we need to consider immediately.

Clearly, the state as an institution is caught in a dilemma. If it is too powerful, it is likely to be resented; if it is too weak, it is likely to be dismissed. The former is illustrated by the Soviet Union during its entire existence; the latter is exemplified by Somalia since the 1990s. Both ends of the continuum require some thought. When the state is too strong, it governs through the fear it can instill in the population. Totalitarian systems may survive for considerable periods of time, but do so at a high price of repression and, eventually, face a strong counter-reaction. If central control can be combined with economic growth, the pressure may be deflected, but it may also result in new demands from entrepreneurial groups and other resource-rich constellations. In addition, totalitarian regimes inject fear into neighbouring countries, not only among its own citizens. Even global relations can be affected. Major power relations changed dramatically when the Communist Party under Mao took control over China in 1949. The same happened when a totalitarian regime under Hitler came to power in Germany in 1933. This shows that working interstate relationships are dependent not only on direct interactions between states, but also on the domestic conditions of the parties. The relationship between totalitarian regimes and democratic powers is particularly contentious. This was a feature during the twentieth century and remains for the new century, epitomized by the West's relations in the past decades to China, Vietnam, North Korea, Burma/Myanmar, Iran, Iraq, Afghanistan and Syria.

When the state is too weak a different dynamic can be observed. It means a state cannot maintain law and order within its assigned area, control the flow of arms and pursue the collection of taxes. These functions of the state are, in fact, highly interrelated. To collect revenue, the state needs to have credible legal means and a reliable police system. In order to maintain an efficient police and legal system, it needs revenue. Revenue is collected from citizens, their economic transactions and from border crossings. To be able to do that it needs to have effective control over its territory. This requires police and military resources. It is an interplay that in industrialized, resource-rich countries is robust and entrenched in the minds of people. In a resource-scarce country, other loyalties are stronger. The provider of security and welfare can be a clan leader who, in addition, may want to enlarge the resources at the clan's disposal. Thus, the state faces challenges. Somalia may, to some extent, represent the case of clans in conflict. It is not the full story, however, as there are examples of clan cooperation and the resort to local forms of conflict resolution (Fox 1999). The competing forces may be other actors, notably companies interested in the extraction of minerals (as seen in other African states, such as the Democratic Republic of Congo). State leaders may play religious groups wanting to institute their own order against one other (which can be witnessed in Afghanistan and Iraq). There can also be ethnically based groups searching for control of strategic assets, such as nodes in pipeline systems (a factor in Chechnya, Nigeria and Iraq). Thus, too weak a state invites intra-state wars; too strong a state may do the same. Both, furthermore, may lead to international repercussions. To find the 'ideal' state for peace is not easy. Democracy has been identified as one element (Russett 1993), but it may not be sufficient for handling all the world's conflict material.

The Global System

The interactions among sovereign states are described as the international system. According to some writers, it is a self-contained system that can be understood through the lens of the security dilemma. Even a state with defensive purposes may be seen as a threat to other states, whose defensive actions in turn are perceived as threatening. This is a security dilemma to which we have already alluded (Waltz 1979). Although strong theoretically, the notion of the security dilemma builds on some assumptions, most importantly that state survival is the prime motive for states, that states are strong and coherent, and that war between states is of basic concern for security policy. A number of these assumptions are not valid when we look at the entire picture of armed conflicts in the world. It is more common to have war inside states than between them (see Table 4.1 on p.74), states do collapse (as just described) and there are numerous other actors. Thus, the *interstate system*, as instituted in international law and in the UN Charter, is but one subsystem, albeit an important one, in a larger framework – the *global system*. This is a messier, less structured, set of relationships that includes a gamut of other actors and interests. In this perspective, the interstate system, often described as anarchic, appears rather structured and based on predictable rules. Let us explore this a little further.

First, *the interstate system* assumes that states can be *easily defined*. The number of states in the world is limited; UN membership (at the end of 2014) is 193. There are some ten additional entities, which are not recognized by the UN majority and, thus, not seated (the Republic of China, Taipei, also known as Taiwan, is one case; Kosovo is another, more successful case, now recognized by half of UN member states). There is, in addition, a category of non-recognized states, which exist de facto, but have not been recognized by the central government and, thus, normally not by other states either: Somaliland, Northern Cyprus, Abkhazia, South Ossetia all belong to this category of state-like non-states. In particular Somaliland, which corresponds to the former British Somali colony and was independent for a week in 1960 before it merged with Somalia, the former Italian colony, clearly has managed to keep state authorities functioning and maintain the country's independence, in spite of the collapse of the rest of Somalia (Fox 1999). No country has yet recognized this entity, however. Partly, this is based on the fear that it would stimulate or legitimize secessionism in Africa. In the case of Eritrea, other states did not recognize the new state until after an arrangement had been made with Ethiopia on a procedure for independence, leading to mutually agreed statehood in 1993. The declaration of Northern Cyprus as an independent state in 1983 led to diplomatic recognition by Turkey, whereas the UN defined the declaration as illegal. The Republic of Cyprus does not recognize this entity. There is a tendency to give the former central, sometimes colonial, power a veto over the recognition of new states emerging from territory nominally under the control of the previous centre. In 1990, several states in the Soviet Union declared themselves independent. At that time, Lithuania was only recognized by Iceland. The major powers did not want to risk undermining Gorbachev's leadership of the Soviet Union as a whole. An agreement on the final status of Kosovo would therefore normally require the consent of Serbia (the successor to Yugoslavia), but Kosovo nevertheless declared itself independent in 2008. Later the same year Abkhazia and South Ossetia took the same step, immediately being recognized by Russia and a few other states. However, the central authority, Georgia, has not agreed. Most states have refused recognition of these two entities, while Kosovo has widespread international backing.

Thus, the attitude among existing states is less than inviting to the formation of new states. Granted this reluctance, it is still likely that a set of new states will be formed in the coming years, eventually to be seated in the UN. The non-recognized states aspire to receive recognition as a way of protecting their security. On many counts they operate as recognized states, and often model themselves on such states. The process of fragmentation of larger ethnically diverse states, which began during the First World War, is likely to proceed. There are today some 200 state-like entities. The number may grow during the coming years with the addition of one or two states per year. A more dramatic rise is only likely if a major, colonial-type empire is dissolved. The record since 1945 shows that there is at least one such event per decade. The dissolution of the British Empire in South Asia took place in the 1940s. The ending of French control in Indochina and Africa occurred in the 1950s and 1960s. The end of British colonial possessions in Africa can be dated to a decade after 1957 when Ghana became independent.

The crumbling of the Portuguese Empire in Africa in the mid-1970s was achieved through liberation wars. The granting of independence to Pacific islands was a process of the 1980s and the breakdown of the communist empires in Europe was a feature of the early 1990s. The process of formation of new states is not at its end, but it is not an unlimited process either. There are countervailing forces, including the possibility of existing states learning to handle minorities in a more respectful way (Gurr 2000a, 2000b).

However, in the 144 armed conflicts since 1989 recorded by the Uppsala Conflict Data Program, it can be seen that the state was only one of the actors in most of the conflicts. This means that there were a host of other parties present. They are defined as opposition organizations, or *armed non-state actors*. The Uppsala Conflict Data Program lists more than 1,000 such actors. Few of these are recognized by states, and certainly not by the states against which they are fighting. They are instead defined variously as terrorists, gangs, bandits, criminal groups, etc. Such descriptions may sometimes be accurate, sometimes not. Some of these organizations enter into negotiations, or even win wars. Their leaders may then appear as reasonable or even enlightened statespersons despite the labels that have been put on them previously (for instance, Nelson Mandela in South Africa, Xanana Gusmao of Timor-Leste, Menachem Begin in Israel).

Sometimes, the organizations turn into political parties or legitimate armed structures (the former liberation army UCK/KLA in Kosovo was, by the international community, converted into a civilian protection corps after the 1999 war). Other organizations have instead been recorded in history as uncivilized, cruel and even illogical. A recent example is the al-Qaida network that was led by Osama bin Laden and generally seen to be the instigator of the attack on the World Trade Center in New York and the Pentagon in Washington, DC, on September 11, 2001. A number of armed groups now claim the al-Qaida mantle, be they located in Morocco, Algeria, Iraq, Somalia, Yemen or Pakistan. Recently, the Islamic State in Iraq and Syria (ISIS) gained notoriety through its brutality, persecution and eviction, particularly against non-believers in areas of its control (a type of religious cleansing, parallel to the ethnic version observed in other conflicts). There are historical precedents. For instance, the First World War followed on from the assassination of the heir to the throne of the Austro-Hungarian monarchy. This was carried out by a terrorist organization harboured by neighbouring Serbia. Indeed, words such as 'assassins' and 'anarchists' refer to terrorists in European history. Such organizations obviously have to be part of an understanding of wars and armed conflict. How did they emerge, what were their goals, how did they get resources to finance protracted wars? These are pertinent and legitimate questions.

The large number of non-state actors illustrates the shortcomings of focusing only on the interstate system, as if states were in exclusive control even of their own territories. It can be argued, of course, that many of the non-state groups would not have been able to sustain themselves without access to other countries. This may be true, but it does not mean they are always and purely puppets of others. They may in reality be strong enough to coerce regimes and even become involved in wars with the host countries (as happened in Jordan in 1971 and in Lebanon in 1982 with Palestinian groups and the PLO as actors). In the 1990s, there emerged a market for mercenaries and private security companies, which have played a role in wars in Africa, South America and the Middle East. There are militias or para-military formations, that is, informally or formally organized groups. These are locally recruited, operate with unclear mandates and obscure finances and are often directed by a determined leadership, motivated by political and/or economic gains. Such groups are reported from Colombia, Central Africa, in the Bosnian War, in pre-independent East Timor, in Chechnya and in Middle Eastern conflicts. Thus, we see that insecurity and security dilemmas abound, and they are created also by actors other than states.

Third, the global system includes actors who do not have arms but still have a role in conflict. In the emerging global civil society, *non-governmental organizations* (NGOs), increasingly called civil society organizations (CSOs), have gained in significance since the end of the Cold War. They have an ability to act legitimately in a transnational way that few other actors can. One of the most successful is the Doctors Without Borders, or Médecins Sans Frontières (MSF), the Nobel Peace Prize Laureate 1999, which at the same time delivers humanitarian support and brings global attention to atrocities and disasters. With skilful access to conventional media, use of Internet connections and social media, NGOs are able, in a short period of time, to mobilize support globally for particular actions and causes.

Fourth, there are also actors who profit from the messiness of the global system and who operate across borders without any fear of interdiction. This is a category of *trans-state actors*. There are, of course, multinational companies operating all over the globe. They may be involved in the early phases of conflict, as the exploitation of resources may be at the heart of social dynamics leading to armed conflict (as seen in the protracted conflict over Bougainville, Papua New Guinea). The supply of major weapons involves such trans-state organizations, and some of these transactions may be concealed in obscurity, evading laws, with or without the consent of governments. These actors seldom appear in the armed stages of the conflict, and rarely participate openly in negotiations to end the conflict. Other actors, however, may represent their interests, be they states, non-state actors, NGOs or law firms. In addition, there are informal networks. Arms dealers trading in small arms, merchants dealing in valuable minerals controlled by governments or non-state actors, drug traders engaged in international cartels and coalitions, or monetary transfers and money laundering to support war efforts. There are reports of entire ships loaded with weapons that have been captured by factions and used in their armed struggles. Support groups may extort 'revolutionary taxes' from compatriots living far from the war scene to demonstrate their professed 'solidarity' with particular causes. Often, such pressures have a mafia-like quality. Support groups for different sides may even fight each other, thousands of kilometres away from the battlegrounds. Thus, linkages may extend globally, in what might be termed ethnic internationals or global 'tribes' (Kotkin 1992). In addition, conditions of lawlessness give rise to human trafficking and enhanced drug trade, not the least organized across borders.

Thus, there are good reasons for using the term 'global system' for these connecting webs with numerous different types of actor. On the basic level of conflict analysis, the focus is on warring parties. This is the relationship that has to be settled for the conflict to be resolved. It is a necessary element and is dealt with in Part Two. It may not be sufficient, however. That is why the global system, with all its actors and its disorder, enters into the complex level of analysis (Part Three).

4.3 Introducing the Trichotomy of Conflict

Our concern is the resolution of conflict. Although the origin and dynamics may be similar for many conflicts, for each party *its* conflict is unique. In many important respects this is also the reality. There are no conflicts which are entirely similar, and special features always have to be kept in mind. Still, there are rules, norms and understandings that try to equalize conflicts so that they can be treated in similar ways. This is true for violence in any society. One murder is not likely to be identical to another; there are still norms which treat them in similar ways. When society wants to contain violence and inflict punishment, it strives to do that in a fair way. Equal punishment for equal crime is a basic rule. These are general rules created for handling unique events. In the process, similarities are emphasized so as to make events comparable. The argument for dealing with conflicts in the global system is parallel. There are large-scale conflicts that are sufficiently similar to allow them to be handled in comparable fashions. Through international law, such a differentiation has already been introduced and has gained considerable acceptance in the international community.

Traditionally, a firm distinction has been drawn between international and internal conflicts. The first can be handled by, for instance, the international institutions, such as the UN, the International Court of Justice and regional organizations. Internal conflicts are, in this thinking, left to the domain of the states themselves, and placed outside the purview of the international bodies. Internal affairs may only become the affairs of the international community if the legitimate authority in the country, that is, its government, asks for such an intervention. This is a basic tenet of the UN Charter and was seen as an untouchable principle during the Cold War. It does not deny, however, the possibility of making rules for internal conflicts. The distinctions drawn have been ones of expediency rather than matters of principle. If interstate conflicts can be compared, this should also be true for internal conflicts. Indeed, otherwise it would not be possible to draw a general distinction between internal and interstate conflicts. Furthermore, the political climate has changed. The lively debate on humanitarian intervention since the Cold War has questioned the validity of the distinction, both normatively and in practice. By the end of the 1990s, humanitarian arguments resulted in large international support for NATO bombings of Yugoslavia during the Kosovo crisis in 1999 as well as for the international involvement in East Timor, formally a part of Indonesia. The UN extended general support for such actions as part of its new responsibility to protect exposed populations, as agreed by the General Assembly in 2005. This document gave such authority only to the Security Council and the principles were applied in the Libya conflict in 2011. By limiting international action to the Council, the interstate system was maintained, even if internal conflicts have become central in the debate and policies on international peace. The question of international terrorism has also led the Security Council to make decisions that actually transcend traditional sovereignty, for instance, in the commanding decisions on financial sanctions in 2001. Even so, implementation rests with the member states individually, even if they are exposed to heavy external pressure.

The separation of interstate conflicts from other conflicts is entrenched. It will be maintained here because it is a simple differentiation, which reflects realities of importance for conflict resolution. It needs to be seen, however, together with other conflicts, as well as within a larger framework to lead us to a complete picture. Thus, Chapter 5 is devoted to the interstate conflicts, whereas Chapters 8 through 12 present the larger picture.

This leaves us with a group of conflicts which are 'internal'. It is a broad category. Much of what goes on in 'normal' political affairs are interactions among individuals, groups and peoples inside the same borders. The disagreements can be many, as can the conflicts. Internal conflicts, argues Zartman, 'begin with the breakdown of normal politics' (Zartman 1995a: 5). Thus, there are a large number of issues that can be combined in such a way as to make conflict serious and escalatory. There are probably more such concerns inside a particular country than between a given pair of states. Thus, it would be logical to expect more conflict inside states than between them. Decisive for how situations will develop are prevailing and historical social and economic conditions, the governance system for accommodating changes of such conditions, etc. These are matters that will be of concern to the ordinary citizen. To the citizenry, international affairs are often separate and distant. With increasing globalization, their importance may become stronger and more obvious, particularly for small and dependent countries. However, to most inhabitants, what goes on in their own country is likely to be primary as it immediately affects income, well-being and freedom. It is noteworthy that all countries seem to have an internal conflict, which at times is the dominant one. It is also readily identifiable by the citizens of that country. Conflict is a common experience in any society and not necessarily something that is outside 'normal' affairs. Almost to the contrary, as observed by Coser, conflict may contribute to keeping society together (see Chapter 3 and Coser 1956). What is not 'normal' is the resort to arms. There is likely to be a universal preference for peaceful politics, within as well as between states.

Thus, for the population of this planet, internal conflict is as important a category as international conflict. It needs to get as much attention and to be treated in an equally thorough way. It may be true that international law instruments have been restricted from dealing with internal issues, but legal rules are becoming more numerous and more intrusive. It is sufficient to think of the human rights issues, the convention on war crimes tribunals, the many democracy-promoting agencies, as well as the general integration through the global market. Internal affairs are a legitimate object of study and are amenable to conflict resolution that also involves outside parties.

Let us now complement the dichotomy of interstate and intra-state conflict. So far we have presented a dimension which deals with the actors in conflicts – whether they are states or other parties. In Chapter 3 we introduced an equally important notion, incompatibility. This has theoretical and practical implications, particularly for intra-state conflicts. The distinction has turned out to be a fruitful dimension in the Uppsala Conflict Data Program. It separates incompatibilities that concern control over territory from those dealing with government. As we have also seen, the Correlates of War project now applies this distinction for intra-state conflicts (Sarkees and Wayman 2010). Territorial conflicts have always been central in interstate conflicts. Military authorities are important for the control of territory. State security often depends on control over particular areas. Such areas are defined as strategic or vital and thus come to justify military action. The same, of course, is true for internal conflicts. If particular groups claim control over certain areas and want to change their status, it affects the inhabitants of the state as a whole. It might mean drawing new borders and altering established rights of all citizens. It impacts on access to particular areas. It has implications for control over resources. The interest in maintaining the existing territorial arrangements is strong in interstate relations. International consensus is highly resistant to territorial changes which do not have the consent of the parties. The government of a state is likely to be highly conservative with respect to the territory it is set to administer. Challenges are likely to be taken very seriously. Thus, territorial issues also acquire a particular meaning in internal affairs. Studies point to the significance of territory in explanations of interstate war (Vasquez 1993, 1995; Gibler 2012) and we suggest that the same is true for internal conflict. The incompatibility over territory, in other words, cuts across the distinction between interstate and intra-state conflict.

This also applies to the second incompatibility, control over government, referring to the command over the existing central government authority and the composition of the government. The most serious disputes in this category are those where an opposition challenges the existing authority and wants to have it removed, rather than just achieve a change in a particular policy. Repression by governments aims at keeping a particular group in power. Criticism of government policy may be interpreted as a challenge to its authority. Repression can set in at an early stage. In fact, a larger number of incumbent governments have come to power through non-democratic means. Coups, revolutions, civil wars and dynastic arrangements are still routes to power and they are as frequent as are democratic procedures. The struggle over governmental control is classic in politics and continues to be an important aspect of conflict. The state, as we have just seen, contains such attractive resources that many will find it worthwhile to fight to stay in power or take over power. Thus, it draws on a different dynamic from territorial issues, which focus on particular areas or regions, not the state as a whole. In internal affairs, this incompatibility makes sense.

Is this incompatibility also of value for the analysis of international conflicts? Yes, the Cold War demonstrated this convincingly. The interventions by the Soviet Union and the United States were not motivated in terms of territorial gains but with regard to government control. The ambitions of both sides were to promote particular types of regime, not change borders after the territorial realignments of the Second World War. The return of Soviet authority in Ukraine, Belarus and the Baltic states actually met strong armed resistance going on until the early 1950s and explains why these countries were the first to opt out from the Soviet Union in 1990–91. (It goes without saying that the events in Ukraine 2013–14 have actualized these historical experiences.) During the Cold War, Soviet policy aimed at the installation of Soviet-style governments. There were, no doubt, military and strategic considerations, but the conflicts placed local communists loyal to the Soviet Union against non-communist members of the same society. The USA and the West were supporting or establishing particular governments in Iran and other places in the Middle East, as well as in South America and Indochina, but without the idea of changing borders. The hot wars that were part of the Cold War focused on the control over government: which type of regime should there be in a particular country? Some countries may have had a more crucial, geographical position in these global strategies (for instance, Cuba and Turkey). Nevertheless, it was the allegiance of the country as such that was disputed, not the idea of breaking up existing units.[1] The Cold War dualism is no longer present on the global level, but the issue of regime types remains important, both regionally (there are still communist regimes in East Asia) and in particular situations (exemplified by the West-led intervention of Iraq in 2003 and Libya in 2011). The West remains committed to promoting democracy, also with military means, and other actors pledge to resist this, or argue for the right to make counter-actions (even justifying terrorism). Thus, we can observe that both intra-state and interstate conflicts have similar incompatibilities when conflicts are armed and serious. The distinction of territory and government as two separate incompatibilities is fruitful.

This gives us four categories of conflict to consider, but we will merge two into one, making three categories. This creates the trichotomy for conflict analysis. The first category consists of *the interstate conflicts around territory and government*. It is treated as one category, as this is an established group of conflicts, identified with criteria used in international law. Then there are *intra-state conflicts over government* and a third category containing *the intra-state conflict over territory*. It can be said that this trichotomy follows the distinction of international law, but develops it with respect to the intra-state conflicts. Interstate negotiations between sovereign states are similar no matter what the incompatibility concerns, but this, we will show, is not the case for intra-state conflicts. The trichotomy also makes sense as the number of interstate conflicts is limited, and much of today's conflict materials are of an intra-state nature. Furthermore, in the case of intra-state conflict resolution, there are likely to be different arrangements depending on the incompatibility.

It is interesting to note that this distinction for internal conflicts applied here is parallel to the one made by Zartman (1995a) between 'regional' and 'central' conflicts. However, there is no understanding here that conflict resolution, in Zartman's words, necessarily leads to the 'restoration of normal politics' (1995a: 24). The political realities after a serious conflict are likely to be dramatically different, depending on the incompatibility. The solution to a conflict over government may aim at achieving integration and thus some form of restoration and 'normalcy'. A negotiated settlement of a conflict over territory is not likely to have such an outcome. It is not going to be a return to the conditions that prevailed before 'the troubles', but rather involve different forms of separation, even to the point where new states are created. Relationships are changed in a fundamental way. There are, consequently, strong arguments for making the distinction between government and territory particularly important for internal conflicts.

Locating Conflicts in the Trichotomy

It is not necessarily simple to separate one category from another. Thus, the following questions can help to sort out the categorization of the conflicts. For finding a conflict of the first type, it is helpful to ask the following:

Does a particular conflict have a significant interstate component? This can be decided primarily by observing if there are troops from different states involved, meaning that the direct command goes to a particular decision centre. If there are two regular armies fighting each other from two different states, the conflict is a classic inter-state confrontation. Most important is whether the troops of one or the other party are there as part of an alliance or have an internationally legitimate authorization (for example, by the United Nations or an international regional organization). This shows an additional component of the interstate character of the conflict. The issue becomes more complicated if the 'foreign' troops are fighting on the territory of a country with the consent of the government. The problem is to decide whether this is a collective defence arrangement and, thus, a case of legitimate assistance, or whether it is a case of intervention, to which a particular government cannot but agree. An even more complex situation is if the external actor is supporting a non-state actor in the other country. Is this then to be regarded as intervention into an internal conflict between a non-state actor (the rebels) and the government? Or is this, in fact, an interstate conflict, where the external actor is only using the non-state actor as a Trojan horse, or an excuse for expansionism? Determining the true state of affairs is often easier than may first appear, if one applies strict criteria. By observing where the non-state actor gets training for its forces, how its finances are raised, how logistics are set up, how weapons reach the rebels and where political support is expressed, a picture emerges. Key questions are: who can stop the fight-ing, and who will sign an agreement that will be implemented? Two states in direct or indirect conflict are likely to prefer to settle the conflict between themselves and not allow space for others. Armed conflicts which meet these criteria are interstate conflicts, and their solution is discussed in Chapter 5.

The second type of conflict can be identified by asking: *Does a particular intra-state conflict have a significant component of being an incompatibility over government?* In this case, we are considering a conflict between a government and a non-state actor, and the conclusion is based not only on the military actions of the parties, but on the stated purposes of the parties. If the goal is keeping or taking power within the same country to which both sides claim allegiance, it is clear that we are talking about a conflict that traditionally has been identified as *civil war*. It is a struggle for power within a particu-lar state, not only a fight for a change in the policies pursued by a government.

Recent developments indicate that non-state actors may not be primarily inter-ested in taking state power as such, but may settle for control over particular areas or want to make external supporters withdraw so that internal change can be achieved. For example, the peace agreement in Sierra Leone in July 1999 gave the non-state actor, RUF/SL, access to the mining resources in the country. The war was, however, fought on more general grounds and there were no stated intentions of breaking away a particular piece of territory from the country. On the contrary, the peace agreement reaffirmed the unity of the state. This conflict, therefore, is a part of new wars, where public welfare questions are no longer the primary driving forces. These are cases of *'warlordism'* (Duffield 1998; Reno 1998). In practice, they concern access to particular resources in a country, and aim to achieve this by forci-bly removing the incumbent government from attractive areas. They challenge government control.

A second case in this category is *internationalized terrorism*, where the ultimate goal is change in particular societies but where the armed attacks are directed primarily against international supporters of the incumbent regimes. A typical case is the al-Qaida grouping attacking the USA on September 11, 2001, with the hope of achieving US withdrawal from the Middle East. This was in turn expected to lead to regime change in the region. In Chapter 6, the conflicts over state power will be analysed in more detail.

The third type of conflict can be found by asking: *Does a particular intra-state conflict have a significant territorial component?* In this case, the conflict posits a government versus a non-state actor, where the former demands the upholding of the integrity of the state. Its opponent, however, wants to break away a particular piece of territory from the existing state. This may come in different forms. It can include either demanding significant constitutional changes, achieving full sovereignty or attaining integration with the neighbouring state. These aspirations are here subsumed under one: the question of territorial control. More refined labels can be given, such as separatism, secessionism, liberation, irredentism, reunification, restoration, but all these labels have strong value connotations. Discussing them under the heading of territory as incompatibility makes possible a less charged analysis. These conflicts are labelled *conflicts over state formation*. From the government's point of view, it is a matter of keeping the present state form intact. To the non-state actor, it is a question of changing this very set-up in a profound way. These are the conflicts to which considerable attention will be devoted in Chapter 7.

4.4 Applying the Trichotomy of Conflict and Peace

Armed Conflict Since the Cold War

The three types of conflict identified in Section 4.3 are applied to the armed conflicts reported in the Uppsala Conflict Data Program since 1989. The result is seen in Table 4.1. It shows the empirical validity of merging interstate conflicts into one category. There are few such conflicts in the period, in all only nine. This has been observed before and has often been regarded as a prime hallmark of the post-Cold War period. In fact, there have probably been few interstate conflicts for a long time. During the Cold War, however, internal conflicts were internationalized in such a way as to make the local issues subordinate to the global confrontation. It appeared that there were more interstate conflicts. Furthermore, in those days, government issues were probably more important. Although the distinction government–territory is not systematically applied in Table 4.1, it does have a strong impact on the data. We can note that most interstate conflicts dealt with territorial issues, notably changes of borders (Ecuador–Peru, Eritrea–Ethiopia), more complex relationships focusing on particular territories (India–Pakistan) and the resurrection of an occupied state (the Gulf War over Kuwait in 1991). There were two interstate conflicts over government, both of them involving the United States. One was its intervention in Panama in 1989. The other case was the 2003 Iraq War to remove the regime of Saddam Hussein. The Panama case may, in fact, have been the last of a typical Cold War pattern. The Cold War saw many interstate interventions to remove or support incumbent regimes (Hungary 1956, Dominican Republic 1965, Czechoslovakia 1968, and Afghanistan and Nicaragua in the 1980s are but a few examples). It has been argued that such unilateral interventionism by a major power may be something of the past. There was an international operation to remove the military regime in Haiti in 1994 in order to bring back the democratically elected government. It was a US-led activity, but under a mandate of the United Nations. The 2003 Iraq War would then have to be an exceptional event. The issue initially concerned the removal of any potential Iraqi capacity for weapons of mass destruction, but in the final round came to concern the regime itself. The war was not sanctioned by the UN, although it had a limited collective ring to it, being supported, for example, by troops from the United Kingdom and Australia. As the formal occupation ended in 2004, the war in Iraq continued, but then it is recorded as an internationalized intra-state conflict over government. At that time it also had the support of the United Nations. Thus, this example may not signify a return to a pattern of unilateral interventionism.

Table 4.1 presents the armed conflicts during the 25 years since 1989 in five five-year periods. We can see that the total number of armed conflicts actually is declining, most sharply in the 1990s, and with a flattening out in the 2000s. The increase in the fifth period in conflicts over government can partly be attributed to the aftermath of the Arab Spring. However, also in African countries promising trends towards democracy and growth seemed threatened, as was also the case in Eastern and Southern Europe. It might be possible to attribute this to the global economic crisis that followed the financial breakdown in 2008.

The table also shows that the bulk of the conflicts deal with incompatibilities that are internal. At no moment in time did the interstate conflicts constitute more than around 5 per cent of the total number of conflicts. Even among the wars of the period (that is, conflicts with more than 1,000 casualties in one year), only four were interstate (the 1991 Gulf War, the Ethiopia–Eritrea border war 1998–2000, India–Pakistan in 1999 and the 2003 Iraq War) of a total 47 wars in the period (Themnér and Wallensteen 2014). Nevertheless, the interstate category is important. Such wars may have a stronger potential for escalation and diffusion. They may become more destructive and more unsettling for entire regions, in a shorter period of time, than intra-state conflicts.

Table 4.1 Basic types of armed conflicts, 1989–2013 (absolute number of conflicts active per five-year period)

Type	1989–93	1994–98	1999–2003	2004–08	2009–13	Total 1989–2013
Intra-state conflict over government	44	33	30	24	28	64
Intra-state conflict over territory	46	39	23	31	24	70
Interstate conflict	3	4	3	1	2	10
Total	93	76	56	56	54	144

Note: The column 'Total' does not constitute the sum of each row as it refers to conflicts active over the full 25-year period.

Source: Uppsala Conflict Data Program. Armed Conflict Dataset downloaded November 24, 2014.

The other two categories include the largest number of all conflicts and wars in the period. Many have become very protracted and the accumulated destruction is immense. It is likely that Afghanistan is the most serious case, with more than 1 million deaths. The war in Bosnia, as horrible as it was, still does not compare. The genocide in Rwanda stands out as the humanly most destructive of the events of the decade. The killings were directed at defenceless individuals. Shelters and churches were not spared. The genocide took place in a short period of time. In this case, the killings were not even part of the armed conflict, nor did they serve a strategic, military purpose. It was an attempt to wipe out an entire population (Prunier 1995). In the Uppsala Conflict Data Program, this is treated as a case of one-sided violence, in addition to the armed conflict. The protracted war in Sudan ceased with the peace agreement in 2005, and the long war in Sri Lanka ended with government victory in 2009. Both cases saw considerable cruelty against civilian populations. The peace agreement in Sudan, however, did not settle all the issues. In 2011 South Sudan seceded, becoming the 193rd member state of the United Nations. However, armed conflict still took place within the two state entities, particularly destructive in 2014, as well as between the two.

Table 4.1 shows that the two categories of internal conflict that we have identified in Section 4.3 are of about equal size, although with a slight numerical advantage for the territorial conflicts. Many of the latter are protracted and localized conflicts, for example, in India and Myanmar. Conflicts that have drawn heavy casualties in the most recent five-year period concern struggles over government: Syria is likely to be the most devastating one, but in this category are also located the conflicts in Afghanistan, Iraq and Pakistan. Table 4.1 reinforces the importance of separating the two for purposes of analysis. As is the case with all three basic conflicts, there are likely to be interconnections, and to them we shall return in Part Three.

There are some distinct regional differences. Conflicts over territory are almost non-existent in South America. The conflict between Ecuador and Peru indicates that there are a number of unsettled interstate borders on the continent. Indeed, the Falklands/Malvinas conflict of the 1980s was an important reminder of that and there are minor episodes reported around this dispute throughtout the period. There is, however, limited resort to separatism and autonomy in South America, which is common in other parts of the world.

On the other end of the spectrum is Europe, where almost all conflicts are concerned with territorial issues. This is most marked for the wars, that have all been about territorial issues. This includes Northern Ireland. For most of the period the conflicts were concentrated in the Balkan and Caucasus regions. During the Cold War, conflicts around government were central; thus, the promotion of democracy was focal in political and academic thinking, apart from the standard defence considerations. The European integration project stemmed from a desire to denationalize European affairs, something which has been relatively successfully achieved in Western Europe. However, East, Central and Southeast Europe came out of the Cold War with a strong nationalistic fervour, as part of the popular mobilization against the communist regimes (an example is Croatia), and where such regimes quickly took on a nationalistic rhetoric (notably, Serbia). The EU enlargement process, making the European Union into an association of 28 states with the inclusion of Croatia in 2013, has been a check on such tendencies. By emphasizing democracy and human rights, countries aspiring to become members have had to adjust their policies accordingly. However, the financial crisis since 2008 affected the EU's ability to act and the proposal of an extension of the union into an Eastern partnership with, among many, Ukraine, led to serious conflicts within the country and with Russia. Thus, in 2014, Europe saw a new war, where the territorial issues around Crimea and Eastern Ukraine strongly affected regional and major power relations.

Other regions find themselves between the South American and European patterns. The Middle East and Asia have somewhat more conflicts dealing with territory. Africa, surprisingly, largely exhibits conflicts framed in terms of government. There has been a political taboo against breaking up states in Africa, a shared policy that has been pursued on the continent by the African Union (AU, until 2003 the Organization for African Unity, OAU) since 1964. The two exceptions have been Eritrea and South Sudan, but this may have sparked others to ask for the same. Thus, new territorial conflicts erupted in Mali, Niger and Nigeria, with regional as well as religious ingredients.

The trichotomy used in this book is based on the incompatibility in the conflict and this is drawn from the parties' own descriptions of the conflicts. It means it does not treat 'ethnic', 'religious' or 'ideological' as separate categories. Such labels are analytically difficult to compare from one situation to another and not necessarily useful from the viewpoint of conflict resolution. It is political demands for change that are crucial for the outcome of a conflict. 'Ethnic', 'religious' or other identity variables may cut across the categories and perhaps help to understand the intensity of demands, the mobilization of social groups, or interconnections. The resolution of the conflicts, however, has to depart from the specific demands made by the parties. These are captured by the trichotomy.

Peace Agreements Since the Cold War

The Uppsala Conflict Data Program contains systematic information on the outcomes of conflicts and on peace agreements. In Chapter 2, different outcomes were presented (Table 2.1), and an overview was given of the relative frequency of peace agreements. The trend data of Table 4.1 show a gradual reduction in the total number of active armed conflicts, from 93 in the first period after the Cold War to 54 in the fifth one, a reduction of 42 per cent. One explanation given for this is an increased international commitment to peacemaking (*Human Security Report 2005*).

The peace agreements can now be related to the trichotomy of conflict. A first observation is that such an agreement may be concluded long after a particular conflict was active. The almost simultaneous ending of the war and the signing of a peace agreement in Bosnia-Herzegovina in the last months of 1995 is not typical. There were peace agreements concluded in the 1990s for conflicts that had not been armed for many years. There was a peace treaty in 1994 between Israel and Jordan. The most recent, severe military encounters between these parties were in 1967. Also, a peace agreement may be concluded one year, while the armed conflict is still not ended nor the agreements implemented until the following year, or even later. Thus, there is a discrepancy between peace agreements and war termination. This makes it more reasonable to deal with longer periods rather than focusing on the annual shifts. Table 4.2 lists the peace agreements concluded for armed conflicts that have been active in the post-Cold War period.

Table 4.2 Peace agreements in armed conflicts, 1989–2013

The number of agreements is shown in parentheses	*The year marks the latest agreement*
Peace agreements in intra-state conflicts over government:	*Peace agreements in intra-state conflicts over territory:*
Afghanistan (3) 1996	Angola (Cabinda) (1) 2006
Angola (4) 2002	Bangladesh (Chittagong Hill Tracts) (1) 1997
Burundi (8) 2008	Bosnia and Herzegovina (Croat) (1) 1994
Cambodia (1) 1991	Bosnia and Herzegovina (Serb) (1) 1995
Central African Republic (4) 2013	Comoros (Anjouan) (3) 2003
Chad (11) 2006	Croatia (Serb) (1) 1995
Colombia (6) 2002	Georgia (Abkhazia) (1) 1994
Congo (1) 1999	India (Bodoloand) (1) 1993
Côte d'Ivoire (9) 2008	India (Tripura) (1) 1993
Democratic Republic of Congo (7) 2013	Indonesia (Aech) (2) 2005
Djibouti (3) 2001	Israel (Palestine) (8) 2007
El Salvador (9) 1992	Mali (Azawad) (2) 1992
Guatemala (16) 1996	Moldova (Dniestr) (1) 1997
Guinea Bissau (1) 1998	Niger (Air and Azawad) (2) 1995
Haiti (1) 1993	Papua New Guinea (Bougainville) (3) 2001
Liberia (11) 2003	Philippines (Mindanao) (8) (2013)
Macedonia (1) 2001	Senegal (Casamance) (1) 2004
Mexico (1) 1996	Sudan (Abyei) (1) 2011
Mozambique (5) 1992	UK (Northern Ireland) (1) 1998
Nepal (1) 2006	Yugoslavia (Slovenia) (1) 1991
Niger (1) 1993	Yugoslavia (Kosovo) (1) 1999
Philippines (1) 1995	*Peace agreements in interstate conflicts:*
Rwanda (6) 1993[a]	Cameroon–Nigeria (1) 2006
Sierra Leone (3) 2000	Djibouti-Eritrea (1) 2010
Somalia (5) 2008	Ecuador–Peru (1) 1998
South Africa (5) 1993	Eritrea–Ethiopia (1) 2000
Sudan (10) 2011[b]	Sudan-South Sudan (1) 2012
Tajikistan (5) 1997	
Uganda (8) 2008	

[a] The two agreements on August 3, 1993, are treated as one.
[b] The three agreements on May 26, 2004, are treated as one.

Note: Peace agreements are defined as signed treaties which regulate (resolve or find a process for) the incompatibility, which are concluded between the warring parties and put an end to conflict behaviour. Cease-fire agreements are not included. Agreements signed by the end of 2013 are included.

Source: Uppsala Conflict Data Program, downloaded on August 27, 2014.

Table 4.2 shows the tangible outcomes of considerable international, national and local efforts to deal with armed conflict. Many of the agreements are part of peace processes with mediators, facilitators, experts, civil society representation, public debate, as well as the politically responsible actors. These 194 agreements were often signed under solemn conditions and generated high hopes. Many actually fulfilled the expectations, others became part of further learning on the requirements for durable peace.

There are many difficulties in defining a peace agreement. The war between Iran and Iraq ended with the two sides accepting a resolution by the Security Council in 1987. There was no treaty signed between the two heads of state. Their support for the arrangement was a result of a decision by the Security Council. Still, it regulated important aspects of the contentious issues, adhered to by the two parties, and there was no further fighting between them. Neither side could be said to have won the war, but both could claim that they prevented the other from winning. The Security Council resolution was the main modality through which war termination was expressed.

The case of Kosovo is similar. It ended with official negotiations between the Western powers and the government in Yugoslavia through intermediaries. It was a document that both NATO and Yugoslavia could accept. It led to the cessation of air warfare and a withdrawal of Yugoslav forces from Kosovo. It left central issues unresolved. Most notable was the absence of a solution for the status of Kosovo, which was the focus of the conflict. It was agreed that the forces of Yugoslavia were to be replaced with an international force (KFOR), and that the opposite side, Kosovo Albanian forces (UCK/KLA), were to be disbanded. It outlined a process for settlement. Thus, it is comparable to other peace agreements which also have this element and it is included as a peace agreement. In 2008, Kosovo declared itself unilaterally independent and, by 2014, about half the world's countries had accepted Kosovo as a new state. It remains for it to get sufficient majority in the UN General Assembly, however, to get the final mark on sovereignty, including avoiding a negative vote from two veto powers (Russia and China). The most noteworthy peace process is the one between Israel and the PLO in 1993. In this case, a number of interim agreements had been concluded during the 1990s, seven of which are included here as peace agreements. A restart of negotiations took place in November 2007 resulting in a new agreement on a peace process and a new attempt was initiated by the Obama administration in September 2010. However, by early 2014, the US Secretary of State, John Kerry, gave up on his latest attempt to broker an agreement between the two sides.

Another noteworthy case, which is not included in Table 4.2, is the termination of the Gulf War. It ended through UN Security Council Resolution 687 (1991). It was an asymmetrical document. It specified the conditions to which Iraq had to adhere for international forces to withdraw and economic sanctions to be lifted. Iraq had virtually no input into the document, and was not expected to influence the process that followed. This included the disarmament of particular weapons systems, acceptance of a procedure for drawing the boundary between Iraq and Kuwait, and the payment of compensation. It is a document written by a victorious coalition. Thus, it cannot be regarded as a peace agreement. It makes clear who won the war. There was little ambiguity. The outcome of the Gulf War in 1991 was more a victory than the Kosovo conflict in 1999.

A further complication is that there may be many agreements in the same conflict. Agreements are overturned, reworked or extended. This is why notions such as spoilers and spoiler management became valid for the international community (Stedman 1997, 1998). In Table 4.2 there are 194 agreements for 55 armed conflicts, an average of more than three per conflict with a treaty. The highest number is found in the conflicts in Burundi, Philippines (Mindanao), Uganda and Israel (Palestine) with eight each, El Salvador and Côte d'Ivoire both with nine each, Sudan with 10, Chad and Liberia with 11 each and Guatemala's 16 testifying to considerable complexities, failures, mistrust and renewed efforts for a solution. In fact, these ten conflicts have a total of 98 peace agreements, that is slightly more than half of all agreements. By 2013, only three of them had an ongoing minor armed conflict.

If we concentrate attention to the conflicts with agreements and relate this to the trichotomy, Table 4.3 emerges. It compares the frequencies of conflict resolution in the three categories of conflict.

Table 4.3 Armed conflicts and peace agreements, 1989–2013

	No. of conflicts with peace agreements	*No. of armed conflicts*	*Proportion of peace agreements to armed conflicts (%)*
Interstate	5	10	50
Intra-state over government	29	64	45
Intra-state over territory	21	70	30
Total	55	144	38

Note: Armed conflicts with at least one peace agreement.

Source: Uppsala Conflict Data Program, September 4, 2014.

Table 4.3 shows that there is considerable similarity in the ability to conclude peace agreements no matter what type of conflict. About two-fifths of all conflicts appear likely, sooner or later, to find a negotiated settlement, sometimes even more. There is, however, a consistent pattern of such settlements being somewhat more common for intra-state conflicts over government. It is reasonably common that agreements will be reached to make such accords a most serious aspect in any analysis of war and peace. Also, the fact that there are some differences – although not very strong – among the categories in the trichotomy suggests that it is valid as a guide for conflict resolution.

Further Readings

Go to the *Understanding Conflict Resolution* web page at https://study.sagepub.com/ wallensteen4e for free access to journal articles listed.

Peace Agreements: General Understanding

There is considerable work on peace agreement with respect to individual conflicts. More general treatments are rarer. However, the Peace Accord Matrix at the Kroc Institute, University of Notre Dame is a particular resource for the implementation of such agreements. It can be reached on https://peaceaccords. nd.edu

For an overview as well as definitions of peace agreements, see Harbom, L., Högbladh, S. and Wallensteen, P. 2006. 'Armed Conflict and Peace Agreements', *Journal of Peace Research*, 43 (5): 617–31.

Bell, C. 2008. *On the Law of Peace: Peace Agreements and Lex Pacificatoria*. Oxford, UK: Oxford University Press.
In this work Bell presents the legal aspects of peace agreements, which often are absent in the more political treatments of such arrangements.

Stedman, S.J., Rothchild, D. and Cousens, E.M. (eds) 2002. *Ending Civil Wars: The Implementation of Peace Agreements*. Boulder, Colorado: Lynne Rienner.
Here a number of researchers study peace agreements in political terms and in particular conflicts.

Note

1 This is a broad generalization. The four most glaring exceptions are Germany, China, Korea and Vietnam. It is noteworthy that none of these cases was seen by the Cold War superpowers as a question of separatism. The Western support for West Germany was built on the idea of a reunification in the future under a democratic, federal system, the East's support for East Germany emphasized a new legitimacy, not separation of an 'East German' identity. Similarly, the divisions of China, Korea and Vietnam follow such Cold War lines of legitimacy, not separation of identities. This can be seen also in the attitude to reunification. In Germany, it was the West that pressed for unification. In Vietnam, it was instead the communist side that favoured this option, as has also been the case for China in its relation to Taiwan, particularly pronounced when the latter was ruled by a pro-independence party.

PART TWO
BASICS OF CONFLICT RESOLUTION

5

THE RESOLUTION OF
CONFLICTS BETWEEN STATES

5.1 Armed Conflicts and Peace Accords between States

Are wars between states disappearing? They are fewer, but were such wars frequent during the Cold War? If they always were few, then the changes may not be so dramatic. Either way, finding solutions to interstate war remains important. In this chapter, wars and peace settlements among states will be analysed. Of particular interest is the way incompatibilities between states are handled. We will begin by recording the experiences of the last decades of the Cold War, then see what has happened in the 25 years since 1989, to get a basis for a discussion on how interstate conflicts can be solved.

The Last Decades of the Cold War

The global conflagration between East and West made any country or area an object of strategic consideration. Even highly local disputes acquired an interstate quality. Judging from incompatibilities, we find that many Cold War conflicts actually concerned the control over government *in* particular countries. This is true for the events in Nicaragua in the 1980s, in Chile in the 1970s, Czechoslovakia and the Dominican Republic in the 1960s, Hungary in the 1950s, etc. To major powers, these situations had relevance for strategic and tactical calculations, all stemming from a concern with a nuclear confrontation. Direct or indirect interventions were common. The logic was that if the 'other side' is involved 'so should we'. Still, there were classical interstate conflicts during the last two decades of the Cold War.

In the 1980s, some interstate wars received global attention. Among the most devastating was the Iran–Iraq War 1980–88, whereas most press coverage may have been extended to the more limited Falklands/Malvinas War between Argentina and the United Kingdom in 1982 and Israel's invasion and occupation of large parts of Lebanon 1982–85. There was a short war between Chad and Libya. There was also a US intervention in Grenada (1983), in the Caribbean, defined as a minor armed conflict. There were four interstate conflicts during the 1980s. In the 1970s, there were more interstate wars, notably between Vietnam and Cambodia, Vietnam and China, Vietnam and the United States, as well as between India and Pakistan (over the creation of Bangladesh) and the October War between an Egyptian–Syrian alliance and Israel. Israel took control of a part of Lebanon at the end of the 1970s. In 1974, Turkey invaded the sovereign state of Cyprus, and still continues to hold almost 40 per cent of the island's territory. Indonesia occupied East Timor, a territory that formally was under Portugal, in 1975. There was also a war between Ethiopia and Somalia over the Ogaden area and an intervention by Tanzania into Uganda to remove the regime of Idi Amin. In this decade there were ten interstate wars. This clearly was more than we saw in the 1980s and 1990s.

The interstate conflicts in the 1970s and 1980s could not all be subsumed under the heading of the Cold War. Some of them involved major Cold War actors and became part of global politics. But the origins and the incompatibilities were often more specific, concerning territorial issues (islands in the South Atlantic, the status of East Pakistan and East Timor, relations between communities, border questions, etc.) or governance (who should rule in South Vietnam, Uganda, Cambodia, Grenada, etc.). There were strong local dynamics. Major powers may have involved themselves although the conflicts had different origins. Often this contributed to an escalation of conflict. The US engagement in Indochina is one such case. When a major power sends in troops, helps finance one party or in other ways interferes substantially, this is likely to become the main feature of the conflict. In many conflicts, however, the Cold War opponents refrained from provoking each other. Where one was strongly involved, the other might stay out (the Soviet Union was cautious in the Falkland/Malvinas conflict, for instance). There were instances of them supporting the same side (Iraq in the Iran–Iraq War is an example) and cases where both restrained themselves from too heavy involvement (India–Pakistan in 1971).

What does this entail for conflict resolution? It means lessons from these interstate conflicts are relevant also beyond the Cold War. Furthermore, the conventional wisdom has it that it is easier to negotiate peace agreements among states. Thorny issues of recognition and legitimacy that plague parties in internal conflict are not as significant. Classical wars take place between states which are recognized at least by some members of the international system, if not directly by the warring parties themselves. Thus, contacts should be easier to establish. In addition, the UN Charter and other international instruments are available to handle such conflicts. What is the record from the last two decades of the Cold War?

Victory and defeat were the more frequent outcomes in the 14 interstate wars. Many resulted in the withdrawal of one party. Argentina evacuated the islands in the South Atlantic. China pulled out its troops from Vietnam. Pakistan left East

Pakistan, ultimately recognizing the independence of the new country, Bangladesh. The PLO had to leave Lebanon and Somalia withdrew from the Ogaden desert. There were deals or agreements behind these moves, but they cannot be defined as peace agreements arrived at through symmetrical negotiations between equal parties. The developments on the battlefield made clear that one party had prevailed.

When victorious endings were not forthcoming, the conflicts resulted in protracted territorial occupation. Many lasted for several decades. Examples are Israel in South Lebanon (22 years), Sinai (15 years) and still continuing in the Golan Heights. Similarly, Turkey kept control in Cyprus, Indonesia in East Timor (ended in 1999 after 24 years) and Vietnam in Cambodia (11 years). In the case of Iran and Iraq, the parties controlled different parts of the opponent's territory as long as the war lasted. Territorial conflicts, in other words, were difficult to solve in a speedy fashion through negotiations, although the parties have been internationally recognized states.

In conflicts where the regime issue was central, the conflicts resulted in the defeat and removal of these regimes (Ugandan leader Idi Amin escaping to Saudi Arabia, Cambodian leader Pol Pot continuing resistance from the jungles on the Thai border). This, in a way, made the wars shorter. Once this was accomplished, the intervening state was often willing to withdraw its troops, or at least to take measures to mask its presence. This does not speak in favour of negotiated settlements. On the contrary: as the issue was the control over government, negotiations were ruled out. Often both sides regarded the other as an illegitimate actor who could not be dealt with through direct contacts. Thus, we find that interstate conflicts are not easily amenable to international diplomacy, although some objective conditions would speak in favour of that proposition.

Actually, among the 14 conflicts, there are only 2 with mutually developed peace agreements. The one receiving the most attention was the Camp David Accords between Israel and Egypt, negotiated in 1978 and 1979 and implemented in the following years. This agreement meets the criteria set out in Chapter 3 for a conflict resolution ending to a conflict. The same can be said for the arrangement to terminate the war between Chad and Libya. It took the form of a process that lasted into the 1990s. The deal between Ethiopia and Somalia in 1988 can be regarded as a settlement. It took place ten years after actual fighting had ended and the agreement confirmed the outcome of the war. The ending of the Iran–Iraq War, through the auspices of the United Nations, included a cease-fire, an exchange of prisoners of war, and an investigation of responsibility for the conflict. It is still difficult to classify as a peace treaty. It is noteworthy, as it was done through the UN Security Council and the UN Secretary-General. This particular war has many lessons for conflict resolution and we will return to them in this chapter.

Thus, the notion that states have fewer problems negotiating among themselves is not borne out, at least for the Cold War period. The 14 wars followed their own dynamics. In some cases, Cold War parties aligned with conflict actors, for strategic and other reasons, thus reinforcing tensions. The chances of peaceful settlements became intertwined with the overall relations between major powers. It is interesting to note that many of the conflicts are still not solved, two decades after the Cold War ended.

This underlines their origin as being different. From this test, it appears that conflicts in Indochina, after the US withdrawal in 1973, were closely related to major power dynamics between the Soviet Union and China. As this tension subsided, these conflicts found solutions. Many other conflicts remained on the agenda and peace initiatives stemmed from other dynamics: India–Pakistan continued to be a contentious relationship, with a short-lived peace process in the early 2000s; the Cyprus question remained on the agenda, with a UN attempt failing in 2004, and later directly contacts between the Cypriot actors, but yet without solution; the East Timor conflict found a solution after the fall of the Suharto regime in Indonesia, not as a result of the end of the Cold War.

The Post-Cold War Period

It is important to note that the frequency of interstate armed conflicts is low and this is not a novel phenomenon. It remains, of course, true also for the period after 1989. Table 5.1 reports on interstate conflicts and peace agreements.

There were 10 interstate armed conflicts since the end of the Cold War and by 2014 none was active as a typical interstate war. The US war on Iraq, however, had been transformed into an internationalized civil war, with the return of US forces to fight ISIS, a rebel group active in both Iraq and Syria. The status of some wars could be discussed. For instance, the Gulf War was not over as air strikes on Iraq by the United States and Britain continued throughout the period. The war of 2003, however, was not a simple escalation from this, but instead concerned the regime in Iraq itself. Four interstate conflicts rose to the level of war. It is fewer than in the previous periods, but not significantly so. It is difficult to judge if there is a long-term trend towards fewer interstate conflicts.

Three conflicts resulted in victory of one party over the other (USA–Panama, the Gulf War, USA–Iraq). Two were taken to the International Court of Justice for settlement (Cameroon–Nigeria, Cambodia-Thailand). Two were concluded through a negotiated process resulting in a peace agreement, signed by the two sides (Ecuador–Peru, Eritrea–Ethiopia). India and Pakistan initiated a peace process in early 2004 and violence on the border diminished, but without solution. The terror attack on Mumbai in 2008 and political instability in Pakistan prevented further advances. Similarly, there was no settlement between Djibouti and Eritrea, although violence ceased. There was an agreement between Sudan and South Sudan on the common border and fighting subsided but tensions remained, also involving the implementation of the solution. Of the 10 conflicts, five ceased through a process of conflict resolution and there were negotiations in several others. Ending through settlement was a more frequent outcome than military victory. Also, military victory was the outcome only in conflicts that were very asymmetric. The USA was a party to all and its intervention capacity was crucial to the result (Panama, the Gulf War, Iraq 2003). In Iraq, the USA and its allies, chiefly Britain, encountered unexpected and protracted resistance. Still, this period shows different ways of ending conflict compared to the preceding decades.

Table 5.1 Interstate armed conflicts, 1989–2013

Parties	Incompatibility	Outcome	Intensity
Panama v. USA	Regime in Panama	Victory	Minor
India v. Pakistan	Border, Kashmir	Peace process	War
The Gulf War	Kuwait's independence	Victory	War
Ecuador v. Peru	Border	Settlement	Minor
Cameroon v. Nigeria	Border	Settlement	Minor
Eritrea v. Ethiopia	Border	Settlement	War
Iraq v. USA, allies	Regime in Iraq	Victory, civil war	War
Djibouti v. Eritrea	Border	No settlement	Minor
Cambodia v. Thailand	Border	No settlement	Minor
South Sudan v. Sudan	Border	No settlement	Minor

Note: Chronological order, parties listed alphabetically in English, issues indicated, outcome or status by end of 2013 and highest intensity reached during this period.

Source: Uppsala Conflict Data Program Conflict Encyclopaedia, UCDP/PRIO armed conflict dataset.

The incompatibilities in the armed conflicts were related to territorial issues, with the exception of the interventions in Panama and Iraq. In the Panama case, the USA captured the country's strong man, General Manuel Noriega, and brought him to an American court for violation of US drug laws. The political issue of who rules Panama was turned into a police issue. Objections to US actions were vetoed in the Security Council. In the Iraq case, the leader, Saddam Hussein, was captured by the end of 2003, sentenced by a special Iraqi court and executed in 2006. The other conflicts concerned border questions and issues of territorial integrity of states. If it is correct, as reported, that the total number of land borders in the world is around 300, seven border conflicts is a small number (Blake 1999: 150). As most of the armed conflicts have remained on a low level of intensity and also found solutions, there seem to be ways in which border conflicts can be handled. This means that those conflicts that were not managed, but turned into wars, need particular attention.

The four interstate conflicts that became wars point to the propensity of military escalation in interstate conflicts. This might distinguish them from other types of conflict. There might even be a tendency for earlier and less reluctant use of military capacities in such conflicts. The escalation of conflicts was rapid. Within a few weeks the resources amassed by the parties were immense. This is the more striking as one case involved two poor agricultural societies (Ethiopia and Eritrea). In the 1991 Gulf War, the swift deployment of US and Western military resources to the Middle East was used to apply pressure on the government in Iraq at the same time as it was part of war planning. A similar tactic was used in the months leading up to the Iraq War that started in March 2003. Relations between India and Pakistan have been on the brink of war several times during the decade. Nuclear weapons tests by the two countries in 1998 increased tensions, and for some months in 1999 the countries were close to a major conflagration. In interstate conflicts, the parties have military organizations, which are trained for conflict options, at their disposal and, thus, the ability actually to use them is higher. Military options are more tempting, more credible and, thus, more likely to be applied.

The escalatory potential of interstate conflicts is well known and is particularly felt in the regions that are affected. This means that the early activities by neighbouring countries to contain conflicts are important. Such actions were taken in the Gulf War, without a solving formula being found. In the case of the 2003 Iraq War, the alleged presence of weapons of mass destruction or capacity to produce such weapons was an issue. An alternative route existed, supported by the UN Security Council from November 2002: weapons inspections by capable international experts. Thus, the Council was not willing or ready to authorize an attack on Iraq by March 2003. In the case of India and Pakistan, neighbours have been effectively barred from involving themselves, as India consistently has seen the problems as a bilateral or internal issue. The official peace attempts have been strictly bilateral. In the case of Djibouti v. Eritrea, the UN Security Council demanded that the troops of the parties withdraw to the status before the armed conflict. Djibouti did, Eritrea did not and was subsequently exposed to an arms embargo by December 2009. The conflicts between Sudan and South Sudan, following the dissolution of the shared stated, immediately sparked mediation efforts by neighbours and by the African Union. There was a peace agreement, but tension was not ended. In the temple dispute between Cambodia and Thailand, there was an established process in the International Court of Justice to which the parties could defer. These conflicts were contained on a low level of intensity.

The peace agreements during the post-Cold War period are listed in Table 5.2. Settlements take time. Table 5.2 also lists armed conflicts which saw little or no fighting in the 1990s. It means that peace processes have been protracted. By 1994, the conflict between Chad and Libya over the Aouzou strip was settled. The final issues were handled by a UN mission, following a decision by the International Court of Justice (ICJ) (Merrills 1999: 105–6; Shaw 1999: 51). By then there had been no armed conflict since the mid-1980s. Similarly, the border issues between Russia (succeeding the Soviet Union) and China found solutions through a series of agreements, the first one concluded in 1991 (Kotliar 1999; Su Wei 1999). The most severe confrontation between these countries took place in 1969, more than 20 years earlier. A peace agreement was signed between Israel and Jordan in 1994, but the countries had not been at war since 1967, more than a quarter-century earlier. Why was there a lack of concerted efforts to settle these conflicts earlier? A high level of tension between states is but one answer. Tension in the surrounding region is another. But the answer could also be found elsewhere. Although conflicts may have their own dynamics, their ending requires efforts by the international community. When victory is preferred among leading states, there will be little interest in local settlements.

Some disputes, which did not result in severe casualties, found settlements since the end of the Cold War. Table 5.2 includes Eritrea v. Yemen, which had a dispute over the Hanish Islands and associated maritime boundaries in the Red Sea. Instead of letting the conflict escalate or linger, it was brought by the parties to the International Court of Justice. International arbitration was used for the conflict between Botswana and Namibia, again a dispute not qualifying as an armed conflict. In an earlier era, there may not have been the same swiftness in finding a solution.

This underlines that there is a stronger emphasis on peaceful settlement in the post-Cold War period than earlier. Whereas most conflicts in the last two decades were

Table 5.2 Peace agreements in interstate armed conflicts, 1989–2014

Parties	Solution through the use of	Highest intensity 1989–2014 (or earlier)
Iran v. Iraq	UN Security Council	War
Chad v. Libya	ICJ, UN peacekeeping	War
Mauritania v. Senegal	Bilateral agreement	Dispute
China v. Soviet Union/Russia	Bilateral agreement	(Minor)
Eritrea v. Yemen	ICJ	Dispute
Israel v. Jordan	Bilateral, US support	(War)
Ecuador v. Peru	Four guarantors	Minor (War)
Cameroon v. Nigeria	ICJ	Minor
Botswana v. Namibia	ICJ	Dispute
Eritrea v. Ethiopia	UN, OAU	War
Cambodia v. Thailand	ICJ	Minor
South Sudan v. Sudan	AU, Neighbour	Minor

Note: Peace agreements concluded by parties since 1989, where the parties have been in an armed conflict with one another at some point since 1946. The table also includes three disputes, that is, conflicts below the intensity of an armed conflict. Parentheses indicate that the highest intensity was recorded before 1989. The order of the two parties in each dispute is alphabetical in English and does not imply a statement on the initiator of hostilities.

Source: Uppsala Conflict Data Program Conflict Encyclopaedia.

ended through victory/defeat outcomes, the most common ending since 1989 has been through settlement. This says something about a changed climate, perhaps also a shift in practice, at least for some types of conflict. It means that conflict resolution is higher on the agenda for interstate conflicts than earlier. The attempts by many states to use the UN as a way to resolve the Iraq situation prior to the beginning of the 2003 war also testifies to the willingness to find peaceful solutions. The fact that Iraq has been at war with the USA twice in this period also indicates the limits of such ambitions. This makes it most important to explore how negotiated settlements of conflict issues between states actually have been dealt with, in this era as well as previously.

Geopolitik, Realpolitik, Idealpolitik and Kapitalpolitik

The Cold War was a global power conflagration, entangling all major powers. It did not result in an armed conflict between the leading two. With the experiences of the First and Second World Wars in mind, a peaceful outcome of the Cold War could not be taken for granted. The polarization between East and West was a high-risk policy venture. Major power relations since then are different. There is now a frequency of summit meetings. The UN Security Council, as we will see in Chapter 9, found a new position as a forum for managing some of these relations.

Indeed, also after the Cold War, there are complicated relations between major powers. Much attention has lately been given to China's relations with its neighbours and with the Western powers. This includes questions over the status of Taiwan and control in the South China Sea. Equally or more important for the East Asia region is the China–Japan relationship. Japan participated for the first time in a peacekeeping operation in 1992, sending personnel to Cambodia. Russia remains significant and recently more assertive than in a long period. It is an actor in several world regions. Germany, mostly working with the EU and NATO, for the first time sent ground troops outside alliance areas in 1999, when a German contingent was stationed in Kosovo. In 2014 it agreed to send weapons to a war situation, when supplying Kurdish forces in Northern Iraq to fight the threat from the rebel group ISIS. We should note that major powers have not had any direct territorial or other confrontations among themselves since the end of the Cold War. The tensions around Ukraine in 2014 and the Russian annexation of Crimea thus break an established pattern.

The wars and armed conflicts since 1989 have involved regional or local issues. This has given rise to new questions. For instance, should major powers, or an international organization where major powers are crucial, act to contain or resolve a particular conflict between states? There is no definite answer: in interstate wars since the end of the Cold War – the Gulf War, the Eritrea–Ethiopia War, the India–Pakistan War in Kargil in 1999, and the 2003 Iraq War – the states not strategically involved pursued distinctly different courses of action. In the first case, the UN authorized an armed intervention, in the second, international mediation was preferred. In the third, there was little involvement at all. In the fourth, two major states were allied in the war (the USA and Britain), four others were against it, but did not act militarily on the issue (France, Germany, Russia and China). The answer is more varied today, in general giving settlement and diplomacy higher priority. In the face of a determined major power, this may not necessarily be an effective alternative. Nevertheless, let us see what the settlement response entails. The duty of the UN is to deal with interstate conflicts wherever they occur and this ambition is no longer frequently blocked by permanent member states in the Security Council. The existence of an internationally agreed framework also means that there are particular procedures for the settlement of interstate conflicts. Chapter VI of the UN Charter is devoted to this. Article 33 recommends member states to take a number of measures: 'negotiation, enquiry, mediation, conciliation, arbitration, judicial settlement, resort to regional agencies or arrangements, or other peaceful means of their own choice'. It is a mixed group of activities, where some more readily relate to certain types of interstate conflict. For instance, for boundary conflicts, arbitration is frequently used. In this case, the parties commit themselves in advance to accept the outcome of a court of arbitration. Arbitration is, however, difficult to apply to conflicts dealing with governmental control, regional or global balance of power.

It is likely that the danger of conflicts spreading inadvertently is more immediately apparent in cases of interstate conflicts today. Earlier, conflicts were held in check by the global powers. Today, there are new patterns of arms trade, unsettling interruptions in civilian trade, and a less controlled flow of refugees. This means there are heavy pressures on neighbouring governments to take sides or to take their own defensively motivated actions, thus spreading the conflict. There are also neighbours being challenged by the warring actors or by groups linked to the ongoing war. Furthermore, interstate conflicts often involve challenges to principles of international law. This implies that a particular settlement may create precedents that affect active or potential conflicts in other member states.

The interstate security dilemma takes on a new meaning after the Cold War. Its original formulation assumed that sovereign states feared the attacks of other states whose intentions were difficult to read and, thus, they prepared to defend themselves. These very preparations created fear and induced the opposite side also to prepare for war. It could give an advantage to the one that would attack first, a first strike option that would be intended to pre-empt actions by the opponent. In a world dominated by superpower rivalry and global tensions, such dilemmas seemed to repeat themselves throughout the planet. However, in a world which instead sees conflict as an aberration, a peculiar exception, fears of attacks should diminish. With evidence that wars become protracted conflicts, rather than military victories, the incentive to strike first should reduce. With increasing difficulty of finding allies for war efforts, again fears may be reduced. With an emphasis by major international actors to find solutions, local actors may see fewer reasons to prepare for military attack.

However, September 11, 2001, has created a new security dilemma which clearly affects international relations. The insecurity of the leading state, the United States, induced insecurity throughout the planet. The 2003 Iraq War has been explained as part of the campaign on global terrorism. This intervention in itself, however, fuelled insecurities in Iraq, leading to a seemingly protracted internal war with heavy outside engagement. Such internal security dilemmas will be considered in the following chapters.

Although the interstate conflicts are few, their significance for the international system is very high. This means they have to be scrutinized in considerable detail. In so doing, it is also apparent that they exhibit different origins, incompatibilities, dynamics and solutions. The interstate conflicts are purposefully divided into four categories (Wallensteen 1981, 1994a, 2011b) to simplify comparability. The four categories are *Geopolitik, Realpolitik, Idealpolitik* and *Kapitalpolitik*.

First, there are *Geopolitik* conflicts, where particular types of territory are afforded such significance by one or more states as to give rise to war or serious armed conflict. The concept of *Geopolitik* goes back to classical thinking on international relations. Certain areas were seen as so important that control over them would also mean control over an entire continent or even the globe. Candidate territories have been certain areas on the Eurasian landmass, control over the High Seas, and today control over outer space. On the local level, states may regard particular border areas as rightfully theirs, for historical as well as strategic reasons.

Second, there is a category of *Realpolitik* thinking, where prime importance is attached to power and the power capabilities of the actors. Mostly, this refers to military instruments and the latest military technology, as well as the quantitative strength that can be mustered. This logic also has classical roots. *Realpolitik* has primarily been seen as a driving force for major powers. It may, however, be applied equally well to regional conflicts, where issues of balance of power may be as important. A goal of the fighting parties could be to gain the upper hand as regionally dominant.

These two notions are often closely related to each other, as power has implications for territorial control, and vice versa. Thus, we treat these aspects together in Section 5.2, although they will point to different solutions of conflicts.

Third, there is a category of *Idealpolitik*, meaning an emphasis on ideological and legitimacy issues. Two governments may dispute each other's rights due to the way in which they have been created or gained legitimacy. It is often maintained that there is a built-in tension between democracies and non-democracies. The appeal or fear of political thought on one side of the border may affect the politics on the other. There are often conflicts arising from revolutions in one country affecting neighbouring states. Indeed, revolutionary changes in one major power affects its relations to all the other major powers and is, thus, an event of significance for global affairs. The revolution in China (actually, the military victory by the Communist Party in 1949) certainly had a global impact, as did the coming to power of Hitler in Germany in 1933 and the Bolsheviks in Russia in 1917, just to give some examples. The legitimacy issue needs to be dealt with, particularly in the light of the democracy–peace proposition, stating that interstate relations between democratic states are more peaceful than all other types of relations (Russett 1993).

Fourth, there is a category that is not given as much prominence as it probably deserves, and that is here called *Kapitalpolitik*. This means that economic issues are central, be they questions of oil prices, the drawing of pipelines, transportation routes, or relations between rich and poor, industrial and non-industrial producers. Some theorists see these as fundamental for the formation of conflict patterns, and with capitalism as the global guideline for economics, it is a pertinent issue to consider.

The *Idealpolitik* and *Kapitalpolitik* conflicts are dealt with together in Section 5.3. As is often the case, of course, a particular conflict may well contain strands of all four elements, and we will have to see how that impacts on conflict resolution possibilities.

5.2 Conflict Resolution: *Geopolitik* and *Realpolitik*

Geopolitik, as we have defined it, is concerned with territories of particular interest. In its original form, dealing with major powers, particular regions would gain pre-eminence in global strategies. This was also the situation during the Cold War, where locations strategic to the movement of fleets, troops or aircraft could readily be identified. In the post-Cold War era this is no longer as clear-cut, although arguments for its significance can be made (Cohen 1999). Indeed, areas which are close to major powers continue to be important in strategic considerations. There are some straits and islands which acquire such significance, but now probably more because of their role in the global economy than for their intrinsic military value. In the vocabulary introduced here they are *Kapitalpolitik* assets rather than *Geopolitik* ones. To these belong the Persian Gulf, the South China Sea, the Cape of Good Hope, perhaps the Suez Canal and the Strait of Gibraltar. Also, locations along major pipelines for oil or natural gas take on significance. In the South Caucasus region, much of the politics is concerned with the routes through which oil from the Caspian Sea can reach the world market. Ukraine finds itself at similar lines. Geopolitically interesting areas are possible to identify and would, in themselves, be a worthwhile subject for study. Certainly, such considerations will have an impact on the major powers and their attention to particular areas. In the last analysis, what matters are the lenses through which decision-makers view these territories.

Territorial issues remain important as conflict issues (Diehl 1999; Starr and Thomas 2005; Vasquez 1993, 1995). The settlement of such disputes is important for shaping of future relations between the countries involved (Gibler 2012).

In the 1990s, interstate war was associated less with grand strategies of *Geopolitik* and more with local territorial issues. Some of these, in fact, have little economic significance to the involved parties, but border questions have proved to be rallying points for action. As can be seen from Table 5.1, most of the recent interstate conflicts were border disputes. Some, such as Ecuador–Peru, had a previous history which influenced the prospects for their settlement. The ending of this dispute in 1998 was thus of historical significance (Einaudi 1999). Other conflicts that were new still turned out to be difficult to handle, as the parties grappled with their own positions, trying to locate historical evidence and contemporary precedents for their case. The repeated conflicts between the United States and Iraq, first over Kuwait 1990–91 and then the full-scale invasion in 2003, gave rise to global attention, illustrating some of the dimensions identified above: Iraq is located in a region that is a leading producer and exporter of oil.

Status Quo or Status Quo Ante Bellum?

The key question from the point of view of resolving such conflicts, once an armed conflict has occurred, is what is the point of departure for the settlement? Shall those interested in a settlement use the (new) status quo created by actions of one party or shall they demand a return to status quo ante bellum before negotiations can be considered? Accepting the newly created situation, status quo, is the more convenient, less demanding approach. It is a realistic position. It could be said that it would provide a speedy way of resolving a conflict and undo the effects of war, for instance, by allowing an immediate return of refugees. The demand for a return to the situation before the war started, status quo ante bellum, has many complications, but it rests on a normative imperative. It makes clear that international relations are not entirely ruled by raw might, but follow certain agreed rules. It can be argued that strict adherence to this principle contributes to deterring future conflicts of the same type. If we follow the wording of the UN Charter, we would expect this perspective to dominate. It is a matter of undoing aggression. The most obvious understanding of aggression is when one country without permission comes into a territory held by another state and claims that it intends to hold on to the area. The principled stand is attractive. However, the demand that territorial conquest is to be undone before any talks can be considered is not an easy proposition to maintain, in spite of its attraction. Realities may force conflict resolution promoters into more complicated strategies. Let us look at some situations among the wars we have recorded in Section 5.1 and in Table 5.1 as a guide to the experiences of the most recent three decades.

During these years, the status quo approach was applied in a series of situations, but often with some qualification. The UN Security Council resolution of 1967 demanded that Israel return occupied territories in exchange for a lasting peace with Egypt, Syria and Jordan. Thus, the Council took the more convenient approach, but not without conditions. There was an obvious difficulty: there were no international boundaries to return to, only armistice lines negotiated in 1949. It would not have been acceptable to either side to define these as international borders. Only in the case of Egypt have the intentions of the Security Council materialized, in a land-for-peace deal. There is also a peace agreement between Israel and Jordan, but it was simplified by Jordan's decision in 1988 to abandon its claim to the West Bank. Syria maintains that peace with Israel requires that Israel commit itself to returning to the exact previous lines, before negotiations can take place. Thus, although all agree that the conditions prior to the war should serve as a basis, soon 50 years have passed without the parties finding an agreement for the full implementation of this principle.

A second case is the one of Turkey versus Cyprus, where also a withdrawal is expected, but this is tied to a solution to the communal problems of Cyprus. The withdrawal of Turkish troops is one demand, but there are other security concerns (for the Turkish Cypriot community) as well as demands for freedom of movement, settlements and property (for the Greek Cypriot community). It leads us into the security concerns of the parties. In the cases of Cyprus and Palestine, the demand for withdrawal has been coupled to a settlement of the conflict as a whole, suggesting that the particular circumstances of each case have been attended to. It means, at the same time, that the militarily established status quo has been maintained for many decades. Thus, they turn into near permanent situations and new generations adapt to their existence. It makes some comfortable, others highly frustrated.

An important test on the application of this approach is found in the war between Iraq and Iran. When the war broke out in 1980, the UN Security Council demanded a ccase-fire and did not specify a force withdrawal to the international boundaries. This meant that the Council was satisfied with the less demanding position, but instead faced a situation where the authority of the Council was badly damaged in the eyes of one warring party, Iran. From an Iranian perspective, a cease-fire meant that Iraqi troops would remain on Iranian territory, and only withdraw through negotiations. Iran would have to make additional concessions to achieve this. Iran rejected this stance, and thus preferred to work only with the Secretary-General or the special representatives appointed by him (Pérez de Cuéllar 1997).

The demanding principle of status quo ante bellum was specifically raised and implemented, sometimes with superior military force, in some of the conflicts recorded in Section 5.1. Argentina was forced to withdraw from the Falklands/Malvinas Islands. Iraq left Kuwait after being militarily defeated. Vietnam removed its troops from Cambodia after ten years. Somalia pulled back from Ogaden. Israel withdrew unconditionally from Southern Lebanon in May 2000 when the government was led by Ehud Barak. Thus, the principle has general acceptance and its application is seen as the end point of a particular conflict. In none of the examples quoted, however, has it been an easy process. The role of force in achieving this has been obvious.

In the conflict between Ethiopia and Eritrea, the third parties, in particular the Organization for African Unity (OAU), worked from a normative framework on border changes. According to this, there has to be a return to the status that existed prior to the onset of the fighting in 1998. In the words of the OAU Framework Agreement presented to the parties: 'the armed forces ... should be redeployed to the positions they held before 6 May 1998 as a mark of goodwill and consideration for our continental Organization'. The OAU summit meeting in Cairo in 1964 took the fundamental decision to accept the borders that were inherited from colonial times. African states have avoided international border revisions by force. The OAU peace plan built on this consensus. The reference in the Framework Agreement to the organization itself appeals to this legacy, its continental significance and its ability to talk 'on behalf of Africa'. These elements were additional pressures on Eritrea and Ethiopia. However, the parties continued to raise questions on the Framework Agreement and later documents derived from it. As part of the process, a high-level delegation from the OAU concluded that the disputed territory around the town of Badme, where the conflict originated in 1998, was administered by Ethiopia at the time the fighting began. Thus, the demand was on Eritrea to withdraw. It is also 'understood that this redeployment will not prejudge the final status of the area concerned'. The choice of words was important: 'redeployment' not the same as 'withdrawal', or 'evacuation'. A later, legitimate decision could award the territory to Eritrea. This is also what happened. As part of the peace settlement a border commission was created and in 2002 awarded Badme to Eritrea. Since the end of the war, this territory had been held by Ethiopia, which showed no inclination of giving it up. The UN peacekeeping mission was ended in 2006 without a settlement. In the Eritrea–Djibouti territorial conflict, Eritrea is accused of having occupied areas belonging to its neighbour. The UN Security Council in 2009 explicitly demanded a return of Eritrean forces to their 'status quo ante' positions (UN Security Council Resolution 1907).

As this case illustrates, both the UN and the OAU (now African Union – AU) have enunciated clear principles against forceful change of borders. The same is true for many other international and regional organizations. Territorial integrity is built into the normative framework on which these organizations operate. By bringing a particular conflict to one of these organizations, the parties will know what principles will be applied. There is a common interest among most states in favour of keeping the present boundaries and, thus, to support peace processes on that basis.

The principles are only applicable if the cases are reasonably evident, which means they have to concern fairly sizeable territories and not appear to be merely border adjustments. The occupations by Israel in 1967, Turkey in 1974 and Iraq in 1990 had high visibility. This made it imperative for the international community, chiefly the UN Security Council, to take a marked position on the return to the previous dividing lines. Whether such decisions are followed by effective measures to change the situation on the ground apparently is a separate matter as the mixed record suggests. In cases where a status quo approach has been applied, explicitly or in practice, there is little international interest in bringing about a visible change in the disputed territories. This frustrated the Arab states in their conflict with Israel; Greek Cypriots in dealing with Turkey; and Iran in dealing with the Security Council. In contrast, the conflict between Ecuador and Peru, highly important to both countries, drew less international attention. The dispute concentrated on the treaty of 1942, with many complexities in interpretation. The fighting in 1995 was kept on a low scale, not least due to the efforts of neighbouring countries to contain the conflict. International peacemaking did not have to confront withdrawal issues as the cease-fire was instituted. Instead, diplomacy could concentrate on the incompatibilities.

Although there is an ambition to uphold the demanding principle of a return to the previous status quo before negotiations, the successes in achieving this have not come easily. The record shows that it is not enough with diplomatic persuasion. In the case of Argentina, the occupation resulted in war and the defeat of the Argentinean forces. The islands were returned to British control only a few months after being taken by Argentina. The war was a military and political victory for Britain and there was a return to status quo ante bellum. The costs for this were high. Furthermore, Argentina has not accepted the new (or restored) situation. The umbrella agreement of 1989 made possible the return to diplomatic and commercial relations without solving the incompatibility. In the case of Vietnam, a unilateral withdrawal was implemented in 1989, that is, 10 years after the troops entered the neighbouring country. By that time, a new regime had been able to establish itself in Cambodia. It was evidently strong enough to maintain control on its own, as it remains in place 25 years after the withdrawal. Somalia held on to the territories it conquered in Ethiopia for about one year, but in the face of close cooperation between the United States and the Soviet Union it withdrew. Still, it took until 1988 for Ethiopia and Somalia to conclude an agreement on the basis of the restored status quo.

From these experiences, it can be concluded that the conflict resolution policy in the UN Charter – the demand for a restoration of the status quo ante bellum – in reality is subject to interpretation and evasion. It is obvious that other factors are also relevant. For instance, political proximity to the United States may appear to be an important factor for states to avoid being pressured to comply with the principle. For Israel, there are special arguments for its security, undoubtedly with considerable support in the Western world. With respect to Turkey, there has been a similar 'understanding', taking into account Turkey's strategic location even after the Cold War, and as a NATO member. It is not necessarily shared in parliamentary assemblies throughout Europe, however, where the debate on Turkey's human rights record has been lively. In the Iran–Iraq War, Iraq was the preferred party of the USA, but interestingly enough also for the Soviet Union. Thus, the UN resolutions were consistently biased, and Iran reacted to that with arguments based on international law.

However, the correlation between strategic affinity to the USA and acceptance of the status quo is not always that simple. The United States opposed Argentina's actions in the Falklands/Malvinas but might have been expected to respond negatively to a forceful British reaction. The USA had a tradition of objecting to extra-Hemispheric interventions in South America. After a period of mediation, however, the United States chose to support Britain. That the USA opposed Iraq's actions against Kuwait may have come as a surprise to the Iraqi leader, Saddam Hussein, remembering the support he received in the war with Iran, which had just ended. The leaders in Iraq and Argentina may have thought of themselves as so close to the USA that no effective counter-actions would be forthcoming. It is less surprising that the USA opposed Somalia's actions in Ogaden (Somalia by that time was regarded as a Soviet client state) and Vietnam's war in Cambodia (Vietnam's alliance with the Soviet Union was opposed by China and the USA alike). Arguments on conflict resolution principles are evidently not the full story.

However, on issues of territorial change, there has often been a remarkable consensus among the major powers. Defending the territorial integrity of states is a cornerstone of the UN Charter. States are likely to be resistant to forceful changes in principle, as they may also affect them. The status quo ante bellum principle is, consequently, the one most easily agreed to by the major powers and UN member states. In instances where this is not so, we can suspect that a member state has a particular interest in a given conflict. We would, on the whole, expect a permanent member of the Security Council to support the more demanding position of a return to the pre-war lines, except in cases where it sees particular reasons for not doing so. The creeping occupation and annexation of Crimea by Russia in 2014 (largely without bloodshed) constitute a violation of these principles. Russia's veto power prevented Council action. Western countries as well as Cina refused to recognize this development, maintaining that the peninsula belongs to Ukraine.

For interstate geopolitical conflicts, questions of status quo and status quo ante bellum are highly relevant. There is a general preference for demanding a return to the situation before the outbreak of hostilities. However, we find exceptions to this rule, weakening its consistent application and, thus, also reducing its deterrent effect. We have seen that the exceptions are connected to the stronger global powers.

Punitive or Integrative Solutions?

Realpolitik conflicts build on the power of the parties. In this analysis, power is what ultimately decides the outcome of conflicts. Such outcomes, furthermore, are formed in clear alternatives, preferably victory or defeat. If a conflict results in negotiations and compromises, this is because none of the parties is strong enough. Furthermore, the analysis emphasizes that the objectives of the parties involve power and domination. Power is both a means and an end.

When the British government decided to reconquer the Falkland Islands, this was not only a question of the islands and their status. It also involved regional and global influence. To regain control meant that Britain would continue to have a role in South America. To project force across large distances is an indicator impressing other actors. Obviously, it would have been more difficult for Britain to react in a similar way had, for instance, Hong Kong been occupied by China. Guatemala, on the other hand, may have refrained from challenging British control in Belize, knowing that it would encounter strong opposition. Argentina underestimated Britain's likely response.

Territorial issues have power implications. Whether Iran or Iraq prevailed in their war in the 1980s was thought to affect influence in the Gulf region. Iran, during the reign of the Shah, had been the dominant actor in this sensitive locale and the Islamic revolutionary leadership preferred to maintain this position, albeit with a different ideological content, as we shall see in Section 5.3. Iraq, on the other hand, was likely to use a victorious outcome of the war to bolster the position of radical pan-Arabism. It might tilt the regional balance against Israel, for instance. This analysis leads to a cynical attitude, where a major power perspective would make it desirable if the two regional actors weakened each other. This provides little incentive for major powers actively to bring a war to a speedy end. Would there ever be a *Realpolitik* interest in conflict resolution?

Yes, there are such concerns as it is the *Realpolitik* tradition to consider relations between major powers after a war. The same logic applies to other interstate conflicts. The key question is whether a losing side should be dealt with in a punitive or integrative way. What is the 'best' approach for terminating a war and avoiding a future repetition of this particular war? It is a discussion with roots in Machiavelli's writings and it continues to have validity. Kegley and Raymond have formulated this as an issue of whether one should prefer a punitive or lenient peace (1999: 33–6). Let us consider these two lines of thought in some detail.

In punitive, or harsh, peacemaking a firm distinction is made between winners and losers. The idea is to establish such a strong power asymmetry that the winners will rule for the foreseeable future and the losers, therefore, willingly accept their roles as subordinate members of the international system. It means that a war is likely to be waged until the complete capitulation of one side. The destruction is the price for a lasting peace after the war, it is argued. The winner has to keep up its superior military, economic and political position after the war. Peace requires heavy military expenditures for a long time to come. In *Realpolitik* understanding, there are always actors who are interested in challenging the stronger ones and who will try to locate its weakest spots. Only permanent preponderance can remedy this.

There are critics of this line of thinking: there is a danger that even after a severe and humiliating loss, the loser will rise again, and now be more bitter and frustrated. Thus, there will be a new round of conflict, new attempts at revenge, new victories and new defeats. Such a cycle of events may be broken by the superiority of one party, a realist may argue, but, the critics will respond, this requires heavy armaments, invites arms races and prevents the development of civilian sectors of either of the societies.

The integrative approach, in contrast, argues that it is important to reintegrate the loser quickly into the new international or regional order. This means that, once the loser has met stated demands, normalization should follow, with rewards for good behaviour, an extension of respect and incentives for non-aggressive stances. There is an asymmetry also in this relationship, but it is less pronounced, and there is a willingness to contribute to reintegration. The perspective is long term and reformist. The purpose is to change the asymmetric relationship into a mutually beneficial partnership, something which, it is assumed, is also in the interests of other parties. The hope is that in this way there will be fewer reasons for a resurgence of conflict. It could be objected that this strategy might be self-deceptive and wishful thinking. It is even dangerous if it leads to early disarmament, encouraging uncompromising elements on the other side. Opportunities are created for the defeated to strike back. Even a defeat with a human face is a defeat, and is going to be felt as such. War is likely to result anyway, a *Realpolitik* critic may argue. Neither argument is without its logic as well as plausible critique. This makes it interesting to study the historical record. An overview of the experiences of 200 years of major power relations shows how different strands of thought have dominated at different times (Wallensteen 1984, 2011b). In periods of universalist or integrative thinking, the frequency of major wars has been reduced; in periods of more particularist thinking, major wars have been more numerous. This means that the overall approach major powers take to each other does have important effects on their international relations.

An account of the German–French relationships is instructive. The war between the two countries in 1870–71 ended in a humiliating way for France. Not only did Germany take control of two important provinces, Alsace-Lorraine (in German, Elsass-Lothringen), but it also proclaimed the new German Empire in the halls of Versailles, the French monarchical residence. These actions made it evident that the conflict would not go away. Any form of partnership and alliance was excluded. Instead, the conflict between Germany and France became the axis around which European international affairs operated for the following seven decades.

The First World War ended in a similarly humiliating way, but this time the outcome was reversed. Now, it was France that could dictate – in Versailles – the conditions for Germany's post-war situation. These involved the return of territory to France (Alsace-Lorraine), the acquisition of new territories (colonial areas), and the creation of new states in the territory formerly held by the losing powers (the new states in Central Europe emerging from German, Austrian and Hungarian territories). There was also a requirement of heavy financial compensation and restrictions on German military power. It was meant to be a punitive peace and, by any standard, it was. The treaty has been much debated. For instance, it has been noted that it had to be implemented by a newly created democratic regime in Germany that had not been responsible for the war. Thus, it came to be seen as a treaty against all Germans, not just the elite who controlled the country in 1914. Hitler used this and, aided by the economic crisis, came to power on an agenda for undoing the Versailles Treaty. The Second World War followed.

The allies in the Second World War demanded unconditional surrender by Germany. There was never a peace agreement signed with Germany after the war. Instead the country was divided. This was only in part a strategy for dealing with Germany. The original plan among the allies was that Germany would be treated as one unit, although each of the victors would control certain parts for a period of time. Their disagreement precluded the unification and resulted instead in two German states, the Federal Republic in the West and the German Democratic Republic in the East. The de facto solution of two German states may have served a purpose, as it focused German attention not at the victors, but at ways of overcoming the cleavage. Unintentionally, the Cold War led to a more rapid integration of the two German states into the international system, albeit in opposite camps, than would otherwise have been the case. There were additional elements, which served to break the cycle of punitive peace. One was the Marshall Plan. Instead of demanding economic compensation from Germany, the allies resolved to rebuild West Germany as fast as possible. An economically strong Germany, connected with the other Western countries, was seen as a more promising arrangement. It was argued in terms of a struggle against communism and prevention of the spread of revolutionary ideas. The measures were also to prevent a return of neo-Nazism, drawing on the lessons learned from the economic crisis of the early 1930s. The Soviet leadership took a more punitive and less integrative attitude to 'its' Germany. Entire industries were dismantled to be used in the reconstruction of Russia after the war. The Soviet Union chose not to participate in the Marshall aid programme. If it had, Europe might have developed differently.

The emphasis on reconstructing democracy was an important element of the post-1945 policy towards West Germany. This meant learning some of the lessons from the First World War. The democratic system had become too weak, and was identified with the defeat. In the post-Second World War period the tribunals against Nazi war criminals made clear that some Germans were more responsible than others and, thus, a new political elite could act with fewer constraints. It included building a new Germany. The demilitarization of Germany was another important aspect of the changing relationship. Only in 1955 was a German armed force again set up, but within the NATO alliance and with innovative democratic features. Not until the conflict in Kosovo in 1999 were German soldiers stationed outside the country. Since then German troops have also been used in Afghanistan, well outside the traditional NATO area of operation.

The integration of Germany into two major frameworks of international cooperation was also important. The creation of the European Coal and Steel Community in 1950 was a first aspect of this, and Germany has since then been an active, powerful member of what is today the European Union (EU). In 1955, West Germany became a member of NATO. Ten years after the end of the Second World War it had gone from loser to allied partner. This again shows how differently the allies reacted after the two world wars and the consequences of this basic attitude for the future of relations. The attitude towards Germany shifted from a punitive to an integrative strategy, and it appears that the latter has produced more promising results for a future without war between the same parties. Remarkably, (West) Germany continued to pay the First World War reparations and could celebrate paying the last instalment in October 2010.

The distinction of punitive and integrative endings of wars thus has empirical application. Is this framework relevant for interstate conflicts since the Cold War? Looking at the war endings we have mentioned, it is clear that the attitude has been more punitive than integrative. The Iran–Iraq War displays that fully. The Iranian side, feeling that it was victimized by Iraq and the world, initially demanded the elimination of the regime in Baghdad and compensation for the destruction it had inflicted on Iran. In the end, it had to accept the regime, but the hostility remained. On the Iraqi side, the ambition was to eliminate a regime built on the Shiite version of Islam. The majority of the Iraqi population is Shiite and was seen as a threat to Saddam Hussein's hold on power. The war did not have this result. Thus, two antagonistic parties had to accept each other. It was bitter to their leaders. It also meant that the war could have been concluded much earlier, had a realization of the likely outcome been predicted. The lasting, punitive attitudes are reflected in the parties' interpretation of the cease-fire arrangement, where both sides have been as strict as possible, for instance, in dealing with the exchange of prisoners of war. It is as if the war was continued in the implementation of the peace.

The Gulf War of 1991 ended in a similar way, with a cease-fire resolution by the Security Council. Its strict enforcement reflected the sceptical attitude of the parties. The UN was not going to reward Iraq for good behaviour, only punish it for bad actions. Iraq had no interest in being forthcoming to the UN, for instance, in the disarmament provisions. The ending of the war was punitive, and Iraq's interstate relations continued to be difficult, until the regime was overthrown in March 2003.

There are few examples of integrative thinking in wars between smaller, neighbouring countries, but one of the most daring initiatives is found in this category. The visit by Egypt's President Anwar Sadat to Jerusalem in 1977. It was a remarkable gesture, and the negotiations that followed were difficult. The Israeli government was not prepared to meet the Egyptian leadership on the generous level the visit initiated. Without the intervention of the Carter administration in the USA, the initiative may have failed. It did not, but came to be an important, though still controversial, breakthrough in Israeli–Arab relations (Carter 1992). It has resulted in a cold peace, rather than close integration, however. This might be attributable to the fact that other elements of the conflicts around Israel have not been settled. It is instructive to observe the important role of Egypt in promoting peace talks among other actors. Relations may take a different turn once there is a complete set of peace agreements on the Palestinian issues.

Conflicts defined in *Realpolitik* terms tend to be dealt with as matters of bilateral relationship. There are many examples of very difficult negotiations and careful implementation. The parties themselves seldom seem to view the solution to their common conflict as a way of establishing a novel relationship for a particular region. Consequently, the wars have not resulted in novel regional orders, only in temporary endings of one war in a series of wars. If this is true, it means that the parties expect a repetition and will do little to prevent this through innovative thinking. South Asia is a case in point, with repetitive conflicts between India and Pakistan over almost 70 years. There is a particular challenge to search for ways in which this can be changed. Integrative solutions may require a regional approach to conflicts in several conflict-prone regions, for instance, the Middle East, the Gulf region, South Asia, Indochina and the Horn of Africa. In some, there are embryonic organizations on which to build. The history of the French–German relationship suggests that changes are possible. There is, furthermore, little evidence that the punitive approach can bring a conflict to a lasting termination.

The Seven Mechanisms

Turning to the solutions to interstate wars, to what extent are the seven mechanisms identified in Section 3.5 relevant and useful? Let us look at them one by one and apply each to recent conflicts and settlements between states.

The first one concerns the *change of a basic position* by one or several parties. There are instances of demands being dropped. In the war termination which is closest to a peace agreement, the settlement between Iran and Iraq, both sides abandoned key demands, particularly those pertaining to the question of the legitimacy of the regime in the other country and to issues of compensation. Thus, the negotiations came to concentrate on the sequencing of issues, particularly whether a cease-fire should come first or not. In the end, the cease-fire, implemented in August 1988, was followed by the first direct meeting between officials of the two sides some days later.

This meant that the two sides accepted the other as the party to talk to. The positions changed without a shift in the leadership. The key issues that remained concerned recognition, responsibility and compensation. They recognized each other, found a formula for determining responsibility and left the issue of compensation. Thus, a war ending was possible. No doubt, this can be attributed to war weariness. There was little prospect of any side winning and, thus, there was little point in continuing. But that had been obvious much earlier. It was told to the parties by the international mediators. It is also possible to attribute the final agreement to changes in the international environment. The West as well as the Soviet Union united in demanding an end to the war, whereas they previously, by individual calculation, had supported the same side against the other. This was manifested in the unity of the Security Council. In the face of this change, the warring parties could comply only by giving up the demands they learned were the least acceptable to the other side as well as to the international actors. In so doing, it also became clear which demands were the most significant in the conflict, as a political choice had to be made.

A second way of transcending the incompatibility is by *dividing the contested values*. In a conflict driven by *Geopolitik* considerations, this would mean dividing a particular territory between the contestants. Such outright territorial deals have been rare recently. They seem to belong to a previous era. In the Munich accord in 1938 and the Hitler–Stalin agreement in 1939 this was a prominent feature. Perhaps, popular considerations today make such agreements impossible. It would suggest, however, that they are doable in unpopulated areas, typically for maritime disputes. We also need to consider the possibility of dividing authority. In a major power perspective, this means creating geographical spheres of influence. Major powers have historically been uninhibited in dividing areas, openly or in secret, to reduce the frictions between themselves. The Cold War had such features. The USA was unwilling to challenge Soviet control behind the lines drawn at the Yalta and Potsdam conferences in 1945. Both sides kept their forces off these divisions, as both sides perceived a danger of escalation and nuclear war.

Horse-trading is identified as a third mechanism. Geopolitically, this would mean yielding control over one area in exchange for control in another. Sometimes this is what is done in delimitation and demarcation of new borderlines. It is seldom explicit, however, and may be observed only with a close scrutiny of the results. A problem in the Iran–Iraq War was the return to previous international borders. These were regulated in a 1975 accord which Iraq had unilaterally abrogated. Iraq was not willing to return to this document. The final outcome did not envisage a border change, however. Instead, it said that forces should be withdrawn to the internationally recognized borders, although these were technically not agreed. In fact, the borders from 1975 were used. It meant both sides had to leave some areas to gain access to others. The occupied territories, in a sense, were traded against each other.

Horse-trading may also involve the trading of one issue for another. A party can agree to drop a particular question, to be rewarded by receiving full support on another. As we have just seen, in the interstate conflicts there has been little of such give-and-take in the last three decades. It could well be that horse-trading requires better relations than these cases exemplify. We can observe that it is more likely to be taking place between major powers. Their vast interests make such actions more possible, as commitment to particular actors or issues vary in strength. The negotiations on major arms and nuclear weapons reductions do contain many such arrangements, where entire categories are exchanged. The deal of 1987 on intermediate nuclear forces (INF) is instructive. The USA promised to eliminate all of its new cruise missiles (Tomahawk) and ballistic missiles (Pershing II) in return for the Soviet Union eliminating its numerous SS-20 missiles. The weapons systems were seen to have similar functions and could thus be traded. Each side had publicly committed itself to the elimination of the other's weapons of this type. The INF included considerable verification measures. The USA was willing to yield on some of these in order to gain Soviet acceptance of the complete elimination of all missiles (Woodworth 1999: 188). As we observed in Section 2.4, this ability to deal with armaments far surpassed their willingness to deal with ongoing conflicts.

A fourth way of transcending an incompatibility is by *creating shared rule*. Again, there is a difference in dynamics among conflicts between major powers and those among non-major powers. In the former cases, there is a history of creating shared organizations. The UN is, in itself, the outcome of such an effort. The key elements were agreed directly between the American and Soviet leaderships in the negotiations of 1944–45. The UN has, as we have indicated, set standards for resolution of *Geopolitik* conflicts (notably the inviolability of boundaries of states), which has had a profound impact on relations between states. In direct deliberation between major powers there are joint organizations, such as inspection teams for arms control agreements, for instance, in the INF agreement in December 1987. These were strictly bilateral arrangements; no third party was let in. In conflicts between non-major powers, such arrangements appear difficult to create. Between India and Pakistan there are agreements pertaining to nuclear installations. Between Iran and Iraq no joint organization was set up between the two, for instance, for operating the important waters of Shatt-al-Arab. This would have been a reasonable way of handling a shared waterway, but was not part of the concluding negotiations. Thus, the issue of control over this international waterway remains unresolved. In the agreement between Israel and Egypt some shared organs were created. The same is true for the agreement between Israel and Jordan. In both cases, the agreements have run into difficulties.

If the parties cannot share control, a logical possibility is *to leave control to another party*; this is the fifth form indicated in Section 3.5. This is a frequently used form in interstate relations. From a major power perspective, this could mean neutralization or the creation of buffer zones. This is how it was possible for East and West to agree to the reintegration of Austria in 1955. Its neutralization was a solution that met concerns among the major powers. There are other examples of such measures, solving at the same time a *Geopolitik* and *Realpolitik* question. In the 1991 Paris accords on Cambodia, the country was defined as non-aligned. Thus, neither China nor Vietnam nor Thailand could count on the country as a potential ally. This was satisfactory to all parties. It meant, for Vietnam, that it would not face a two-front challenge from a Cambodia allied to China. The gain for Thailand was that it would not have Vietnamese forces close to its borders. For China, the advantage was that the influence of Vietnam was reduced or less visible. Furthermore, it was also preferable to most Khmers, as it ensured the independence of the country. The stationing of peacekeeping troops along exposed borders, as has been done in the Sinai and Lebanon, or the creation of demilitarized zones are examples of partial neutralization. The expectation is that they will be withdrawn when general peace exists. It can be a long-term commitment. In 1993, Sweden and Norway decided to dismantle their demilitarized zone, stretching along both sides of the border. It was part of the agreement on Norway's independence and had been in effect since 1905.

These are successful examples. However, one of the modern wars relates to a failed agreement: Cyprus. The agreement on independence in 1960 made Cyprus an independent and neutral state. It could not align with any of its neighbours. It was part of an arrangement whereby Greece and Turkey agreed that they would not forcefully incorporate Cyprus into their own territory (in whole or in part). This was a form of neutralization of the island, in spite of the majority population (Greek Cypriots) wanting to reunite with Greece (*enosis*) and the minority group (Turkish Cypriots) interested in uniting with Turkey by dividing the island (*taksim*). None of the actors achieved their main objectives. Instead, an independent state, Cyprus, not desired by any side as their first choice, was created. It had a constitution that balanced the various interests, and it also gave the right to the neighbours to interfere in the affairs of the independent state. The conflicts on the island escalated dramatically in 1963. UN forces were stationed there from 1964 onwards, but still an invasion took place by Turkey in 1974, de facto dividing the island. A proposed peace agreement in 2004, the Annan Plan, creating a federal state, was accepted by one community but resisted by the other in two separate referenda.

These examples illustrate that neutralization is a difficult course of action. It may function, particularly as long as the surrounding states support the arrangement and it can be upheld by strong local opinion. However, it can also mean that neighbours will anxiously watch what is happening and react rapidly if the agreed order is unravelling. Turkey in 1974 acted after the pro-Greece junta had taken over Cyprus. In its view, the island was about to be incorporated into Greece. Quick, pre-emptive action was seen as necessary. Rather than deterring action, the neutral status spurred action. Thus, leaving important territories outside the control of strongly interested parties may work, but it may also create new dangers. Could such measures be used to solve disputes around areas that are of a particularly high value? For instance, could Jerusalem be handled according to a formula involving internationalization? The 1947 UN plan passed by the General Assembly made Jerusalem an international territory, separated from the states in the region. It was not possible to get full support for this idea. Jerusalem is today regarded by the State of Israel as the country's capital. Similarly, Palestinians regard Jerusalem as their capital. There are few precedents for solving such disputes. Many peace plans have proposed that parts of the city would be international. The Oslo peace process resulted in creative suggestions, but none has yet been accepted by the two negotiating parties. There is only one city which is the capital in two states: Rome. It is shared between the Republic of Italy and the Holy See (the Vatican). This case might provide a better model than the original UN plan. Such a solution has to assume that a part of Jerusalem is an autonomous unit, and there have to be arrangements for unhindered access to the holy places. Still, there is an issue of control and sovereignty that has to be handled in such a way as not to invite a division of the city. Lessons need to be drawn from the fate of neighbouring Cyprus, where even the capital, Nicosia, is divided, although mutual access is now available.

A sixth form for transcending incompatibility is the resort to *conflict resolution mechanisms*. There are a number of such experiences. It may mean that conflicts are handed from a political to a legal level and, thus, are treated in accordance with precedence and the parties do not have to invent the solution themselves (Corell 1999: 33–4). There are also *ad hoc* mechanisms created for particular occasions, such as arbitration courts. The most central issue is whether a mechanism has legitimacy with the international system and the parties. In reality, actual solutions may integrate the first five mechanisms we have just recounted. The conflict resolution mechanism adds a procedural and argumentative level to the resolution, which helps to make the outcome more acceptable.

The legal means of conflict resolution are those that have been described most carefully. One of the most interesting is arbitration, where the parties commit themselves to accept the outcome, whatever it is, before the deliberations begin. Since 1945, Bilder claims, there have been 'at least several dozen significant arbitrations'. Here there are more cases from relationships among non-major powers. There are arbitrations handling some of the aspects of the conflicts listed in Tables 5.1 and 5.2, notably between India and Pakistan over the Rann of Kutch area in 1968 and Egypt and Israel over the Taba area in 1988 (Bilder 1997: 161). In none of these cases can we say that the mechanism dealt with the central, often political, aspect of the conflict. It was useful, however, in avoiding further tension around implementation. It is particularly applicable to issues that concern territory. The most recent case is worth a closer analysis.

In the Eritrea–Ethiopia peace agreement of December 2000, the border issue was handled through the creation of a special Commission (Article 4 of the peace treaty). In fact, 17 (out of a total of 47) paragraphs were devoted to this Commission in the final peace agreements. Its composition and mandate were crucial, as this was what the conflict was originally all about. In the text, the parties agreed, for instance, that this neutral Border Commission would consist of five members, with two appointed by each side. It was stated that neither of these 'shall be nationals or permanent residents of the party making the appointment'. These four members were then to agree on the fifth one, who would be the President of the Commission. If they could not agree, the UN Secretary-General was given the role of selecting the president, who would be 'neither a national nor permanent resident of either party'. The parties took special precautions to ensure that the members of the Commission would have no connection to either party. It was also specified that decisions by the Commission were to be made by a majority of the Commissioners. It suggests that the parties did not expect consensus and that, in severe cases, the President of the Commission might become the sole arbiter of the outcome. In 2002, the Commission nevertheless was able to deliver a unanimous decision on the border delimitations. Ethiopia chose not to abide by the decision claiming procedural objections. Its position was weak, as it had agreed to the arrangement. By the end of 2014, the decision had still not been implemented and there was little pressure on Ethiopia to do so.

The solution to the conflict between Ecuador and Peru was made through a special procedure, which in essence was arbitration. The Guarantor countries to the 1942 treaty that was in dispute were asked to solve the remaining issues. They provided a package deal where the parties had already agreed to certain matters (navigation rights, border integration, confidence-building measures). The Guarantors resolved the outstanding territorial issues by giving parts to Peru, but one crucial square kilometre to Ecuador (as private property), thereby meeting a central Ecuadorian demand. Interestingly, the area surrounding this, a total of more than 50 square kilometres, was made an ecological reserve (Einaudi 1999: 425). Thus, the solution contained elements of a division of territory, but also relinquished control (the ecological reserve). Most important was that the final decision was left to others than the parties themselves, thus reducing domestic criticism of the governments. Importantly, both the Congress of Ecuador and the one of Peru had accepted this procedure in advance.

Arbitration may not solve matters of power directly, but can have an impact indirectly. Using such a mechanism might be the way to reduce the centrality of a particular issue. The border between Ecuador and Peru was a highly sensitive question in Ecuador, where it took on existential dimensions. It related to the self-perception of being a state of the Amazon basin. Thus, the solution was of vital importance to the standing of the country in the region. Similarly, Peru was not willing to yield, as it had a record of lost wars. Its regional position would be affected, at least in its own eyes, if territory were yielded once again. The conflict resolution mechanism thus solved an issue while maintaining the parties' self-respect and position in the regional context. It did not make any of the parties more or less powerful than before.

The UN and International Atomic Energy Agency (IAEA) missions on issues of weapons of mass destruction in Iraq were reactivated by the UN Security Council in November 2002. UNMOVIC was led by Dr Hans Blix and the IAEA team by Director Mohamed ElBaradei. This was seen, by many member states, as a mechanism for dealing with the contradictory facts of the case, and possibly as a way to avoid war. The US actions on Iraq in March 2003 effectively ended this route. Interestingly, US teams later reported on the issues, demonstrating that no such capacity existed in Iraq at the time of the war.

Finally, we noted that there are ways in which issues can be *left to the future*, without the parties changing their views on a preferred outcome. This requires, of course, that the parties not commit themselves to a settlement by a certain date, thus preventing the easy resort to this mechanism. By leaving the question open, time is gained and options are maintained. To defer issues to commissions is a possibility. An example is the ending of the war between Iran and Iraq where Iran demanded that the responsibility for the war be determined. The agreed solution in 1988 was to appoint a group to document this. It presented its report, by December 1991, at a time when much had changed in the Gulf area. To many actors the findings had only historical interest. However, it showed that Iraq had committed the initial aggression and should be held responsible for damage inflicted on Iran. In short, it vindicated Iran's position. By that time, however, this had been overtaken by other events and the impact was not the one that Iran had expected.

Similarly, in the peace treaty for the Eritrea–Ethiopia War, it was agreed that an investigation into the origin of the conflict was to be carried out. Article 3.2 gave this assignment to an 'independent, impartial body appointed by the Secretary-General of the OAU, in consultation with the Secretary-General of the United Nations and the two parties'. The Commission reported in 2005, saying that Eritrea's attack on Ethiopia in May 1998 could not be justified as lawful self-defence and that the country, thus, should compensate Ethiopia.

These commissions proceeded at such a pace that the verdict would come later, and thus not raise obstacles in implementing other, more pressing provisions of the agreements. In the case of Eritrea–Ethiopia, however, the implementation of the border decision had not been completed. Nevertheless, in two of the most destructive recent wars, issues of responsibility for the initiation of hostilities have been central. They have even been so important that they were maintained by the parties to the very end of the negotiation process. It returns us to the issues of legitimacy and the right to initiate war. Undoubtedly, it has become increasingly difficult for states to be involved in wars, unless it can be clearly attributed to self-defence (as accepted in the UN Charter, Article 51). When convincing arguments cannot be made, and this can be determined by commissions, it opens the possibility of compensation as well as increases the obstacles to renewed war.

5.3 Conflict Resolution: *Idealpolitik* and *Kapitalpolitik*

Ideological matters and economics are often seen as driving forces in conflict. They require closer scrutiny. We need to see to what extent such factors have been important in the origins of conflicts, thus having implications for the issues with which peace agreements will have to grapple. Given the dynamic character of conflicts, however, issues may also arise as the war proceeds and generate new issues that have to be remedied. Let us look at the role of *Idealpolitik* and *Kapitalpolitik* in general in interstate conflicts, and then proceed to the use of the seven mechanisms for solving the issues.

In two of the interstate armed conflicts of the 1990s an incompatibility over government can be clearly identified (Table 5.1). Obviously, the US intervention in Panama aimed at removing a strong force behind the government. The purpose was to enhance the prospects of democracy in Panama. It was also thought to improve stability and secure the operations of the Panama Canal. The war on Iraq in 2003 also aimed at removing the incumbent regime, which was seen by the US government as a potential terrorist threat, as a negation of democracy as well as ruling a country with important oil resources. The interventions had several purposes, one of them dealing with *Idealpolitik* (furthering the ideals of democracy) and one with *Kapitalpolitik* (that is, safeguarding economic interests). This does not exhaust this dimension in interstate conflict, however.

We have also seen that *Idealpolitik* was an important consideration in the Iran–Iraq War. Both sides feared being overthrown by the other. A change of government in Iraq was also an explicit demand by Iran. It stalled negotiations. The same concerns were voiced in Eritrea and Ethiopia, each accusing the other of supporting designs on the government or planning to attack the capital of the other. The fact that both leaders were present in Algiers, Algeria, in December 2000, to sign the agreement also made clear that they accepted the other's hold on power. Similar concerns were an aspect of the Cold War confrontation in particular countries. A country might have a role in the global strategy of the two superpowers. Both had a record of attempting or actually overthrowing governments in other countries. The US intervention in Panama was the last one related to the Cold War. Its explicit motives pointed to a new era, where concerns were no longer with governments' alleged communist inclinations, but their ability to combat the drug trade or deal with terrorism. In this way, concern over government continues to be a valid dimension for interstate relations.

Idealpolitik and the Settlement of Conflicts

There are two major debates in international affairs on *Idealpolitik* issues. The first concerns the democracy–peace hypothesis. It maintains that democratic states rarely fight wars with each other. If this is so, as statistical evidence shows, does it mean that, if democracies nevertheless are involved in wars, these will be settled more easily? The second debate concerns the alleged clash of civilization, where the argument can be translated into saying that deep cultural or political differences are likely to generate more conflict and make settlements less likely. A less ambitious formulation is that ethnic divisions are central for interstate conflict. Let us what this brings for the possibility of ending conflicts.

The *democracy–peace hypothesis* is the one most easily handled with the available evidence (Russett 1993). Of the 14 wars identified during the last two decades of the Cold War and the 4 wars following it, democratic states were at least one party to 10 of them. This means that they were involved in more than half of all armed conflicts that escalated to war. In 9 conflicts the opposing sides were non-democratic states. This observation confirms that democracies are not peaceful under all circumstances. The point in the democracy–peace hypothesis is, however, that they are at peace in the relations among themselves. This is also borne out by the data presented here. There is only one case where it could be maintained that both sides were democratic societies: the Turkey–Cyprus War in 1974. Let us, consequently, investigate this conflict a little further.

The democratic systems were, in both Turkey and Cyprus, less well entrenched than the systems normally studied by the democratic peace writers. Clearly, both societies were exposed to considerable internal strain, from the military in one case, and from the conflict with the minority in the other. The Cyprus dispute, furthermore, had a long history. The country became independent from British rule in 1960. It was equipped with a special democratic constitution that gave most power to the majority population, the Greek Cypriots, which constituted four-fifths of the inhabitants. Within this framework, strong measures were instituted to protect the rights of the minority, the Turkish Cypriots. In July 1974, the democratic government of Cyprus under Greek Cypriot President Macharios was deposed in a coup masterminded by the military junta ruling in Greece. The coup leaders controlled the island for a short period of time. The situation was used by Turkey, led by an elected prime minister, to

launch a military intervention. In two consecutive military moves, Turkey took control of 40 per cent of the island. Turkey's objective was not to restore democracy on
the island, but to safeguard the interests of the Turkish Cypriots and meet strategic
Turkish concerns. The government it faced was in disarray. It is difficult to define this
as a conflict between two democracies of the type postulated by the democracy–peace
hypothesis. It was more a question of state collapse in Cyprus and the grasping of a
window of opportunity by an outside power. Thus, it does not challenge the basic
proposition on the improbability of war between stable democracies.

The following developments are interesting, however. The intervention stimulated the downfall of the military regime in Greece. A stable period of democracy
followed in Greece. Also, the elected government in Cyprus was returned to power.
The case, thus, is important in a discussion on conflict resolution, as all the parties
to the conflict have now been open societies for more than a quarter of a century.
The same is true for those particularly interested in a settlement: Britain, the USA
and the EU. Still, the conflict remains unsettled. There is no war, but there is no
peace either, among these democratic states, in spite of considerable international
efforts. There are even arguments saying that the very openness of the societies prevents a solution, as each proposal immediately is available to everybody. Doctrinaire
objections prohibit serious discussion. Thus, although democracies may not make
war, they certainly have difficulties making peace.

Several of the more recent interstate conflicts may testify to this conclusion.
Cambodia-Thailand saw an escalation of the temple dispute, while both sides had
elected government. It was possible to defuse the tension. The regimes in Sudan and
South Sudan may also be defined as elected, but their democracy score would be
even lower. These cases help to complicate the hypothesis, but none of these newer
situations have escalated to war, and none of them have seen a lasting settlement.

There is an *Idealpolitik* divide among the parties in a number of the other wars in
the three decades. Leaving Cyprus aside, there are cleavages along the democracy–
dictatorship dimension in nine conflicts, a high share of all conflicts. In two more,
an objective for one side was the removal of a dictatorial regime in the other
(Tanzania aimed at overthrowing the government in Uganda; Vietnam had similar
goals in Cambodia). Of the remaining conflicts, four belong to the Cold War divide
(two strongly so: Vietnam–China, Somalia–Ethiopia; two more weakly connected:
Indonesia–East Timor, Chad–Libya). Two have a strong dynamic of their own, Iran–
Iraq and Eritrea–Ethiopia, not least as the government issue was present in both.
Iran believed that Iraq wanted to undermine the new and not yet consolidated
Islamic leadership in Tehran. Iraq feared that the new Iranian leadership was insti-
gating an uprising among the large Shiite population in the country. Both sides may
have entertained such ideas. Eritrea continued to worry that Ethiopia would not
accept its newly-won independence, while Ethiopia accused Eritrea of fomenting
unrest among different ethnic groups in Ethiopia. In neither case was democracy a
question, but there was definitely an issue of the government's political standing in
society. This element can also be seen in the India–Pakistan War in 1999, which
resulted in the later removal of the shaky, and only in a very formal sense democratic, government in Pakistan. However, many governments probably constantly

worry about their standing. This does not mean that they would want to go to war, as this would rather serve to increase their vulnerability (Heldt 1996).

From this we need to conclude that *Idealpolitik* considerations are important in the origins and dynamics of conflict. The settlements have, however, seldom referred to these matters. As they are done between states, such matters are the internal affairs of each state. If one side raises them, it is likely that the other will reciprocate with similar issues. Thus, both sides are likely to avoid the matter, or ask for adherence to principles of non-interference in internal affairs. Sometimes it may go a bit further, as there are likely to be nationals on both sides of the border. This was an issue in the Eritrea–Ethiopia War and the agreement in December 2000 makes reference to it: 'The parties shall afford humane treatment to each other's nationals and persons of each other's national origin within their respective territories' (Article 3). This aims at protecting the rights of Eritreans in Ethiopia and vice versa. There are no mechanisms specifying the implementation of this agreement, but the statement still acknowledges that certain internal matters are of concern to the other side.

The record of imposing a new, democratic regime after a war is not impressive. In the wars where ruthless regimes were deposed (the regime under Pol Pot in Cambodia and Idi Amin in Uganda), the governments that followed were hardly democratic. The US interventions in Grenada and Panama have fared better; even suggesting to some that highly asymmetric military interventions may serve to promote democracy. The Iraq War of 2003 has been followed by a bloody and complicated internal conflict at the same time that a democracy-building effort was being pursued. In fact, the conflicts across the democracy–dictatorship divide involve just four democracies: the USA, the UK, India and Israel. Only in the Vietnam War did their war involvement result in a defeat. The United States led the wars in Vietnam, in the Gulf, and on Iraq in 2003; Britain was involved in the Falklands/Malvinas conflict; and Israel was a party to wars with Egypt, Syria and Lebanon. India's wars all stem from the conflict with Pakistan. India has for most of the period retained its democratic system. Pakistan sometimes experienced more open forms of government. The Vietnam War was waged in the name of democracy, but the US-supported regime in South Vietnam crumbled, partly due to its lack of national legitimacy. The Gulf War led to the restoration of the emirate in Kuwait, and only later did a more open society emerge. The complexities of Iraq are still unfolding. In 2014, a third democratic election took place in spite of considerable domestic strife and a widening rift between the dominating Shiites and many of Iraq's other groups. The Falklands/Malvinas conflict resulted in a new democracy, as the military junta in Argentina lost legitimacy and was replaced by a democratic regime. India's involvement in East Pakistan was in support of a popularly based independence movement, and led to a democratic constitution in the new country of Bangladesh. But it was not until the 1990s that a more stable democracy took root. The record of democracies creating democracy by war, in other words, is not striking. Wars between democratic states and non-democratic regimes end at points which have military significance, not when they have led to new governments. The democracies may be successful in their war-fighting, but war is still different from the expansion of democracy. It may also strengthen regimes building on nationalist or authoritarian legitimacy.

The regimes the USA confronted in Vietnam and Iraq, remained, the one in Iraq being removed by force 12 years after the first war. *Idealpolitik* considerations are important in ending wars but, even when democracies are on the one side, does it mean wars lead to the creation of new democracies. Post-war dynamics are difficult to predict.

An analysis of *civilizational dynamics* as a clash between 'the West and the rest' (Huntington 1996) largely becomes parallel to the one of democratic versus other forms of government. If it is defined to mean an Islamic challenge towards non-Islamic societies, it is more interesting. Among the 18 interstate wars during these three decades, societies with a predominantly Muslim population were party to 14. Three were between Muslim societies (Iran–Iraq, Chad–Libya and Iraq's invasion of Kuwait, as the first part of the Gulf War), and three involved Israel's relations with its neighbours. It means that in eight cases there was a Muslim/non-Muslim divide. If we look at societies at war which have Christian leadership, defined in an equally wide sense, the list becomes equally long, with ten cases where one was between two predominantly Christian states (UK–Argentina). Islam and Christianity, in other words, have long lists of war involvements. The civilizational clash, as a conflict between Christianity and Islam, is possibly relevant for the wars over Cyprus and East Timor, where the primary parties may be described as 'Christian' and 'Muslim', respectively. Even so, their self-descriptions would probably be more secular. The Muslim character of the Turkish Cypriot society has not been strong, and Islam in Indonesia was, for most of the period, moderate. Even so, international alliance patterns do not follow this divide. The USA did not side with the Greek Cypriots (Greek Orthodox Christians) and for a long time it supported the regime in Indonesia (although Muslim) against the East Timorese (largely Roman Catholic). Also, some of the more devastating wars were not part of this particular divide at all (Vietnam–China, the USA–Vietnam, Vietnam–Cambodia, Eritrea–Ethiopia). The Iraq War has sometimes been seen in this light, but the fact is that the majority in Iraq, being Shiite Muslims or Kurds, were the chief beneficiaries of the removal of Saddam Hussein, who for most of his rule, took a secularist approach, but had a basis in the Sunni community. Furthermore, there were agreements terminating wars across these very divides, for instance between Israel and Egypt, and Ethiopia and Somalia. In none of these was religion or civilization important in ending the wars. Thus, this perspective neither captures the dynamics of conflicts, nor the ability of settling conflicts.

In a version of civilizational divides which emphasizes *ethnic* differences between actors, a theme that will be further elaborated in Chapter 7, the patterns are not striking either, even in the post-Cold War era. There were such elements in the dispute between Mauritania and Senegal. They may also be found overlapping with the civilizational paradigm in the conflict between India and Pakistan. It is more interesting to observe that some conflicts strengthen ethnic differences or even create them. The conflict between Ecuador and Peru may have been important for the identity of these parties. It made people on both sides more aware of their own preferences. The same may be the long-term result of the war between Eritrea and Ethiopia. For peacemaking, the ethnic dimension introduces complicating elements. Seldom, however, has it been the origin of interstate conflict.

A more general pattern that can be observed when considering *Idealpolitik* dimensions is the importance of *domestic political change* for conflict dynamics and conflict resolution. Revolutionary regimes create regional repercussions that affect neighbouring countries and give rise to considerable tension, rearrangement of alliances and wars. The victory of the revolutionary Khmer Rouge in Cambodia in 1975 initiated such a series of events, ultimately resulting in the occupation of the country by Vietnam. The attempts to repress the results in the Pakistani elections in 1971 led to resistance in East Pakistan against rule from West Pakistan, an uprising, India's intervention, and the disintegration of the bifurcated country. The civil war in Lebanon affected the neighbouring countries and made them intervene, making the conflict into an interstate war. The coup in Cyprus led to the Turkish invasion. The coming to power of a new and revolutionary regime in Iran initiated a sequence of events that eventually led to war with Iraq. Ethiopia and Eritrea were both governed by victorious, revolutionary governments. Although this pattern is unable to capture all the conflicts, it points to dynamics which affect entire regions. As the new regimes are the ones that later will have to enter into the agreements, the internal dynamics of peacemaking have to be considered. It may be more difficult to convince revolutionaries of the need to settle scores with former enemies. Successful revolutionaries are likely to believe more strongly than others that they will prevail even under difficult circumstances. Thus, their resistance to negotiated agreements, short of victory, is likely to be solid. The difficulties in ending the Iran–Iraq, Eritrea–Ethiopia and Indochinese wars testify to this.

Thus, we find that the *Idealpolitik* component is important, particularly as it introduces the question of legitimacy and governance inside states. *Idealpolitik* considerations contribute to an understanding of the origins of conflict, not least the impact revolutionary changes have in regional settings. For interstate agreement-making, internal affairs have to be taken for granted. Increasingly, more democratic regimes are likely to have a long-term impact on interstate conflict, but ending wars will require having to deal with regimes of many different kinds.

Peacemaking and *Kapitalpolitik*

Much theorizing assumes that economic matters are decisive for human action. Indeed, very little happens without economic considerations. However, the exact linkages between economic factors, the onset of conflict and conflict resolution are not easy to disentangle. Even more problematic is to estimate their significance when there are other factors in the picture, such as those we have mentioned earlier in this chapter.

It is obvious that an armed conflict is a costly undertaking, and it involves high risks. It is unlikely that there will be a 'return on the investment' in the same way as is the case when building a factory, launching a new product or hiring new workers. From a strictly economic perspective, other opportunities are more predictable and, thus, preferable. There are, of course, certain industrial interests which have war as their particular 'niche': arms manufacturers, arms traders, armed forces, intelligence operations. During the Cold War many of these interests learned that most profit is actually not made from war, but from continuous rearmament and the *threat* of war. An arms race may be economically more lucrative than the actual use of weaponry in armed conflict. Wars, we have repeatedly argued, are waged on decisions made by political actors. Wars are explained and legitimized in ways which relate to political affairs. The issues of *Geo-*, *Real-* and *Idealpolitik* all belong to this sphere of 'legitimate' explanations. Economics do not. A slogan in the American opposition against the Gulf War in 1991 was 'no blood for oil', expressing exactly this. The same slogan returned after 2003. It is not possible, particularly in a democratic and open society, to argue for a military intervention based on the economic gains that it is likely to generate. Armed conflicts involve the death of people and the destruction of investments, and these cannot be publicly defended with economic calculations. Thus, little will be openly stated on economic considerations for particular courses of action. Does it mean that there are no economic considerations? Probably not, but it suggests that there are also other concerns when countries go to war.

Let us first look at the economic arguments in the wars presented in Section 5.1. The discussion concentrates on two economic assets: oil resources and transportation routes. Oil is such a significant aspect of the energy supply of industrial economies that it takes a special role. Reductions in oil supplies or strong increases in oil prices (or both, as the former would lead to the latter) will unsettle economies in most countries, particularly those which rely heavily on oil imports. This afflicts rich as well as poor countries. No other single commodity has such a global impact. Transportation routes are important, meaning that, for instance, the blocking of certain waterways would affect economies in many countries, as they are used not only for oil shipping but also for general trade. It is possible to mark resources and routes on a map. This means that *Kapitalpolitik* assets have a geopolitical component. They are not the same. There is a difference in time and pricing. New sources of oil are still discovered. Alternative energy technologies can be developed. New routes can be found. More rapid transportation can be created. With increasing prices for one source, incentives are created for development of alternatives. Thus, *Kapitalpolitik* concerns can adapt. All this takes time and it will gradually shift political considerations. However, an economy is a daily operation and it reacts to short-term prospects. Thus, in a short-term perspective, *Kapitalpolitik* concerns over resources and transportation can be close to traditional *Geopolitik* interests.

The presence of oil resources was evident in three of the wars in the last three decades: the Iran–Iraq War, the Gulf War and the 2003 Iraq War. Oil also figured in other wars. There were expectations of oil discoveries around the Falkland/Malvinas Islands, and drilling has taken place since the war. In the Vietnam–China relations, access to potential oil resources in the adjacent waters has been mentioned. Among the lower-level conflicts reported in Table 5.1, the potential for oil discovery was an element in the Cameroon–Nigeria border dispute. Even so, most of the interstate conflicts have no relationship to oil production. If we include the issue of transportation routes, two more conflicts can be added: Israel–Egypt across the Suez Canal and the Panama–USA conflict, on the site of the Panama Canal. It is not obvious that the economic benefits of the canals were primary motives for decision makers. Thus, among the interstate wars and armed conflicts of these three decades, there is no strong evidence in favour of a simple *Kapitalpolitik* hypothesis that such concerns always are present and even paramount. It gains significance in particular conflicts, not in the overall picture.

In the cases where economic motives are important, the question still remains: how? For instance, it is not theoretically clear whether economic growth or economic decline is the primary motive for why economic considerations move countries into conflict. The Iraqi experience is a good illustration. Iraq gained from the high oil prices in the 1970s. At the start of the war against Iran in 1980 it had considerable financial strength, a well-equipped army and a functioning administrative system. The war soon ended most of this and Iraq became a debtor state. It had to borrow from its wealthier neighbours, not least Kuwait and Saudi Arabia. When the war finally ended, these countries asked for repayment. Iraq responded that this was unfair, as it had been fighting, as it were, for the entire 'Arab Nation' against external 'Persian aggression'. Besides, Iraq argued, to repay its debts the international oil prices had to increase. This was the central aspect of Iraq's dispute with Kuwait in 1990. Neither Kuwait nor Saudi Arabia was willing to increase the price by lowering its own production, thus giving more room on the market for Iraqi oil sales. By mid-July, the Iraqi leadership raised issues of the border with Kuwait and accused Kuwait of stealing Iraqi oil by drilling holes from the Kuwaiti side of the border. On August 2, 1990, Iraq invaded and occupied its neighbour. Thus, on top of the economic issue was placed a question of *Geopolitik*. This is instructive and shows how economics can enter into the decisions that lead to interstate military conflict. The key observation is this: in 1980 the Iraqi economy was in good shape, in 1990 it was in crisis. In both these years the same leadership decided to launch the country into an unpredictable war. There is no straight line between economic performance (or lack thereof) and the onset of war. We have to conclude that economic questions need to be seen in a larger perspective, not just as economic matters in their own right.

This appears to be a promising way to understand the *Kapitalpolitik* element in armed conflicts. It enters in combination with other concerns. As long as economic issues are handled in isolation, they are likely to find solutions. After all, economic aspects of social life are those that are most easy to divide. That is the point in having economic values translated into currencies, such as dollars and cents. It is when combining economics with any of the other three types of issues that it becomes deadly. This is what happened in 1990 when Saddam Hussein began to invoke territorial issues. This was a clear warning signal, not picked up by leaders around the world. They continued to see the dispute with Kuwait as bargaining over oil prices and oil production. The impending escalation was missed.

Thus, economic issues, taken by themselves, are more readily solvable than any other issue. This suggests a negotiation strategy for interstate conflict resolution, where economic questions are separated from other issues, improving the chances of agreement in at least one sphere of incompatibility. In the negotiations between Ecuador and Peru, agreements on navigation rights and development projects were dealt with first, while the border issue remained to the very end. Still, these agreements may be important to clarify that a final deal has many components, and that there are economic benefits to the peace arrangement. Economics can help forge larger package deals, but these are not complete unless they also solve the other matters. After all, the purpose is not to make lucrative trade arrangements, but to solve important incompatibilities between nations.

An informative example relates to the process ending the Cold War, the Helsinki process. It aimed at reducing tension between East and West during the Cold War and was agreed on in Helsinki, Finland, in 1975. In this case, different 'baskets' and fora were created for the four types of issues that we have identified here. One basket was concerned with border issues, a second one with economic cooperation, and a third one with human rights. A separate forum was created for reduction in troop strengths. Agreement was first reached in the second basket. The *Geopolitik* questions of borders were handled in a deal that also involved the *Idealpolitik* questions of human rights. By accepting Soviet demands on the status quo of borders in Europe, the West achieved an agreement from the Soviet Union on human rights. In the West, the treaty became known as a treaty for human rights, and Helsinki human rights groups continue to be important. This is also the way it was read by dissidents in Eastern Europe. In the official circles at the time, however, it was hailed as a way of consolidating Soviet control in Eastern Europe. Fifteen years later, it was clear that they were wrong.

Thus, economic matters can be important elements in peace agreements, and oftentimes there are compatible interests in such arrangements. Since the Cold War there has been a contentious matter, as a result of war: the issue of compensation. This has been an age-old problem in peacemaking. The winner has often demanded resources from the loser, in order to cover losses, or even to make war profitable. It has been less common in the twentieth century. It was an important element in the Versailles Treaty ending the First World War. Germany was subjected to reparations. They were part of the punitive approach described in Section 5.2. It has been argued that this prevented the recovery of the German economy. It was exploited by Hitler and other critics of the agreement. Thus, compensation issues did not become important after the Second World War in how the West treated Germany. The Soviet Union, however, demanded reparations from its defeated enemies. For Finland, for instance, this was a heavy burden, which actually was turned into an asset, as it gave Finland access to a Soviet market that no other Western states had. In wars during the following decades, economic compensation was not of central concern.

The Paris treaty ending US involvement in Vietnam in 1973 actually included such provisions, but they were not implemented by the USA. Following the Gulf War, a special institution was created for recovering the losses Kuwait had suffered under Iraqi occupation. In this case, compensation could be paid from funds maintained by the UN as it was controlling the income from Iraqi oil sales. A version of this formula has been agreed in the peace agreement between Eritrea and Ethiopia. A Claims Commission was created, seated in The Hague, Netherlands. The parties, that is, the governments, submitted their claims to the Commission, which considered them. In its final award the Commission found that Eritrea and Eritrean individuals should be compensated by US$163 million, whereas the corresponding award for Ethiopia was US$174 million. As the Commission said in its press release on August 17, 2009, this was 'probably much less than each Party believes it is due'.

Kapitalpolitik considerations play a role in origins of interstate conflict, primarily with respect to certain commodities. In many conflicts, such concerns have not figured prominently, however. In the wars on the Horn of Africa or in Kashmir they had no direct role. In peacemaking, other concerns are likely to step forward and become the object of negotiations. However, we find that matters of compensation are significant in the processes that end wars. Even though the *Kapitalpolitik* dimension is seldom directly confronted in peacemaking, it is important to keep in mind.

The Seven Mechanisms

The seven mechanisms have different implications for *Idealpolitik* and *Kapitalpolitik* issues, as the following systematic overview shows.

The first mechanism deals with *changes of priority*. In the case of *Idealpolitik,* it might be that the parties go from a rigid to a more flexible interpretation of what their demands are. All ideological systems contain the possibility of making 'hard' or 'soft' interpretations. A hard interpretation means that the thought-system is regarded as entirely correct and exclusive, and cannot entertain alternative ideas. This is likely to be a position associated with conflict. In a soft version, an open, searching and more tolerant approach is preferred, including an ability to accommodate other views. The positions maintained by the parties will be crucial for conflict resolution. The ability to accommodate debate is key for reaching understanding and respect. It may even result in a change among the parties on *Idealpolitik* issues. An interstate negotiation process is unlikely to come that far. The development of alternative positions is important in a long-term perspective. It suggests that peace agreements would need to include the possibilities of changes, opening the possibilities of dialogue and meetings on levels other than the strictly political one. This has rarely been an element in inter-state peace agreements. As observed above, it may be a side-effect of a war ending. It is important for long-term relations, even if such discussions are shared only among a small group. It becomes a way of broadening the spectrum of options in a society.

The ending of the Cold War is closely associated with the ability of developing new perspectives on communist ideology and finding its compatibility with democracy (at the time termed 'Euro-Communism', *glasnost* and *perestroika*). It led to the demise of an empire and a party, but also to the rise of new organizations, specifically combining a communist agenda with a democratic society. Softer interpretations mean that a party accommodates changes. They are often described as 'moderate' positions. Such developments are important, particularly in societies which have long experience of rigid ideological systems. A 'nationalist' does not need to be a 'chauvinist', for instance, but retaining a national identity can still be important for conflict resolution and for its acceptability in society.

In the *Kapitalpolitik* field, the first mechanism might point to the need for a deliberate decoupling of economic issues from those that are more immediately political, for instance, building on the realization that economic issues are more manageable. It is also easier to shift position if it is based on an economic calculation. When the benefits of agreement outweigh the benefits from confrontation, deals can be made.

Dividing the values, the second mechanism, appears difficult to apply to secular and religious ideologies. It is interesting to ask, however, what actually goes on in a debate.

It is a give and take. Positions may be found that are halfway between the parties. It is notable, for instance, that new 'religions' emerge where thought-systems clash geographically. It might not be a coincidence that the four most influential mono-theist religions all developed in the area stretching from the Mediterranean to the Indus River (Judaism, Christianity, Islam, Sikhism, all probably drawing on ancient Zoroastrian thinking). Also, *horse-trading* may be seen to take place between these thoughts, reformulating ideas into entirely new combinations that transcend some of the previous dichotomies. Such rethinking is not arrived at quickly, however, and rests on a societal ability for open discussion.

These two forms, division and horse-trading, are easily handled in *Kapitalpolitik* conflicts through a process of bargaining, and using economic values as a baseline. It becomes a matter of fixing the price of the commodities in question, and then working out an arrangement that is mutually acceptable. None of the other issues has a similar scale of values that all sides agree to and that can be used in negotiations.

The fourth mechanism concerns *sharing of assets*. By pointing to shared values, *Idealpolitik* considerations may be able to develop unexpected links with an opposite side. History has seen many surprising alliances. Even in the Cold War, there were some shared values between East and West. For instance, both sides looked negatively on fascism in Spain and Portugal. There was a shared understanding in favour of decolonization and against apartheid South Africa. This was not based on power considerations, but stemmed from the same *Idealpolitik* positions that made the two sides allies during the Second World War. Sharing some values can lead to joint action. Initially, both sides were supportive of the creation of Israel; only later did they become separated on questions of peace in the Middle East. The opening of the Soviet system in the late 1980s built on giving a new priority to environmental concerns, matters that also stretched beyond the borders of the Soviet bloc. In the peace agreements since the Cold War, there are few references to such shared values. However, in the case of the Ecuador–Peru settlement, the creation of ecological reserves in the disputed area obviously was something the parties could agree to.

In the *Kapitalpolitik* field, this is less problematic. It is simply a question of creating a joint company, through which profits can be reaped and shared according to a formula set up at the founding of the company. Many disputes over oil resources could probably be handled this way, if other issues did not enter into the considerations.

The fifth mechanism, of *turning control of contested values over to other parties*, is perfectly well designed for *Kapitalpolitik* issues. This is sometimes seen as privatization. This has rarely been used in peace agreements, but the Ecuador–Peru accord includes the solution of making a key territory private property. *Idealpolitik* issues are not resolvable in this way. Ideas live their own lives and are only replaced with other ideas, as has happened partly with the democracy–dictatorship divide. However, environmental issues have brought in concerns which create new challenges to governance and legitimacy.

Similar reflections can be made on the sixth form of transcending conflicts, the *use of courts and other conflict resolution mechanisms* outside the parties. On ideological issues, it would mean that there is a legitimate authority to decide the 'correct' interpretation of particular thoughts. In countries with a sizable Catholic population, the Pope's ruling on different issues will be a possible way of transcending internal debates. This authority of the Vatican was used for settling *Geopolitik* disputes, for instance, between Argentina and Chile. In the Islamic world, the Al Azar University, in Cairo, Egypt, plays a similar role (particularly for the Sunni branch of Islam). Its statement of the compatibility between Islamic teaching and the Camp David agreements between Egypt and Israel was important for the peace process. It made clear that unspecified 'temporary peace' is possible between Muslims and non-believers. In *Kapitalpolitik*, the resort to conflict resolution mechanisms is very important and common. The World Trade Organization (WTO) contains clauses for arbitration. For the five years of 2006–10, 82 cases were brought to the WTO, while the International Court of Justice, largely dealing with non-economic issues, added 15 new contentious cases for the same period (according to the websites of these institutions).

Finally, the issues can be left to *oblivion*. This is probably what happens to a considerable number of *Idealpolitik* issues. Confrontations that seemed important fade away or diminish in significance. In that sense, *Idealpolitik* concerns do not have the same permanence as those of *Geopolitik* or *Realpolitik*. As a class of phenomena, they remain, but their influence changes. Ideas of fascism, Nazism and communism are not central in debate on government legitimacy in much of the world, but they still have appeal to some groups, also in the Western world. Fascist and neo-Nazi groups constitute a problem in Europe. Nationalism has been growing in Russia. Chauvinism that was part of the European experience in the early twentieth century unexpectedly came back as the Cold War was waning. Communist parties still rule in parts of East Asia, and less reformed communist parties are still significant in Eastern Europe. Thus, ideas do not disappear; they change in relevance and popular attraction. Globally, democracy has gained in significance as a legitimate value. In a way, it has sharpened the dichotomy between democracy and non-democracy. It can be seen in the discussions on humanitarian intervention. The rights of states to intervene in another state to protect human lives threatened by their own governments are given increased salience. It rests on the value of human survival, but also on the strength of democratic thinking and democratic powers. There is a transformation of *Idealpolitik* concerns. *Idealpolitik* as such is not disappearing.

In *Kapitalpolitik* matters, economy has a prosaic quality. It is not an issue which easily translates into conflict and war, and for which it is worth risking life, at least not on the public level. Various mafia-like structures exist, and their violence is directly connected to economic interests. For international relations, however, this is seldom the case. Economic matters are often regulated, and renegotiations are possible at agreed intervals and levels of government. Thus, economic matters become routine and part of daily life in ways which are not open for *Geo-*, *Real-* and *Idealpolitik* concerns. For much of the 1990s, large-scale economic negotiations were pursued without much public debate. The economic crises since 2008 have an impact, by making fewer resources available for peace agreements, and reducing employment possibilities for millions of people Thus, economic concerns remain important in shaping actors and agendas. What we find is that *Kapitalpolitik* matters are not strong forces behind the interstate wars we have seen lately and, consequently, do not appear in the peace agreements, except with regard to particular resources (oil!) and to compensation.

5.4 Conclusions for Interstate Conflict Resolution

Interstate conflicts continue to be a problem for international affairs and international organizations, although it has not been as dominant an issue as it were 20 or 30 years ago. There have been fewer interstate wars and the global confrontation between East and West has disappeared. However, interstate conflicts are still occurring, and there is no reason to expect them to cease. Although the spread of democracy and integration may ultimately result in an international system which is less war prone, as implied by the research on the democracy–peace hypothesis (Russett 1993; Russett and Oneal 2001; Weart 1998), this is far from a linear process. There have still been wars involving non-democracies and democracies. Forcefully removing a dictatorial regime, in the name of democracy, still does not make a democracy, and is more likely to lead to severe internal conflicts. We have even noted a complex situation, the one over Cyprus, now involving only democratic states and still waiting for a solution. More important for the future is probably the potential rise of major power conflict, involving Western actors, China, Russia and India. The crisis over Ukraine has highlighted problems in the relations between the West and Russia. Interstate conflicts still need to be attended to with great severity. The analysis and resolution indicated in this chapter remain important for the foreseeable future.

We have seen that there are four matters that are continuously pointed to in studies of the risk of interstate war. *Geopolitik* concerns over borders and other territory, *Realpolitik* interest in power and armaments to maintain power, *Idealpolitik* considerations of legitimacy and governance, and *Kapitalpolitik* interest in particular resources and other economic assets. As this chapter has made clear, issues of territory and power remain the most frequent ones. Questions of ideology and economy gain significance, particularly as causes of conflict combine with these factors. Thus, peace agreements have to find ways of dealing primarily with territorial and power considerations.

There is, however, a lesson also in this. Economic conflicts, if dealt with in isolation, are likely to find a solution. The seven mechanisms are applicable to all forms of *Kapitalpolitik* conflict. In this area, parties are able to change positions, find ways of dividing or horse-trading, sharing or handing over matters to others, including conflict mechanisms. The simplicity of the measurements (dollars, cents and corresponding measures) makes this easier. The moral obstacles for fighting wars over money contribute as well. In this, *Kapitalpolitik* contrasts in particular to *Idealpolitik,* which has a higher potential to inflame populations and spur humans into action. It is more attractive, it seems, to die in the fight for a higher value (be it the Nation, God or Democracy). Thus, *Idealpolitik* has a higher mobilizing ability than any of the other categories. Nevertheless, *Geopolitik* and *Realpolitik* seem to be at the core of much interstate conflict. This is where the parties have the largest difficulties in finding agreements, and these are the issue areas where agreements are the most likely to break down.

It is encouraging to find that agreements have been made also in these more cumbersome areas. We have shown that the international community is equipped with principles for handling *Geopolitik* issues. There is a strong preference for negotiations to depart from the status quo ante bellum position. Territorial gains in a war are to be undone, either prior to or as part of a settlement. The UN Charter emphasizes territorial integrity as a fundamental principle for international peace and security.

The seven mechanisms of conflict resolution are all relevant for the settlement of *Geopolitik* disputes. Parties do change their positions, although simple deals of dividing or horse-trading territory today appear less common. There is also a resort to conflict resolution mechanisms even for handling highly sensitive matters (as seen in the settlement between Ecuador and Peru in 1998, and Eritrea and Ethiopia in 2000). The creation of neutral states, that is, situations where none of the major contestants gets their way, has both positive (Cambodia) and negative (Cyprus) recent experiences. Buffer zones, controlled by outsiders, may be a more promising venue, but require long-term commitment from the parties and outsiders (Sinai is an example). Although border disputes may be old, they are often kept alive and become part of the national conscience. Under these circumstances, they are not likely to be forgotten. They require a peace process. Ecuador and Peru could finally reach a settlement in 1998 using some of the seven mechanisms we have mentioned.

Realpolitik issues are seldom properly addressed in peace agreements. The closest we come is the regulation of armaments. These can be measures directly dealt with by the parties in special arms control deals. The Cold War saw many of these. Since then there have been fewer arrangements for nuclear weapons. The ending of interstate conflict has involved little disarmament. A general impression is that weapons issues are manageable through agreements. Weapons can be counted and weighed. There are often agreements among military experts on what different weapons systems can accomplish. Thus, parties can change position, divide and horse-trade in armament negotiations. They can also agree to bilateral and multilateral inspections.

The most important lesson may instead be another. How are the parties dealing with one another after a war? It is tied to issues of responsibility for the war. Is there accountability for the destructive events in a war between states? In several agreements this issue has been raised and prevented early deals (Iran–Iraq, Eritrea–Ethiopia). The compensation arrangement in the Gulf War also built on the assumption that one side was more responsible. It is less likely to be something the parties agree to in interstate negotiations. Responsibility is related to the need for court procedures and international criminal legislation. This has developed in the 1990s, culminating with the convention on the International Criminal Court in 1998. Now ratified and in operation, this Court might have an impact on interstate peacemaking, but its primary focus so far has been on intra-state situations.

Further Readings

Go to the *Understanding Conflict Resolution* web page at https://study.sagepub.com/wallensteen4e for free access to journal articles listed.

Inter-state War

Buzan, B. 1991. *People, States and Fear* (2nd edn). Boulder, CO: Lynne Rienner. Buzan's classic work constitutes an eloquent theoretical explanation for the dynamics in inter-state relations.

Geller, D.S. and Singer, J.D. 1998. *Nations at War*. Cambridge: Cambridge University Press.
In this work, the two authors associated with the Correlates of War project recounts empirical findings for how the international system actually operates.

This theme is further elaborated in Vasquez, J.A. (ed.) 2012. *What Do We Know about War?* (2nd edn). Lanham, MD: Rowman and Littlefield.
This volume brings together a number of authors working in the Correlates of War tradition on inter-state relations.

In contrast to the concern with security matters, state revenue is given a heavy role in this seminal contribution on the emergence of states in Western Europe: Tilly, C. 1990. *Coercion, Capital and European States AD 990–1990*. Cambridge, MA: Blackwell.

Inter-state Peace

Holsti, Kalevi J. 1991. *Peace and War: Armed Conflict and International Order, 1648–1989*. Cambridge: Cambridge University Press.
In a very long historical perspective Holsti brings out the variations in how interstate relations are organized and the importance of this for war and peace. For a shorter period than Holsti applies, and with a different systematic, this short article also discusses the importance of international orders and relations between major powers for war as well as peace:

Wallensteen, P. 1984. 'Universalism vs. Particularism. On the Limits of Major Power Order', *Journal of Peace Research*, 21 (3): 243–57. Also reproduced in Peter Wallensteen 2011b. *Peace Research: Theory and Practice*, London: Routledge, where also the notions of Geopolitik, Realpolitik, Idealpolitik and Kapitalpolitik are analysed at some length.

In an important work two authors explain not only how democracy is important for peaceful interstate relations, but also integration and international organizations, in what they call Kantian Peace, drawing on a classical text by philosopher Immanuel Kant:
Russett, B.M. and Oneal, J.R. 2001. *Triangulating Peace: Democracy, Interdependence, and International Organizations*. New York: W. W. Norton.

6

CONFLICT RESOLUTION IN CIVIL WARS

6.1 Armed Conflicts and Peace Accords within States

Civil war, or more specifically intra-state conflict concerning the control over government, has been a constant feature in the global conflict picture. It has received particular attention in its own right since the end of the Cold War.[1] It consists of many different phenomena, only one of which is the narrowly defined armed conflict. There are also military coups which sometimes are swift and result in limited violence, attempted coups, short-lived rebellions, actions by militias, armed gangs, bands, freedom movements and terrorist organizations. There is also government action as an important component and often in a close relationship to the actions of opponents. There are forms of repression, police measures, legal instruments such as preventive detention, human rights violations and unwarranted arrests. Indeed, there is a close relation between police brutality and violent riots. This is a pattern that can be observed in rich and poor countries alike. A considerable share of all violence in the world can be attributed to conflicts dealing with control over governmental power in particular states. It is an old issue to which much political analysis has been devoted. The events of September 11, 2001, demonstrated the international implications of such dynamics. An organization primarily concerned with change in particular countries (Saudi Arabia, Egypt) chose to attack the main external supporter of the incumbent regimes. Global terrorism mostly has its roots in internal conflicts, some of which deal with government control, some with territorial issues. The Arab Spring further emphasized the importance of governance, with a series of popular revolts for change that in many cases resulted in civil wars. Let us now examine the situation of internal conflict during and after the Cold War.

Civil Wars during and after the Cold War

Civil war is sometimes described as the most important feature of the period after the Cold War. This is not entirely correct, however. As we have noted in Section 5.1, many of the Cold War conflicts dealt with intra-state conditions and control over the government apparatus. The contention centred on whether a particular state was controlled by the 'left' or the 'right', by pro-Soviet or pro-Western groups. The conflicts were perceived to be part of the Cold War. Thus, they became of international concern. Various forms of intervention took place, internationalizing the civil war. Actions included the dispatching of troops from a bloc leader. Some examples are the US interventions in Guatemala in 1954, in the Dominican Republic in 1965, in Grenada in 1983 and in Panama in 1989; and Soviet troops were used to change governments in Hungary in 1956, in Czechoslovakia in 1968 and in Afghanistan in 1979. There were other, clandestine forms of intervention, as well as support to particular governments or groups doing the actual combat in internal conflicts. Intervention in internal conflicts was a marked feature of the Cold War. Some of its most severe confrontations grew out of such situations, for instance, the conflicts around Cuba (with a US-sponsored intervention in 1961) and the war in Vietnam (particularly following a US-supported coup in Saigon in 1963).

Although the UN Charter specifies that issues which are 'essentially within the domestic jurisdiction' of a state (Article 2.7) should not be of concern to the UN, and thus not be internationalized, they were. The Charter provision was often only barring the UN itself from involvement where a host of other actors were heavily engaged. Article 2.7 was principally used by the Soviet Union to obstruct international actions in situations among members of its bloc. Even obvious Soviet interventions, such as those in Hungary, Czechoslovakia and Afghanistan, were excused as invitations of a legitimate government. The West was barred from intervening by the fear of a crisis escalating into a nuclear confrontation. Similarly, US interventions were kept from the UN agenda by Western dominance in the Security Council and by referring situations to regional organizations controlled by the USA (for instance, in the case of Guatemala). The strict interpretation of Article 2.7 was also used by military regimes to minimize external and internal criticism and fend off interference into their brutal rule. Newly independent states in Africa and Asia used it as a legal defence of their independence against former colonial powers. Thus, the UN and other international actors met severe constraints in entering into internal conflicts.

Since the Cold War, the picture has changed. In the early 1990s, the UN and other international agencies were authorized to go into a series of intra-state conflicts and peace processes, notably in Central America, Indochina, Africa and Southeast Europe. Many of these situations would, during the Cold War, have been defined as outside the parameters of international action, with reference to Article 2.7. This may explain today's conventional wisdom that there are more internal conflicts than ever before. It is more accurate to say that there are now more internal conflicts in which international organizations are involved.

Internal conflicts are often seen as particularly difficult to handle. A civil war means the breaking-up of existing social relationships. Families may be divided, friendships are destroyed, and local communities are shattered. Thus, socially and psychologically, they are more devastating than many interstate wars. This is true for situations where the interstate conflicts take place between states that have long been separated. In cases of states being neighbours or when states are newly created, there may, however, exist similar networks across borders as there are inside states. The distinguishing features of civil wars and other internal conflicts is primarily not the brutality or the social impact. All armed conflicts have such effects, which makes war a shared phenomenon across cultures and continents.

The mark of the internal conflict is instead found in the incompatibility and in the primary parties. Civil wars are a matter of keeping or taking control over a particular government and its state machinery. Furthermore, the primary parties are rooted within the same state. Thus, initial conflict dynamics tend to build on internal grievances, such as the ones indicated in Section 3.3. Many of these relate to power relations, economic interactions and the internal social fabric. To a larger degree than is the case in interstate conflicts, the actor will have a longer shared history of conflict and cooperation prior to the war experience. This is one element in the perception of internal conflicts as more socially devastating than other conflicts. The lines drawn between people are ideological, economic or social. Civil wars may also be 'ethnic' or 'racial'. The civil strife in South Africa and the genocide in Rwanda concerned the control of state power in these countries. The actors were largely, but not entirely, formed along lines of historically ascribed identities. Thus, the conflicts were 'ethnic' but did not include ambitions of territorially dividing the state.

This means that internal conflicts raise two particularly sharp and interlinked questions for conflict resolution and a durable peace settlement. First, there is the problem of how to construct a social and political system which gives reasonable social and political space to all groups in a society. This is necessary as civil wars concern the distribution of power in society. Answers will have to deal with *participation* and influence in a society. This points to the question of democracy as a solution, theoretically and empirically. The second problem is the one of *security*. The experience of a civil war raises a pointed internal security dilemma, which the actors may put in the following form: 'If I win, you lose,' and thus as a consequence: 'As you may act against me, I had better act before you do.' This is the logic of repression and terror prior to war. It is the reasoning of armed action. Thus, ending violence in a way which removes this security dilemma has to be part of any settlement. Without the parties being secure, subjectively and objectively, a peace agreement is unlikely to be sustained. This involves control over government, as government resources can be used to maintain the security dilemma or to transcend it. Indeed, we may locate the phenomenon of corruption in the same insecurity. It will pay for leaders to accumulate personal wealth, as this is a way to bribe others, whether contenders or loyalists. To put money abroad is providing for an alternative exit in case of challenges. Kleptocracy, in other words, finds its roots in the internal security dilemma. Solutions to the dilemma might improve the chances for honest government.

Peace Agreements in Civil Wars

Before proceeding we need to approach the experiences since the Cold War in ending civil wars through peace processes. Table 6.1 lists all such peace agreements entered into from 1989 to 2013.

Table 6.1 lists 29 countries with armed conflicts that were ended, at least for a period, through a peace agreement. Most of them are in Africa, some in Central Asia and South America. There are different dates given in cases where agreements were later abandoned or a new one added. Some failed completely, meaning that fighting soon broke out again. Even in such cases, however, the parties may revert to the original agreement, as happened for instance in Cambodia. In Chad, changes of government resulted in new agreements, and in Liberia the agreement in 2003 is the most recent in a long series of agreement experiences. It should also be noted that some agreements concerned only some of the parties in the internal conflict.

One of the chief lessons since the end of the Cold War is the extraordinary complexity of peacemaking. This is further illustrated in Table 6.1, in the many cases with repeated agreements. Some of these attempt at solving the problem stated by the parties (for example, dealing directly with an issue, such as finding a power-sharing formula) and others indicate a process for how the parties are going to continue peacefully (such as an electoral process). There is often also an interaction between the two, as can be seen from a number of cases mentioned in Table 6.1. By the end of 2013, there were functioning peace agreements in most of the conflicts with an agreement. Agreements have been lasting, suggesting that the parties mostly are serious when signing a treaty. This, however, did not necessarily include all conflicts in a particular country (in Colombia, for example, there was a durable agreement between some parties in 1991, and failed peace processes with one actor in 2001–02, but leading to a restart of negotiations in 2012).

It is interesting to observe that many cases show a continuous process of new, more elaborate agreements. The notion of a 'peace process' accurately describes what many peace agreements are all about. The original idea of conflict resolution efforts was to reach an agreement that would regulate conclusively all the aspects of a conflict. The experience since the end of the Cold War has made clear that such comprehensive and final settlements often are unlikely. There are nine cases in Table 6.1 with only one agreement. Most of them were later overturned, without being replaced with a new arrangement. However, the agreements on Macedonia and Nepal were still in place by 2014. It might be true that the longer a conflict has continued, the greater the need for a durable process for restoring peaceful conditions. This might even be more pronounced for internal conflicts. Furthermore, the longer the peace process the more dangers there will be of a relapse into war, due to activities of 'spoilers', effects of unmet expectations or external intervention. Peace processes are fragile routes to peace.

The total number of civil wars for the period 1989–2013 is 64 (see Table 4.1). Comparing this to the lasting peace agreements in the same period, it means that half of all internal armed conflicts saw an agreement (45 per cent, see Table 4.3).

Table 6.1   Peace agreements in civil wars since the end of the Cold War

Conflict location	Year of agreement	No. of agreements
Afghanistan	1993, 1996	3
Angola	1989, 1991, 1994, 2002	4
Burundi	2000, 2002, 2003, 2006, 2008	8
Cambodia	1991	1
Central African Republic	2008, 2012, 2013	4
Chad	1991, 1992, 1993, 1994, 1995, 1997, 1998, 1999, 2002, 2005, 2006	11
Colombia	1991, 1999, 2001, 2002	4
Congo, Republic	1999	1
Côte d'Ivoire	2003, 2004, 2005, 2007, 2008	9
Dem. Rep. Congo	1999, 2001, 2002, 2003, 2009, 2013	7
Djibouti	1994, 2000, 2001	3
El Salvador	1990, 1991, 1992	9
Guatemala	1990, 1991, 1994, 1995, 1996	16
Guinea Bissau	1998	1
Haiti	1993	1
Liberia	1990, 1991, 1993, 1994, 1995, 1996, 2003	11
Macedonia	2001	1
Mexico[a]	1996	1
Mozambique	1991, 1992	5
Nepal	2006	1
Niger	1993	1
Philippines	1995	1
Rwanda	1991, 1992, 1993	6
Sierra Leone	1996, 1999, 2000	3
Somalia	1993, 1994, 1997, 2008	5
South Africa[b]	1990, 1991, 1992, 1993	5
Sudan	2002, 2003, 2004, 2005, 2006, 2011	10
Tajikistan	1995, 1996, 1997	5
Uganda	2002, 2007, 2008	8

[a] The agreement was not implemented, but fighting did not resume.
[b] Strictly seen, this case should not be included as the armed conflict between ANC and the apartheid regime took place prior to 1989.

Note: Peace agreements in armed conflicts concerning the control over government, active in the period 1989–2013. The table includes treaties that have been signed, that regulate (resolve or find a process for the solution of) the incompatibility, and have been concluded between the warring parties, and have ended armed conflict behaviour. Cease-fire agreements are not included. The parties are listed in English alphabetical order.

Source: Uppsala Conflict Data Program Conflict Encyclopedia; Table 4.2 in this volume; Högbladh (2006).

This is higher than other researchers report from civil wars in previous periods. The definitions of 'civil war' are not the same as applied here, as they often include state formation conflicts as well. Also, 'agreement' or 'negotiated ending' is determined slightly differently. Still, there are some interesting long-term patterns. For instance, Mason and Fett (1996) report that there were 13 peace agreements for the period 1945–92 in a total of 56 civil wars, that is, 23 per cent of the cases. Licklider gives an even lower number, finding that for the period 1945–93 there were 14 conflicts which ended through negotiations out of a total of 84, that is, 17 per cent. Stedman finds that for the period 1900–89 there were solutions through negotiations in 15 per cent of the civil wars in this century (Licklider 1995: 684; Mason and Fett 1996; Stedman 1991: 8).[2] The negotiated agreements have been few, and even fewer in cases which have concerned the civil war category as here defined. It suggests that peace agreements are more common as ways of ending such wars today than previously. Given that the time span for the cases reported in Table 6.1 is much shorter, it definitely means that peacemaking in civil wars is now a higher priority. For the periods covered by the three studies, a peace agreement was concluded every third to eighth year. Table 6.1 shows that there was an average of around six peace agreements reached every year in the post-Cold War period. Terminating civil wars through negotiations has become very important.

This notwithstanding, a number of internal conflicts ended in the elimination or capitulation of one party, that is, victory. The share of such endings is somewhat lower than previously. For the post-Cold War period this outcome is evenly distributed between victories for the opposition (for instance, in Panama, Paraguay and Romania in 1989, in Ethiopia in 1991, in Zaire in 1997, in Libya 2011) and for the government (for instance, Sri Lanka in the non-Tamil conflict in 1991, Venezuela in 1992, Russia, and Georgia in 1993). In two cases, peace agreements were never implemented, instead resulting in victory (in both cases by the opposition): Haiti (the Governor's Island Agreement) and Rwanda (the Arusha Peace Accord), both completed in 1993. In the first case, it nearly resulted in an intervention by a multinational force; in the second case, the world was standing idle when an unprecedented genocide followed. It was directed against the Tutsi minority and stopped only when forces composed largely of Tutsi rebels took over the capital. In a more recent internal conflict there was no room for negotiations: Afghanistan 2001. In this case, victory could be declared as the incumbent government was deposed, the capital taken by the forces of the other side (the 'Northern Alliance' with US support) and a new regime was recognized. A peace agreement of sorts was signed, the Bonn Agreement of 2001, with broad Afghan participation but without representatives of the deposed Taliban. The agreement has been basic for subsequent events in Afghanistan, but Taliban resistance has continued. These examples notwithstanding, we can conclude that clear-cut victory for one or the other side is not as common as are peace agreements.

However, many internal conflicts have 'other outcomes', meaning that the fighting recedes to levels which are below the Uppsala Conflict Data Program inclusion threshold of more than 25 killed in battle per year. In reality, this means that governments remained in power. The conflicts may have ended in de facto victories for the status quo, the government side, without this being clearly acknowledged by the losing side. For either side, perhaps more for the weaker one, a peace agreement may actually provide a greater chance for survival and, thus, there might be an incentive for a peaceful solution. In an interstate conflict, the sides can withdraw behind an internationally recognized boundary and the survival of that side is not directly threatened.

These observations are further underscored by the fact that many intra-state conflicts continued at the end of the recording period. This means that some civil wars have persisted for a considerable period of time. Situations which have received ample international attention at times, but without a sustained programme of international action, are, for instance, Algeria, Burma/Myanmar, Peru, the Philippines (the conflict involving the Communist Party, NPA), Rwanda, Somalia and Uganda. These internal conflicts are old. Many have been going on for decades. There are some newer conflicts which may have the potential to become equally entrenched if no solutions are found (for instance, in Central Africa, Mali and South Sudan). Some protracted conflicts have, at times, drawn much interest, notably Somalia, Afghanistan, Burundi and Sudan. A conclusion is that if the parties in an intra-state conflict cannot solve their incompatibilities, it is more likely that a conflict will become protracted than end in victory.

It should be noted that most of the intra-state conflicts concerning government are taking place in classical Third World countries, many of which are poor, overpopulated or marked by stark contrasts between rich and poor. This is also where regimes have turned into kleptocracy. The resources of the state have been used to corrupt leaderships and opponents alike. There are armed conflicts in some oil-rich or industrialized states but, interestingly, many have been of a shorter duration (Venezuela, Azerbaijan and Russia) except when connected to religious or racial dimensions (Algeria, South Africa). In predominantly agricultural economies, control over the state may be a particularly valuable asset, as there are fewer alternative sources of income. Some studies also point to environmental degradation as a source of internal conflict, particularly if connected to other factors (Hauge and Ellingsen 1998; Wantechekon 1999).

There is one striking change in internal conflict and that is the reduction in military coups. Military regimes and transition to democratic institutions were an important topic throughout the 1980s. The problem has not lost its relevance, although the patterns have changed. South and Central America, which used to be the focus of the discussions, now have few such military governments. There is considerable popular resistance to them. The coups that have taken place during the 1990s include the one in Haiti in 1991, the President's actions in Peru in 1992, Guatemala in 1993 and the failed coup in Venezuela in 1992. By 1994 these coups were undone. The coup leaders were forced to leave power in Haiti. President Fujimori in Peru retreated, won a second period in office but his third victory in 2000 was highly fraudulent. He resigned and was later put in prison. The chief plotter in Venezuela, Hugo Chávez, was brought to court, later freed to embark on a political career, and took power in 1999 by democratic means. He survived a short-lived coup attempt in 2002 and stayed in power until his death in 2013. There is now reluctance – nationally, regionally and internationally – to accept military intrusion into political life. This was clear when facing the coup in Honduras in 2009. Latin American opinion was overwhelmingly negative.

The same trend can be seen in the Middle East, where there were 21 coups in the period 1950–69 and 6 in 1970–89.[3] In early 2011, an unprecedented wave of peaceful, democratic protests swept through the Middle East, the Arab Spring. The protests unseated the regimes in Tunisia and Egypt. They were strongly repressed in Bahrain and led to armed conflicts in Yemen, Syria and Libya. Particularly in the case of Libya it resulted in UN and NATO action to protect civilians, based on the principle of the international responsibility to protect exposed populations. The incumbent leader, Muammar Gaddafi, was killed in October 2011.

Another coup-prone region has been Africa, but it has seen fewer military takeover attempts in recent years. In Sudan in 1989, a military junta based on a stricter interpretation of Islam took power from a civilian government. A new brand of leaders emerged through revolutionary wars in Uganda, Ethiopia, Eritrea, Rwanda and Zaire. Established one-party states were replaced through democratic elections (for instance, in Zambia and Malawi). Although the plotters in Burundi in 1993 failed in taking control of the government, their actions unsettled domestic relations not only in Burundi, but also in Rwanda. A new coup took place in 1996. A coup in Lesotho in 1994 was rejected by its neighbours, the previous regime was reinstated and peacekeeping troops from the region were posted in the country in 1998. A military regime yielded to democratic procedures in Nigeria in 1999. There was an unsettling coup in the Côte d'Ivoire in December 1999, followed by an armed conflict in 2002. The peace agreements included new registrations of voters and new elections. The elections in 2010 clearly gave the opposition the majority of the votes, but the incumbent, Laurent Gbagbo, refused to step down. After a short, internationally supported war in March and April 2011 he capitulated, accepted the election-winner Alassane Ouattara as president and is now at trial in The Hague. A coup in Togo in 2005 was rejected by African states and led to demonstrations, forcing an election. The phenomenon has not been eliminated, but the frequency is clearly lower. In 1960–69, forced removal accounted for close to three-quarters of all regime changes in Africa; in the first five years of the 2000s the share was down to one-sixth (Southall et al. 2005). Unconstitutional removal of leaders remains a problem and the African Union (AU) has instituted a sanctions policy against such events (Eriksson 2010a; Hellquist 2014).

There were some coups and attempted coups in Southeast Asia. The military takeover in Thailand in 1991 led to a successful, popular uprising and democratization in 1992. A military attempt against the democratic regime in the Philippines in 1989 failed. The Asian economic crisis in 1997 hastened the downfall of oligarchs in South Korea as well as in Indonesia, at the same time as it strengthened democratic tendencies in Thailand, Taiwan and the Philippines. The trend towards democratization has been pronounced in much of Asia. The only typical military intervention in a South Asian country occurred in Pakistan in October 1999, when General Pervez Musharraf took control of the country in a bloodless coup, but then staged another coup in 2007 when the High Court annulled his victory in the elections. He was forced out by popular uprisings in 2008. Such movements have repeatedly affected the governments in Thailand. In 2010 the so-called Red Shirts were violently repressed by a government, later won in the elections, but faced a new military coup, in 2014.

As this overview suggests, the coup phenomenon has become more rare in a world of democratization. Political leadership changes, in many parts of the world, have taken more constitutional forms in the post-Cold War era than before. Also, authoritarian regimes have been challenged by mass-movements which have been able to defy police repression by turning out in huge numbers. Mobilization through the Internet in general, and through social media in particular, is a new feature in politics, as seen in Iran in 2009 and in Arab countries in 2011. It is interesting because there is a debate over whether, for instance, Islam is intrinsically incompatible with democracy. Certainly, the democratization of Indonesia (the country with the largest Muslim population in the world), the democratic transitions from one party to another in Bangladesh during the 1990s, and the rise to power of an Islamic party in Turkey in 2004, qualifies such notions. The spring of 2011 saw wide pro-democracy movements in a series of Arab countries, further confirming that demands for democracy transcend such cultural differences.

The decline of the military coup does not mean it is a phenomenon of the past, or that military influence over political life has disappeared. Instead, military establishments are finding novel ways of influencing democratic policies. In some countries, the military remains, according to its own view, the sole guarantor of the 'order' of the day. Thus, the Turkish armed forces have historically acted to ensure a secular, Europe-oriented state in a country with a predominantly Muslim population. By the mid-2010s, however, military power seemed curtailed by the dominant political party, AKP, the Justice and Development Party. The failure of military leaderships to maintain open political control in the early 1990s suggests that times are changing. A less visible, but still effective role may be what military establishments hope for in South Korea, Taiwan, Indonesia, the Philippines, Bangladesh and Burma/Myanmar. For the outside observers, it means that the analytical tools have to be sharpened to discern the influence of the armed forces.

There are many ways in which military leaders can adjust to democratization, and they do not necessarily have to be hostile to it. The democratic system assumes civilian control over the military, but also that a workable arrangement can be found between a professionally defined military establishment and democratic authorities. Normally this means that the tasks of the military are separated as clearly as possible from civilian responsibilities. This appears to be a global tendency. The ability of the civilian state to control the military will depend on the competence and strength of the state. Some argue that economic and technological globalization might undermine the state and weaken its hold over the legitimate use of force (Desch 1999: 128–30). Ultimately, the strength of the democratic system rests on its support from the population. This requires state structures that are strong and autonomous enough to set the agenda for a society. The weakening of state institutions in the 1990s has implications for the performance of peace agreements as well as for managing the civil–military relationship.

At the same time, overly strong states become repressive and create new conditions for revolt. The terrorism seen in recent times stems from both ends of this spectrum. Closed political systems (such as in Saudi Arabia and Egypt) stimulate opposition, which in turn may draw energy from unsolved regional issues (the Palestinian issue, for example) and find allies in states in turmoil (such as Afghanistan and Pakistan) where it might be possible to establish bases for dramatic actions (such as those on September 11, 2001, suicide attacks or even establishing territorial control). Some roots of terrorism, in other words, come from ongoing conflicts and prevalent political conditions. The solution is neither a very weak state nor an overpowering one.

In this chapter we are dealing with democracy as a solution to internal war, theoretically in Section 6.2 and empirically in Section 6.3. The question of internal security dilemmas and state failure are approached in Sections 6.4 and 6.5. Newly created democracies have to rest on considerable popular support to manage the balancing act with the military, at the same time sustaining transitions from internal war to peaceful conditions. The role of civil society is crucial for the survival of democracy. We shall return to this in Section 6.6.

6.2 Dealing with Incompatibilities over State Power

Most peace agreements listed in Table 6.1 include democratization as a central element in the settlement. It is logical as these wars involve a struggle for power and influence in society. This is a way to handle the *participation of parties* in a society after a war: to give space to a host of actors who have previously been suppressed or excluded from influence. A solution may encompass procedures for transferring the struggle into constitutional and non-violent forms. This typically means a system of political parties, with freedom of association, safeguards for human rights, access to media, security for election campaigns, independent election commissions, fair elections and the free forming of new governments on the basis of election outcome. In other words, democratization is not a quick fix, but a multidimensional process. It is not only a matter of arranging an election. It also relates to an underlying balance of forces in a society, where parties realize that they cannot monopolize power. They have to adjust their demands in accordance with their electoral strength. It means that the incumbent government may lose power, due to the outcome of a previously agreed upon process (as happened, for instance, in Nicaragua, Cambodia and Iraq). This contributes to making a new system of governance credible and improves its attraction to political forces. This notwithstanding, newly created democracies are likely to remain fragile. We need to analyse how a democratic system, once established, can handle disputes that are likely to arise over the distribution of power in a society.

This aspect is particularly important in connection with the second problem indicated in Section 6.1, the one of *the security of the parties*. Can the democratic system simultaneously solve a basic incompatibility and move a society away from the sharp internal security dilemma where 'If A wins, B perishes – if B wins, A perishes'? There is no doubt that in conflicts with a clear-cut victory/defeat outcome, this is the logic that will apply: Nicolae Ceaușescu, leader in Romania, was executed, almost on television, in 1989. Mengistu Haile Mariam, the losing leader in Ethiopia, fled to Zimbabwe in 1991 to avoid being captured. Mobutu Sese Seko, the deposed leader of Zaire, escaped with his family and died in Morocco in 1997. Charles Taylor was 'persuaded' to leave Liberia in 2003, later being captured and sentenced in The

Hague-based court for Sierra Leone. Sometimes, the loser is in mortal danger, but there are other examples. The coup leader in Venezuela was jailed, but later made a new political career. The losers in armed conflict in Moscow in 1993 disappeared from politics but remained alive as ordinary citizens. There is a reality of an absolute internal security dilemma, but it can be modified. We may ask whether it takes a resource-rich or diversified social system for accepting another outcome (as was the case in Venezuela and Russia) and thus make the conflict shorter. An answer is that if the shift in power goes in the direction of democratization, the security dilemma is mitigated. In such cases, other outcomes are reported, notably in Thailand, South Korea and Indonesia, where the leaders could stay in the country, sometimes being convicted for crimes or corruption, but having their lives, families and dependents protected by the new system.

The question of human rights has entered into the settlement in a new way since the Cold War. It affects particularly the issue of what happens to the parties after a settlement and after a loss of power. The emphasis on accountability introduces higher criteria for what is an acceptable peace agreement. This was brought out strongly by the peace agreement for Sierra Leone in 1999. It provided amnesty for perpetrators of some of the worst violations of human rights and dignity. It served to end the war, for a time, but it was also unacceptable to the international community. In a reworked peace agreement, the conditions were changed and a tribunal was created specifically for Sierra Leone. UN negotiators are now instructed not to accept amnesty provisions.

Still, the democratic system appears to be a social system with possibilities of handling political losers and the changing fortunes of political forces. The human rights criteria help to draw a line between those who can participate in the democratic system and those who are to be brought to trial. Let us see how, in principle, a democratic system works.

The seven ways of conflict resolution we have identified in Section 3.5 are typical of the way a democratic system operates. The first form concerns *changes of priorities*. In a democratic system, the electoral outcome gives party leaders the chance to change their goals. They can claim that they have insufficient votes or seats in order to carry out the promises made. Such excuses are not available to the leaders of authoritarian regimes. Instead, the credibility of an absolute ruler hinges on the notion that he/she knows what should be done and is capable of delivering results. The fact that in authoritarian regimes there will also be (hidden) power struggles is not part of the image. The democratic system, furthermore, has the advantage of actually giving the loser a second or third chance. New elections are an agreed, regulated, intrinsic element, and this gives a defeated actor another chance. In fact, the best indicator of a functioning democratic system is the second or third election, not the first one. Alternative political systems neither give nor protect such a second opportunity. The possibility of a comeback can be regarded as the single most important instrument for breaking out of the internal security dilemma. It is a strong point for a democratic system.

The second solution, *dividing the values* in conflict, as well as the third one, *horse-trading*, are integral parts of any parliamentary system. Compromises, trade-off deals and multi-issue packages are continuously the substance of politics. A struggle for power can be solved through ingenious divisions of power (over years, over functions), trade-off arrangements (according to the logic 'I support you on issue A, you support me on issue B') or combinations of the two. A society does in fact contain many attractive positions that can be part of a deal of power distribution. Some ministerial posts are customarily regarded as more important than others (for instance, portfolios as prime minister, or foreign, defence, interior or finance ministries). There are also posts such as speaker of parliament, head of particular committees, control of particular functions in society, governor positions, etc. In a one-party system, these are all available, but the difference is that they are only distributed to loyal party members to prevent them from becoming the basis for critics or attacks on the government. In the democratic system, however, they may equally likely go to opponents and to generally competent personalities. They also give a position of power to opponents, and thus serve to protect their security.

The fourth solution, *ruling together*, is represented by coalition governments, which are necessarily formed in a democracy in a multidimensional state and where proportional representation is the formula. A special aspect of this is the power-sharing arrangement, to which we shall return shortly.

The fifth solution, of *leaving control* to a minority or third force, is also a common feature in any established democratic system. Minority governments may in fact be the most common form of governance, particularly if minority is defined as representation of the general population. For example, if 80 per cent of the population votes in an election and those getting the majority, say 55 per cent of the votes, take control of the government, this still does not represent more than 45 per cent of the electorate. The key lies in the way the minority government is formed. An open process provides assurances to the population as well as to competing political leaders.

The sixth solution, bringing issues to a *conflict resolution mechanism*, is also available to the democratic system. It can be done, for instance, in the form of a referendum on a particular issue or new elections to break a political stalemate. Some systems do not have this possibility, which means there is more pressure on using the five other mechanisms.

Finally, there is the seventh way: *postponing issues*, by referring them to commissions. This is more difficult in a direct power struggle, but such struggles can be contained if the main contenders agree to let a minority run the government, that is, using the fifth way as a temporary measure. Leaving constitutional issues to commissions for later proposals can be a way of handling transition questions. The expectation is that once a commission presents its findings, the struggle has lost some of its intensity.

These examples illustrate that the incompatibility over government can be handled in ways which serve to remedy the internal security dilemma. More theoretically, we may ask, what is it actually that the democratic system does? The answer is easier said than translated into practice: it enlarges the number of options to the conflicting parties. There is no longer only a choice between (1) winning and (2) perishing. The democratic system provides intermediate options such as (1.2) winning, but not gaining complete dominance, (1.4) being strong enough to play a role, (1.6) having some strength which can be enough to prevent undesirable developments, or (1.8) losing, but still keeping a position in society. Democracy expands the political alternatives in society. The actors have more real choices, which is to the benefit of the society as a whole. Still, the system is capable of making decisions. It may be slower, but decisions are more likely to be more durable.

For this to function, however, three conditions must be met. The winner must be committed to respecting the rights of the loser to be a loser, even to have a chance to make a comeback. This might be in the enlightened self-interest of the winner, if the winner realizes he/she could be the loser at a later stage. Furthermore, the loser must feel secure enough to accept defeat and not risk annihilation at that moment of conceding defeat. In an intra-state war, these are two conditions not easily met in a credible way. In a democratic society, respect and guarantees are customarily extended and the control of weaponry is restricted. The period immediately after a civil war is uncertain for all actors. There are plenty of weapons around. There may be anger and frustration. Economic conditions are often chaotic. This is why a reasonably strong and efficient international peacekeeping force can be important for a peace process in a civil war. It provides a neutral power resource which can extend guarantees to all sides.

Behind these two conditions there is a more deep-rooted notion, a third condition. It is that the state is not seen to 'belong' to any of the parties. Even a given government is only a temporary custodian of the state machinery. State resources are not at the unlimited disposal of the government or the winner. This is the essential meaning of the expression 'the rule of law'. The uses of state resources are limited by rules: there are safeguards, watchdogs and ombudsmen that protect the citizens. If generally accepted, the principles of the rule of law will make the state apparatus less attractive as a resource in society. It means that the significance of the state is deliberately restricted. In this way, the democratic system creates its own guarantees. For instance, the loser, if it is the former government repositioned as the opposition, is as important for the continuation of the rules of society as is the winner, who moves in to assume government control. The limit of what the state can do is what provides guarantees for the survival of the system. The struggle for state power, however, often stems from an ambition to gain control of an unlimited resource. To accept the principles of such limits is not easy for any contender.

How can such a transformation take place in a situation where the actors are entrenched in a deadly conflict over the state? How did it take place in the countries that today have democratically stable systems? The solution may be found in a special balance of strength where neither side completely wins or loses all its resources in a society. This means there is a balance among contending forces, giving them a chance to formulate the rules of the game. This is normally done in a constitutional reform with assemblies that bring together influential strands of a society. The agreed rules create a way of life which affects and helps to maintain the underlying societal balance. Some of the peace agreements in Table 6.1 are such formative documents, which become frameworks as the political system evolves. The fate of such peace agreements also gives insight into how democracy can be established under extreme conditions. Few, if any, of today's entrenched democracies in Western

Europe and North America evolved directly from such strong internal conflicts as several of the countries in Table 6.1 face today.

Clearly, it is a process that is little understood.[4] After the parties have signed a peace agreement they face the difficult phase of implementation. The former warring parties are still the paramount actors and they will attempt to control the developments. As they are the signatories to the agreement, their interpretation is difficult to challenge, as long as they agree on the process. Their disagreement can imperil the whole arrangement. Thus, this is a period requiring considerable trust and confidence. Also for this reason, an international presence may be conducive for the continuation of the process. It should be clear, however, that the primary actors themselves are responsible for the progress of implementation. It is a learning period, where the parties discover new traits about each other as well as how different building peace is from waging war.

After this comes a period where the previous conflict may no longer seem significant, but where the new conditions in themselves create tensions. This is when the peace treaty is consolidated, but also exposed to unforeseen tests. There may be topics that were neglected or not understood at the time of the peace accord (Stedman et al. 2002). There may be problems which arise as a result of the agreement, for instance, the problem of how to handle the former military forces. As we are interested in peace agreements after war, the latter aspect is particularly pertinent. Is it possible for the parties that were fighting a war among each other to integrate into the same societal framework again? The fact that there are more peace agreements in the post-Cold War period than previously means that there is little historical precedent on which to build. This, furthermore, is probably more true for civil wars than any other category. Thus, the questions of physical security and ability to cooperate are put at particular strains. Seen in this way, the fact that so many peace agreements actually survive is an achievement.

The physical security of the fighting parties is of particular concern in the settlement of internal conflicts. Such settlements do not normally establish dividing lines within a country behind which the parties can withdraw, as is the case in interstate conflicts. There is a limit to dissociative solutions. Sooner or later, the accord assumes that the parties reintegrate or relate closely to each other. Thus, transition requires special measures to provide sufficient security for leaders and to familiarize the general public to their presence in public life. Their freedom becomes a symbol of a new reality of peaceful cooperation. Let us proceed by looking at the experiences since the Cold War in this light.

6.3 Democracy and the Settlement of Civil Wars

The peace agreements in Table 6.1 were concluded in societies with important differences in political institutions on which to build democratic solutions. First, there were cases of conflicts going on in countries which already had limited forms of popular participation in politics. For instance, elections, party competition and media independence were accepted principles. Thus, the question became largely one of reforming this system so as to accommodate the demands arising from the civil wars. The peace arrangements in Colombia, El Salvador, Guatemala, and South Africa could all use existing legal structures. The peace agreements meant fundamental changes in these constitutions so as to allow for a broader participation, as well as the dismantling of structures that were antithetical to the new democratic system (more specifically, the military institutions and all apartheid institutions, respectively). Although basic changes took place, institutions could remain and transcend themselves into the new realities. Particularly in South Africa, the changes in power in all central institutions meant considerable social change. Accountability for repression and war crimes were issues raised in the peace processes and resulted in a path-setting institution in South Africa (the Truth and Reconciliation Commission). In all three cases, public security concerns were high following the ending of the armed conflicts. El Salvador faced a test in 2009 when a leader of the former rebel movement (FMLN) who was not a commander, Mauricio Funes, was elected president and again in 2014 when another party member won the following election, with a slim majority.

Second, there were civil wars in societies which had had elections and appropriate institutions, but where one-party rule had been the dominant feature for a considerable period of time. To these cases belong, for instance, Nicaragua, Angola, Mozambique and Macedonia. As part of the peace initiatives, constitutions were amended to allow for multiparty politics. The agreements could build on existing structures, but also had to consider that these institutions were likely to be biased. The credibility of an open multiparty system was questioned. In the cases mentioned, the conflict was also strongly polarized into opposing camps. In Nicaragua, polarization has remained. The Sandinista leader Daniel Ortega, who lost elections in 1990, was elected President in 2006 and in 2011. In Mozambique, polarization from the war appeared to have been defused, only to resurface in fighting in 2013. The long-term ability of eliminating the war divides through democracy may be limited, but the likelihood of renewed violence might be reduced and measures in place to prevent escalation.

Third, there was a category of states where the agreements entailed more or less a complete reconstruction of state institutions, including the training of electoral staff, supervision of new institutions, etc. The peace agreements on Lebanon, Cambodia, Chad, the Democratic Republic of Congo, Liberia, Sierra Leone and Tajikistan had such elements. While the agenda for implementation of agreements, needless to say, becomes more extensive, the less there is for institutions to build on. For instance, the application of principles of accountability and war crimes has met difficulties.

It is probably correct to say that the countries in the first category, today, are functioning more democratically. Thus, it is less likely that there will be a return to the previous wars. Three examples (El Salvador, South Africa, Guatemala) are post-war societies which have found themselves engulfed by considerable violence, often criminal in character and with some roots in the civil war itself. Many social inequities that originally motivated the war linger and may give rise to new parties with new sharp demands. There are seeds of possible revolt, but along different lines than before. A settlement in Colombia would be an addition to this category, as it has a remarkably entrenched democratic system.

The second category includes some successes, but also a repeated failure (Angola). Nicaragua has seen several shifts in government; Mozambique has yet to experience such a test of the strength of its reformed institutions.

The most difficult processes can be expected in the third category. It is also a group of societies which will depend most on external support for success. Cambodia was the object of a largely successful UN peace operation in 1992–93 (Hampson 1996: 200–4), but low-scale wars and coup behaviour have been part of the experiences since then. In Haiti, the international commitment was high in the mid-1990s, then waned and the country relapsed into conflict in 2004. Not until the devastating earthquakes of January 2010 was there significant attention. This is to suggest that democratization following a civil war is more likely to succeed if there is a previous legal system building at least on some principles of rule of law. Also, sustained international support is likely to be required for countries such as Liberia and Sierra Leone. These countries were on roads of recovery; however, in 2014, they were challenged by the devastating Ebola epidemics.

The seven forms of conflict resolution help us to illustrate the process of change more closely. First, there is the gradual acceptance by the governments of, as it were, new principles for ruling society. This means that new priorities are made. The National Party in South Africa had to accommodate to a new situation. What mattered to the party was no longer to keep power for itself, but to maintain the social positions of the white minority. In the words of Zartman, the party had to make 'a trade-off of power for position'. Similar moves of accommodation had to be made by other parties. For the ANC, there was a choice between demanding a pact with power-sharing or taking full control by itself (Zartman 1995a: 149, 162), where the ANC, in the end preferred the former. The agreements were predicated on such shifts in position by the parties. This meant that one party agreed on the legality of other parties and, thus, opponents were able to enter into negotiations. It also implied that the view of the outcome changed. The possibility of losing power or not achieving complete state control was part of the understanding, thus making it important for a dominant actor to appreciate the need of safeguards for the losers.

For all the peace agreements, it is obvious that the negotiations leading to settlement involved considerable compromise, including locating middle points and horse-trading deals, that is, the second and third forms of transcending the incompatibility. This could, for instance, concern issues of the length of transition periods, timetables for demilitarization, changes in institutions with hostile mandates, introduction of human rights provisions, etc. In some cases, it also involved agreements on dividing cabinet posts according to particular preferences.

Most interesting is the use of the fourth and fifth forms for solving incompatibilities: power-sharing or leaving control to another actor. Obviously, rebel groups are suspicious of the government and fear its potential power in, for instance, manipulating upcoming elections. In some of the agreements, innovative arrangements were made. In the case of South Africa, a multiparty Transitional Executive Council was instituted to oversee the government's activities for a period of about five months, up to the elections held in April 1994. In the case of Cambodia, a Supreme National Council was created with representation from all four leading groups as well as a strong UN presence supervising five of the key ministries in the central government (Hampson 1996: 178–88). Thus, forms of power-sharing were instituted before the elections, and there were expectations of coalitions or national unity governments after the elections. Such inclusive arrangements may have contributed to the durability of these peace agreements. It is interesting that in some conflicts, the opposition did not demand a share in the government, but preferred to be able to participate securely in the political process. This was the position of the FMLN in El Salvador (not winning Presidential power until 2009). Instead, a National Commission for the Consolidation of Peace (in Spanish, COPAZ) was agreed (Hampson 1996: 140; Pérez de Cuéllar 1997: 419–20, 434). In the 1991 Angolan agreement, both sides expected to win the elections, and only a weak joint commission was instituted. The next agreement contained more cooperative arrangements, but without leading to a full implementation of the peace agreement (Ohlson 1998: 74–82). It took until 2008, six years after the war ended, for the government to arrange parliamentary elections.

In civil war agreements, there is little resort to formal conflict resolution mechanisms, apart from giving room for negotiations or referenda. This is understandable. Such mechanisms are often legal, and the legal institutions are often part of the dispute. Their roles have frequently been tarnished by the incumbent regime or its predecessors. There is considerable use of international mediation, however, and the involvement of the UN in the Nicaraguan settlement was a breakthrough for UN actions in internal conflicts. The supervision of Nicaragua's elections in February 1990 was the first time that the UN monitored elections in a sovereign state (Pérez de Cuéllar 1997: 405–16). It has, since then, become an important practice. It is remarkable, however, that there are few international institutions to turn to for settlement of internal conflicts.

Postponing issues, the seventh model, is also a frequent approach, in order to reach an agreement on other topics. In the case of El Salvador, the armed opposition coalition, the FMLN, agreed not to push the land reform issue at this stage (Cañas and Dada 1999; Hampson 1996: 141), although it had been a key demand for its entire political and military campaign. It was partly a matter of giving priority to reforms of the military institutions and gaining access to political institutions. The party remained free to return to the problems. The issue remains contentious in El Salvador. In the case of Cambodia, the incumbent government, known as SOC (State of Cambodia), gradually reduced its demands to insert words on 'genocide' in the concluding document. The question of possible trials on human rights grounds against leaders of the Khmer Rouge regime in Cambodia did not subside, however, and later a combined international and national court was set up, delivering its verdicts more than 35 years after the events.

These examples illustrate that the democratic framework is helpful in handling conflicts over power in society. It is also noteworthy that the transitions have been made possible by temporary power-sharing arrangements. These may well have contributed to introducing parties, previously excluded from decision-making, into the real financial, administrative and international constraints under which governments have to operate. Power-sharing has an educational effect. It is noteworthy that the agreements that have failed have not had such elements. In Angola, the first peace agreement was a 'winner-take-all' arrangement, whereas the second accord allowed for power-sharing. It was never implemented in full, mostly because of actions by UNITA, the armed opposition party (Ohlson 1998: 152). The use of power-sharing for democratization involves a conversion of views. It 'moves towards success when it shifts elections from being a mechanism to award victory denied on the battlefield to being the means to admit all parties to legitimate and ongoing participation in the future political system' (Zartman 1995a: 339). As a transition from civil war to civil peace, power-sharing may be a useful device, but if instituted for too long a period, it may have stifling effects.

What this overview shows is that the central provisions in peace agreements have dealt with procedural issues and government institutions. Particular ways of sharing power have been important. Underlying issues, such as land reform questions, poverty and other questions of economic and social justice, and economic policies, which many would deem as important, have seldom been solved through peace agreements. Human rights issues have not always been important. It seems that the opposing sides have had a similar belief that with access to government power, they will be able to deal with substantive matters according to their goals. The democratic systems that follow, however, do not only represent the voices of change, but also the voices of the status quo. The reverse is also true: democratic systems do not necessarily protect the status quo, but provide opportunities for social change. Either way, societies change, perhaps more slowly than many would expect, more quickly than others would want.

Decisive for the fate of the agreement are the priorities of the carriers of the peace, the parties that signed and committed themselves to its implementation. Their attention to the procedural aspects and the substantive matters will mix with the new realities following the ending of the war. These actors will have to make a choice among the many elements that any peace agreement entails. For instance, the peace agreement for Guatemala included 13 separate agreements. To implement them all, at the same time, is clearly impossible. Some matters get more attention and more support, others meet more resistance. Furthermore, the direction of society may turn out to be very different from what any of the warring parties had expected. The more open a society, the more will voices other than those of the warring parties make themselves heard. For instance, the issue of justice and human rights is one of the concerns that often gets more attention than the warring sides may prefer. Their primary interest is often with their own security under peacetime conditions.

6.4 Dealing with the Internal Security Dilemma

A major issue for the origin of civil wars, we have said, stems from the intra-state security dilemma. To the parties, this is a major concern. What will be their future following the end of the war and the accompanying demobilization of soldiers, closing of bases and other measures that are necessary for the reconstruction of peace and the formation of an integrated society? The parties that sign the agreements are likely to be highly suspicious of each other. They have good reasons. In their agitation, they have often emphasized that the other side is criminal, illegitimate, corrupt and/or untrustworthy. To negotiate, conclude agreements and, perhaps, even share power, with such an actor is a difficult transition. Thus, the conclusion by Ohlson in his analysis of the peace agreements in Southern Africa is to the point. Agreements are more likely not to fail if the 'physical and organizational security concerns of the primary parties are addressed to their satisfaction' (1998: 186). There are likely to be some security guarantees for the parties to sign the accords.

Such guarantees and reintegration among the parties might work better if leaders on both sides come from the same social class or share a normative system. This is not often the case. Many civil wars have revolutionary origins, meaning that they pit an established regime against an organization of previously marginalized persons and groups. For the regime, it means fighting people who come from unknown circumstances and are understood only to have ambitions to wrest their power. To make deals and even yield power is frightening and likely to encounter criticism in the regime's camp. For the opposition, the war means getting closer to power and a chance to change society. Not to win might be perceived as failure. If leaders have difficulties in adjusting to a compromise agreement, it is probably even more frustrating for the followers on the opposite sides. To them, it may appear that leaders are betraying the causes for which the lower echelons have risked their lives. For many, victory will be the only acceptable outcome. The leaders, in other words, have a major educational task in explaining their strategy and why a peace agreement will suffice. They may be aided by war fatigue, economic deterioration, death tolls and rampant destruction, which make the general public responsive to peace. The soldiers, officers and leaders, however, may not necessarily share the perspective of the public at large. The educational task, in other words, has to deal with the internal dynamics of an actor, rather than the general public.

The need to make the rank-and-file follow the leadership into a peace agreement adds strains to the negotiations. The settlement has to include sufficient security guarantees, as well as benefits, to make peace acceptable to the party's internal sceptics. The negotiations need not only to solve the problem with the opponent, they must also address the inner concerns of the party itself. This is where the outside world may have a particular role, as it can commit resources to smooth transitions.

Studying the peace agreements since the Cold War, we find that they attempt to manage the security dilemmas of the transition from war to peace with the help of five different measures. These are: (a) a general demilitarization and creation of a unified army; (b) specific guarantees for leaders; (c) international presence, for instance, peacekeeping forces; (d) transitory power-sharing; and (e) amnesty to leaders, officers and agents. These measures are used, whether the agreement is one of depriving a military regime of its power or giving power to a successful guerrilla movement. In the case of victory, these five measures are likely to be used in a one-sided manner. Demilitarization will be only for the opponents, privileges only for the winners, international presence only for legitimization of the new status quo, power-sharing only for those who cooperate and amnesty only for the supporters. In the peace agreements of Table 6.1, there are many examples of these five measures being used, but in a less biased manner. The five measures do not exclude one another. There is so far little evidence to suggest that some are more successful than others, or that certain combinations are more optimal. An exemplification will suffice.

Demilitarization deals directly with the ability of one side to threaten the security of the other. A rapid reduction in armed forces and firepower is necessary in order to reduce insecurity among the parties. In many peace negotiations, these are issues which are agreed at a late stage. This indicates that the more obvious 'political' elements are central and that the military force is there to back up the parties' position on these issues. By delaying the security issues, some leverage is kept on the other side. It means also that a cease-fire may be late in coming (as was the case in El Salvador). Alternatively, if there is an early cease-fire, the parties may retain the option of restarting the war (a more common approach). Either way, the timing suggests that the security issues are among the most difficult to deal with. For instance, demilitarization means removing troops from positions conquered in deadly battle, or giving up hard-earned and strategic weaponry. To some military leaders this may appear close to defeat, not victory or peace. Political gains must be considerable to convince the military side to make such concessions.

From an analytical point of view, demilitarization is almost a definitional necessity for ending a civil war. Without it, there will be the threat of a resumption of war. The military forces have to be part of a new setup. Particularly important in civil war endings is the idea of combining the fighting forces into one large, new unit. The definition of a state is the existence of *one* military force under one central command, the government. However, simply combining the two sides into one unit would create an unbearably large army. If integration is successful, this force might become an overwhelmingly powerful factor, potentially to be used against the new political order. It might even become threatening towards neighbours.[5] Demilitarization and the creation of a new army is a logical outcome of these concerns and of the peace process. It has the additional advantage of making it possible to screen the new military forces so as to include only officers willing to cooperate with the new conditions and integrate with the former opponents. Involvement in war crimes is another obvious criterion for exclusion.

However, the experiences from Southern Africa do not suggest that there has always been complete demobilization (Ohlson 1998: 181). Most important may well be the possibility of reducing the threat to the other side. The formation of a unified army may be a protracted process. In some agreements, such as the one in El Salvador, an important FMLN demand was the elimination of certain officers or certain units in the regular army (in El Salvador this was called 'purification'). Also in this case, three police services were disbanded and a new force created (Cañas and Dada 1999). This integration process proceeded surprisingly well. The more difficult problem has been what to do with the decommissioned officers and soldiers. When turning in their weapons they have sometimes been paid (which risks starting a local arms trade) or been given implements to start a new life (land, seeds and fertilizers, for instance, plus assistance in reintegrating into villages or towns of their origin). These approaches were used in Mozambique and El Salvador. Counter-reactions by decommissioned soldiers who have kept their weapons have become a problem in the aftermath of some peace agreements. The former soldiers have demanded jobs and payments or joined underground groups. It turns out, however, that this is a dilemma also in cases of victory. It is not only something facing a losing army, but also the victorious military force has to be reduced once the fighting is over. The problem of decommissioned soldiers reflects the availability of weapons, the breakdown in social fabric and the disturbed economy that any protracted war is likely to produce. Lately, donor attention has focused on these issues, termed DDR (disarmament, demobilization and reintegration of ex-combatants). Recent studies point to the importance of the networks among former combatants for their ability to become engaged in military action again (Themnér 2013). A particular aspect is the fate of former child soldiers.

Security guarantees for leaders are a particular problem, arising as an important factor in the peace agreements in Southern Africa (Ohlson 1998). The leaders entering the accords find themselves in exposed situations. Those who see the outcome as betrayal may turn against their leaders, who thus are vulnerable not only to revenge by their enemies, but also to assassination attempts by their (former) supporters. There are examples of leaders being killed during the peace process. This gives incentives for some leaders not to pursue demilitarization in full. There is a temptation to hide weapons or 'civilianize' units which, in practice, have para-military functions. A distinction between different types of weaponry probably would help sort out this problem. If larger, offensive and provocative weapons are banned and handed in, smaller and defensive ones might be allowed during a transition period, for a smaller unit geared to the protection of particularly controversial leaders. This, however, has to be a transitory phenomenon; otherwise, it becomes a privilege with a negative effect on popular acceptance of the agreement. Seen in this light, many of the peace agreements in civil wars have turned out to be more manageable than expected. They have seldom resulted in mass killings, contrary to some reports for earlier periods (Licklider 1995). The return of refugees is an indicator of this. There may be a larger problem in cases of clear-cut victories, where losers are in immediate physical danger and have little political future.

International military presence, in the form of a new generation of peacekeeping operations, can contribute both to demilitarization and leader security. The prime motive for peacekeeping, however, is a different one: to provide a measure of security to the process as such. It gives time for adjustment and for building confidence. The international presence leads to international attention which may assist in reducing the insecurities. Obviously, peacekeeping operations have more specific functions in the implementation of elements in the peace agreements, but that is a separate matter. In the peace agreements reported here, peacekeeping has typically been part of the transition from war to peace and then it has been withdrawn. This is logical, and also in line with the commitment that the international community makes. The goal is to return the primary parties to a 'normal' situation, where they have to work out their relations among themselves. Some agreements had no international troop presence at all (most obviously in South Africa).

There is a debate, however, as to the ability of the international peacekeepers to achieve their task. The mandates, for instance for UN troops, are often very limited and the priority is often to protect the security of the force itself, rather than the peace process it is there to guard and promote. The mandates are set by the UN Security Council and it may have other concerns in mind than a particular crisis, notably the well-being of the national forces that are committed to the international force. There have also been complaints about the quality of the military training of some troops. Much of the credibility of the international presence rests on the ability of the peacekeepers to act effectively and quickly. Also, they are there to indicate the possibilities for additional support from the international community, that is, to be a tripwire for further international support if necessary. In several instances since the end of the Cold War, this support has not been forthcoming. When challenged, the forces have instead been withdrawn. This was illustrated in Somalia in 1993, when the United States withdrew its force after 18 US Army Rangers had been killed, something which affected peacekeeping for the rest of the decade.

Most of the peace agreements contain some element of *power-sharing* or influence on the process, either before, during or after the implementation of the agreement. This aspect is primarily there to transcend some of the incompatibilities in the conflict, as we observed above. Power-sharing also contains a degree of physical protection for the leaders, as they are included in official institutions and, thus, are to be protected by them. In such capacities, the leaders will find ways of protecting their followers. This is, from a security perspective, preferable to the suggestions that leaders keep their own security force. Its usefulness hinges on the normalization of society after the war. There is a risk that one part of the government apparatus will become controlled by one of the former fighting parties. A change in the composition of the cabinet would then have security implications for certain actors, for instance. It could lead to resistance and state institutions would turn into resources in a potential renewal of the civil war. Such a scenario unfolded in the civil war in Lebanon from 1975 to 1989. Again, a repetition could be seen in Iraq. Following the US withdrawal in 2010, Sunnis became fearful of the Shiite-dominated government and associated militias that did not provide for their protection. Some allied with ISIS, the US demanded an inclusive government that was installed following elections in 2014. It remained to be seen if confidence in the central government could be recreated.

Finally, several agreements have wrestled with the issue of *amnesty*. Are those leaders, officers and soldiers who are responsible for atrocities during the war to be brought to trial or not? In civil wars which end as victories, the victor may use the legal system to prosecute the losers. This is a factor which may make losers reluctant to accept an agreement. The security dilemma in this legal form may be a powerful incentive for a leader to fight on. In the end, capitulation may include some form of amnesty as the loser's last demand. It means that there is a high likelihood that a peace agreement will include protective clauses, often for all sides. It makes it possible for the fighting parties to conclude an agreement. For instance, in the peace plan for Central America that Costa Rica's President Oscar Arias proposed in 1987, and which was essential for ending the wars in this region, amnesty was among the conditions given (Pérez de Cuéllar 1997: 402). This was immediately accepted at the time. It was complemented, however, with ideas of national dialogue and reconciliation.

Ten years later, the issue of amnesty in civil wars is more complicated. As was mentioned in Section 6.2, in the peace treaty for Sierra Leone of July 1999, some of the perpetrators of war crimes during the civil war were granted amnesty. It was a condition for them signing. But there was no longer international acceptance of this and the counter-reaction was overwhelming. The war crime tribunals for former Yugoslavia and Rwanda have made impunity less acceptable. The convention on an international permanent court on war crimes was concluded in Rome in 1998 and the court is now operational. For the fighting parties, amnesty may no longer be a convenient way out. Even if agreements are signed by the parties, international law may eventually overtake them. In 2005, key members of the Lord's Resistance Army in northern Uganda became the first to be indicted by the International Criminal Court (ICC). Previous negotiations have held out the chance of amnesty. As mediation did not end the war, the ICC issued its indictments, asking for international support in capturing the indicted. The conflict, however, continued unabated. At the same time there was evidence pointing to the durable effects of amnesty provisions (Melander 2009a; Wallensteen et al. 2012).

Since the end of the Cold War there have been a number of innovative ways of dealing with the issue of human rights in the conditions of war, severe conflict and military government. This has important implications for the prevention of renewed war. It affects the security concerns of the fighting parties, and points to the emergence of new norms which make impunity less acceptable. The creation of truth commissions is one of these. There is experience with such commissions from many different conflicts (Hayner 2011; International Center for Transitional Justice 2005). Most of these relate to conflicts over power in society, that is, civil wars and repressive governments. They are important elements in forging a society after a devastating experience. For the society to function, a process of healing and reconciliation is necessary. It runs counter to the demands of particular leaders. Interestingly, such commissions are rare in peace agreements for interstate wars as well as for state formation conflicts.

It is important to note that many peace agreements in civil wars have provisions for human rights commissions, investigations into brutalities and war crimes. Such provisions may appear as a threat to some leaders, but in particular it gives a role to the civil society that exists beyond the fighting parties. These are instruments that can be used. There are examples of governments making unilateral amnesty decisions, thus pre-empting later legal procedures. This difficult issue has led to innovative solutions. One of the most celebrated ones was actually a political compromise, the Truth and Reconciliation Commission in South Africa. It has been heralded as a new model. It does provide amnesty for those who agree to have their cases processed through the Commission. The Commission was only a temporary measure, which meant that the process started immediately, not waiting for the new political situation to consolidate. Other forms, such as the Commission for Truth in El Salvador, have a broader mandate, but have also led to political counter-measures, where some persons were protected from prosecution by the government. This was only the first in a series of measures that prevented the implementation of recommendations on justice (Cañas and Dada 1999; Hampson 1996: 157).

The international war crimes tribunals now give particular emphasis to this issue. It is applicable to all three forms of armed conflict with which we are dealing in this book. The longest functioning tribunal for a civil war is that on the genocide in Rwanda. It is based in Arusha, Tanzania. The present Rwandan government is simultaneously pursuing its own legal processes and a process of local reconciliation, the gacaca. For former leaders, there may be a preference to go to Arusha, as the international tribunal does not hand out capital punishment. The tribunal is restricted to the events of one year, 1994, which means that only one part of the Rwandan conflict dynamic is captured, basically the genocide of that year (Johnson 1999: 193). There was a civil war before this tragedy and there remains a complex regional situation with huge numbers of refugees outside the borders of Rwanda. The impact of the gacaca can be debated. Psychologically, it means a retraumatization that may impede reconciliation (Brounéus 2008). The most prudent solution is a generally applicable, permanent international court for war crimes, the ICC.

These are five ways, reflected in peace agreements, of mitigating the immediate internal security dilemma. Thus, it was possible to enter into the agreements. But the agenda was often broader than this. As the agreements are recent, it is difficult to draw long-term conclusions. The hope was to transcend the classical security dilemma. We cannot say what the societies will look like 10 or 20 years after the peace agreements. In some countries there has been a rise in public insecurity, with criminal violence more widespread than before (South Africa). There have also been political assassinations, often directed at former guerrillas (El Salvador) and against independent voices (Guatemala). This points to the dangerous period that follows an accord. It certainly is not the same as the war breaking out again, but it is also far from the peaceful conditions and expectations of development that sustained the peace processes.

A key question for the internal security dilemma in the long run is what happens to the armed services. The peace agreements expected that constitutional authority would grow by, for instance, enhancing the role of parliament. It would make the armed forces (police, military) subordinate to civilian authority. To restructure a military force would be necessary, but not easily done. A new armed force would need considerable training, find new ways for recruitment, implant a new understanding of the role of the armed forces in society and integrate human rights in the self-definition of these forces and in society as a whole. Such restructuring was initiated in El Salvador, Guatemala and South Africa. It means that the military forces are to be separated from police functions. The rule of civilian leadership is taught to new generations. It is made clear that army, air force and navy are to be used for external defence only. In the end, a professional army with a different ethos will be established. Part of this is, of course, that the armed forces are to operate professionally, and thus refuse to be involved in political projects of particular, unauthorized leaders. In Liberia and Sierra Leone there has been considerable international support for such efforts, entirely reconstructing the armed forces after the civil wars. In short, the propensity for military coups should be reduced. In fact, there have been few coups after the peace agreements listed in Table 6.1.

It is interesting to note that reforms of the military institutions could be part of an international preventive strategy. In development cooperation, security sector reform (SSR) has become a novel undertaking, unusual for foreign aid donors who have previously deliberately preferred to be civilian in their approach. By infusing professional values into the military establishments worldwide, the likelihood of military coups may gradually recede. Today it appears that such programmes are undertaken, notably in the Philippines (learning from a long experience of martial law) and in some of the newly independent states in Central and Eastern Europe (as part of a Westernization of the military forces). Such programmes may meet more resistance in countries where the armed forces are strongly entrenched, and may be seen by many as the guarantors of the existing order and the cohesion of the state (Indonesia, Thailand and Turkey).

The solutions to incompatibilities indicated in this section are those that the parties have agreed on in serious negotiations and where implementation is under way. Thus, they are measures deemed by the parties to be necessary for ending a war. The agreements may have been difficult to reach and that could be a good sign that they are taken seriously. This has also been understood as an indication of their willingness to implement what is agreed. This cannot, however, always be taken for granted. In reality, there is a difficult period from the conclusion of an accord to its full implementation. This period is crucial for the creation of goodwill among the parties. Thus, monitoring implementation is an important aspect of peacebuilding. Failure to pursue what is agreed was an element in the developments leading up to the Rwandan genocide in 1994. It also gave rise to the notion of spoiler and spoiler management (Prunier 1995; Stedman 1997, 1998). There are parties who see their interest threatened by a peace agreement, and who are willing to pursue their own agenda, even at very high cost.

6.5 State Failure, State Reconstruction and Non-State Terrorism

In extreme but not infrequent cases, civil wars have resulted in the collapse of state institutions. In such a case, the legal system has broken down, extortion and murder have taken place with impunity, normal operations in society have ceased to function (from garbage collection to tax collection). This is a case of state failure. As was observed in Section 6.3, peace agreements will then face entirely different challenges. Peacemaking will have to include state building or state reconstruction. Some such cases since the Cold War are Angola, Lebanon, Cambodia, Chad, Liberia, Sierra Leone, Tajikistan, the Democratic Republic of Congo and most recently Libya, Mali and the Central African Republic. There are also cases where no such reconstruction took place, Somalia being the most notable case, but others include Afghanistan and Burundi. Rwanda may suggest an alternative route to state recreation after war: the victory of one faction then creating its own state machinery.

If we depart from the political science definition of the state as the sole authoritative user of physical violence (see Section 4.2), it might be reasonable to conclude that a state which cannot keep order throughout its territory, for all practical purposes, is a failed or, more diplomatically, a fragile state.[6] Theoretically and practically, state failure, then, is separate from the phenomenon of civil war. It can take place without civil war, and there can be a civil war without a state failure. As we are concerned with situations after civil wars, state failure is one such possible outcome. It may not be the most frequent one, but one that is among the most difficult to repair. We have already concluded that if legal systems and institutions are intact, rehabilitation after war is more likely to succeed. This means that there is a special challenge to peacemaking if state institutions are no longer in place. Some lessons have been learned on the possibilities of recovery from state failure after civil war.

For a long time, Lebanon was seen as the archetype of a state failure. It is normally attributed to the onset of the civil war in 1975. In a rapid series of events, central state institutions ceased to function, the armed forces and the territory of the country were divided along the lines of the contestants. Prior to this, Lebanon had been held together through a delicate political balancing act. It was a permanent power-sharing arrangement. When this began to unravel, the constituent parts started to operate as separate actors. The integration was limited among the parties carrying the state. Add to this family ties, old alliances and enmities, ideological convictions and the involvement of actors with other agendas, for instance, Palestinian liberation organizations, Cold War intelligence agencies, Egypt, Syria, Israel, Iran, and the completeness of the fragmentation can be understood. What followed was a series of changing alliances, local power struggles, de facto self-ruling areas, and a proliferation of warlords. Lebanon became an arena for vicious bombings and for capturing, keeping and trading Western hostages. What was once a prosperous financial and entertainment centre turned into ruins. After 15 years of wars, a peace process gained momentum. The full extent of state failure can be understood from the fact that in the peace negotiations in Taif, Saudi Arabia, there were no representatives of the government as such. It was not a 'distinct actor' in the negotiations (Deeb and Deeb 1995: 126). Lebanon was recreated, through the passage of the peace treaty reforms in 1990. The state was again a functioning entity, but under heavy Syrian tutelage. After a decade, the state was once more performing basic internal functions. It had taken Lebanon 15 years to reach a peace from which recovery could be initiated. The regional setting was not conducive to recovery either: first, in getting Syria's troop out of the country; then conflicts with Israel over South Lebanon; third, a strong militarized actor in the country (Hezbollah); and, more recently, a protracted civil war in neighbouring Syria.

A slightly older case that has been seen as a success in recovery is Uganda. Its predicament rose from internal mismanagement. The regime of Idi Amin has to take the blame for the state's deteriorating conditions. Amin took power in a military coup in 1971, forced the entrepreneurial Asian population out of the country in the following year, and the country subsequently saw the economy sharply decline. He involved the country in a war with Tanzania (1978–79), only to find himself chased out of his own country by Tanzanian forces. The ensuing regime, under Milton Obote, did not improve matters. Inter-ethnic conflicts arose, and the state gradually lost all legitimacy. From this crisis emerged an entirely new leader and a new movement: Yoweri Museveni and his movement for reconstruction. In 1986 his troops conquered Kampala, the capital. An important element in his victory was the generous attitude of the victor. Museveni initiated a process of reintegrating opponents and competing movements into society. The first government was a broad-based coalition. With this there was political predictability. Economic recovery followed. The state failure lasted for about 15 years. The reconstruction has gone on for an equally long time. The situation improved, but remained fragile, particularly at election time. In 2006 Museveni was elected – in a debatable electoral campaign – for a third term as President and a fourth one in 2011. There is a reluctance to give up control. Democracy is still not entrenched.

This time frame for reconstruction in Uganda is parallel to the one of Lebanon. The political management used for recovery is also similar. It is a version of a power-sharing scheme to include many factions of the society. The two experiences indicate the need for at least one strong actor interested in recovery. It could be an external, neighbouring power (Syria), or a victorious movement not tainted by the previous rivalries (Museveni). However, at some time there has to be a role for the rest of society, and that transition is constantly delayed, not the least with references to events involving the region as a whole.

These lessons are applicable to other cases, but also suggest the difficulties. Afghanistan had a chance of recovery after a protracted war, but its disunited leadership failed to grasp it. The withdrawal of the Soviet troops by February 15, 1989 did not result in the fall of the Soviet-supported communist regime, as anticipated. The internationally supported Afghan coalition could not take power until 1992. The coalition, furthermore, remained divided. In 1996, a new force, the Taliban, supported by Pakistan, entered the scene and captured the capital, Kabul. Although it had, by 1999, taken control over most of the territory of Afghanistan, it was not internationally recognized. In 1999, UN sanctions were instituted on Afghanistan for its support of terrorism as the country had become a refuge for Osama bin Laden and his al-Qaida network, which was responsible for attacks on the American embassies in Dar-es-Salaam, Tanzania, and Nairobi, Kenya, in 1998. American air strikes were directed against Afghanistan in 1998, and then, of course, for the attacks on September 11, 2001. The Taliban leadership refused to hand over Osama bin Laden and his followers made the country a target for sanctions and war. The war resulted in the removal of the regime by the end of 2001, a broader government was installed, freer elections were carried out, but security rested on NATO, the USA and local warlords. After a few years, the Taliban managed to reassert itself, while the Western countries prepared to withdraw. The prospects of peace appeared bleak at the end of 2014.

The role of the international community is significant. It often looks for a movement of locals to take power and to whom it can extend its support. This is particularly true if these are local movements that have basic support in the society, and are not associated with the previous regime, the downfall of which led to the state failure. For the international actor this avoids direct interference, while still providing for a friendly government or at least reduced chaos. There have been many disappointments for such an international strategy over the years.

Civil wars resulting in state failure are clearly more difficult to handle through the usual mechanisms of conflict resolution. There have to be actors who are willing to break the cycle of violence. Too often it is likely that surrounding states will engage themselves in a particular civil war to pursue their own goals, and thus soon find themselves in new conflicts, rather than in solutions. However, non-interference may not be an option either. Thus, the focus is turned to new groups, emerging from the local society, that can provide a chance for a break in the reproduction of conflict dynamics. We also can see that a recovery will not be possible unless the new social forces are able to include and incorporate elements of the old system. There is an intricate balance that has to be made between being revolutionary and maintaining continuity.

Not only neighbouring states but also non-state actors have taken advantage of the turmoil that is created by state fragility. This has been typical for the way organized crime has acted historically. In the post-Cold War period also, non-state actors using terrorist tactics have seen this possibility. Al-Qaida found its base in Afghanistan and later in Pakistan. The protracted civil war in Iraq has provided conditions that are close to state failure and, thus, further new terrorist acts. This confirms the thesis that the breakdown in the state machinery may provide opportunities for rebellious groups using terror tactics. In the examples given, this has had unsettling conditions beyond the state.

There is still no global consensus on a definition of terrorism, but the one provided by the High-Level Panel on UN reform may suffice: 'any action … that is intended to cause death or serious bodily harm to civilians or non-combatants, when the purpose of such act … is to intimidate a population, or compel a Government or an international organization to do or to abstain from doing any act' (High-Level Panel 2004: para. 164). An objection to this definition has been whether it applies under occupation and, thus, possibly, defines some forms of resistance as terrorism. Still, there is consensus on the illegality of targeting civilians or non-combatants in most circumstances. The suggested definition would apply equally to actions by states and non-state actors.

Let us conclude that civil war may result in state failure, which at the same time requires sustained efforts for recovery and can generate conditions for new armed conflicts and terrorism that will have an effect beyond the borders of that state. In other words, the peaceful solution to civil war is an international interest. This has gradually been understood since 1989, and increasingly so since 2001. The options may still be narrow, and so is often the understanding of the conditions under which peace can be constructed.

6.6 Civil Society in Internal Conflict Resolution

The endings of civil wars, military regimes and state failures have some common traits. They all require the reconstruction of societies on principles which are inclusive, provide some broader participation in state affairs, and offer a sense of security to leaders and citizens alike. The political arrangements are necessary also for solving the problem of refugees that all civil wars, military repression and state failures produce. They lay a foundation for economic recovery. They can be used to provide the rise of a new kleptocracy. From the point of view of future conflicts, most important is the opening they may provide for an active civil society.

Many peace agreements have clauses stipulating the unimpeded return of refugees. There is a record of people moving back to their countries and areas. Also, in cases of victory, refugees begin to re-enter their country of origin. However, the outcome of the war may make it difficult for many to return. They may fear for their own safety, or they may be blocked from returning by groups who believe their return would hamper a particular cause.

In the Cambodian conflict, refugees were stranded on the borders of Thailand for more than a decade. Only with the peace agreement in Paris in 1991 and with international assistance was it possible for them to return. On their return they became part of the new political system, not only with the right to vote, but also to organize themselves as pressure groups. In the aftermath of the genocide in Rwanda in 1994, the Tutsi army took control of the country. Fearing revenge, huge numbers of Hutus fled across the borders to Zaire (now the Democratic Republic of Congo) and Tanzania. Particularly in Zaire, they ended up in camps controlled by Hutu militias. When a war erupted in eastern Zaire, these militias withdrew further west. Refugees, freed from militia control, could return in large numbers to Rwanda 30 months after they left. The fears of revenge were less than the plight of the camps. Reports show that they rapidly reintegrated into society and the economy. Their role in the political life was minimal, however (Sollenberg and van Dassen 1998). Thus, the two examples illustrate the different positions of refugees. In the first example, the peace agreement allowed for their return as well as for an open political system. Measures were instituted to ensure this and they were integrated into the society, although they had been outside the country for a considerable period of time. In the second case, there was no peace deal, only a victory by one of the parties. The refugees could return, but on the conditions set by the victors. To return was still preferable for most.

The issue of the return of refugees is important, as this signifies, more than many other actions, that the extreme conditions that gave rise to their flight have been remedied to some extent. As most of the cross-border refugees in the world stem from conflict situations, peace is also important for handling the world's refugee problem. Stipulations in peace agreements or the conditions offered by victorious parties are important, and deserve closer scrutiny. As the civil wars end with a reconstruction of the same political unit, the return of the refugees needs to be as unrestricted as possible. This separates the refugee situation in civil wars from those in state formation wars (which are dealt with in Chapter 7), where the purpose often is to remove some people from a particular area in favour of others. Unlike civil wars, when refugees are regarded as legitimate citizens of the society, state formation conflicts sometimes distinguish between those with a right to the territory and those who will not be given such a right.

The conditions created by peace agreements are also significant for economic recovery. Without the predictability that peace accords and democratization provide, large-scale investments are not likely to come. It will instead risk making societies dependent on international assistance. The agreements since the Cold War are still too recent for making observations on their ability to actually change the economic conditions. The experience from democratization in South America in the 1980s suggests that economic development became positive. These experiences also point in the direction of the significance of a more participatory democratic society, for the stability of the society. An active civil society, that is, the existence of numerous independent (non-governmental), civilian-based organizations non-violently and freely pursuing civilian values on issues of societal significance, is important for sustaining democratic society (Putnam has termed this 'social capital', 1993). Thus, voluntary organizations, professional associations, student movements, trade unions, religious groupings, clans, tribes, women's movements, environmental groups, etc., would be part of such an independent civil society. It can be debated whether political parties, military-based associations, exclusivist groupings and sects are to be included as part of 'civil' society. In sum, it may all be important for democratic life, and it is definitely a part of the picture of what makes established democracies vibrant. Civil society in this form has been instrumental in bringing down autocratic regimes, as witnessed in repeatedly in Thailand since 1992, in Indonesia in 1998, in the Philippines and Yugoslavia in 2000, in Georgia in 2003, in Ukraine in 2004 and 2013–14, Pakistan in 2008, Tunisia and Egypt in 2011 and in the opening of the military regime in Burma/Myanmar since 2012.

This is to suggest that a strong civil society can be a barrier to military control. It probably assumes that the civil state is seen, by the civil society, as a protector of civil values. It has been remarked that there was no public support for the government in the wake of the military takeover in Pakistan in October 1999. There were no celebrations of the coup either. The indifference of the population was remarkable. The ten-year experience of democratic rule in Pakistan did not seem to entrench institutions and did not result in general support for them. Instead, it appears that these institutions were identified with the political parties of the day and thus were part of a societal polarization. The disputes between leading civilian politicians were detached from the needs of the population. They were perceived as ways for leaders to gain access to governmental resources. The democratic system generated kleptocracy, not popular participation. In 2008, the military government met the same critique and was brought down, being replaced by a democratic regime that soon was exposed to the same concerns. Legitimate democracy requires social forces to improve honesty and accountability.

The implementation of peace agreements gives a special role to civil society. As we saw in Section 6.3, human rights provisions have been important ingredients in the peace accords since 1989. Their implementation directly depends on the existence of a civil society. Governments may institute investigatory commissions and ombudsmen. However, it has to be the civil society that takes up violations and brings them to the attention of the institutions. For this to happen, the environment must be sufficiently secure. The stronger the civil society, the more such security is created. The government may, by its actions, reduce security and thus act to curtail the civil society. In the implementation period after a peace agreement, there may often be a preference for not taking up human rights issues. The consolidation of the peace is given priority. This attitude is strengthened if some of the chief culprits escape from responsibility by the granting of amnesty or pardon. As we have seen, this has been part of some agreements.

However, few peace agreements prohibit the publication of material on what has happened. Human rights commissions often have the mandate of describing violations that have taken place. Such documentations are crucial, as are their publication and dissemination. As peace is consolidated, there may emerge various ways in which court cases can be pursued. The arrest of the former Chilean dictator General Augusto Pinochet in London in 1998, as a court in Spain demanded his extradition, is suggestive. There may be ways in which cases can be brought without jeopardizing the particular peace agreement. The international arena provides such a possibility. Also, after the consolidation of peace, peace agreements may be reworked or made obsolete. As observed, with the international criminal court, it provides the possibility of trials outside the country, making it possible to manage peace and justice at the same time. It is more likely that a civil society will pursue matters of justice. Governments may find excuses and other interests may impinge on their ability to act. There is, however, also a point in holding such trials inside the state where crimes have been committed. It can make the proceedings more accessible and credible to the local community. Since 1989, the options for war crime prosecution have been dramatically enlarged.

The international connections are increasingly important. The civil society of one country is often linked to those of other countries. The emerging international civil society provides new ways in which peace agreements, civilian control and state institutions can be sustained. First, it provides a network for early warning, if matters threaten to go in the wrong direction. The possibilities of instant communication mean that information can be transferred quickly. Thus, it may be difficult for actors to say that they 'did not know'. Second, it provides opportunities for quick action. There may be official visits which can be affected or used to raise particular civil concerns. There may be contracts which are about to be signed, and which can be blocked or postponed. Thus, it might be difficult for decision-makers to say that there 'was nothing that could be done'. International diplomatic conferences and meetings, to which issues can be brought, are constantly being held. These are only some examples of how the international civil society is increasingly able to affect the internal affairs of countries, in a direction that is favourable to peace, civilian control and functioning state institutions.

Recent experiences demonstrate the impact of the Internet and social media on the flow of information as well as the ability to mobilize a population. Together with strong local organizations, this gives civil society a possibility of effecting change that opens up society and at the same time may improve the quality of peacemaking. A defender of the 1999 coup in Pakistan asked: 'Is democracy an end in itself or a means to an end? What do you do when democracy leads ineluctably to chaos?' (quoted by Safire 1999). The answer is that democracy is a way in which a society can be governed so that all competing interests are given a chance. It is not an end in itself, but a way in which inevitably arising conflicts can be steered in constructive directions. For many parties, it took a protracted war, a long period of military rule or the experience of state failure to realize this.

Further Readings

Go to the *Understanding Conflict Resolution* web page at https://study.sagepub.com/wallensteen4e for free access to journal articles listed.

Recurrence of Civil War

There is an increasingly complex literature on the issue of recurrence of civil war. A good overview of the literature and the discussions is provided in:

Newman, E. and DeRouen, Jr., K. (eds) 2014. *Routledge Handbook of Civil Wars*. New York and Abingdon: Routledge.

For an interesting way to investigate the dynamics of recurrence consult Walter, B.F. 2004. 'Does Conflict Beget Conflict? Explaining Recurring Civil War', *Journal of Peace Research*, 41 (3): 371–88.

Peace in Civil War

The literature on the possibilities of peace after civil wars is more limited. Insightful ideas can be learned from particular cases, whether failed or successful. One is the Iraq experience of the 2000s. A good starting point is the following article:
Diamond, L. J. 2005. 'Lessons from Iraq', *Journal of Democracy*, 16 (1): 9–23.

For more general understandings of peace agreements and their implementation, the presentation of the Peace Accords Matrix is a valuable tool. It is introduced in Joshi, M. and Darby, J. 2013. 'Introducing the Peace Accords Matrix (PAM): A Database of Comprehensive Peace Agreements and Their Implementation, 1989–2007', *Peacebuilding*, 1 (2): 256–74.

Notes

1   A note on the term 'civil war': in the United States, it is a common label for the war of 1861–65. However, that was not directly a war about control over the central government. Instead, it was a conflict over state formation, where the right to secede was central. In some parts of the USA, it is still referred to as the 'War between the States'.

2   Licklider reports seven conflicts that ended too close to the cut-off date, of which four were terminated through negotiations. Adding them would make 18 negotiated endings out of 91 civil wars, that is, close to 20 per cent (Licklider 1995: 684). This confirms that peaceful endings are more common since the end of the Cold War.

3   For instance, there were smooth dynastic transitions in Jordan and Morocco in 1999. In effect, this is also what happened in Syria in 2000. The regime changes in Iraq in 2003, Tunisia and Egypt in 2011 are different stories.

4   The Peace Accords Matrix at the Kroc Institute, University of Michigan, is a new development that will help bring the analysis of implementation forward, see Joshi and Darby (2013).

5   There are no examples of such threats to neighbours arising from peace agreements, however. In the cases of victories, there is evidence of such fear in neighbouring countries (meaning an interstate security dilemma is created as an result of an intra-state victory). In the 1990s this happened, for instance, in the case of Ethiopia and Eritrea, and following the victory of Kabila's forces in Zaire in 1997, which affected civil wars in Congo-Brazzaville and Angola.

6   This is the definition given by Snow (1996: 100): 'The failed states are those in which governance has broken down and virtual anarchy … has persisted across time.'

7

CONFLICT RESOLUTION IN STATE FORMATION CONFLICTS

7.1 State Formation Conflicts

State formation conflicts put a government against an identity-based, territorially focused opposition, where the key issue is the security of a particular group. Often such conflicts are tied to a geographical region of an existing state, but they may also involve questions of discrimination in the society at large. These conflicts are linked to some form of nationalism, and thus relate to European history of the nineteenth century, when nationalist ideologies were first presented. During the 1920s and the 1930s, the League of Nations sought to find strategies for handling nationalistically defined conflicts. The formulation of the principle of national self-determination by US President Woodrow Wilson during the First World War was one such measure favouring nationalist aspirations. At the same time, there was a need to consolidate newly created states and avoid further fragmentation. Territorial integrity of existing states was the counter-principle. The tension between these two concepts coloured much of the twentieth century.

Nazi Germany included a racial project of uniting all Germans into one state, thus breaking up other states. It also wanted to develop hegemony based on German power and lineage. It resulted in the Second World War, the largest war ever fought on the planet. It also led to the Holocaust, primarily aimed at the Jews, wherever they were. This was the largest, most systematic killing of innocent people in history. The suffering and destruction were enormous. The lessons still have to be learned.

One conclusion was to make issues of ethnic homogeneity contentious. Exclusive nationalism was discredited. When international relations were reconstructed after the Second World War, it could be seen, for instance in the UN

Charter, that territorial integrity was given a stronger role than self-determination. Expansionist intervention for nationalist reasons was not to be allowed and, thus, fewer state formation conflicts were to be expected. At the same time, democracy and human rights were given a stronger position in international relations, manifested, for instance, in the Universal Declaration of Human Rights in 1948. It was meant to counter authoritarian regimes, but some nationalist aspirations had a popular following. Let us review the record of state formation conflicts during the Cold War, then proceed to the present era.

State Formation Conflicts during the Cold War

For four decades, from 1948 to 1989, the territorial dividing lines that were in place after the Second World War remained unchanged. The last changes seemed to be the internationally agreed or accepted divisions of India and Palestine into two states, both decided on in 1947. Following this, no new states which required the adjustment of borders were recognized. The demands for border revisions for national self-determination reasons that had plagued Europe and East Asia in the period between the world wars were no longer common, and certainly not legitimate. Still, a number of new states became independent. This took place through the agreed process of decolonization. It was a dramatic change in international relations, most clearly indicated in the change in membership of the United Nations. It went from around 50 members during its first years of existence to 170 as the Cold War ended. It was done almost entirely without border changes. A key aspect was that independence was granted within the borders drawn by the colonial powers. Even the creation of Bangladesh from Pakistan in 1971 took place within the lines of 1947. A remarkable stability was maintained at the same time as it allowed for change. This requires a closer analysis.

The arguments for maintaining territorial integrity and political sovereignty of the existing states, as written into the UN Charter, Article 2.4, were supported by an unusual international consensus on the preservation of existing territorial units. It was a result of the lessons drawn from the actions of Nazi Germany, Fascist Italy and militaristic Japan. All major powers had been victims of actions of one or several of these states. Furthermore, none of the five permanent members of the Security Council saw a benefit in supporting separatist movements in other countries. It could only complicate matters or even hit back at the major powers themselves.

The strongest supporter of non-interference and territorial integrity was the Soviet Union. It was also the country that had made the largest territorial gains as a result of the Second World War. This included the annexation of the Baltic states, the incorporation of territory which formerly was part of Eastern Poland and Germany, and taking over Bessarabia from Romania. The return of Soviet control often met severe resistance, notably in the Ukraine and Lithuania. The Soviet Union became a strong defender of a territorial status quo. Soviet concern led to constant actions to secure borders and political influence in Europe. The anti-colonial movements provided a potential dilemma and challenge as they argued in terms of self-determination. At the same time, these movements were anti-Western and anti-capitalist, thus being potential allies of the Soviet side in the Cold War. It made it necessary for the Soviet Union to support this principle. Soviet support for it, however, applied only to colonial situations. A distinction had to be introduced between state formation conflicts in Europe, which were not to be allowed, and those in other parts of the world. Other major powers were also interested in such a distinction.

The consensus among the major powers was to describe anti-colonial conflicts as a particular category of conflict. The goal in the decolonization process was the creation of new states from the territories legally and militarily held by colonial powers. Thus, the issue was control over territory within what was, formally speaking, one state. Some colonial territories were highly integrated into the colonial 'motherland', even with representation in the National Assembly. This was true for Algeria and other French possessions in Africa, and it was the way the United Kingdom regarded Ireland, India and the dominions, for instance. Mostly, however, the legal status of colonial possessions made clear their subordinate position. The degree of integration was not comparable to those of territories closer to the centres. It was not too difficult to distinguish between what was a significant 'colony' and what was not. It also made it possible to distinguish between countries that did not have colonies and those that did. The United States and the Soviet Union put themselves in the first category; a host of European larger or smaller states were in the other. The USA actually could define itself as the first country to rebel against European colonialism; the Soviet Union argued that it was the first to break out of European capitalism through its Socialist revolution in 1917. Either way, the two dominant states of the time supported the decolonization process.

Decolonization conflicts constituted a sizable fraction of all conflicts during the Cold War period. They were located in the Middle East, South and Southeast Asia in the 1940s and 1950s, in North Africa in the 1950s, in sub-Saharan Africa in the 1960s and 1970s, in Pacific and Caribbean waters in the 1970s and 1980s. The momentum was strong and rolled irresistibly across the southern continents. There was also an important element of solidarity between the anti-colonial movements. With increasing success in achieving independence, they turned into a distinct and united force in international affairs. This was the origin of the Third World, a group which was independent and not aligned to either side in the Cold War. In particular, it became a strong coalition in international organizations building on the one-state-one-vote principle. Thus, decolonization profoundly changed international affairs.

It is important to observe that the nationalist movements for decolonization were often heterogeneous coalitions of ethnic groups, educated urban dwellers and visionary intellectuals. The focus was not on the rights of one particular ethnic group, but on the collectivity, united in a struggle against a dominant, mostly distant, white colonial power. Self-determination was a matter of removing one form of control, more than taking control by a particular, determined ethnic group that expected to replace colonial domination with its own power. The liberation movements that pursued anti-colonial struggles were fronts and coalitions. They built on an ability to unite different interests into one cause. Thus, this form of nationalism was different from the exclusive and chauvinistic version seen in the 1920s and 1930s. Furthermore, once the cause was achieved, the fronts often turned into one-party systems building state legitimacy on the anti-colonial struggle. In matters of territorial change, they became highly conservative adherents to the principle of territorial integrity of the state. Thus, they did not challenge the established territorial consensus, but instead joined it (Kacowicz 1994: 67). One of the few states that pursued a traditional nationalist agenda was Somalia, aiming at the creation of one state for all Somalis. The merger between the former Italian and British possessions was achieved in 1960, but the continuation of the programme involved the country in war with Ethiopia and conflict with Kenya, for instance.

The decolonization era was seen as finished after the southern continents had been liberated from colonial domination. This verdict, of course, depends on the definition of colonialism. The one used to separate 'colonialism' from traditional occupation, annexation and conquest contains several elements. The distinguishing feature is that a metropolis exerts control over a territory populated by people of a different ethnic background, located at a considerable distance and geographically separated from the metropolis. Some settlement of the centre's population in the colony may also have taken place, creating an interest of a settler community. The most obvious differentiation between colonialism and traditional conquest, it has been said, is the saltwater between the metropolis and the periphery. With this definition, the colonization by Western and Southern European powers of the Americas, Africa, the Middle East and Asia, is a distinct phenomenon. Furthermore, it arose at a particular historical moment, often associated with victorious capitalism. These elements distinguish colonialism from traditional military conquest of a neighbouring territory. However, only with such a definition is decolonization a finished process. If another form of colonization, such as traditional conquest, is included, it is not. Also, if other elements are included, such as economic dependence, colonialism and neocolonialism, it is still an important feature. Furthermore, the notion of self-determination was always wider than only colonial situations. In the 1920s, it was applied to adjacent territories in Central Europe. Thus, the colonial era may not have been finished as easily as is often argued.

There are, in fact, a number of definitional questions that make this a matter of general interest. For instance, was the issue of British control over Ireland to be seen as colonialism or traditional conquest? It certainly took place before the phenomenon of colonialism was defined, but the different elements in the definition would apply, including colonial-type settlements. The Irish revolt and the creation of the Republic of Ireland preceded the international movement of decolonization, and was seldom seen to be part of it, but in essence aimed at the same goal.

Another case is the Soviet annexation of the three independent Baltic countries in 1940. The centre of Moscow was distant, control was ethnically separate and there were deliberate settlements of Russians in the areas. There was no saltwater between the metropolis and these areas, but would that change many of the consequences? Certainly, the Soviet Union voted in favour of the famous decolonization resolution in the Fifteenth UN General Assembly in 1960 (Resolution 1514) in the belief that it did not apply to its own situation. It could argue that the annexation had taken place after colonialism, was done under a banner of socialism and that the Baltic states became 'sovereign' units within one functioning union. During the Cold War, the charge of colonialism against the Soviet Union seldom received significant support.

A similar challenge could be made to the United States where, for instance, Hawaii and Alaska became states with equal rights only the year before the UN resolution was passed. The two territories were defined not as colonial possessions, but as integral parts of the United States of America. They had freely entered into this association. Certainly, their accession to the union was done democratically. But in that case, it meant that democratic procedures could have more weight than decolonization. Actually, the second UN General Assembly resolution on this issue (Resolution 1541) did suggest types of decolonization other than independence. During the Cold War, however, independence was seen as basic decolonization and the experiences of Hawaii and Alaska were seldom part of the debate. It was, of course, feared that such arguments could be used by settler communities to block decolonization.

Challenges to the definition of colonialism are many and not only theoretical. The discussion may seem obsolete today, but some conflicts have their roots in how decolonization was handled also among the newly independent countries in the Third World. An early challenge was posed by Biafra, in the southeastern part of Nigeria, dominated by the Igbo community. It declared independence in 1967, following massacres of ethnic kin in other parts of Nigeria. It led to one of the most destructive wars in Africa. Some African states recognized Biafra on humanitarian grounds (for instance, Tanzania). Others feared that their own states could meet similar threats and supported the central government. Biafra was defeated in 1970. In the same year, East Pakistani leaders objected to the control of the country from the distant centres of West Pakistan. Military repression followed, a war resulted, India intervened and by 1971 Bangladesh was created as a new state. West Pakistan acquiesced. After this, international recognition followed. This outcome said that if the metropolis accepts independence, so will the international community.

In the Helsinki Final Act of 1975, signed by all states directly party to or neutral in the Cold War, only peacefully agreed changes of territory in Europe were accepted. The story of East Pakistan was not to repeat itself in Europe, or anywhere else. This was strongly encountered by the Eritrean liberation movements which demanded independence from Ethiopia. They argued that their country was also a victim of colonialism, first under Italian rule, then under Ethiopia. This was accepted neither by other African states nor by the larger international community of the time. The established view of colonialism made that clear. To other states, such wars threatened to invite fragmentation and weakened state authority. They were dangerous precedents. The consensus on the abolition of 'saltwater colonialism' did not extend to questioning established borders. Eritrea did not gain its independence until after the Cold War.

State Formation Conflicts after the Cold War

State formation conflicts after the Cold War have some features in common with those witnessed in the earlier era. They are often seen as justified anti-colonial and/ or historical struggles for self-determination (the rebel perspective) or fights to preserve territorial integrity of a state for the benefit of all inhabitants (the government's view). However, they have less simple solutions. The cutting of a formal link across distant waters is no longer an available option. The centres in today's states are not easily allowing dissolution of their territories, as the colonial metropolises were willing and able to do after the Second World War. One reason is that the territorial cutting points are difficult to locate and that people are interspersed throughout the entire territory. Sometimes these are recent and deliberately created settler communities, such as the Jewish settlers in the West Bank (and until 2005 also in Gaza); sometimes they go further back in history, as has been the case with Serbs in different parts of former Yugoslavia. Still, the number of new states has continued to grow. In 25 years, the UN membership increased to 193 (by 2014), that is adding more than 20 states since 1989. It is a rate of state creation that is comparable to the Cold War era. A new aspect is that new states are mostly found in Europe. This is the continent which already had the highest incidence of states in relation to its territory. The opposite effect of state formation, (re)unification of states, has also taken place (Germany, Yemen), but the net effect is still an increase in the number of states. In addition, there are today (2014) about a dozen unrecognized de facto states (such as Northern Cyprus, Somaliland, Abkhazia and South Ossetia) as well as Taiwan, Western Sahara, Palestine and Kosovo, to which a larger number of countries have extended diplomatic recognition.

Still these trends in state formation have been remarkably peaceful. Three-quarters of the new, recognized states were created without a major war, as was also true for the decolonization process. Neither the ending of the Soviet Union nor Czechoslovakia required a major armed conflict. This, of course, was not the experience of the dissolution of socialist Yugoslavia. It is interesting to ask why the processes were so different.

The main reason can be found in the attitude of the centre of the state being dissolved. When Boris Yeltsin took over leadership in August 1991, it was on a platform of Russian independence from the Soviet Union. The centre, in other words, was in favour of dismantling its own empire.

In Yeltsin's view, the Soviet state had deliberately discriminated against Russia in order to have the cooperation of the other republics. It was claimed that Soviet authorities had invested more in the non-Russian areas. Russia's independence would be beneficial to Russia itself. Thus, there was no reason for Russia to object. Russian populations outside Russia would be in less danger if the demands for self-determination were met. In fact, Russia had an interest in speeding up the process. By the end of 1991, the Soviet Union ceased to exist. In a similar way, the largely Czech leadership of Czechoslovakia did not object to Slovakia leaving the shared federation, and a peaceful separation was in effect from 1993. Although there were no water divides, the break-up could follow what used to be internal administrative lines.

In Yugoslavia, the story was different. The Serb leadership objected to the dissolution of the state and acted militarily to prevent it. It feared the consequences for a dispersed Serb population, but it was also a matter of self-interest. Following the demise of Soviet-style socialism, the regime built on exclusive nationalism to keep itself in power. The resulting inability to find an agreed formula for dissolution involved the area in four armed conflicts in less than ten years (in Slovenia in 1991, in Croatia in 1991–92 and 1995, in Bosnia-Herzegovina in 1992–95 and in Kosovo in 1998–99). The consequences of the wars for the Serb population were uniformly disastrous. The results were the creation of new states, a separated region turning into a state (Kosovo), a reconfiguration of the state into a federation between Serbia and Montenegro, and eventually also its dissolution (in 2006). The borderlines sometimes could follow previous administrative divides and sometimes (as in Bosnia) were new creations. Major population movements resulted, and the chances for people to return to their homes were low, affecting also the Serb populations.

The conclusion from these experiences is that a leadership that favours or accepts the dissolution of a state can accomplish a peaceful transfer of authority. It requires that it sees this to be in its own interest. Often, however, the self-interest is different. Thus, a leadership that is against such a policy, while meeting an equally determined opposition, is likely to face a protracted conflict. Both government and opposition should have an interest in finding better solutions.

The post-Cold War period shows that there have been more than 70 armed state formation conflicts. These have put an incumbent government against a regionally based, armed opposition demanding a radically different status for a particular territory. The demands concern autonomy, federalism, independence or joining a neighbouring state. Often they followed a weakening of state authority, with groups demanding further autonomy (Chechen groups in Russia) or a return to centralization (the Sunni-based rebellions in post-Saddam Hussein Iraq were initially demanding a stronger centre, while Kurdish groups and many Shia Arabs wanted more power to the constituent parts. With Shiite control over the centre, these patterns are now reversed). The armed phase of some of these conflicts predate the end of the Cold War. This is the case, for instance, for Northern Ireland, the Basque provinces, the Kurdish disputes and the Palestinian conflict. The same can be said of conflicts over Namibia in Southern Africa, and several of the conflicts in India, Sri Lanka and Burma. Also in Southeast Asia there are protracted conflicts, such as those over Mindanao (the Philippines) and East Timor (Indonesia). The examples show that most regions of the world have some experience of state formation conflicts. They also indicate that the conflicts may become protracted. The ferocity of some conflicts has been extraordinary. This type of conflict war has long been regarded as marginal, part of an earlier era, and thus not important. They did not fit the established paradigm of state formation conflicts. They had some features which made them different from anti-colonialism.

The actors appeared to be driven by sentiments of self-determination and anti-colonialism that were sharper than in many decolonization struggles during the Cold War. In particular, the close connection between political demands and certain ethnic identities was striking. The new political fronts and constellations were pursuing the causes for one ethnic group within a nationalist umbrella, rather than cutting across many identities in a multi-ethnic nationalist formation. They played on sentiments that were largely avoided in the anti-colonial struggles. It appeared that the new conflicts were neither new in terms of history, nor accepted the conclusions on the dangers of nationalist war that had governed Cold War thinking. The notion of 'ethnic conflict' came to be associated with this type of conflict. This notion, furthermore, became synonymous with separatism and the quest for ethnically homogeneous states. All this appeared to throw the world back to the pre-1939 era.

It is necessary to reiterate that most of the new state formation conflicts were located in Europe. It strongly affected a European self-understanding of having successfully left a dark time of chauvinist nationalism. Europe was not prepared to deal with this new reality. Africa, which often is understood as a continent of ethnic conflict, actually had fewer such conflicts.[1] In Africa, opponents seldom directly challenged established state units. Differences in regional, historical or cultural identities resulted in struggles over government rather than in the break-up of states. The same was true of the Middle East, where the Kurdish strive for independence was the only one following historically and linguistically determined lines. The Palestinian situation is, for instance, not a quest for the break-up of an existing Arab state, but has features of an anti-colonial struggle. Thus, it is possible for Arab countries to support the Palestinian cause for self-determination and statehood at the same time as they oppose Kurdish desires for such goals.

The state formation conflicts of the post-Cold War era often involved neighbour states. This was novel, as states previously avoided entangling themselves, at least openly, in state formation conflicts in neighbouring countries. There used to be little official sympathy for separatist movements. In the post-Cold War period, such inhibitions have declined and neighbours have been heavily engaged in what goes on beyond their borders. Furthermore, in the Cold War era, there was a measure of solidarity across regions and even continents, between different liberation movements. The anti-colonial ambition united them. In the present epoch, this is not the case. Each struggle is separate from others. Each nationalist struggle sees itself as, in principle, unique and only a few generalizations are made, for instance, if the same ethnic group is involved in several different struggles, or if the opponent is the same. The search for international allies builds on allegiances that can be exploited, rather than on a sentiment of being part of the same global cause. In addition, the major powers normally stayed out of nationalist or 'ethnic' conflicts. This makes the events around Ukraine 2013–14 remarkable. Russia's President Putin began to talk about the plight of Russians outside the country and also acted accordingly, when taking control over Crimea in March 2014, ultimately annexing the area into the Russian Federation. This way of acting broke a Russian (and Soviet) policy since the end of the Second World War.

The state formation conflicts confronting the international community after the Cold War have some features which are different from the colonial experience. This has had an impact on their solution. Decolonization struggles ended in the withdrawal of the metropolis. This ending has not been available in conflicts without obvious geographical features that separate the opponents. Other dividing lines have been resorted to, with mixed success. Often, solutions have to be found within the confines of a shared territory. This may seem difficult, but a remarkable phenomenon is that such conflicts have found solutions through negotiations. Let us turn to these.

Peace Agreements in the Post-Cold War Era

There are 18 countries that have seen peace agreements on territorial issues after the Cold War, all agreed by the parties and with some lasting impact. They are listed in Table 7.1.

The settlements of Table 7.1 are testimony to the possibility of finding solutions to conflicts which have a long history, and where the understanding of that history seldom is shared among the parties. Different, if not contradictory, historical narratives are integral to the conflicts. Thus, the peace agreements are part of a shift in historical relationships. That is also often the way they are understood by the parties themselves. This historical dimension is something that sets state formation conflicts apart. They often concern peoples that live close to each other. They are aware and informed of each other. In most of the conflicts there is evidence of close neighbourly cooperation. There are also accounts of intimidation and repression. These are narratives passed from one generation to the next, thus solidifying themselves as stereotypes of the other side. The ambivalence of neighbourly cooperation and tension may be a factor that makes these conflicts particularly volatile. It is easier to mobilize action along these dimensions than others. This has given rise to the notion of an 'ethnic security dilemma', as a conflict-driving force (Kaufman 1996; Kaufmann 1996; Melander 1999). On the local level, minority groups will be insecure *vis-à-vis* a dominant group, and from this tension, militant action can begin, sometimes quickly accelerating conflict dynamics. For instance, if violence takes place against members of one group, this can (correctly or not) be attributed to the other group as a whole. That group in turn will take action to prepare its own defence, which then – to the first group – confirms expected hostile intentions and justifies pre-emptive action. Such dynamics have been reported from some, but not all, conflicts in Bosnia-Herzegovina (Melander 1999).

The ethnic security dilemma operates on a local level, making it exploitable by leaders. This is parallel to the internal security dilemma described in Sections 6.2 and 6.4, as well as the interstate situation for which it was originally developed (Chapter 5). Peacemaking in state formation conflicts faces problems which are manifestly different from those encountered in other types of conflict. To these problems belong the return of refugees to their original homes, from which they may have been forced out and replaced by others. Comparing Tables 6.1 and 7.1, we can also note that the agreements on state formation conflicts more frequently appear to solve the problem, rather than leading to a process of renewed conflict

Table 7.1 Peace agreements in state formation conflicts since the end of the Cold War

Conflict location	Years of agreement	No. of agreements
Angola (Cabinda)	2006	1
Bangladesh (Chittagong Hill Tracts)	1997	1
Bosnia-Herzegovina (Croat)	1994	1
Bosnia-Herzegovina (Serb Republic)	1995	1
Comoros (Anjuan)	2000, 2001, 2003	3
Croatia (Serb)	1995	1
Georgia (Abkhazia)	1994	1
India (Bodoland)	1993	1
India (Tripura)	1993	1
Indonesia (Aceh)	2002, 2005	2
Indonesia (East Timor)[a]	1999	1
Israel (Palestine)	1993, 1994, 1995, 1997, 1998, 1999, 2007	8
Mali (Azawad)	1991, 1992	2
Moldova (Dniestr)	1997	1
Niger (Air, Azawad)	1993, 1994, 1995	3
PNG (Bougainville)	1991, 1994, 2001	3
Philippines (Mindanao)	1996, 2001, 2012, 2013	8
Senegal (Casamance)	2004	1
Sudan (Abyei)	2011	1
UK (Northern Ireland)	1998	1
Yugoslavia (Kosovo)[b]	1999	1
Yugoslavia (Slovenia)	1991	1

[a] This agreement was concluded by other actors, implemented by warring parties.
[b] Different agreements signed by different parties, conflict terminated 1999.

Note: Peace agreements in armed conflicts concerning the control over territory in a state, active in the period 1989–2013. The table includes treaties that have been signed, that regulate (resolve or find a process for the solution of) the incompatibility, and have been concluded between the warring parties, and ends armed conflict behaviour. Cease-fire agreements are not included. The parties are listed in English alphabetical order.

Source: Uppsala Conflict Data Program Conflict Encyclopedia; Table 4.2 in this book; Högbladh (2006).

and settlement. These agreements are fewer, less frequently challenged and thus not reworked. This illustrates some of the differences between internal conflict over government and territory. The former deal with constitutions and political arrangements that are likely to change, also under 'normal' circumstances. Solutions to territorial issues, however, are more permanent: a border is drawn, a federal structure is created, thus changing the conditions for future politics in a way that is more difficult to change once again. There is irreversibility to such agreements. The agreements, in other words, may be fewer, more difficult to reach, but also involve more lasting changes that are visible on a geographical map. The exceptions are the protracted settlement process over Palestine and over Mindanao, in the Philippines. By 2014, the former saw a new breakdown in talks, while the other arrived at an agreement.

The record show that close to one-quarter of the conflicts of this type have reached an agreed settlement or an agreement on a process to such a settlement, comparing Tables 4.1 and 7.1. This is of particular interest, as victories are less common. For the same period, there are only a handful of situations where one side has clearly defeated the other, forcing, for instance, its withdrawal, capitulation or surrendering of demands on the disputed territory. Among the victories are, in effect, Slovenia's and Croatia's exits from Yugoslavia, although involving negotiations and agreements as well (1991, 1992), Eritrea winning Ethiopia's acceptance of its independence (agreed in 1993), India's subjugation of the Khalistan independence movements in Punjab (by 1993), Yemen's victory over South Yemen's attempt at secession (in 1994) and Sri Lanka's victory over the Tamil Tigers (LTTE) (in 2009). The few examples show that victory is not easily achieved. The commitments are strong on the opposite sides of the divides. Some of the victories include mass-eviction of the members of the losing side (most notably the eviction of Serbs from Krajina, Croatia, in 1995).

Several of the peace agreements in Table 7.1 are linked to the decolonization process and, as a consequence, to the United Nations: Palestine and East Timor. Before 1989, there were also such agreements for Namibia and Western Sahara. With the exception of Israel/Palestine, the security dilemma has stemmed from distant control, not from the direct influence of locals over locals. This is true for Namibia's independence as well as for the agreement on Western Sahara. The Palestinian struggle has been seen in that light, as has the East Timor conflict. The internationalized disputes over the status of some of these territories emanated from them being mandates by the League of Nations (Namibia, then known as Southwest Africa, a former German colony; and Palestine), and thus legally a concern for the UN as the successor. South Africa and Britain held these mandates. Western Sahara was a colonial territory under Spain; East Timor was under Portugal. Both colonial powers gave up control in 1975. Morocco then took control over Western Sahara, its neighbour to the South, and Indonesia occupied East Timor, as it already held West Timor. These actions were resisted by local movements and gave rise to considerable international opposition. Through the deliberate settlement of people, local ethnic security dilemmas were created. This has been most obvious in the case of Palestine, with an eviction of the former inhabitants, a massive settlement of Jewish immigrants and, following the outcome of the war in 1967, Jewish settlements also in the West Bank and Gaza (until Israel's unilateral withdrawal in 2005). In these areas, particularly strong escalation could be observed during the First Intifada (1987–93) and even more so during the Second Intifada (approximately 2000–06), two major uprisings of Palestinians. These issues continue to be of international concern.

The UN played an important role in the search for solutions for Namibia, Western Sahara and East Timor. The conflict over Namibia was the first to come to a generally accepted ending. Western Sahara is to have a referendum, but the composition of the electorate has not yet been determined. Morocco has managed to prevent the process from moving forward. East Timor became an independent country, Timor Leste, in 2002. This was the will expressed by the overwhelming majority in the referendum of August 1999, leading to carnage by Indonesia-supported militias.

It gave rise to a UN peacekeeping operation, first by Australia, to protect the agreed outcome. In the Palestinian issue, the UN has mostly been on the sidelines. Particularly since the Camp David agreements in 1978–79 between Egypt and Israel, the United States has been the leading outside actor for a settlement. However, we can still conclude that in conflicts relating to decolonization, as defined in the Cold War era, the UN is likely to have a particular role.

Sometimes, UN-led processes takes special forms, including that leading actors were not party to agreements. The key actors were sufficiently informed and accepted what was agreed, but did not sign documents. This is true for Namibia, where SWAPO, the leading liberation movement for Namibia, was not a signatory, and for East Timor, where the agreement was concluded between Indonesia and Portugal, as the former colonial power. In both cases, the UN was party to negotiations and implementation. It is not likely to be of great consequence, as these very actors were heavily involved in the following implementations, and were treated as legitimate parties.

It is also important to note that several settlements were reached without the input of the international community (Mali, Niger and Chittagong Hill Tracts). The issues were seen by the governments as internal affairs. This view was accepted internationally. For a long time, Britain resisted international participation in the settlement of the conflict in Northern Ireland, but eventually an arrangement was found involving the Republic of Ireland as well as the United States. It still is managed outside any international or regional organization. Similarly, Indonesia did not want to see the situation in Aceh as a parallel to East Timor, and thus did not involve the UN as a third party. Instead, a group led by the former President of Finland, Martti Ahtisaari, brokered a deal in Helsinki and its implementation was supervised by EU observers. The great tsunami disaster of December 26, 2004, leading to the demise of almost a quarter of a million people on Sumatra, contributed to galvanize the interest in a settlement. For the conflict in Chechnya, for which a cease-fire agreement was found in 1996, to be overturned by 1999, Russia refused to have any international participation. It is likely to be difficult for international organizations to get involved if it is resisted by a major power that also happens to be party to the conflict. As we can see, however, small or weak states also may prefer to deal on their own with their state formation conflicts and they may succeed in finding agreement.

In contrast, the conflicts over Yugoslavia and the settlements agreed to in 1994 and 1995 all became highly internationalized. The same is true for the war in Kosovo in 1999 where there was considerable negotiation in the events leading to the unilateral declaration of independence in 2008. The European Union, the Organization for Security and Cooperation in Europe (OSCE), the UN, NATO and a number of NGOs were heavily engaged in the search for solutions. Although it is generally true that solutions to state formation conflicts have considerable international interest, this does not automatically lead to international involvement in the settlement process. In the Balkan conflicts, governments and oppositions alike appealed for international support and, thus, succeeded in internationalizing the conflicts. It led to isolation of one party, Yugoslavia under Slobodan Milosevic. Only after his resignation in 2000 was this ended. Still there is no agreement by Serbia to Kosovo's independence, although the de facto situation is acknowledged.

These outcomes do not suggest that there is now international consensus in support of national self-determination for state sovereignty as a way of solving the ethnic security dilemma. The international actors were unwilling to endorse this principle for the settlement of the conflict in Kosovo. However, there may no longer be as firm a consensus on the ways of settling state formation conflicts. The decolonization principle is still applied in some instances. The notion of prior recognition by the previous centre can be used in others. The democratic principle – that is, to accept what the majority of the population in a particular territory favours – has been applied in some instances. But there are contradictions. Bosnia-Herzegovina was recognized as a sovereign state although there was no prior recognition from the previous unit, Yugoslavia. East Timor, Western Sahara and South Sudan in 2011 were given the right to vote on independence, but why would this not apply to Kosovo or to Chechnya?

In Section 7.2, we discuss the possibility of finding solutions to identity conflicts which do not directly involve a territorial issue. In Section 7.3, the different forms of territorial divisions within existing states are presented, particularly autonomy and federalism. Section 7.4 discusses possible solutions in conjunction with international integration, and Section 7.5 reflects on state formation conflicts and democracy.

7.2 Identity Discrimination and Conflict Resolution

It is often assumed that, at the heart of intra-state conflicts over territory, there is an experience of discrimination. Groups and peoples who will not have their rights respected by the governmental authorities, according to their own understanding of what such rights should include, are likely to become dissatisfied and this gives rise to action. This way of understanding ethnic conflicts is an application of the social frustration model presented in Section 3.3. A fuller explanation would rest on all the models given in Chapter 3. The argument would then be reformulated in the following way. There are certain basic needs that are not met. These may not necessarily be material, but also immaterial, for instance, cultural. Often, in reality, there is a close connection between these two. For instance, if a person cannot use his or her own language to pursue a particular grievance with official authorities, this person is at a distinct disadvantage against those who command it, and thus the person is more likely not to receive a fair share of, say, social services or business deals. Repeated experiences of such differentiated treatment may lead some in the identity group to mobilize for action. Thus, a leadership emerges and the options are calculated according to the rationality of the resulting movement. Actions are initiated, conflict escalates and after a while a state finds itself in an increasingly complicated conflict situation.

What are the needs that could give rise to such dramatic escalation? They are not obvious from the outset. There are some 6,700 languages in the world. Many are rapidly disappearing. Some argue that only with a state is it possible to protect languages and, thus, linguistic nationalism has become a feature in analysis. People's identity is sometimes strongly connected to language. The linguistic differences may be small, as is the case between Croatian, Serbian and Bosnian, but they may be sufficient for locating a significant element in an identity profile. However, it should be clear from the outset that language is not the typical factor that makes one state different from another. There are a great number of states that share the same language, although differently spoken. English is the official language of a number of states, as is French, Spanish, Portuguese, Russian, Arabic and Chinese. A number of languages are strongly related, making it possible to understand spoken idioms across borders. This is the case among the Nordic countries and between India and Pakistan (Hindi/Urdu). Also, there are states that manage well with two (Finland), four (Switzerland) or more than 20 official languages (India). The close connection between state and language is, thus, not as strong as might first be thought. Although nationalism often invokes history and language, conflict formation and the quest for a state probably has more complicated origins. Societies clearly are able to accommodate considerable language diversity, and states can survive with other states using the same language.

There are other identity carriers that might result in violence-prone discrimination. Among those are access to education, right of worship, discrimination built on race, gender, sexual orientation, legal discrimination, economic discrimination, oppression by police or military forces dominated by other groups, lack of access to public administration, lack of political representation and human rights, difficulty to cross borders, etc. In short, many of the matters mentioned in the Universal Declaration of Human Rights from 1948 and the Convention on Human Rights from 1966 are potential elements in the escalation of conflict. Most likely, none of these, alone, would give a full explanation. In a given state, there may be groups discriminated against for different reasons which find sufficiently common cause to combine in support of a particular movement, whether this movement is in power or a challenger. Any society is likely to react early and search for appropriate measures. This means that escalation is not necessarily driven by the movements pressing the anti-discriminatory demands, but by the government's reactions to these demands. If the reactions go in the predicted direction, that is, repressive, dismissive or intolerant, it is likely that an opposition movement gains strength. If that attitude, furthermore, is one of using violent repression, legal harassment and special sanctions, the chance of escalation is likely to increase. Thus, the most appropriate early-warning indicators would be the government response to identity-based demands.

There are many options for governments, and only some result in an escalation of conflict. Early action for accommodation would have the greatest chance of channelling such demands into constructive societal development. A responsive government has to consider demands from many groups and, in a resource-scarce society, this dilemma will be more difficult to handle. Table 7.2 presents some ways in which such demands are dealt with in responsive societies. These solutions can be reached with the help of the seven ways of conflict resolution given in Section 3.5. They particularly aim at finding compromises and horse-trading between competing demands arising from discrimination.

To remove discrimination for one group may affect rights of other groups; simply replacing the rights of one group with the rights of another is no solution. It perpetuates discrimination. Thus, measures have to transcend discrimination in ways

171

where the reconciliation of opposing demands are seen to be of interest to all groups as well as to the general concern of the state. Legitimate principles have to be found. There has to be a commitment to review the actions after a time with a chance of revision. The procedures for instituting solutions are important. Imposition, even of reasonable propositions, will not do. Imposition may, sooner or later, be seen as violation in itself.

Practical applications of the solutions in Table 7.2 can be found all over the world. They are attempts to handle difficult conflicts. Issues can be resolved in ways which are satisfactory to the involved parties. On the whole, there are two basic strategies used. One is inclusive and integrative, trying to make all groups work within the same unified system. It requires particular care so that all concerns are met, the approach is understood by all involved and it finds a practical application that functions in daily life. Another approach is more exclusive and decentralized. Special arrangements are made for particular groups. The overall framework remains the same, but some individuals are treated positively differently from others in order to

Table 7.2   Solutions to non-territorial, identity-driven conflicts

Incompatibility	Solution
Acceptance of language	Several official and administrative languages Shared 'superlanguage', a lingua franca
Access to educational system	Several parallel systems of equal quality Recruitment quota for unified system
Application of religion, morals	Freedom of religion Secular state, separated from religion
Legal system	Shared legal system, with certain allowances Separate legal system for defined groups
Economic inferiority	Positive action for specified period of time Earmarked resources for regions or sectors
Access to natural resources (land, water, subsurface)	National law with specified conditions Local administration of natural resources
Population movements (migration, refugees)	Protection for indigenous settlement Rights of return Significance of documentation
Access to police, armed forces	Recruitment quota for unified system High admission requirements Training in human rights Transparent procedures for redressing issues Disbanding of questionable forces
Access to administration	Recruitment quota for unified system High admission requirements
Oversight of implementation	Independent ombudsmen International review
Political representation	Minority rights, minimum representation Electoral system with equal access
Constitution	Human and minority rights Guarantee against rapid constitutional change
Human rights	Human rights for all, positive action for some
International transparency	Review of implementation International access accepted

remedy past grievances and create an equal platform for the future. Each of these strategies can be evaluated, with respect to its short- and long-term impact on society.

The solutions have normally not been instituted as preventive measures in order to avoid future conflict. Rather, they are the result of considerable thought and struggle, particularly by the groups that have a strong grievance against the way society functions at a particular moment in time. Issues of discrimination have given rise to considerable internal conflict the world over. Much conflict action has been non-armed and has affected government policies, without resulting in civil wars. A model-forming experience was the civil rights movement in the United States in the 1960s. The demands by the African-American population changed politics locally and nationally. It also changed the reality for all segments of the population. It was pursued largely with non-violent means. The Nobel Peace Prize was given to a prominent leader, Martin Luther King, Jr. The creativity of this movement led to an interest in non-violent methods. The systematization of such methods made the experiences useful in other contexts, injecting new thinking for other struggles (Sharp 1973).

However, violence was also part of the picture. Sometimes it was spontaneous and badly organized, but nevertheless highly destructive, as in the riots that followed the assassination of Dr King in 1968. At other times it was more deliberate, and regarded as a necessary defence, as advocated by the Black Panther Party. This resulted in gunfights with police units as well as between members of the movement. It was seen as a necessary, revolutionary, way for changing society. It increased the pressure on the government and threatened to turn the issue into a civil war. Severe discrimination, in other words, could lead to the types of conflict we discussed in Chapter 6. In the US case, however, it seldom translated into a demand for secession. This is worth exploring further.

It takes two to conflict. Thus, we have to observe that discrimination in a society affects most groups in a particular state. Some are favoured and others are discriminated against. Thus, there are vested interests in discriminatory practices, which makes it possible to maintain such policies over a long period of time. Regimes desiring to keep power may exploit ethnic divides for their own advantage, as was witnessed in the Milosevic reign in Yugoslavia (1987–2000). Such regimes are likely to be repressive and manipulative in order for a leading group to retain advantages. They may be ruthless when meeting resistance. They can play different groups against each other. Some can be invited to join the government, others can be severely harassed. Thus, opposition will be diluted and divided. It is difficult to organize opposition under such circumstances. It requires strategies that focus on particular matters and an ability to pursue them with vigour and creativity. Only then is it likely that governments become interested in solutions. Sometimes they implement reforms which are genuine; many times they remain window dressing. Achieving an end to discrimination requires an understanding of how power is exerted in a society, and whether that power structure is affected by measures such as those listed in Table 7.2. Ending discrimination, in other words, is not only a matter of possessing the right instruments, but also in applying them in the right ways.

Matters may develop differently if there is a significant, regional concentration of a particular group. It may provide a closer-knit experience of discrimination. It makes resistance easier. It may also invite more repression, as the incumbent power realizes this potential. This, furthermore, makes the fate of the area more important for those who are outside this territory. Regional concentration of discriminated groups may provide for escalation. If, in that region, there are also members of other groups, which in fact benefit from the policies, an additional element is added. The conflict over Kosovo illustrates this.

In the Kosovo conflict, a key Albanian demand was access to education in the Albanian language. The actions instituted by the Serb authorities in 1989–90 in Kosovo meant a reduced, public role for Albanians. Instead, the Serb language gained in significance, even to the point where street signs were changed. Instead of Albanian street names on the top, Serb names were given that position. This signified a loss of control for Albanians in running their own affairs in Kosovo, at the same time as they could see the Serb inhabitants getting better access. Street signs were daily reminders of a new society. From the Serb point of view, however, this was simply redressing the previous situation, when Albanians had dominated. Thus, the educational issue became a symbol of what the conflict was all about: self-rule, but for whom?

The Albanians were the majority in the province, Serbs argued that Kosovo was part of the Republic of Serbia (the largest unit in the Federal Republic of Yugoslavia, as the country was called at the time) and, thus, Serbs were in the majority. After Kosovo lost its autonomy, the Kosovo Albanian leadership refused to cooperate with Serb and Yugoslav authorities, as this would imply the recognition of their legitimacy. The non-violent methods were supported, but in late 1997 armed groups began to appear. By 1999 there was full-fledged war in the country, including NATO bombardments all over Yugoslavia. This resulted in an international administration, the armed groups were reconstituted as a force under civilian control, but relations between the remaining Serbs and the Albanian majority remained tense. Kosovo's independence in 2008 has not yet changed this, although recent EU connections may.

From this history, we can conclude that the issues of discrimination can be closely linked to political and territorial control. Tight connections between issues, such as those listed in Table 7.2, are likely to escalate a situation into a state formation conflict. This, furthermore, would be particularly strong if some of the issues concern territorial control. The discriminatory experience provides the frustration, the territorial concentration, the shared community, the boundaries, the majority–minority relationship and, if the territory is close to an international border, it provides for access to weapons, finances and international assistance (Cornell 2002).

These arguments find support in the work by Ted R. Gurr (1993), which shows that the removal of autonomy has been strongly associated with the onset of a higher level of armed conflict within a decade. Probably, the loss of control is in itself the most distinguishing experience a political unit can suffer, if it is done without the consent of the governed. In the Kosovo case, there was no consultation and it was done with intentions that were threatening to the majority population in the area. That questions of discrimination were important in the conflicts can be seen from a cursory review of the peace agreements in Table 7.1. It is possible to find strong identity groups as governmental and, particularly, as opposition actors. All these cases concerned areas where the population had a shared experience of losing territorial control, recently or in historical times. This provides an element of self-righteousness that can sustain a political battle. The forms of discrimination may vary. It can be based on race, as in the case of Namibia. Negative memories went back to German colonization. It can be based on religion, as in the case of Mindanao, an area with a large Muslim population finding itself subject to discrimination from a Christian majority of the Philippines. Again, this dates back to Spanish colonial conquest. It can be based on economic opportunities, as was the way the civil rights movement began in the late 1960s in Northern Ireland (housing was a first key issue).

Also, in the cases of state formation conflicts resulting in victories, we find similar experiences. Eritrea was initially defined as an equal partner in union with Ethiopia, but was relegated to a province by the Ethiopian government in 1962. Tamils continue to point to their exclusion from political life in Sri Lanka, perhaps made even more severe after the defeat of the Tamil Tigers (LTTE) in 2009. In this, as in many other cases, there are alternative movements, something to be dealt with in Section 7.5. Since the fall of Saddam Hussein the Iraqi Shiite population has reasserted itself, pointing to its experience of religious discrimination as well as political exclusion. In this case, instead, violent opposition has stemmed from the previous powerholders, secular or Sunni Arabs fearing discrimination in the future.

Discrimination issues have importance in their own right. They can be addressed in political life, either as challenges to the existing state (state formation conflicts) or against government policies (making them into conflicts over government, that is, intra-state conflicts). When connected to territorial control, they are likely to be more entrenched and difficult to settle. In other words, not all questions of discrimination lead to armed conflict and challenges to the state. Those that do, however, will require particular efforts to identify solutions. Thus, we are moved to study the ways in which solutions can be found to the territorial security dilemmas of the state formation conflicts. This we will do in the following sections.

7.3 Autonomy and Federalism: Territorial Solutions within a State

Discrimination was an essential motive for the opposition in the conflicts listed in Table 7.1. It is given as a cause for action. Of course, there can be other motives and, indeed, whether such a grievance results in armed conflict depends on a host of other conditions. There is no straight line between the depth of a grievance and the onset or continuation of an armed conflict. Still, the reasoning in Section 7.2 leads to the conclusion that the territorial control question is essential. The ethnic security dilemma takes on a territorial dimension that needs to be handled. A state with more than one identity group formed on the basis of a territorial dimension will have to give thought to possible solutions. The following overview exemplifies remedies, using the seven mechanisms of conflict resolution identified in Section 3.5.

The first way points to the possibility of *reducing the significance of the territorial dimension*. This means that the parties, and particularly the opposition, will find that it would benefit from regarding the conflict as one purely of discrimination, equal opportunity, improved legislation, etc. This would mean reverting the conflict to the questions dealt with in Section 7.2. As we can assume that this already has been on the minds of the leaders – indeed even been an earlier phase of the conflict – this shift is less probable. Once a territorial demand has been raised, it is difficult to remove it from the agenda. Even if the original instigator gives it up, others may well follow. If it has come to a sustained armed conflict, this is even more unlikely. It is more possible that the demands for independence can be scaled back and that autonomy, for instance, can be acceptable as a final or interim solution. Nevertheless, there are interesting examples of policy shifts. One is the redefinition of the aims of PKK for the Kurdish cause in Turkey. In a statement to his followers while imprisoned, the leader of the organization, Abduallah Öcalan, argued that the struggle was no longer about a separate Kurdistan. Violent rebellion was, thus, to end (Kinzer 1999). The new approach was supposed to transform the struggle from a territorial issue to one of participation in the existing Turkish state. The armed conflict continued but in 2012 negotiations began with the Kurdish party in the parliament and in 2014 it became legal to discuss peace also with PKK. The approach to the Kurdish issue was as a non-territorial issue. Positions had changed.

A second form that was mentioned is to find *ways in which territory can be divided* within the state's present confines. To some, this is seen as partition. An important issue is the impenetrability of the borders. Another is whether it leads to further division. This is where autonomy and federalism come in. Table 7.3 suggests all forms of internal and international partition to provide as complete a picture as possible. The basic idea is that an area – and its inhabitants – are given a degree of self-rule of their own affairs. It means that it affects not only the territory, but also the functions that this entity is going to handle. There can be various ways in which such functions can be divided as well.

The first five solutions in Table 7.3 are located within the existing state; the last three assume sovereignty and international recognition of the outcome. Also an autonomy arrangement can be internationalized if there are strong international guarantees. Federalism, furthermore, can provide the right to secede to the constituent units, giving them powerful levers against the central government. Independence can be restricted and conditional, as is the case with two of the options in Table 7.3. The agreement on independence may include the right for guaranteeing powers to intervene or even keep forces in an independent country. It may actually be asked if an autonomy arrangement sometimes gives more self-rule than a sovereign state would have, if particular restrictions were applied. Notions such as 'confederalism' are diffuse and find themselves somewhere between federalism and independence. In reality, the authority provided for the constituent units is decisive, not the labels.

Table 7.3 Territorial solutions to state formation conflicts (with examples from cases mentioned in the text and in Table 7.1)

Status of unit	Characteristics of self-rule	Examples
Self-administration	Devolution of powers from the centre to local, communal or provincial levels	Niger, Mali
Autonomy	Given from the centre and subject to policy changes of the centre; exists in weaker or stronger forms	Mindanao
Autonomy	Given or guaranteed by outside actors, thus not subject only to the policy of the centre, but to international developments	Åland, South Tyrol, Northern Ireland
Federalism	Created for many units, uniform constitution, central government composed of the constituent units	India, Switzerland
Federalism	Created for a few units, with equal rights	Bosnia-Herzegovina (two forms)
Independence	Created with international guarantees, close monitoring	Cyprus, 1960–63
Independence	Done without formal guarantees, but with integration in a regional framework	Within the EU?
Independence	No restrictions except adherence to regular international conventions	Eritrea

Note: The distinctions in this table concern territorial control. Each form could contain a range of self-rule authority over particular issues, for instance, taxation, policing, international representation, external security, etc.

Among the agreements in Table 7.1, decentralization was a chief element in two solutions in the 1990s (Niger, Mali). Various forms of autonomy were instituted, temporarily or permanently, in a number of cases (Palestine, as an interim arrangement, Chittagong Hill Tracts, Aceh and Mindanao as more permanent institutions). In some instances, the population has been given a choice between 'independence' and 'integration'. In Western Sahara, this is to be the subject of a referendum that is still being awaited due to disagreement on who should be in the electorate. East Timor in August 1999 had such a choice and the population overwhelmingly voted for independence. In Bougainville, such a vote is promised in 2015. South Sudan's referendum on independence in January 2011 led to a new state.

It is noteworthy that there is only one case of a federal solution after a war. This is the status given to Bosnia-Herzegovina in the Dayton Agreement of 1995. The new State of Bosnia-Herzegovina has a presidency (three presidents, one from each community), a two-unit federation, where one actually is another federation (the Federation of Bosnia-Herzegovina and the Serb Republic), and where the units were maintaining separate armies. The statewide federal level has been difficult to implement. So has the unit-level federation, concluded between the Bosniak (Bosnian Muslims) and Croat leaderships a year before the Dayton Agreement.

For post-Saddam Hussein Iraq, federalism was seen as the only viable solution to reduce the power of Sunnis. For the Kurds and Shiites it provided a guarantee for their identities. But it had other disputes with a territorial dimension: which areas should be part of which federated unit and where should multi-ethnic and oil-rich Kirkuk belong?

The solution to Northern Ireland, found in the Belfast agreement signed on Good Friday 1998, can be seen in this light. It gives considerable autonomy to the province, and it maintains the territory in the United Kingdom for the time being. It is a unique solution as it provides a functioning autonomous unit, which actually can switch its allegiance to the Republic of Ireland, while retaining its self-rule arrangement. The agreement also makes a connection between the North and the South of Ireland, and institutes a new regional council for the British Isles. There is a federal-like order developing for the United Kingdom as a whole, but the Belfast solution is more complex, as it combines different elements in Table 7.3 in a creative way.

There are objections to such territorial solutions. It has been argued that autonomy may, in fact, result in an area being ruled by illegal and criminal groups. This charge was levied in Russia against the solution for Chechnya in 1996. The bombings of apartment buildings in Moscow in 1999 were explained in this way, and thus it undermined the credibility of the arrangement in the eyes of the centre. Instead of instituting democracy and working for economic development, it is possible that various armed groups could take control, exploiting the fact that there would be no interference of a legitimate superior authority. There has also been the opposite charge, that the autonomies often become too dependent on policies of the centre. The centre may choose to abolish the special status of a particular territory. This would serve to undermine the credibility of the solution in that particular area. For instance, Eritrean movements claimed that an autonomous status within Ethiopia was no longer acceptable as Ethiopia had abolished the self-rule the area had in the 1950s.

A third way is the issue of *horse-trading*. In this context, it would refer to the possibility of agreements on exchanges. Such exchanges, only some of which can be part of a treaty, may occur in state formation conflicts through a process where a people changes identity, there are population exchanges across internal borders and exchanges of territories. None of these is attractive following the experiences of the Second World War. In the post-Cold War era, however, they have returned as possible options, although their legitimacy is low, as they run counter to principles of human rights and conflict resolution. The three forms can be illustrated in the following way.

The first refers to a process of integration into the society of previously marginalized groups. This is assimilation, meaning that these groups take on the traits of the dominant side. It is possible, as a long-term result, but it is difficult to see assimilation resulting from an agreement. In reality, assimilation is the strategy a victor prefers to use towards the conquered. In a less harsh form, however, there could be stipulations in an agreement as to the rights of the populations on opposite sides of internal frontiers.

The exchange of populations has sometimes been agreed in international treaties, thus being part of a state creation process. Between Turkey and Greece, there are examples of agreed population exchanges. In the 1920s, a total of more than half a million people were forcibly moved, either from Greece to Turkey (more than 350,000) or from Turkey to Greece (more than 190,000) (Ekstrand 1944). Some see this as an achievement and as a contribution to a reduction in hostility. However, tensions have remained between the peoples and the states. The experiences of being forced to move (by the other side, under international supervision, notably) served to fuel the conflict, not dampen it. There are writers who regard such population transfer, humanely done, as a way of solving the problem of minorities on one side of a border being loyal to a majority living on the other side (Bell-Fialkoff 1996).

The third approach would mean that one side holds a territory the other one wants, for instance, as a result of a recent war. It would be returned in exchange for concessions on other issues. Such horse-trading is today probably not legitimate, except in the immediate aftermath of a war, and then relating to military arrangements rather than population resettlements. It would today appear more like hostage-taking.

The fourth and fifth mechanisms for solving territorial conflicts within states point to the possibilities of *providing access to government*. This can take place on the local or national level. It means that solutions may be found, without resorting to territorial divisions. Examples are powersharing arrangements and coalition governments (Jarstad 2001; Sisk 1996). The Belfast agreement created a government for Northern Ireland composed according to the strength of the parties in elections. The minority was assured its seats. Sinn Fein, seen to be close to the Provisional IRA, was thus seated and has, since then, exerted influence on the developments of the area. Similarly, the Dayton Agreement includes an ethnically defined composition of leading bodies in Bosnia-Herzegovina. In federal arrangements, it is customary that one of two chambers in a federal parliament provides over-representation for certain areas. A federal arrangement gives more influence on state affairs to a particular group through such representation than does autonomy. This suggests the need for a national government for the period of transition.

The sixth model for conflict resolution would mean that a territorial issue is settled through the resort to *conflict resolution mechanisms*. Some such decisions have been made, but only with respect to territorially limited disputes. The status of the town of Brcko was decided through a process of arbitration (making the city a unit directly under the State of Bosnia-Herzegovina, not belonging to either the Federation or the Republic), as the last remaining issue in the Dayton negotiations on peace in Bosnia-Herzegovina in 1995.

On the seventh way, *postponing issues or the creation of timetables*, we can note that, although territorial issues are at the heart of state formation disputes, there are certain issues that tend to come last. As just mentioned, this was the case with Brcko. It was known in advance that this would be a strategically important decision. By keeping it as the last agenda item, negotiators may have believed that it would recede in importance. Then a solution could be found, particularly as the alternative would be to jeopardize the entire agreement. As it turned out, the parties were close to doing just that. The resort to arbitration became the last possibility. As a form of brinkmanship it is a high-risk game that could easily go wrong.

A central question in the Israeli–Palestinian negotiations concerns the status of Jerusalem, which both Israel and Palestine are committed to as the capital in their state. It was left to last in previous negotiations, for instance in Camp David in 1978. In the Oslo process, it was again defined to belong to the final status issues. There was a limit to how long this issue could be postponed, however, and when a solution was presented, in July 2000, it may have been too late. It involved elements of what we have suggested above on the division of functional influence, sovereignty and guarantees. It was still not enough. Too many other matters have not worked out according to expectation, leaving little confidence for settling this issue. Leaving important matters to last, it turns out, may be counter-productive. But so is the opposite strategy, of solving the most difficult issues first. Difficult questions have to be tackled when confidence and momentum are at their highest.

Judging from the record since the Cold War, autonomy solutions have been of increasing interest. From Table 7.1, it can be surmised that it is one element – under different names – in at least ten agreements. It has also been an important proposal in the search for solutions in some other cases, for instance, for Nagorno-Karabakh within Azerbaijan, Jafna and adjacent areas in Sri Lanka, and Basque areas in Spain. It was proposed for Corsica in France. The strength of the autonomy solution is its ability to provide a tailor-made solution for a particular problem. It meets simultaneously the interests of self-determination of a people and the interest of the centre to keep the state together, thus upholding its territorial integrity. From the point of view of the centre, this is important as it perceives a danger of other units also demanding self-rule. In its worst-case scenario, there is a threat of break-up of the entire state. Thus, a special arrangement can be defended as a particular measure which does not set a precedent for others. The history of the conflict may assist to provide such arguments. For the territorial unit itself, autonomy creates a direct link to the centre of state authority, thus according it a status no other unit has. Furthermore, if this linkage is sufficiently strong, it may provide the guarantees of self-rule and security that the inhabitants of the unit require (Nordquist 1998). However, mistrust is likely to be high. After all, there has been a war. There are often pertinent questions of the return of people of other identities to which the centre will give priority. Thus, solutions may not always be found only between the centre and the region. It may involve international actors, acting as guarantors. Regional arrangements, the UN or particular states can take this role, although there are not many examples in this period.

The interest in autonomy solutions may have other origins as well. For the opposition, it may be the first step to independence. This is the way East Timor resistance movements saw autonomy, for instance. It would be a way of building up an administration, shaping a functioning economy and forming a police system of its own. It would make the option between autonomy and independence a real choice. This plan was pre-empted by the Indonesian authorities, however, who in January 1999 gave the same choice to the East Timorese, without first acquainting the population to the practical experiences of self-rule. As it appeared to be a final offer and the only chance, the choice was easy for these movements. They had to take the chance for independence. The outcome of the internationally observed referendum in August 1999 was predictable. The violence that followed showed that the Indonesian government might not have fully understood the local political situation. It also underestimated the will of the international community to intervene after it saw the overwhelming support for independence.

The experience of East Timor may make central authorities in multi-ethnic societies less inclined to vie for autonomy solutions. In the 2005 solution to the conflict in Aceh, the independence option was also ruled out by the liberation movement, GAM, no doubt under the impact of the tsunami disaster. This made an agreement possible. This is underscored by the Kosovo crisis of 1999, where international action created a de facto independent unit, but for nine years maintained that it was part of Serbia. However, by declaring independence, Kosovo ended this fiction. Similarly, the self-government afforded to Palestinian-ruled areas of the West Bank and Gaza is seen as a prelude to independence.[2]

Under such circumstances, autonomy becomes a first step to independence, not a final settlement. However, this is not true for all the solutions. There is no expectation that Northern Ireland will become independent, but it could very well become an autonomous part of the Republic of Ireland. Independence is not likely to come to Mindanao and Chittagong Hill Tracts. In the agreements in Sudan and Papua New Guinea, a vote would determine the fate of South Sudan (as it did in 2011) and of Bougainville (to be held in the period 2015–20). An idea is that this gives the central authorities an incentive to please these regions so as to keep them inside the present state. It remains to be understood what separates the self-rule situations from those where autonomy is but a stepping stone. Most of the functioning autonomies have not seen ethnic cleansing on their territories or considerable refugee flows, as was the case with Palestine, Bosnia, Chechnya, East Timor and Kosovo. It is also interesting to ask if autonomy is more likely to gain local support under a stable democratic centre. This is true for each of the first four cases mentioned, whereas the last four have been exposed to semi-democratic or dictatorial regimes (former Yugoslavia, Russia, Indonesia and post-1995 Yugoslavia). This might suggest that Sudan will become another case of secession (which is what happened), while Papua New Guinea might not. Democratic government provides for more transparency and predictability. With such experiences, less extreme measures may be sought. This argument would, interestingly enough, apply also to the Palestinian case. Nobody can refute the democratic strength of Israel. It is, however, an exclusive democracy, not willing to accommodate a large Palestinian population. In this case, a separate-state solution is the only viable one.

The federal solutions are theoretically attractive but obviously not frequent in the settlement of state formation conflicts. Bednar (2009) lists 26 federations for the period 1990–2000 and, at most, two can be seen as solutions to conflicts between parties that became units of the federation. Tanzania was formed to integrate Tanganyika and Zanzibar in 1974 in a peculiar coup episode. This leaves the Bosnia-Herzegovina federation as an exceptional case and its future is still in question. The Dayton Accords from 1995, ending the three years of war in Bosnia, included an elaborate constitutional structure, with one central government and a federation parallel to an autonomous republic (the Bosnian Serb Republic). It builds on legal symmetry, in which each unit is on the same organizational level. It was argued in the Dayton negotiations that constituent units of the United States, for instance, use terms such as 'Commonwealth' and 'Republic', but still legally are on the same level (Holbrooke 1999: 131). This might not be the chief obstacle for the functioning of the solution, however.

Federal solutions involve a division of territory. In a federation with a strong central structure, such lines are less important, but the weaker the centre, and thus the stronger the constituent units, the more important are the territorial arrangements. According to accounts from the Dayton negotiations, considerable time and energy were expended at drawing boundaries. It is remarkable as they were supposed to be internal lines in a central state. The significance of the border issue suggests that the parties were not really contemplating the creation of a strong unitary state. The formula agreed to beforehand of a territorial division of 51 per cent for the Federation (that is, the Bosniak and Croat areas) and 49 per cent for the Republic (the Serb areas) was guiding the procedure. The maps were continuously adapted so as to arrive at this formula. Matters of constitutions and elections were dealt with more easily than the one of territory. It is illustrative that the final agreement, concluded in the morning of the last day of negotiations, was on a territorial question, the Brcko district (Holbrooke 1999: 302–9). Clearly, the negotiators expected the borderlines to be as important as between separate states. The borders were going to be 'hard', not 'soft' as inside a state, where the same sovereignty extends on both sides of the border. The implementation has had to face this problem, trying to 'soften' the borders by finding agreements on border crossings, common institutions and a common currency. The survival of the state may depend on the success of such measures. What was created at Dayton was not a 'normal' federal state.

Thus, it is not surprising that the Bosnia-Herzegovina federation is marred by problems. But they not only stem from the sharp boundary cutting across the country, or even the existence of hostile armies. The main problem is that the solution has little foundation in the minds of the population, even among the leaders. The Bosnian Serb population would still prefer to be united with Serbia, something explicitly excluded in the Dayton Accords. Croats would still prefer to be with Croatia. The carriers of the State of Bosnia-Herzegovina are the Bosniaks, and they are not the majority. The international support the central government receives is crucial for the federation. It means that independence is severely circumscribed with respect to international relations and as to what state leaders can do inside their state. The commander of the international peacekeeping operations and the Office of High Representative (OHR), appointed by the international community, are the sources of real authority.

Federal solutions may still be of interest, but more as preventive measures than solutions after a war. This form of solution requires an arrangement for the full state, as its idea is that there are many units balancing each other, but also reflecting diversity in the country. Thus, a two-unit federation is at the bare minimum and may in fact lose a significant element of its contribution to conflict resolution, or actually become a de facto autonomy solution (Zanzibar is highly separated from Tanzania). Although there are only four languages in Switzerland, the units in the federation are many times this number. Also, territorial conflicts may not be of concern to all areas in a given state. It is problematic to extend federal rights to areas which have not asked for them, but get them as part of a solution to a problem in another part of that state. In the case of Bosnia-Herzegovina, the Dayton Accords were drawing a constitution for a new country. In post-Saddam Hussein Iraq a federal state is being constructed by two of the largest communities, together representing a dominant majority – the Kurds and the Shiites. The opposition comes from Sunni Arabs and worries are expressed by some smaller ethnic communities, in all around one-fifth of the population. This is a risky experiment that is being carried out as a constitutional process in the midst of a terrorist civil war. Federalism may appear intellectually and technically feasible. However, a common result of studies of the durability of federations is that they require a 'federal consensus' (Bednar 2009: 216; Duchacek 1977: 13). A war rarely creates such a consensus and, indeed, federal solutions have not normally emerged as solutions between the opposing sides in a state formation war.[3]

Thus far, the territorial solutions negotiated since the end of the Cold War using autonomy or federation have not failed. Some are still in an early phase of implementation (Bosnia-Herzegovina, Northern Ireland), others are in place but under review (Mindanao, Chittagong Hill Tracts), still others are seen as first steps (Palestine) and, thus, only to be judged with respect to that. We have also observed some of the difficulties, for instance, it seems hard to find a balancing point that can uphold autonomy. It is a compromise between independence and integration. It has strong intellectual appeal, but may be difficult to manage in situations of stark conflict. It might function under conditions where peoples of different identities live intermingled, where there is no experience of ethnic cleansing and where the centre is democratic. Also, we can observe that federal solutions are few and face severe difficulties in recreating an identity-divided state. The Dayton Accords attempt to do this, and so far have been upheld through the Bosniak community and a strong international presence. To this should be added findings which suggest that federations that also decentralize military forces may face quicker and more devastating wars, if an armed conflict were to break out (Regan and Wallensteen 2013). In the case of Iraq, for instance, locally operating well-armed militias constitute a problem, something compounded by the threat from ISIS in 2014.

7.4 Independence with or without Integration

When parties are involved in war the original goal is to win or prevent the opponent from winning. In conflicts over territory within one state, the end result should be obvious. Either the existing state wins, order is restored and no changes of international borders are made, or the existing state loses, new states are born and borders are changed. There are victories that also fit into these two outcomes since the Cold War. Slovenia, Croatia and Eritrea all attribute their independence to military victories; the movement for an independent Khalistan for Sikhs was routed by Indian forces targeting the leadership. Coercion is not necessarily the only way to independence, however. It is noteworthy that negotiated solutions do not rule out the possibility of independence, as can be understood from Table 7.1. Independence would solve the ethnic security dilemma by creating borders between the opposing parties, thus alleviating the tensions of being in the same state and ending competition for the same recourses. As independence is an option, we need to ask what the experiences are in achieving independence in an armed conflict without victory.

Independence was an alternative for Namibia, as agreed before 1989, as well as East Timor. That is also what the majority chose. It remains a likely option for Western Sahara and for Palestine. The way the Bosnian conflict is defined in Table 7.1 assumes that Bosnia-Herzegovina was an independent country from 1992. However, as the Federal Republic of Yugoslavia did not extend recognition with diplomatic relations, there remained an uncertainty in the minds of the Bosnian leadership. The Dayton Accords reaffirmed the independence of the country. A different outcome to the war may have resulted in a division of Bosnia between Serb and Croat forces with linkages to Belgrade and Zagreb. Diplomatic and military actions blocked such outcomes. Bosnia's independence was secured through a military stalemate. These examples show that independence can also be achieved in armed conflicts without a complete military victory.

For the many stalemated and ongoing armed conflicts this may be an important lesson. It means that governments may not necessarily fear to enter into talks. It does not necessarily lead only to secession. The opposition may not fear that talks will automatically rule out independence, if that is its preferred alternative. Are there situations in which independence may be the preferred alternative for both sides in a conflict? This can be answered by asking how it was possible for a centre to agree to the dissolution of 'its' state. There are three possible answers. The first is whether there is a solution that reduces the impact of granting independence by finding a regional framework of integration. The second is that this depends on the self-understanding of the centre, something that was mentioned in Section 7.1. A third response is that it depends on the demographic geography, particularly the size and significance of populations ending up on the 'wrong' side of new borders. Let us look at these three factors in some depth.

First, granting independence to a territory is more acceptable to the centre government if it takes place within a context of regional cooperation. It means that the interstate boundaries remain 'soft', allowing the movement of people as well as goods and capital. This all makes sense, for instance, if we discuss autonomy solutions. If the protagonists are members of the European Union, this may make agreements on self-rule less threatening to opponents and centres alike. It may well have been a factor for the agreement on Northern Ireland. The dissolution of the Soviet Union was followed by the quick formation of the Commonwealth of Independent States (CIS). It showed that ideas of regional cooperation were uppermost in the minds of leaders in the former Soviet states. CIS and other links would serve to undo some of the feared negative consequences of the new situation. The peaceful dissolution of Czechoslovakia may also have been helped by the hopes, on both sides, for closer cooperation with the EU and Western Europe. Violence would have reduced the chances of admission.

The possibility of future integration may convince the centre in accepting the ending of a union. The perspective on the seceding side may be different. Whether won through victory or negotiated process, independence still may be seen as the result of a conflict strategy. Thus, the will to cooperate and integrate with the old centre is likely to be modest on the part of the new state. Its first needs are for internal reconstruction, the creation of its own institutions and the development of its own economic and military capacity. The new unit, furthermore, will be busy extending new international contacts. The residual effects of war and separation are pressing concerns for the leadership on both sides. This scenario gains more support from the record since the Cold War than the hope for integration after a conflict. There was little incentive among the newly independent states from former Yugoslavia to work out new cooperative arrangements among themselves. They had gained independence from one tightly knit union, and were looking for different integration projects. Slovenia and Croatia hoped to be early candidates for EU membership. Others were concerned about their international and internal security. Macedonia, for instance, had a conflict with Greece over its name, at the same time as it was exposed to the pressures of state failure in Albania, and increasing war in Kosovo. Thus, regional cooperation was given low priority. If it were to come, it would have to be induced by other actors. For the Balkans, this was left for the EU, which also launched a special cooperative initiative in 1999. The hope of joining EU in the future is also making Serbia more willing to accept Kosovo's independence, at least in practice.

The prospects of regional cooperation may be different if there is also a change in the former centre. This has been the case in South Africa. Southern African cooperation received considerable input from the peace agreements for Namibia, South Africa and Mozambique. It has also been strong enough to handle disputes among member states. The political changes that took place in the first part of the 1990s gave regional cooperation a chance, and the countries in the region were willing to use the opportunity. A similar chance was created in the Horn of Africa, with the 1991 defeat of the old regimes in Ethiopia (Mengistu) and Somalia (Barre). Within one year, however, a process of regional fragmentation unfolded, ending in the collapse of Somalia, the rise of ethnically based violence in Ethiopia and, by the end of the decade, a protracted war between Ethiopia and Eritrea. The regional organization, IGAD, did not have the opportunity it would have needed. In a short period, the Horn of Africa experienced all types of war: civil wars with state failure, state formation and interstate wars. In addition, it has had a recent history of authoritarian regimes, coups and economic mismanagement. Regional integration may follow a war, but only under particular circumstances. At best, regional reconstruction may be a protracted process, no matter what the outcome of the war. Rather, we may be able to identify 'failed regions', as we can discuss failed states.

It is worth noting that in two cases of independence (Slovenia and Namibia) there was considerable economic progress. Slovenia and Namibia belong to the countries that were the least economically affected by the war. In the first case, the armed conflict lasted only ten days; in the latter case, most of the fighting took place in neighbouring Angola, where the armed liberation movement, SWAPO, had its bases. Two other independent countries (Eritrea, Timor-Leste, that is, former East Timor) have experienced wars that have gone on for 20 or 30 years, meaning that vast resources have been destroyed and opportunities lost: young people have died or been crippled, infrastructure wasted and resources plundered. They have expectations of international assistance. In none of these cases is the new state turning to the former centre for support or even compensation. The hopes for regional integration may be important in the minds of the leaders of the centres. It may well underestimate the dynamics behind a struggle for independence. Sometimes regional cooperation can be achieved, but it may be a preferable strategy before a conflict rather than after it.

This brings us to the second aspect. The centre may accept independence of particular territories if this does not damage its self-understanding. It was easier for the Indonesian Parliament in October 1999 to accept the independence vote in East Timor as this did not threaten an Indonesian self-image. In this view, East Timor was a special case. It was not part of the original Indonesian state that was created from the Dutch colonial empire in 1945. West Irian was joined with Indonesia in 1963, but it had also been under Dutch rule. Thus, Indonesia's core self-definition was based on the former Dutch East Indies. The addition of East Timor, a former Portuguese holding, was alien and associated with the deposed military regime under General Suharto. Giving self-government to East Timor was compatible with Indonesia's regime before Suharto. It also made it possible to argue that no other areas were to leave the country. A coherent ideological position could be found. Thus, a settlement on Aceh required a solution within present-day Indonesia, and the same may be implied for West Papua (West Irian).

Similarly, Czech self-understanding made it possible to accept Slovakia's separation. To keep an empire has not been a Czech obsession. We have already observed the Russian self-understanding promoted by Boris Yeltsin while in opposition. Also, Russia had suffered from the Soviet Union, it was claimed, and thus there was a demand for leaving this union. The new rulers in Ethiopia in 1991, EPRDF, had a programme which allowed for Eritrea's separation. They gained power in close cooperation with the Eritrean People's Liberation Front (EPLF). The official view of Ethiopia no longer made control over Eritrea vital for the country's role domestically or internationally.

There are many such changes in self-definition in history. Sweden accepted the secession of Norway after an agreed referendum had been conducted and a demilitarized zone between the two countries had been created. This dissolved a union according to the demands of Norway. The union had been created by force but ended peacefully after lasting 90 years, 1814–1905. Its ending did not affect an emerging Swedish self-understanding, leaving regional power politics in favour of building a modern society of industry, democracy and welfare.

Also, the decolonization process was related to changed self-understanding among many colonial powers. There was a realization that their own economic growth was no longer benefiting from the colonial empires – the costs were increasing. There was a redefinition of their roles in the world. Improving the well-being of the population in the centre became more important than projecting power in distant territories. Some lessons, however, had to be learned the hard way. France lost two wars, in Indochina (1947–54) and in Algeria (1954–62). Britain lost to an ingenious and persistent non-violence campaign in India (led by Mahatma Gandhi, ending in independence for India and Pakistan in 1947) and in the Gold Coast in West Africa (ending in the creation of Ghana in 1957). Together, France and Britain lost in trying to wrestle back control over the Suez Canal from Egypt in 1956. They encountered united opposition from the United States and the Soviet Union. The Netherlands fought Indonesian anti-colonial forces under Sukarno in the late 1940s before realizing the futility in the effort. The last stand of colonialism was by Portugal, where the so-called Carnation Revolution in 1974 ended its colonial ambition. Instead, Portugal gave priority to domestic development and economic integration with Europe, becoming an EU member in 1986.

Changes in self-understanding seem to be important for a more peaceful ending to conflicts over state formation. They may come about as a result of the efforts of the opposition in the controlled areas, but it may also relate to new internal priorities for state and society. Thus, we would argue that a similar self-understanding did not develop in the cases where the conflicts became violent and where independence was only reluctantly accepted. This, furthermore, might also be where regional cooperation has been the most difficult to accomplish. Certainly, South Africa's self-image today is entirely different from the one that existed at the end of the Cold War. This affects relations all over the region.

Third, the human costs may affect the centre's willingness to accept independence solutions. It seems generally true that drawing new international borders is likely to create new problems, not just solve old ones. The state dissolutions we have seen have used previously existing administrative divisions, where such have been applicable. The colonial borders were used for decolonization. There were few Czechs in Slovakia and vice versa, and the same is true with Swedes in Norway. This was not the case in all the situations. Particularly, the new borders among the former Yugoslav republics had the effect of creating Serb minorities in the new states. The notion of ethnic cleansing – by different sides – became the historical imprint of these wars. Serb authorities evicted peoples from their areas of control and, at other instances, Serbs were evicted from non-Yugoslav controlled areas. The rapid escalation of the conflicts in 1991 and 1992 removed any possibility of looking into alternative arrangements. There might have been ways of managing these minority problems, as has so far been possible for Russians outside the Russian Federation, and previously for Hungarians outside Hungary.

Together, these three factors may explain why independence solutions are sometimes peaceful, sometimes not. A central aspect is the dominant unit's understanding of its role. A peaceful dissolution may be more easily achieved if it is done under an expectation of regional cooperation, where the centre has a non-offensive understanding of its role, and where the new borders can be managed so that new minorities, on either side of the border, are given sufficient security. These conditions are not easy to meet, but they have been present at some important occasions.

This means that independence, in order not to create future conflicts, will require accompanying measures, particularly relating to new borders. In general, it appears impossible to draw boundaries which will divide all inhabitants in a humane way. The interconnections between people are many and close, particularly if they are living in an interspersed pattern, as assumed by the idea of the ethnic security dilemma. Also, sources of income are likely to create such patterns. In a somewhat free economy, people of all backgrounds are converging on places of economic growth and new opportunity. Thus, simply drawing thick lines on the basis of population statistics will create unfair and unequal treatment.

Furthermore, one may ask how such a division can be decided in a democratic way. Is a majority decision sufficient or shall the minority be entitled to a veto? How can a referendum without harassment be conducted, particularly if there already is an armed conflict? An examination of the experience of the agreed partitions of former British India and Palestine cannot be avoided. There is a debate on these lessons (Bell-Fialkoff 1996; Schaeffer 1990).

The problem with the boundary divisions is that people have to move permanently and, thus, all their investments, memories and roots are affected. It is not likely to be something about which people are enthusiastic. The blame, furthermore, is going to be directed against the other group, and thus the hatred stemming from a war may become even more deep-seated. There have been two state divisions decided deliberately through legitimate fora. One was by responsible leaders in the case of India, the other by the UN General Assembly in the case of Palestine. Both were implemented more than 60 years ago. Both resulted in wars. The effects have yet to be overcome. The relationship between India and Pakistan has reached a stage of a nuclear arms race. Also Israel is known to possess nuclear weapons capacity. The issue of how to secure the rights of the dispossessed Palestinians remains unresolved. In other words, these are experiences where the solution to an internal ethnic security dilemma actually led to interstate security dilemmas of the type we have discussed in Chapter 5. One solution was bought at the price of a new problem.

The fate of refugee populations is likely to be central in any state division. Some of the settlements since the Cold War have allowed for the return of refugees, but in many cases such a prospect has been bleak. The Dayton Accords stipulated the return of refugees, and many have done so. In this case, there is not only the insecurity of being a minority in surroundings dominated by other ethnic groups, but also the challenge of finding income. As the economies are not developing, it is difficult to return and, thus, the security that a multi-ethnic environment would provide will not emerge.

We see that independence, once achieved and recognized, has provided a measure of stability to a particular conflict. In some cases there is also an experience of economic growth. But the hope of dramatically changing the situation in a region is not borne out. Regional cooperation has become more difficult and the costs to independence higher than anticipated. A new state remains in an area where its old foes also are. New conflicts may follow, as seen in the Horn of Africa. The driving force behind the quest for independence has often been to escape an intolerable situation of dominance. Independence may achieve a change in relations. Whether the result is a less conflict-ridden and more tolerant society or region can be questioned. The record is positive in some cases, negative in others. It is important to observe alternative developments where combinations can be found and have been put in place without armed conflict.

7.5 State Formation Conflicts and Democracy

The solutions to state formation conflicts, which we discussed in Sections 7.3 and 7.4, have concerned territorial divisions between the contending groups, whether their conflict has dealt with decolonization or ethnically based identity issues. The solutions to the ethnic security dilemma have been to create separate units, which provide protection for the different groups. This is in line with much thinking on self-determination. It is likely, however, that this is applicable only to some identity-based conflicts. Most can probably be handled equally well, or even better, through the existing units. Section 7.2 and Table 7.2 suggested some such possibilities. It is only under special circumstances that the ethnic security dilemma will be fully developed and necessitate more radical solutions, such as the creation of new units.

Territorial solutions mean drawing softer or harder lines between peoples in order to create security on each side. A particular ethnic group may feel more secure if it is shielded by a new border. However, some people will be on the 'wrong' side, from the point of view of the new state units. Thus, there are additional security concerns and they are not necessarily solved by the boundaries. Demilitarization and democratization will improve the situation for such groups. The softer the borders the more security will be provided to the new minorities. At the same time, the security demands of the new dominant group make it prefer impenetrable, hard borders. Some tension might be remedied by credible measures for minority rights, for instance, as complements to the independence solutions. The measures in Table 7.2 will be relevant. Also, with harder borders, it will be more difficult for refugees to return. This issue seems more difficult to deal with in the case of state formation conflicts than in civil wars. The restoration of refugee rights in state formation conflicts is more closely associated with security and economic chances for the returnees. For instance, their land and houses may be taken over by others, as part of a deliberate government policy to force them out. The right of return may not be accepted by the new authorities. This risks making the refugee population a permanent issue. Conflict resolution is prevented.

These dilemmas make it necessary to raise the question of whether there are still other possible solutions of state formation conflicts. We would then look for integrative solutions, which give different groups equal rights in the society. For democracies, in particular, this opens new possibilities. A related issue is that conflict situations do not only contain armed actors, who are often part of the final agreements, but a surrounding society of non-armed actors. Some may pursue the same goals as the armed actors, others may have dissenting views. Either way, they are part of the society and their roles need to be considered.

First, there is a possibility of sharing government, or even giving influence to minorities. The example of Finland is instructive. The Åland Islands have been mentioned as a functioning autonomy arrangement. Swedish-speaking inhabitants predominantly populate these islands. In an arrangement achieved through the League of Nations in 1921 and confirmed by the UN in 1950, this autonomy was created to preserve the Swedish language and culture on the islands. In this way, a dispute between Sweden and Finland about the sovereignty over these islands was solved. However, the Ålanders are only a fraction of all Swedish-speaking inhabitants in Finland. Their preference for a separate unit was not shared by others. This is where the story becomes interesting. Let us follow this.

Other Swedish speakers were not interested in autonomy arrangements, or were even sceptical of it, as it could reduce their influence in the society as a whole. They resolved the issue in favour of full participation in the political life of Finland. To them, it was more important that Swedish was recognized and respected as a national language. A political party pursuing Swedish and liberal interests was created and Swedish-speaking politicians emerged in other political parties. Thus, although being no more than 5 per cent of the total population, the Swedish-speaking group managed to exert considerable influence on national politics. At the same time, it could act to protect specific Swedish interests, which largely were questions of culture and language.

This experience suggests an integrative way of handling identity-based conflicts. It is a demanding strategy for a minority, but it also makes it a creative contributor to the society as a whole. It means that the minority is not primarily defining itself as a minority but as a legitimate participant in the affairs of the country as a whole. It escapes the danger of becoming a group concerned only with its own affairs. It avoids a potential danger in autonomy solutions of isolation, ghetto-like conditions and marginalization from the main currents of the state. This is the essence of an integrative strategy. This experience suggests interesting options, where combinations are possible. It could be that the integrative solution gains strength from the simultaneous existence of the autonomy, which in turn also benefits from the minority's participation in national affairs.

It is possible that such solutions are open only to stable democratic societies. It, of course, builds on an important premise: the rights of the minority are accepted in the society, socially as well as legally. Some democratic or open societies have encountered problems on this score. There are examples of minorities with elected representatives who encounter strong resistance when pursuing the interests of the minority. This has been a repeated experience in Turkey for parliamentary representatives of Kurdish origin, for instance. There are similar problems in the State of Israel, where Israeli Arab voters tend to vote for special Arab tickets and, although having their seats in the Knesset, are still not seen among the Israeli general public as a legitimate support-base for a governing majority.

A parallel history is found in the experience of Tamil political representation in the parliament in Sri Lanka. A Tamil party was the leading opposition party in 1977 and initially the government's measures included, for instance, the improvement of the status of the Tamil language. However, the government remained more concerned about its standing in the Singhalese majority community, and negotiations on a solution became increasingly sterile. Following the anti-Tamil riots in Colombo in 1983, the government passed an amendment forcing all members of parliament to take an oath to defend the unitary Constitution. The Tamil members resigned their seats. The negotiations for solutions that had preceded these events had dealt with the possibility of devolution (Wriggins 1995). We have also referred to the experience of Cyprus, also a society working under a democratic framework. Thus, as these experiences suggest, leaders of the majority have at times preferred to marginalize minority representatives, despite their democratic mandates. This is not likely to consolidate democratic procedures in the groups affected.

These examples concern cases where the majority is overwhelming and often able to govern without the support of the identity minority. In Finland, the Swedish party skilfully positioned itself in the middle of the political spectrum. It was party to coalitions with Left, Centre and Right. Its votes have been important for a government's majority. That was also the role earlier performed by Tamils in the parliament in Sri Lanka. In some other democratic societies, such arrangements have been undermined. In Northern Ireland, the Catholic minority was excluded from local political influence, through a de facto one-party system. In Cyprus, the power-sharing arrangement was not allowed to accumulate experience. The dilemma for a democratic system is that democratic policies can either integrate or marginalize groups. As we see in these cases, policies have been pursued so as to keep a minority from influence during longer periods of time. This is done without breaking constitutional rules. The long-term consequences can be negative for the democratic system and for the viability of the state, as can be seen in Cyprus, Northern Ireland, Sri Lanka and Turkey. The societies have found themselves in state formation conflicts from which they have had severe difficulty extracting themselves.

In other instances, where the majority–minority relationship is less clear-cut, the possibility of semi-permanent, broad-based coalitions bridging ethnic divides may be larger. This is part of the formula for the central authority in the state of Bosnia-Herzegovina. In this case, a veto is given to each of the communities. A similar arrangement was made in the constitution for Cyprus (Jarstad 2001) as well as through the Annan Plan in 2004, and both failed to create a necessary atmosphere of cooperation. Functioning examples of such coalitions are found in more authoritarian states. An example is Malaysia, where the National Front, Barisan Nasional, has been ruling the country for more than 40 years. It is composed of parties representing different ethnic communities. As there are opposition parties, the system is more open than might be expected. It means, however, that the society builds on elite consensus, and that basic decisions are made through closed deals between the parties in the National Front. This is in line with the idea of consensual politics for an ethnically divided society (Lijphart also calls this consociational, 1975, 1984). The Malaysian society has functioned remarkably well over a long period of time. The performance in economic growth has been exceptional. At the same time, it has resulted in an ethnicization of politics and society. All parties in the parliament now mobilize support along ethnic lines. The overriding shared interest is to maintain stability, which enhances economic growth. In times of economic crises, this could expose the society to severe strain, as was seen in the late 1980s and in the Asian economic crisis of 1997–98 (Case 2001).

This discussion suggests that there are integrative solutions for state formation conflicts. The prerequisite seems to be that they are instituted early, at a time when ethnic polarization is not developed or entrenched. A tradition of national cooperation can be created. Even at a later stage, it is probably important that the democratic practices are given a real chance for a minority to have an impact on the overall policies of the state. The logic that influence leads to responsibility, commitment and identification is compelling: it is only then that the minority will see the state as 'its' own in much the same way as the majority. Without this, however, integrative solutions in democratic societies are likely to be difficult to maintain. There is a danger of marginalization of groups even under democracy. The bigger such excluded groups are, the more troublesome the future for the democratic framework. This is significant to recall in post-Saddam Hussein Iraq, where the Sunni Arab group is a community large enough to sustain armed resistance.

This leads us to the second issue, the role of non-armed groups in the creation and maintenance of solutions. We referred to this in Chapter 3. As was the case in the settlement of civil war disputes, the incorporation of the larger society has been a feature only in some of the solutions. As we noted, there are solutions where leading actors were not actually signatories to agreements (Namibia, East Timor) with even less involvement of other groups. The fact that these conflicts straddle the dichotomy of interstate and internal conflict means that their management is less consistent. Also, a broader participation requires a democratic system, and several of the settlements concerned countries which were fairly closed. Only a few of the agreements have given rise to a vigorous debate during the peace process. The typical examples are Palestine and Northern Ireland, where options have been discussed while the process was still under way. It is likely that, in both cases, the debate made clear to the negotiating parties the range of opinion and what was acceptable. In some of the ongoing armed conflicts (Sri Lanka, Turkey, Russia) as well as in Cyprus, there are democratic conditions that would be conducive for a broader discussion, but it seems to be difficult to initiate.

Still, the importance of non-armed groups as well as popular participation in the peace process should not be underestimated. The unarmed and largest party on the Irish Nationalist side in Northern Ireland, the SDLP led by John Hume, was instrumental in the furthering of peace. Its informal contacts with Sinn Fein, regarded to be close to the Provisional IRA, made it possible to broaden Nationalist participation in the peace process. There were also groups and parties bridging the gap between the two major communities in Northern Ireland. The main actors on the Unionist side were all, officially, unarmed actors, some no doubt still with links to para-military groups. The non-armed groups were essential in making contacts. At the same time, they also constituted alternative ways of pursuing basically the same demands. It was, for instance, the parties with a clear non-armed agenda that received most of the votes in the elections during the times of armed conflict.

It is likely that non-armed groups can play similar roles in other conflicts, but that makes a cease-fire a necessity – the earlier, the better. Without that, contacts initiated by non-armed groups can be seen as threatening to the solidarity of a particular side, and thus the groups become targets for terrorist attacks. This has been the fate of several early emissaries, for instance, in the Israeli–Palestinian conflict. A cease-fire is not only something that benefits the fighting parties at a certain moment or reduces the strain on the population as a whole, it also gives a chance for a more vibrant society to have an impact on the course of peace. In a study that has explored this issue quantitatively, Desirée Nilsson (2008) found that in a peace agreement which included civil society actors, the peace was more likely to endure.

For states and oppositions alike, there are no simple solutions to state formation conflicts. This chapter has illustrated some of the possibilities that have been agreed between the fighting parties. It has also shown that victory does take place in surprisingly few cases. State formation conflicts tend to be protracted. This suggests that they require early action for a settlement before they become too entrenched, or solutions in which states allow for constitutional variation, perhaps coupled to regional and international involvement.

Further Readings

Go to the *Understanding Conflict Resolution* web page at https://study.sagepub.com/wallensteen4e for free access to journal articles listed.

General Dynamics of State Formation Conflicts

Anderson, B. 1991. *Imagined Communities: Reflections on the Origin and Spread of Nationalism*. London: Verso.

Kaldor, M. 2006. *New and Old Wars: Organized Violence in a Global Era* (2nd edn). Cambridge: Polity Press.

These two books have both contributed to the discussion on the special character of identity-based conflicts. Anderson builds, for instance, on examples from Southeast Asia, and also focuses on the identity-shaping effects of languages. Kaldor discusses 'new' conflicts as those building on ethnic and other identities, often using the experiences of the Balkan wars, to support her theses. It has also given rise to a debate on what is 'new':

Melander, E., Öberg, M. et al., 2009, 'Are "New Wars" More Atrocious? Battle Intensity, Civilians Killed and Forced Migration Before and After the End of the Cold War', *European Journal of International Relations* 15 (3): 505–536.

Solutions of State Formation Conflicts

Cornell, S.E. 2002. 'Autonomy as a Source of Conflict: Caucasian Conflicts in Theoretical Perspective', *World Politics*, 54 (2): 245–76.

Cornell makes a critical evaluation of the autonomy arrangements worked out during the Soviet and post-Soviet times in the Caucasus.

Gurr, T. R. 2000b. 'Ethnic Warfare on the Wane', *Foreign Affairs*, 79 (3): 52–64.

In this article Gurr argues that the international community actually has developed ways of dealing with ethnic conflicts, ranging from the support of

(Continued)

(Continued)

minority rights to self-governance. He also sees a largely successful use of such solutions.

Regan, P. and Wallensteen, P. 2013. 'Federal Institutions, Declarations of Independence and Civil War', *Civil Wars*, 15 (3): 261–280.
In this work the authors see federalism as a solution to intra-state conflicts about territory, but also point to the dangers of armed conflicts becoming more vicious if such arrangements break apart. In particular, they study the organization of military forces and its centralization as a key factor.

Bosnia and Palestine

Daalder, I.H. and Froman, M.B.G. 1999. 'Dayton's Incomplete Peace', *Foreign Affairs*, 78 (6): 106–13.
The Dayton agreement on the Bosnian crisis was concluded in 1995, and this treaty still stands. However, quickly there were critical comments on what was lacking in this agreement. Daalder and Froman is an early contribution, and others have followed.

A different approach is Kostic, R. 2008. 'Nationbuilding as an Instrument of Peace?', *Civil Wars*, 10 (4): 384–412, using national polling data in the search of changing attitudes among the ethnic communities.

LeVine, M. and Mossberg, M. (eds) 2014. *One Land, Two States: Israel and Palestine as Parallel States*, University of California Press.
This is a collection of essays exploring 'out-of-the-box' thinking for a solution to the protracted Palestinian conflict. Particularly it elaborates on the possibility of two parallel states in one territory.

Notes

1 If we include the UCDP category of non-state conflicts, the picture is different. Africa has about three-quarters of these conflicts (Pettersson 2010).
2 A challenging new idea is the one of two parallel states on the same territory (Mossberg 2010).
3 United States of America was created by the victors in the war against the British as a solution to their needs, building on an original confederation that was in effect a defence pact (Bednar 2009: 64–6). After the Civil War, the losing side was simply reintegrated into the existing structure. The Federal Republic of Germany was created by the victors in the Second World War, again their solution to the post-war needs. Both these cases have worked remarkably well and the federations are today profoundly entrenched in the two populations. The same is true for Switzerland, but again it originated as a shared defence pact against outsiders, not as a solution for intra-Swiss conflicts.

PART THREE

COMPLEXITIES IN CONFLICT RESOLUTION

8

CONFLICT COMPLEXES AND CONFLICT RESOLUTION

8.1 Identifying Conflict Complexes

The three basic types of conflict that we have been scrutinizing in Chapters 5, 6 and 7 have to be solved with different instruments intrinsic to each type. This is especially true as long as we can treat them as bilateral relationships between two dominant actors confronting each other. From a solution perspective these are the smallest possible elements into which a conflict can be dissected. However, conflicts are neither this simple nor stable. A particular conflict is rarely left alone to be the concern of only the original parties. Conflicts attract attention, some of which may be benign – outsiders will offer their services to help to solve the conflict; others may be more malicious – there are actors who search for ways of using a situation for their own, highly particular purposes. Still others are involved because they simply want to protect themselves, their economy or their extended interests. This may bring them into a conflict, siding with a party or making them into new parties. The linkages are many and the motives varied. This will have many effects: it may prolong the conflict; it may increase destruction; it may also do the reverse. Of particular concern here is how this affects the resolution process. The more parties with stakes in the outcome, the more difficult it will be to arrive at settlements through negotiations, mediation or other forms of intervention.

To capture these interconnections, the term *conflict complex* is useful. It is a way of describing how conflicts are connected to one another. At a given moment in time, we may observe active conflicts in two different areas but in the same geographical region. Although they may appear separate, closer scrutiny is likely to establish interconnections (Buzan 1991; Buzan and Waever 2003). When applied to geographical and political regions, this gives us the concept of *regional conflict complexes*, where primary and secondary parties are engaged in the same region. The connections between the civil war in Syria and all the neighbouring countries constitute a recent example of this: armed actors and weapons cross the borders, with refugees often going in the opposite direction to find protection wherever possible.

However, here we will also introduce the notion of *global conflict complexes*. By way of major powers and their involvement, conflicts may become connected when this would not otherwise have been the case. The most instructive example is the Cold War, linking distant areas into the same political and strategic thinking. After 2001, the global 'war' on terrorism had a similar effect, most specifically for areas with large Muslim populations. We begin by discussing the regional connections here and in the following section and return to major power dynamics in Sections 8.3 and 8.4 as well as in Chapter 9.

Regional Conflicts since the Cold War

In a study using the Uppsala Conflict Data Program, 16 regional conflict complexes, or regional conflicts for short, could be established since the end of the Cold War. In an updated form they are listed in Table 8.1. They include a large share of all armed conflicts. It means that the solution to a particular conflict cannot concentrate solely on finding ways of transcending the incompatibilities isolated in Chapters 5, 6 and 7. A follow-up study showed that three-quarters of all internal armed conflicts had an outside actor involved – mostly neighbours – further testimony to the significance of the regional dimension (Harbom and Wallensteen 2005).

The 16 regional conflict complexes include approximately half of all armed conflicts since the end of the Cold War. Their share of the most serious conflicts is even higher: more than two-thirds of the wars are in this group (Wallensteen and Sollenberg 1998). Thus, it is important to analyse conflicts in a regional context. Some conflicts have connection to several complexes, and the outer borders of complexes can be discussed. For example, there is a chain of mutual, consecutive connections among conflicts stretching across Africa from Angola to Eritrea, so to say, from the Atlantic Ocean to the Red Sea. The conflict material in this region, which is highly populated and resource-rich, has the potential to fuel conflict, if nothing is done, for many years to come. The three complexes identified in the Middle East may also be quite interrelated, as distances are short and the technological capacities of some actors in the region are considerable. However, it still makes sense, analytically and politically, to separate them. Each displays sufficiently independent dynamics to justify this.

It is interesting to note that these regional conflict complexes also include about half of all lasting peace agreements identified in Chapters 5, 6 and 7, shown in italics in Table 8.1. Conflicts within regional conflict complexes are possible to solve. However, the fragility of some of the solutions has to do with the contentious political contexts in which they find themselves. In some regions, peace agreements have supported each other. This is true for Central America, which developed into a

Table 8.1 Regional conflict complexes with armed conflicts since the end of the Cold War

Regional conflict complex	Examples of armed conflict
Southeast Europe	*Yugoslavia (Kosovo)*, Croatia, *Bosnia*, Slovenia, *East Slavonia*, Albania, *Macedonia*
Caucasus	Azerbaijan, Georgia, Chechnya, Dagestan
Palestine	Israel–Palestine, *Lebanon*, Israel–Syria, *Israel– Jordan*, *Israel-Egypt*, Iraq, Iran
Gulf region	Iraq–Kuwait, USA and allies; Iran–Iraq, Iraq, USA–Iraq, Iran, Saudi Arabia, Gulf states
Syrian and Kurdish complex	Iraq, Iran, Turkey, Syria, Lebanon
Central Africa, West (Great Lakes Region)	Zaire, *Democratic Republic of Congo (Kinshasa)*, *Angola*, *Congo (Brazzaville)*, Rwanda, Central African Republic, *Burundi*, *Uganda*
Central Africa, East	Uganda, *Sudan*, South Sudan, Kenya, Ethiopia, Eritrea, *Eritrea–Ethiopia*
Horn of Africa	Ethiopia, Eritrea, *Eritrea–Ethiopia*, *Sudan*, Somalia, Kenya, *Djibouti*
Southern Africa	*South Africa*, Lesotho, *Mozambique*, Namibia, *Namibia–Botswana*, Angola
West Africa	*Liberia*, Guinea, *Sierra Leone*, *Guinea-Bissau*, *Senegal*, *Côte d'Ivoire*
Sahel	*Mali*, *Niger*, *Libya–Chad*, *Chad*, Libya, Algeria, Mauretania
Indochina	*Vietnam–Cambodia*, *Cambodia*, Cambodia-Thailand, Thailand, Laos
South Asia, West	India, Pakistan, India–Pakistan, Afghanistan
South Asia, East	India, *Bangladesh*, Burma/Myanmar
Central Asia	Afghanistan, *Tajikistan*, Uzbekistan
Central America	*Nicaragua, El Salvador, Guatemala*

Note: Conflicts which saw at least one lasting peace agreement are in *italics*. Some armed conflicts not meeting the thresholds for inclusion in the Uppsala Conflict Data Program are included, e.g. Botswana–Namibia, the peace agreements between Israel and Jordan (where fighting last occurred in 1967) and with Egypt (last fighting in 1973). Also, the table makes no reference to maritime regions, notably the Gulf of Aden, the South China Sea and polar areas. Developed from Wallensteen and Sollenberg (1998).

model of a regionally driven peace process. Politically initiated by Costa Rica's President Oscar Arias in 1987, it resulted, within ten years, in peace agreements in all protracted internal conflicts in the region. It was based on a shared understanding of the leaders of five countries. They agreed to pursue similar policies of national conciliation and non-interference in neighbouring conflicts. By strengthening democratic institutions and human rights in all countries, the armed conflicts were brought to an end, one by one, beginning with Nicaragua.

The Sahel region in West Africa has witnessed something similar, although less coordinated. For a time, conflicts, often connected to Libya, gradually subsided and found solutions. A first case was the Libya–Chad conflict, which was brought to the International Court of Justice, followed by the settlement of Chad's civil war and a creative handling of conflicts in Niger and Mali. The 'Flamme de la Paix' ceremony in Timbuktu, Mali, in 1996 (a big bonfire consisting of thousands of arms turned in by former fighters) became a symbol for attempts to end conflict by eliminating trade in small arms. However, since 2011 the patterns have been reversed. The fall of the Gaddafi regime in Libya led to the spread of weapons and fighters across the region. This affected Mali, in particular, but neighbouring Niger and Mauretania were also threatened. A UN-endorsed military force in Mali demonstrated international ambitions in containing the situation.

Armed conflicts in Southern Africa have all but ceased, partly through negotiated settlements. An example is the verdict by the International Arbitration Court on the Kasikili-Sedudu Island conflict between Namibia and Botswana (1999). The war in Angola connected this region to the complexes of Central Africa but, after the death of UNITA leader Jonas Savimbi in 2002, the parties went back to previous agreements. This also had a beneficial effect on the peace efforts in the Central African complexes. The fact that the actors realize they are part of a larger regional framework makes learning possible. There are many examples of this (Ohlson 1998). In Southern Africa, the earlier failure in Angola had an impact on the settlement in Mozambique in 1992. Renamo, the armed opposition, learned from UNITA's fate in the transition in Angola that it was important to limit the choices of the government side as much as possible. Another element cited was the emphasis in the Mozambique settlement of a sizeable UN presence and early demilitarization, something lacking in Angola's 1991 agreement (Chan and Venancio 1998: 44–5, 63, 66). Thus, when fighting again appeared in Mozambique in 2013 there was considerable international commitment to deal with the situation.

Wars ending in victories also lead to important lessons. Again, the interconnectedness can have the effect of reducing the chance of a decisive outcome. A victory in one conflict can be undermined by the continuation of war in another. Also, a regional conflict complex is likely to be attractive for arms trading. It is most noteworthy that some regions have no examples of war endings other than victory. This is true for the Gulf region, largely also for other parts of the Middle East and the Horn of Africa, and Central Africa. This is in sharp contrast to Central America. As a consequence, the security dilemmas described in the preceding chapters are particularly acute. If there is no practical experience of peaceful endings to armed conflicts, the parties may have very little reason to believe in the realism and relevance of such solutions. War termination through conflict resolution is not likely to be a credible alternative. At the same time, it might suffice to have one case of a successfully implemented peace agreement to change such perceptions. There was, of course, no previous experience of peace agreements in Central America. The Nicaraguan settlement showed the possibility of such a route. The same is true for the accord on Namibia in Southern Africa. The chances of an agreement surviving in an unreceptive milieu of many security dilemmas are not the best, but at the same time it is likely to be necessary to change regional conflict dynamics. The agreement in Burundi 2008 is gradually being entrenched in the society and may stimulate similar approaches in this region.

It is interesting to note that the solutions to regional conflict complexes that have been successful have originated in the region itself. The Esquipulas II process in Central America – named after the second summit meeting among Central American heads of state in Esquipulas, Guatemala – built on previous South American initiatives, the Contadora process. The Esquipulas initiatives were undertaken by the Central American countries themselves. It meant that if united, they could resist diplomatic and other interventions from the United States, the Soviet Union or other states. It turned the established agenda of peacemaking around, and set regional needs first. Outside powers had to make adjustments (Spalding 1999).

Table 8.1 also lists the Syrian–Kurdish complex. It could as well be called the Levant nexus as it involves a host of actors, not only the Assad regime in Syria or the Kurdish actors in many of the neighbouring countries. The protracted and devastating war in Syria has attracted groups with entirely different agendas, ranging from a purportedly more democratic approach of the Free Syrian Army to the notorious Islamic State (variously called ISIS, ISIL, Caliphate or Da'esh in Arabic). Most actors operate within the established borders, and the only one explicitly challenging them is ISIS, building on tenets from al-Qaida thinking. The inability of the Arab neighbours as well as the major powers to find a consistent approach to this conflict is alarming (Wallensteen and Bjurner 2015). By mid-2014, the UN Secretary-General appointed its third consecutive mediator, Swedish diplomat Staffan de Mistura, following on Kofi Annan and Lakhdar Brahimi. Later the US began bombing ISIS positions.

Approaching Regional Conflicts

Disentangling regional conflict complexes typically involves two contrasting approaches to a peace process. A gradual way is to deal with a regional conflict complex *conflict by conflict*. Those conflicts which are open to solution are brought to an ending as speedily as is possible. This is done in the hope that continued conflict in neighbouring countries will not affect the implementation of the accords. By removing one conflict in one country from the agenda, the region has a shared experience that can generate energy to go on to the next conflict. A regional momentum for peace is created as tensions also decline in other relationships. The Sahel complex was handled this way in the 1990s. The first agreement needs to be successful and have considerable support, both inside and outside the region. In this way it can create a new regional reality. Presently, there is no attempt to repeat this experience for that region.

This approach is often the one preferred by stronger regional actors. It gives them a central role. For example, India does not want to deal with its conflicts in other than bilateral negotiations. Similarly, Israel's preference has been for peacemaking with each of the Arab states and actors one by one. In the Israeli–Palestinian process, furthermore, the resolution was sought through a step-by-step approach, where the negotiations aimed at a gradual creation of a functioning Palestinian state next to Israel.

One danger with the conflict-by-conflict approach is that the interconnections in the region might be so strong that it will be difficult to implement an isolated agreement. Despite much effort, it was difficult to find an isolated settlement for Burundi in the midst of all the other conflicts in Central Africa. As can be understood from Table 8.1, this region has seen failed agreements (such as the one in Rwanda in 1993).

Some of these have still resulted in later arrangements with a reasonable potential for the future (Burundi, now with a record of several democratic elections, but still encountering increasing tension). The danger is that the first step will also be the last. This, certainly, has marred the negotiations between Israel and Palestine, where the latter constantly worries whether the goal, a viable Palestinian state, will ever materialize. The same worry may spur others to be more insistent on finding a settlement.

Often, the first steps taken by the parties have been the establishment of a truce of some sort. It makes sense, as it is difficult to pursue negotiations at the same time as violence is continuing among the parties. Nevertheless, there are many negotiations that do not include cease-fire as a first step. Cease-fires often appeal more to a strong party and to regional actors. For the latter in particular, it will reduce acute tensions in the region and make it possible for governments to deal with other matters. It may, however, result in a gradual acceptance of a status quo that will be built on an unsolved conflict. This seems to have happened in the Southern Caucasus, where, 20 years later, the cease-fire in 1994 has not generated a solution to the conflict over Nagorno-Karabakh. A credible step-by-step approach assumes a consistent and coherent leadership as well as extra-regional commitment and a reasonably short time horizon.

There is also a bolder approach, which takes on *the most difficult conflict first*, thus hoping to remove the entire regional conflict complex in a short span of time. This means that the most crucial conflicts are identified and solved, even though they may initially seem to be the ones most difficult to manage. If this succeeds, the rest is expected to fall into place. This is bolder, as it requires a shared analysis of what the central issues are and highly concerted actions to tackle them. Sometimes the issues can be easily identified. The processes that dissolved the conflict complex of Southern Africa provide examples. South Africa had long been identified as a crucial actor by the international system. There were international sanctions on the apartheid regime and considerable attention to its links to wars in the region. Following the settlement of the Namibia conflict in 1988, the apartheid system in South Africa began to open up. As South Africa was central in many conflicts, this had effects on all the surrounding states. Parallel to the democratization process in South Africa, the wars in Angola and Mozambique could find negotiated endings. After the release of Nelson Mandela in 1990 the dynamics of the region changed dramatically, and there was a momentum to build on. It did not immediately, however, carry all the way. Developments in Zimbabwe have resulted in one-sided violence, curtailment of freedoms and economic stagnation in a formerly rich country.

Another case is Indochina, where Cambodia was seen as the core issue in the regional conflict complex. When relations between China and Vietnam improved, Vietnamese troops were pulled back from Cambodia, regional actors approached the different sides and a momentum could be generated. The inclusion of both Vietnam and Cambodia in the Association of South East Asian Nations (ASEAN), the regional cooperation organization for Southeast Asia, served to keep regional stability. Lately, developments in Thailand with repeated coups, elections and demonstrations, have caused concern, but so far with limited regional repercussions. There has been space for regional support to end the conflict in Mindanao, where the Philippine government accepted Malaysia as a mediator.

Identifying such central regional issues, however, may not always be easy. For instance, there are at least two different ways to understand the post-Milosevic situation in Southeastern Europe. Many would argue that the most crucial issue in this complex is the government in Serbia. With democratization and a less nationalist and autocratic rule, many issues in the region have become easier to deal with. Serbia was a key actor in all conflicts in former Yugoslav republics, partly because of the presence of a Serb population, partly due to economic links and military considerations. After the fall of the Milosevic regime in October 2000, there was an expectation of changes in regional dynamics. This is largely what happened. There have been no more wars in the region. Conflict issues have been handled through negotiations. The gradual dissolution of the Yugoslavia that remained, first into Serbia and Montenegro (in 2003) and then independence for Montenegro following a referendum (in 2006), was an entirely peaceful process. Kosovo's unilateral declaration of independence in 2008 resulted in tensions but no armed conflict, and by 2010 Serbia was prepared to de facto (but not de jure) accept the new situation, making possible also personal meetings on the top level. Important was the prospect of ultimately joining the European Union.

There is an alternative view, arguing that the Albanian predicament is the central conflict formation in the region. For example, the Albanians are still the population group most divided among existing states. From this, it follows that finding ways to satisfy Albanian aspirations would be the primary target for a regional process. Certainly, the signs of conflicts in southern Serbia and Macedonia in early 2001 provided evidence for such an analysis. Measures have to be taken within a number of countries to prevent further tension and possible new conflicts. The Ohrid agreement on Macedonia, concluded in 2001, provided reforms and contributed to a reduction in violence. Kosovo remained under international control for nine years before independence was accepted by a significant part of the international community (a number of Western and Muslim countries). A peaceful future requires regional cooperation, perhaps even the formation of interstate connections. For a long time, the attitude in the region was one of promoting separation, self-determination and state formation. However, from an Albanian perspective as well as a Serb one, the possibilities of integration into Europe now hold better prospects.

The bolder settlement approach may be more difficult to implement. It means that it will often have to build on the interest of regional or international powers to pursue such a strategy. It is a strategy that is more often likely to find application against smaller or weaker actors. If a regional power is at the same time identified as central to the solution, its preferences are likely to be difficult to circumvent. There is also a danger that certain issues are left unattended when there is a concentration on key concerns. In the Balkan case, the lack of progress in Bosnia-Herzegovina might be attributable to this. Also, however desirable a bolder strategy may be, it may not be universally applicable. Oftentimes, strategic peace thinking is pushed into the more tactical conflict-by-conflict approach, treating the problems as they emerge or become solvable. As observed, this approach may also appeal to regionally powerful states. It can give them a chance to pursue a divide-and-rule strategy.

The gradual approach of dealing with conflicts has a practical attraction. It will be politically easier to agree that something needs to be done when a situation appears more acute. It becomes a crisis management strategy. The bolder approach means that there is a long-term strategy for regional peacebuilding for states, regional interests and relevant international organizations. It would point to the potential benefit from closer cooperation in other fields than the exclusively conflict-related ones. It will give room for confidence-building and regional learning. Let us see how the two strategies affect broader regional security and the building of regional organizations.

8.2 Regional Conflicts and Regional Organizing

The two approaches to regional conflict complexes generate very different results for regional security when solving conflicts. The conflict-by-conflict approach is likely to result in a strengthening of the different actors in a region, as each solution will be closely fitted to the particular needs of each conflict. It may give rise to weak regional institutions. It would find solutions to particular grievances, but not necessarily shift regional relations to a new level of mutual cooperation. They are likely to result in tailor-made arrangements that can be adapted to the particular circumstances.

Bolder approaches, on the other hand, will have the additional function of creating a security system with rules, guidelines and norms, not only for contemporary conflicts but also for future problems. These could be frameworks for cooperation not only based on the settlement of conflict, but on broader needs. Satisfying such needs is expected to contribute to cooperative relations. Experiences from the peace processes since the end of the Cold War may generate some insights into the effects of these different approaches in regional conflict resolution.

Regional Frameworks

There is a connection between regional conflict complexes and regional security systems. Theoretically, there are a number of such systems, for example, regional security communities, concerts of cooperation among leading states, as well as regional balances of power (Kolodziej 1998). Many of these have come from conflict experiences and sometimes resulted in regional institutions. Regional security systems point to the importance of the distribution of power in particular regions. This should be kept in mind when we pursue the two approaches to regional conflict complexes. Let us clarify these distinctions with some examples and then evaluate the effects of different regional approaches.

First we may talk of *tailor-made frameworks*. These are meetings, fora or other arrangements that are significant parts to solutions of regional conflicts, often originating in regional efforts. Their purpose is to bridge an existing conflict and to provide a venue for discussion and dialogue. Once the framework is established, the parties may find additional shared interests. The presence of extra-regional and supportive actors can be useful for the process. An example is from the Central American peace process. It was a new regional approach. It also gave a role to the United Nations, first in El Salvador (Hampson 1996: 137–44; Pérez de Cuéllar 1997: 402–4) and later in Guatemala (Whitfield 1999). There were previous experiences of regional economic and university cooperation. The wars of the 1980s brought institutional and economic exchanges to a halt. Still, a shared understanding remained of a Central American identity. The process had wider ambitions than only conflict resolution, but settlement of the wars was its primary motive. The composition of the participating states was tailored to fit a regional concept, which included the five states most often cooperating but not, for example, Panama, which was too close to the US, nor Mexico, which could be too dominant.

For the conflicts in Southeastern Europe, a tailor-made attempt was tried with the International Conference on Former Yugoslavia (ICFY), as a forum of UN–EU cooperation. It was convened in 1992 and consisted of 31 countries. It was supplemented with a special Contact Group, consisting of France, Germany, Russia, the UK and the USA (Owen 1995). None of these frameworks spilled over into a regional order for former Yugoslavia after the war. Only in 1999 did a European initiative for the entire region take shape. By 2005, the EU had an elaborate policy of using membership as an incentive for reform and negotiated solutions. It gained attraction, particularly after the inclusion of Bulgaria and Romania in 2007, making credible the promise of an extension into the Western Balkans. In 2013 Croatia was admitted into the EU and arrangements were being made for Serbia and Kosovo.

The Madrid conference in 1991, attempting to find a regional solution to the Arab–Israeli conflict, was a diplomatic breakthrough. For the first time it brought together Arab states and Israel. The United States and the Soviet Union served as hosts. However, it soon ceased to function, mostly on Egypt's insistence on a nuclear weapons free zone for the region.

It is interesting to note that a tailor-made framework, which today is used in a number of conflicts, is the Organization for Security and Cooperation in Europe (OSCE). It originated in the Cold War and was formed by that global conflict complex. After the Cold War it was recreated as an international organization and became important in several regional conflict complexes, notably in Southeastern Europe and the Caucasus.

The tailor-made frameworks we have reviewed were not easy to create. They have been the results of serious efforts on the highest level of policymaking. Still, their success rate is low.

A second approach is to create and build on *needs-based frameworks*. They take a point of departure in shared interests that are not necessarily directly related to the war experience. There are normally many such issues, which can possibly be handled without the interference of ongoing conflicts. It may be beneficial if such a framework exists before serious conflicts are initiated. Issues include providing assistance in times of drought, dealing with shared rivers, managing transportation routes, promoting industrial development cooperation and working out trading arrangements. The origin of the European Union is an example. It built on cooperation in the fields of coal and steel production, followed by atomic energy, agriculture, internal markets, and only slowly approaching the notion of shared foreign policy. The ambition was to tie the two former combatants, France and Germany, as closely to each other as was possible for independent states.

Africa has considerable experience in needs-based frameworks, which have become useful in the settlement of conflict, the Regional Economic Communities, RECs (Adetula 2015). The Economic Community for West African States (ECOWAS) has taken on a role as peacekeeper and peacemaker in the conflicts in Liberia, Sierra Leone, Côte d'Ivoire and Guinea. Its original mandate was not security but economic development.

The conflicts in the complex of Central Africa (West) – the Great Lakes Region – have been handled through a regional process, without a formal organizational framework. It resulted in a series of peace agreements where the ones of 2002 and 2003 may be lasting. The presidential elections in 2006 were conducted in an acceptable manner and the Democratic Republic of Congo had its first elected leader since the 1960s. The fairness of the 2011 elections has been more contested.

The Southern African Development Community (SADC) was created for purposes of economic development in its region, but had something of a mediating role and also kept its own peacekeeping troops in Lesotho in 1998–99, contributing to the management of the tensions in the country. It was not, however, able to deal with the civil tensions of Zimbabwe.

The limits of regional organizations can be understood when looking at the conflicts in the Horn of Africa. They were not dealt with by its regional needs-based organization, IGAD (Inter-Governmental Agency for Development). The two leading member states, Ethiopia and Eritrea, were at war with one another, thus preventing the organization from taking a role in the conflict. It has played a role in conflicts in Sudan and since 2013 is mediating in the internal conflict in South Sudan.

The first initiatives to solve the conflict in Cambodia were regional in character. Indonesia was a prime mover. It gave a role to ASEAN. This organization was formed to meet the needs for economic cooperation among Southeast Asian states. Initially it was a regional coalition against Vietnam and communist control in Indochina. During the late 1980s it took a new role and became acceptable to all the states of the region. It was used as a bridge-builder. Following the end of the conflict in Cambodia, it accepted Vietnam as a member (in 1995). By the end of the decade, the remainder of Indochina and Myanmar/Burma had become members. It has chosen an approach of informal consultations with member states about internal conflicts, thus, sticking to a traditional role of non-interference in internal affairs.

There are other organizations that have been formed on the basis of particular security needs and turned into operations of relevance for conflict resolution. The Organization of American States (OAS) is one case. It was useful for the demobilization, following the end of the war in Nicaragua, and played a role in the conflict in Honduras in 2009 by refusing to seat the unconstitutional government. Still, previous history may make organizations with such backgrounds less useful in conflict resolution. Some of them have been created as alliances against other states in the same region and, thus, they cannot bridge conflicts. They may, however, be important in the aftermath of the conflicts, when agendas are formed (Glaser 1997).

One example is NATO, the chief vehicle for Western defence against the Soviet Union during the Cold War in Europe. NATO was used as a military instrument in the conflicts in former Yugoslavia, both in the war in Bosnia and in Kosovo. After the wars, it maintained troops in both places. In September 2001, NATO was invoked in defence against terrorism. A major engagement became ISAF, the international security assistance force, placed in Afghanistan under a UN mandate of December 2001. In 2011, NATO took charge of the UN-proclaimed no-fly zone over Libya in order to protect the civilian population from attacks by the Gaddafi regime. These actions, however, were seen as more intrusive and led to increasing tensions between the West and Russia over the civilian protection role of the UN.

Another example is the Commonwealth of Independent States (CIS), which was created immediately after the dissolution of the Soviet Union. It was generally seen to adhere closely to Russia's foreign policy. Lately, Russia has pushed the idea of the Eurasian community, incorporating a number of the former Soviet states. The conflict in Ukraine began in 2013 as a question of whether the country should be part of this body or develop its relations with the EU, in the form of a partnership agreement.

Some regional organizations can also be dominated by certain interests that impede peacemaking. The League of Arab States and the Gulf Cooperation Council (GCC) bring together different constellations of Arab states. The League of Arab States consists of the governments of Arab states, and thus represents one side in several of the conflicts in the Middle East. It has backed the PLO against Israel, Iraq against Iran, and Kuwait against Iraq. It has been unreceptive to Kurdish demands. It does have a record of mediating in some conflicts between Arab states. Remarkably, in 2011, it supported the UN no-fly zone over Libya. The GCC has emerged as an active force, particularly in protecting Arab Sunni interests, making it important in the conflicts over Libya, Syria and Iraq, as well as in the Arab League itself.

The Pacific Islands Forum (PIF) has become engaged in conflicts of the South Pacific, particularly taking an interest in preventive measures. It endorsed the Australian police mission to the Solomon Islands in 2003 (RAMSI; Henderson and Watson 2005) and suspended Fiji's membership after the 2006 coup. However, elections did not take place in Fiji until 2014 under a new constitution giving a strong role to the armed forces.

Transregional organizations such as the Non-Aligned Movement (NAM) and the Organization for Islamic Cooperation (OIC) are also relevant. NAM has been important in pursuing the collective needs of the developing world as a whole, thus spanning some contradictory demands. It has not, however, been an actor in managing armed conflicts among member states since the end of the Cold War. The same could be said of the OIC. Both often send emissaries in connection with various conflicts.

Also, when studying the record of regional organizations built to serve particular needs, be they material or security-related, we find that their participation and success in conflict resolution have been limited. This requires further discussion (Wallensteen and Bjurner 2015).

The Limits of Intra-Regional Frameworks

Given the pervasive phenomenon of regional conflict complexes, the utility of a regional framework run by the regional members in creating peace is surprisingly limited. Whether tailor-made or needs-based, such intra-regional approaches have not been at the forefront in conflict resolution, globally speaking. In fact, many efforts have been driven by extra-regional actors, rather than being intra-regionally engineered, as was the case in the Central America model. We may ask why it has been so difficult to develop successful regional approaches.

One factor, mentioned in the literature, is that the aspect of power and dominance might be even more important in a regional context than in a global approach. A regional plan may be perceived to favour one party more than others, which appears to be the way Arab countries reacted to many of the schemes at the Madrid conference. The military might and economic strength of Israel may make many hesitant to choose a regional framework. We have also noted that regional initiatives are difficult to make, as a dominant actor in the region may be central to the ongoing conflict and have other ideas about solutions. The organization for South Asia, the South Asian Association for Regional Cooperation (SAARC), cannot serve to mitigate India's overwhelming power in the region. In such situations, countries are likely to develop support from states outside the region. This has been a pattern in Southeastern Europe, where Bosnia appealed to both the US and to the Muslim world, whereas Croatia drew support from the EU. The same can be seen in South Asia, with Pakistan strongly linked to China and to the United States. Either way, it means that there is a limit to what regional initiatives can achieve.

There might also be strong rivalries between regional contenders, thus paralysing the efficiency of regional bodies. This certainly has been important for the League of Arab States, which was unable to convene a summit meeting until more than ten years after the Gulf War. Similarly, it has not been effective in the Syrian civil war. IGAD could not be used for the conflict in the Horn of Africa and SADC has been hampered by rivalry between the two strongest actors, South Africa and Zimbabwe. In cases where members of the regional grouping are directly involved in the conflict, the regional setting is hard to use. If the strong state is not a direct participant in ongoing conflicts, the situation may be different. One case is West Africa, where Nigeria could take the lead with the support of others in the region in a number of the conflicts in the area.

Nevertheless, we can see that power considerations create a barrier for the utility of intra-regional approaches to regional conflicts. If a regionally strong state is part of the problem, a regional framework is unlikely to be used for peace processes or, alternatively, will be used by this actor to further its own goals.

Thus, it is logical that many regional conflict complexes instead are dealt with by actors outside the complex itself. This gives a role to continent-wide organizations, as seen in the case of the African Union in conflicts in Africa, or informal arrangements. Let us turn to these frameworks.

Extra-Regional Approaches to Regional Conflicts

Intra-regional frameworks have some distinct disadvantages in managing regional conflict complexes. However, the alternative, extra-regional approaches, may turn out to be geographically too broad for smooth operations. The membership of continent-wide organizations is likely to perceive particular conflicts through their own prism. Positions in conflicts may be taken through votes in large assemblies. Thus, there is a danger that too wide a forum will provide arenas for the same regional rivalries that we observed earlier, as well as for attempts to put forward unrelated agendas. The need to take sides will only sometimes be conducive for conflict resolution. This is a problem that afflicted, for example, the OAU in dealing with the conflict in Western Sahara, or prevented it from taking up internal conflicts in member states. The African Union (AU) makes a new departure, however. Since 2004 it has been involved with a peace operation in the Darfur region in Sudan and since 2007 in Somalia.

This is an argument for more informal approaches, that is, approaches that only include some, often neighbouring, countries, together with outsiders. During the 1990s there emerged a number of such specific frameworks. The Contact Group for the conflict in Yugoslavia is one (including the USA, the UK, France, Germany, Russia and later also Italy). Four of these were permanent members of the Security Council, meaning it was a group excluding China, five were members of NATO, thus being able to include one NATO critic (Russia), with important links to the actors in the conflict.

It is instructive to note that the UN has found a role in such regional peace processes. The creation of special envoys, either as Special Representatives or Personal Representatives of the UN Secretary-General, has been one such instrument. More novel is the convening of informal coalitions, sometimes dubbed 'Friends of the Secretary-General', for particular conflicts. There are also 'Friends of Mediation' connecting to the UN Mediation Support Unit in the Secretariat.

This approach has some strength in terms of diplomacy and its ability to mobilize actors with resources. Thus, it may contribute both to finding solutions and financing the post-war period. It is highly efficient. They are frameworks as tailor-made as one can get for handling regional conflicts. It has the disadvantage of being very temporary. Groups are formed on particular needs, thus not necessarily furthering learning from one achievement to the next. Nor are they easily transformed into organizations that can sustain peace after the end of the conflict. At that moment, established organizations will have to be brought in. It may create a problem of transferring the understandings. It will be a less transparent process. Furthermore, it gives a strong role to more powerful members of the international community, in particular, the five permanent members of the Security Council.

This overview shows that it is hard to find an ideal and generally applicable way of organizing peacemaking in regional conflict resolution. The most important lesson is that there are a variety of ways and, thus, each conflict complex may have to find its proper form.

Regional Security after War

Finally, we ask whether the ending of the conflicts in a regional conflict complex also contributes to self-sustaining regional security. Obviously, few of these complexes, listed in Table 8.1, have been entirely resolved. There are four candidates: Central America, the Sahel region (or rather, parts of this vast area), Southern Africa and Indochina. We can note that the ending of these conflicts has not been followed by vigorous intra-regional integration. Rather, the international dependencies that existed previously seem to be intact or even reinforced. For the countries in Indochina, their incorporation into ASEAN may have given additional benefits and new opportunities. In a few cases wars have been followed by economic growth. Vietnam is one example, Cambodia another. Such a pattern may also be found elsewhere. Botswana and Namibia in Southern Africa have had consistent economic growth. Both are rich in minerals. The war effects were limited in both places. However, the stalemated situation in Zimbabwe has affected the possibilities of creating a stronger regional community based on shared democratic values.

The regional systems that can be observed in the post-war period are perhaps closer to a security community model than one of regional integration. The security community builds on the idea that conditions have been created which reduce the expectations that violence will be used to solve conflicts among the members of the community (Deutsch et al. 1957). Openness among the members in the form of democracy would enhance this. That would also be the case with economic cooperation, reduced military spending and more experience in solving conflicts among the members. With these criteria in mind, we can note that there is no expectation of new wars among the members in these four regions. South Africa is unlikely to repeat the interventionist practices of the apartheid regime. Vietnam is reluctant to involve itself again militarily in Cambodia. In a sense, these were the necessary conditions for making the peace agreements in the first place. Those conditions still remain.

This is so since important external threats have declined. The conflicts in Central America and Indochina were associated with the Cold War. The post-war societies in Central America and Southern Africa have become more transparent, which contributes to reassurance within the region. Experiences in solving conflicts are increasing as regional issues are dealt with, without provoking new conflicts. The economic interactions, however, are limited. There are also new threats developing. For Central America, these are associated with the drug trade and gang warfare, and increasing efforts by the USA to reduce immigration from the region. For Indochina and ASEAN, the relationship to China is always important and is watched with great care, even given incentives for cooperation among states in the region. These examples are testimony to the length of time and the amount of effort it takes to create peaceful conditions after protracted war. In the Sahel region, the new threats led to a stronger reliance of the regional elite on the former colonial power, France, a country that took the lead role in Mali in 2013 (Frances 2013).

Thus, we cannot say that these four regions have found new forms of cooperation. At least in three of them there is a wider spread of regional power and a reluctance to engage in war. Thus, these three regions qualify as candidates for regional security communities. A peaceful democratization of Zimbabwe would enhance such a development. The difficulties encountered in the Sahel region, however, demonstrate the continued fragility of the regional frameworks, as well as the states themselves. Unexpected events, such as the fall of the Gaddafi regime, can quickly unsettle an entire region.

8.3 Major Powers and Conflict Complexes

The period after the Cold War is dramatically different from almost all previous decades in the last 100 years. It has been without classical major power confrontation and world rivalry. Only the 1920s are comparable, as major powers focused on implementing the Versailles Treaty and rebuilding ties. It was, however, a period that was devoted to managing economic crisis and economic reconstruction after the First World War. After the Cold War there followed instead a period of rapid economic growth, not only pertaining to North America and Europe, but also to Southeast Asia, China, India and other parts of the world. In this book, it has repeatedly been noted that there are more peace agreements than in previous comparable periods. Conflict resolution is high on the political and scholarly agendas in major powers. New concepts have gained ground, commanding the attention of decision-makers in leading states: humanitarian intervention, preventive diplomacy, war crimes, bans for land mines and small arms, the international responsibility to protect exposed populations, and human security, to name a few. Concepts and issues that dominated Cold War thinking, such as balance of power, deterrence, escalation, pre-emption, strategic and tactical nuclear weapons, and first and second strike capability, have been marginalized. They have not, however, lost their relevance, and have not been thrown on the scrap heap of history. They are still important for arms control measures among major states and for regional affairs, for example, in South Asia or the Korean peninsula. In the efforts to counter internationalized terrorism, matters of nuclear non-proliferation have again drawn attention. Again, the significance of intelligence operations has increased.

The new focus means that the major powers are concerned with the settlement of armed conflicts. Let us explore this by first observing the role of the major powers in the regional conflict complexes that we presented in Table 8.1. A strong presence of one or several major powers makes a conflict part of a larger, global dynamic. In fact, it might turn a regional conflict complex into a global one, if it involves conflict between major powers or their allies. This has implications for conflict resolution. Then we must note that major powers have their own internal conflicts to deal with, and we ask for their record in conflict resolution. Finally, we proceed to study the relationship between the major powers themselves, what legitimately can be regarded as *the* global conflict complexes, as major powers have a reach beyond their own regions. They all have the capacity to impact on other regions. This also involves the question of major power rivalries as well as counter-terrorism policies.

Major Powers in Regional Conflicts

Most of the regional conflicts in Table 8.1 have had major powers engaged with their own troops or through close allies since 1989. This is true for more than three-quarters of the 16 cases. This might come as a surprise, as it is often observed that the era of intervention is over. It was often attributed to the Cold War, with some justification. But the heavy involvement of major powers in this many regional conflicts makes it important to include this aspect in the analysis. If they act together, dealing with regional conflicts may strengthen relations. However, regional conflicts may also expose divergent interests among the major powers and lead to the breakdown of cooperation. Regional issues are not autonomous from global considerations, as far as major powers are concerned. Let us here focus on six major powers, the five permanent members of the Security Council and India as it exhibits considerable military capability, economic resources, intellectual power and international influence.

In some instances, several major powers have been involved in the same conflict. Most notable are the conflicts in Southeastern Europe, where there were significant tensions between these powers, while at the same time, many had troops in the region. In the Gulf region, the three Western states initially acted in concert and with the understanding of other major powers. In most other instances, only one major power has been involved militarily. This was the case with Russia in the Caucasus and Central Asia, Britain in Sierra Leone in West Africa, France in Central Africa, China in the waters of the South China Sea and India in South Asia. The pattern is classical and in line with *Geopolitik* thinking. There are certain areas of concern to major powers, and there is a traditional willingness to respect such areas. The attitude since the end of the Cold War has been just that: to avoid sharp polarization between the major powers. It has meant that the West has avoided interfering in areas of particular significance to Russia (Caucasus including Chechnya), while Russia has acted cautiously in areas of special interest to the West and the USA in particular (the Gulf region, South Asia, notably Afghanistan). The war on Iraq in 2003 displayed considerable major power disagreement over the American and British actions, but not to the point of military counter-reactions. In a longer perspective, however, this unilateral action may have served to undermine confidence between the USA and Russia.

Major power relations during much of the post-Cold War period correspond to a pattern of universalism that can be seen in modern history (Schahczenski 1991; Wallensteen 1984, 2011b). There have been periods in which major powers have acted carefully against each other and been willing to 'understand' the interests of others. The post-Cold War period has traits of such historical periods as those which followed the Napoleonic Wars (1816–48), the Franco-Prussian War (1871– 95), the period after the First World War (1919–33) and in *détente* periods of the Cold War (mid-1950s, parts of the 1960s, much of the 1970s). These contrast with more particularist periods, where the major powers have instead pursued their own narrowly defined interests, even at the expense of other major powers, thus resulting in confrontations and major wars. In the Cold War, this was typical for the late 1940s, early 1950s, early 1960s and first part of the 1980s.

During the Cold War, major powers were prepared to act early for specific strategic reasons when a crisis emerged, and when it was, in their understanding, related to the major power conflict. It oftentimes led to sharp confrontations. The period since then has seen a change in this dynamic. With respect to some of the regional conflict complexes, major powers appear to enter into conflicts at a later stage. The motives are also different, not least a concern for humanitarian considerations. Many of the conflicts that receive considerable attention also have large refugee flows. However, there are situations with an equal amount of refugees but the attention is low. There has to be additional concern for conflicts to trigger resource-demanding actions. These may still not be strategic, but could have to do with domestic reactions to conflicts, thus prompting governments to act. This means that the type of action is different. There has been a surge in international peacekeeping operations. They now include troops from major powers. This was not conceivable before.

Most concern is likely to be given to conflicts, which are geographically closer to major powers, giving them a particular urgency. If there is considerable population movement, this is also likely to trigger action. Thus, it is not surprising to find the Western countries engaging with troops in Southeast Europe, or to find Russian troops throughout the former Soviet empire. In contrast, India and China have seldom sent their troops on unilateral missions outside their immediate region. India most recently had troops in Sri Lanka, but that was 25 years ago; China has had naval confrontations and fired missiles into the waters around Taiwan. However, India has a long record of participation in international peacekeeping missions, a pattern China now seems set to emulate.

The conflicts that are likely to receive the most attention are those where there is a danger of major power confrontation. This was a constant concern during the crises in former Yugoslavia. Different historical connections complicated the efforts of the major European countries in dealing with these crises. In the final agreement on Bosnia-Herzegovina, these powers were all represented. There was support for the arrangements, and all participated with peacekeeping troops to maintain the solution.

The Kosovo War in 1999 made matters even more complicated. The Western strategy led to an aerial bombardment of Yugoslavia that lasted for more than two months. An American missile destroyed the embassy of another permanent member, China, causing further complications. In the end, the Yugoslav forces agreed to leave Kosovo and peacekeepers from the major powers were to take up positions. An indicative episode was when Russian troops unexpectedly and ahead of the Western contingents appeared in Kosovo's capital, Pristina, in June 1999. The Western powers reacted cautiously and refrained from escalating the situation. A confrontation would have defeated the purpose of having both NATO and Russian forces on the ground in Kosovo. The Cold War had many such incidents and they were early indicators of a potential breakdown of relations. It was avoided then, but the West's acceptance of Kosovo's 2008 unilateral declaration of independence, became an argument for Russia both in the crises with Georgia the same year and in Ukraine 2014. Although Russia claimed that Kosovo's action should not be accepted, it used the same arguments favouring the moves by Abkhazian, Ossetian and Crimean leaders: these were expressions of popular sentiments for independence and that has to be accepted. In the case of Crimea in 2014, Russia went a step further and integrated the region into the Russian Federation. This, then, increased the confrontation between Western states and Russia. Thus, we can see how a conflict in one area affects the development in another, through the major power connections. Regions where several major powers have interests may turn into a global conflict complex. So far, however, there have been no direct military confrontations between the major powers.

Such a level of complexity is not found in most regional conflicts. In the Caucasus, only Russia has forces, although Western powers have supported the integrity of Georgia. In the Palestinian and Gulf complexes, only the United States has been strongly present diplomatically and militarily, although its combat forces were withdrawn in 2010. For the Syrian–Kurdish region, the Arab Spring led to increasing complications. With the agreed implementation of a no-fly zone over Libya in 2011, the USA took the initial actions but then handed the daily responsibility to its European allies. The military missions gradually led to an expansion of the original UN mandate and by October 2011 Libyan leader Gaddafi was killed. Russia and China both complained about this extensive interpretation of the original mission, and thus did not want to see new such operations. Most importantly, in the subsequent civil war in Syria, Russia strongly supported the Assad regime, and prevented UN action. The West was reluctant to get militarily involved. The crisis over Syria's use of chemical weapons in August 2013 was handled through a remarkable diplomatic process involving Russia and the US. Syria entered the treaty against such weapons and by April 2014 the last of its declared chemical weapons were destroyed. However, the civil war continued and the surprising military advances by the rebel movement ISIS in Iraq by mid-2014, initiated a reconsideration of Western policy. ISIS at the same time challenged Assad, Iraq, Iran, Kurds, Turkey, Russia and the US. A possibility was that this would lead to an unusual, de facto coalition against the brutality of this rebel movement, demonstrated through videos of beheadings.

In Central Asia complexity may also be on the rise. Both Russia and the USA have forces in Tajikistan, for example. Although there are tens of thousands of Western European troops on the ground in Afghanistan, politically the United States is the leader. The Obama administration has taken a more regional approach to this conflict, emphasizing the connection between Pakistan and Afghanistan, thus also seeing the connections to India, the country about which Pakistan is most concerned. Peace in Afghanistan, in other words, needs to include a regional approach, where neighbours Iran and China also play a role, and the US and NATO withdrawal of combat forces by the end of 2014 will have unpredictable, regional repercussions.

Many of the complexes in Africa, however, have seen military involvement from major powers. France sent troops to Rwanda in 1994 but only after the genocide. French forces in Côte d'Ivoire played a role in the war in the country, and also in the 2011 end-game for the incumbent regime. Britain sent troops to Sierra Leone in 2000. The European Union set up a force to the Democratic Republic of Congo in 2003 and again in 2006. In the aftermath of the Arab Spring we can note more such European involvements, particularly in the conflicts in Mali and the Central African Republic. The US interest in Somalia, which waned after US soldiers were killed in 1993, resurfaced again when Somalia was seen as a safe haven for anti-American terrorists. Since 2007 the USA has used air strikes and commando raids against al-Qaida affiliate al-Shabaab. After the rebels' attack on a shopping mall in Nairobi 2013, Kenya invaded Somalia, no doubt with tacit support from Western powers. For a long period of time major powers took the position that the military dimensions of regional conflict in Africa had to be left to Africa. The appearance of the armed, anti-Western movements such as al-Shabaab (Somalia, Kenya), Boko Haram (Nigeria), AQIM (al-Qaida in the Maghreb; Algeria, Mali), and Ansar Dine (Mali) has resulted in increased involvement by external actors. In many of these situations there is little disagreement among the major powers. To counter what is seen as international terrorism is a shared concern. However, the pattern is not entirely the same with respect to peace processes.

It is remarkable to observe that the USA has at the same time taken a leading role in several of the negotiated settlements. This has been particularly true for conflicts in the Horn of Africa (ending the state formation war in 1991 as well as the inter-state war in 1998–2000), Southern Africa (conflicts over Namibia and Angola), West Africa (particularly for Liberia) and the peace agreement in Sudan in 2005.

In fact, among the major powers, none has such a record of engagement in peace processes since the 1990s as the United States. Its representatives were involved in all the agreements in Southeastern Europe, the Middle East, many settlements in Africa as well as in supporting the Central American processes. The results have been holding up reasonably well. The post-2001 focus on fighting terrorism is associated with a reduced interest in negotiations and peacemaking, particularly in conflicts that can be connected to terrorism. The Arab Spring at times intensified ideas about possible military interventions by Western countries, to counter particular actors, rather than pursuing a discussion on the peaceful ending of these conflicts.

Armed Conflicts in Major Powers

The major powers have their own conflicts as well. Such conflicts are observed carefully as they are most revealing about the military, political and economic capacities of leading states. These conflicts are explicitly defined as 'internal' matters by involved major powers. In some instances, a major power has its territory as part of a regional conflict complex. The conflicts in the Caucasus link to territory of the Russian Federation. In addition, there was a minor armed conflict in the capital of Moscow itself (1993). The outcome of this power struggle was of great interest to other major powers and the international community. Similarly, the Northern Ireland problem has not been seen as part of a regional conflict complex, although it does involve relations between Great Britain and the Republic of Ireland. India's many internal conflicts tend to attract little international attention, but clearly constitute a major problem for Indian states and for the Indian Union as a whole. Several of these are part of a regional conflict complex in the east of the subcontinent. China has conflicts in Tibet and Xinjiang (Uighur) that have international connections, but so far not on the level of a regional conflict complex.

This suggests that major powers are often able to contain conflicts and will act strongly to prevent others from becoming involved. A case in point is the series of conflicts in Chechnya, where Russia's brutal strategy has been criticized in the West but little else has happened. Major powers are often strong enough to fend off 'outside' involvement. It is also part of their strategy to prevent them from being connected to other issues. The conflicts are not only internal matters; they are also 'special' issues, not comparable to others. This, of course, is an attitude that is not exclusive to major powers. It is, however, forcefully maintained only by states that are internally cohesive and have considerable military capacity. These are states that often would want to define themselves as 'strong' states.

This does not exclude international contributions to peacemaking, as indicated by the example of Northern Ireland. The list is not very long, however. More typical is that such conflicts either are subdued with considerable force (or 'excessive' force as the EU has described some actions) or become particularly protracted. An example is India's way of dealing with the uprising in Punjab, which was protracted but ended with much force. China's actions in Tibet have been very forceful. Major powers or strong states may be among those actors most unwilling to compromise in internal conflicts. To some, it might be a challenge to the very notion of being a major 'power' and a 'strong' state. Thus, their record as contributors to new ways of solving conflicts can seldom be built on their experience in their own internal conflicts.

Major Powers and Global Conflict

There are also the direct relationships between major powers. These are sometimes described as global rivalry and – in line with Realpolitik thinking – are built into the international system. We have already observed, however, that they are exposed to important swings, captured by the terms of particularism and universalism. It means that the relationships are formed by conflict complexes, where major power conflicts become interconnected, in the same way as we have seen in particular regions. Thus, we ask: are there major power conflict complexes, rivalries, other than those associated with the regional complexes? How are such relationships handled? Are there rivalries that have ended? As the latter can be answered as a clear 'yes', it means there is also a 'yes' to the first question.

Whatever description one prefers, the Cold War was such a period of global conflict, and it was ended. It is difficult to agree on when the Cold War started. It may have begun in 1948 with the communist takeover of power in Prague, Czechoslovakia. It may have started at the Yalta and Potsdam conferences in 1945 with the disagreements over the composition of the new government in Poland. The Anglo-American agreement in 1941 to start the Manhattan Project on nuclear weapons without informing its Soviet ally may have fuelled suspicion on the Soviet side, once it understood what was going on. It may also be dated to the Bolshevik revolution in Russia in October 1917. It is most common to date the Cold War to events during the Second World War and immediately after. The term 'Cold War' was coined in 1947 by the American analyst Walter Lippman.

When did it end? It has become customary to see the ending as the fall of the Berlin Wall on November 9, 1989. It is a symbolic date for human rights and democracy, no doubt. But if the Cold War was about Poland, it ended with the accession of the Solidarity movement to power in March 1989, breaking the Communist Party monopoly of power. If it was about Czechoslovakia, the 'Velvet Revolution' in Czechoslovakia later in November 1989 may be more appropriate. If, however, the rivalry was over the defeated Germany and its division, the reunification of Germany in October 1990 would be the end point. Still another possibility is the first complete nuclear disarmament treaty, eliminating whole classes of intermediate-range nuclear weapons, concluded in December 1987, as the effective ending of the rivalry. Finally, if the Cold War was about the creation of the Soviet Union, the dissolution of that union in 1991 would be the termination point.

The Cold War may have begun somewhere between 1941 and 1945, and it may have ended somewhere between 1987 and 1991. The selection of an exact date partially reflects an understanding of what the conflict was all about. There is, interestingly enough, a treaty to point to. In Paris in October 1990 the Charter for Europe was agreed, for the first time emphasizing democracy as a leading principle for relations among European states. It is a treaty that also tied communist regimes to the new order. The rivalry between East and West was, over some years, transformed from competition, military posturing and propaganda to one of cooperation, with difficulty at times, non-provocative military positions and mutual gains as key marks.

This is not the first time that major power rivalries have been brought to an end, but it may be the most complete such change without a major power war. The USA established contacts with the People's Republic of China in 1972, followed by diplomatic relations in 1978. It was an end to rivalry, but tensions remained. There was no *Idealpolitik* transformation following the *Realpolitik* and *Kapitalpolitik* changes. *Geopolitical* disagreements remained, for instance, over Taiwan. In the early twenty-first century the relations between China and the USA took on a new dimension of potential rivalry, but also possible cooperation in a configuration of G2, the 'group' of two economically dominating powers. We have also taken note of the changes in Franco-German relations since 1945, although they were heavily influenced by the outcome of the Second World War.

If we go further back in history there are additional examples. The American–British relationship, which started with a state formation conflict (1770–83) and included an interstate war (1812–14), was turned into a close alliance for most of the twentieth century. Similarly, German–Austrian rivalry in the first part of the nineteenth century became a close alliance in the second part of that century. French and British competition in Africa led to a severe crisis in Fashoda (1898), in present-day South Sudan (now called Kodok). This event was creatively turned into a partnership that has lasted for more than a century. Even Great Britain and Russia were serious rivals, particularly in Central Asia, ending with an agreement on Persia in 1907. Oddly enough, these two countries were allies in the two world wars of the twentieth century. Obviously, major powers are not necessarily and always in conflict with one another. Rivals may become allies.

Such transformation requires closer analysis. It is most interesting to study the period immediately before the present. The ending of the Cold War suggests ways in which conflict complexes can be changed. It draws on similar logic that has been found in regional conflicts. It refers, however, to a level where the stakes are even higher. It was not only a process of shifts and changes in major power attitudes to one another, following the particularist and universalist swings that we have identified. It also included the deliberate construction of a framework for dealing with conflict. We need to examine this more closely.

The ending of the Cold War included, first of all, direct relations between the major powers and their leaders. A feature of much major power rivalry is that the leaders have only met sporadically. One meeting can often lead to misunderstanding and misjudgement. Two such failures are widely reported in the history of the twentieth century. First, there is the meeting in Munich in 1938 between the Western leaders and Germany's Hitler. The agreement reached by Neville Chamberlain lacked depth and insight into the personality of the opponent. It was quickly undermined by the German leader. A second case is the encounter between the newly elected US President John F. Kennedy and Soviet leader Nikita Khrushchev in Vienna in 1961. It was followed by a Soviet-driven escalation of the conflict over Germany and resulted in the construction of the Berlin Wall. Thus, bilateral relations should not be entrusted to particular meetings but to regular contacts. The understanding reached at one meeting needs to be followed up with direct contacts immediately afterwards. This is the way political leaders act in internal affairs and international relations are not dramatically different.

The ending of the Cold War is closely associated with the personal and consistent diplomacy of Soviet leader Mikhail Gorbachev. His ability to communicate with his Western counterparts of the time, in particular US President Ronald Reagan and British Prime Minister Margaret Thatcher, changed the customary image of Soviet leadership and its intentions. There was a series of meetings between 1985 and 1990 that were important in bringing the Cold War to an end. It was accomplished in a peaceful manner, but also in a way in which the stronger party, the West, was not pushing the Soviet side into concessions. Rather, changes were brought about by internal forces, and the changes were accepted by the Soviet leadership.

The armament questions are likely to be central to major power relations. In Chapter 5 it turned out that matters within the *Realpolitik* paradigm were of particular importance. In bilateral dealings between the major powers during the Cold War, we have previously noted a surprisingly long record of agreement on such matters. We saw that there were more such arrangements than solutions to ongoing armed conflicts. For the major powers, strategic concerns are linked to the weaponry held by the potential opponent and the ways in which these can be counter-balanced or neutralized. The ending of the Cold War is closely associated with finding ways to stop the continued nuclear arms race. In particular, the newly developed intermediate-range nuclear weapons, which were stationed in Europe and largely targeted the different parts of Europe, were seen to create instability. They shortened the reaction time for each of the major nuclear weapons powers and thus increased the danger of nuclear war. One of the first accords between the two nuclear superpowers was the decision in 1987 to abolish this entire category of nuclear weapons. With the fear of being a victim to a first-strike attack from the other side removed, other changes also became possible.

A third important notion was the ability to act together in particular conflict areas. The *détente* between the major powers set in motion some of the peace processes we have observed earlier. To these belong the ending of the Iran–Iraq War (agreed in 1987, accepted in 1988); the withdrawal of the Soviet Union from Afghanistan (agreed in 1988, finished by 1989) and the settlements for Angola and Namibia (agreed in 1988, implemented in 1989). Most important was also the normalization between Russia and China (begun in 1989, leading to solutions to border conflicts and a peace process for Indochina). Thus, a major power understanding was not only restricted to matters of their direct concern, but also affected their engagement in other parts of the world. It showed that the new policies, primarily in the Soviet Union, were not just cosmetic, but were transformed into concrete action.

A fourth element was the creation of a forum that involved the other participants in the conflict. The bilateral meetings and the nuclear arms reduction talks centred on the USA and the Soviet Union. These were also the actors in some of the peace agreements. However, the European states also had stakes in the Cold War. A tailor-made framework was created that today is the Organisation for Security and Cooperation in Europe (OSCE). Its history is instructive. It began as a discussion on principles of mutual relations, economic cooperation and human rights among the countries that were allies, opponents and neutrals in the Cold War, particularly in Europe. This was possible during a first period of *détente* between the two blocs, early in the 1970s. A founding document was the Final Act, signed in Helsinki in 1975. For 15 years, there were regular meetings on the governmental level in very public, often propagandistic, discussions. It proved successful in the sense that no side wanted to be responsible for a breakdown of the forum, but the meetings were also highly contentious.

An important notion stemming from this, and which directly contributed to the reduction of tension in the Cold War, was the idea of confidence-building measures for conventional armed forces. They are actions that at the same time maintain military security and reduce the danger of unintended armed conflict. Such measures were part of the Helsinki Final Act in 1975 and were later elaborated in close detail in Stockholm, Sweden, in 1986, as the very first concrete measure agreed between the Soviet Union under Gorbachev and the Western countries. It was an issue of common concern for all the participating states and governments.

An important aspect of the ending of the Cold War was popular involvement. The Helsinki Final Act contained clear human rights provisions. The document was widely circulated throughout Central Europe, as agreed. It constituted the basis for the legitimacy of actions taken by dissident groups in Czechoslovakia, Poland and, most crucially, in East Germany. The break-up of the Soviet bloc had already begun in the late 1970s. Only through more repressive measures, such as the imposition of martial law in Poland in 1981, could the leadership keep the bloc together for a longer period of time. With increasing *détente* after 1986, it was again possible to advance issues of democracy and human rights. The acceptance of the Polish opposition as a coalition partner in 1989 signalled the end of the Communist Party monopoly on political life. The fall of the Berlin Wall in November 1989 was primarily a result of internal pressure on the leadership in East Germany. The non-violent domestic opposition made an opening up of society necessary. The same happened shortly thereafter in Czechoslovakia.

Thus, the ending of the Cold War was brought about through a remarkable confluence of factors, all highly related to *détente*, arms control, peacemaking, confidence-building, human rights and democratization. These notions helped to change major power relations, but also created a new period in international affairs. The organization, tailored for this conflict, was in 1994 converted into an international body, the OSCE. It now has 57 members, extending east from Vancouver to Vladivostok, that is, incorporating much of the Northern Hemisphere. With this example of the ending of major power confrontation we have also shown that it is a matter of making many levels of society move in a concerted effort. All conflicts are filled with suspicion. In the case of major powers, there are additional reasons for worry and fear. Their global stature may be at stake. Thus, proposed changes have to be convincingly demonstrated to become credible. The actions on one level have to conform to the actions on another level in order to generate the trust and confidence that is necessary. This has happened throughout history. The ending of the Cold War demonstrates that it is possible even in these times.

8.4 Global Dimensions of Conflict Resolution

As we have seen, many conflicts are connected to developments on regional and global levels. To solve regional conflict complexes it is necessary to bring together many or most parties in a region. If this is done under conditions of intense major power rivalry, the chances of success are limited. Global concerns may make major powers interested in blocking such moves, or embracing them as they serve their purposes. Either way, they are not likely to emphasize the concerns of particular local parties. Global conditions affect regional initiatives and local settlements. Distinguishing between universalist and particularist periods of major power relations seems to make sense as a way of capturing important traits. We would expect conflict resolution to be enhanced by universalist conditions. There is some historical evidence suggesting this (Schahczenski 1991; Wallensteen 1984, 2011b). It means, in particular, that the many settlements the world has witnessed since the end of the Cold War have to be attributed partly to the change in climate created by the ending of that confrontation. Let us explore some of the changes in major power actions in conflict resolution since the end of the Cold War.

First, the very way the Cold War ended may have pointed to new possibilities. There was a resort to procedures that involved negotiations, talks, dialogue, non-violent change, rewards and promises of economic assistance. There were no military threats by one major party against the other. There was an expectation of peaceful change and the furthering of domestic reform. It could be contrasted with a more sinister approach to ending such a conflict, through uncompromising demands, stiff conditions, violent incursions, economic blockades and military threats. Such an ending, if it would have meant one, would leave behind it a legacy of intimidation and humiliation. It would not have ushered in an era of continued peacemaking. The process, in other words, is important for ending any conflict, be it between major powers, in regional complexes or more isolated conflicts.

The cooperation among the major powers that was established during the ending of the Cold War also carried into the new era. The actions in the Gulf War in 1991 are testimony to that. Also later, such cooperation, explicit or tacit, has been a feature in regional conflicts where they have had opposing interests. Competing interests may, however, have stalled initiatives or made actions less effective. The inability of the major powers to act in a concerted way in the Balkan conflicts may have served to prolong the conflicts. At the same time, however, such interest clashes are part of life, and reflect perspectives that also need to be incorporated into actual settlements. We may note, however, that the smooth international cooperation in other conflicts may be due to the fact that major powers have accepted each other's geographical areas of specific concern. The armed conflicts since the end of the Cold War have seldom been located, for example, at the borders of a major power. In cases where they have, caution rather than confrontation has been the prevalent attitude among major powers. There has been reluctance for one major power to encourage rebellion within another major power. This again can be attributed to the universalist attitude. It also means that some struggles, for example, on human rights and self-determination, may not get support in capitals where it might be expected.

There is one area of armed conflict where the major powers have established a new norm of action during the 1990s: the battle with terrorism, however defined. Fighting terrorism has been the argument used by Russia to combat rebel groups in Chechnya, and it builds on a strong national consensus created by the bombings of civilian apartment complexes in Russia in 1999 and reinforced by various deeds since then, notably in Volgograd just before the Winter Olympics in 2014. The United States has found itself a repeated target of terrorism, not only on September 11, 2001: the destruction of a federal building in Oklahoma City in 1995 and the attempt to blow up the World Trade Center in New York in 1993 are but two examples. There were also targets outside the USA. In 1996, 19 American soldiers were killed in the bombing of Khobar Towers in Saudi Arabia. The suicide bombings and explosions in Israel and the Palestinian territories, including the assassination of Prime Minister Yitzhak Rabin in 1995, contributed to combine peacemaking efforts with anti-terrorist actions. After bombs destroyed the US embassies in Dar-es-Salaam, Tanzania, and Nairobi, Kenya, in 1998, the US administration specifically mentioned an organization and a culprit: the Saudi national Osama bin Laden. In response, cruise missiles were targeted against a pharmaceutical factory in Khartoum, Sudan, and at bin Laden's hideout in Afghanistan. In 1999, the UN Security Council imposed targeted sanctions against Afghanistan as the country refused to hand over bin Laden. Sources argued that bin Laden also supported groups in Chechnya. The international unity behind the sanctions against Afghanistan on this score became complete.

On September 11, 2001, a coordinated terrorist attack on targets in the USA marked something entirely new. Four commercial airliners were hijacked by persons with some pilot training and ready for suicide. The planes were turned into flying bombs. Two crashed into the twin towers of the World Trade Center in New York and one went into the Pentagon, the Department of Defense headquarters building in Washington, DC. The fourth plane, with an unclear target in the Washington area, went into the ground in Pennsylvania, after civilian passengers managed to prevent the plane from reaching its goal. In all, close to 3,000 people, mostly civilians, perished in this unprecedented act of terror. Among the dead were citizens of more than 60 nations.

It was an attack with great consequences for the leading power, the United States, but also with effects for the global community as a whole. Temporarily, international air traffic was reduced, the world stock markets went down and oil prices increased. This event further strengthened the international unity against terrorism, expressed through a unanimous vote in the UN Security Council on September 12. In a speech to a joint session of the US Congress on September 20, US President George W. Bush declared that the al-Qaida network headed by Osama bin Laden was responsible for the attack. Training camps existed in Taliban-ruled Afghanistan. In six sharply formulated demands, he asked the Taliban to deliver to American authorities the al-Qaida leaders, to close the camps and to allow the US access to inspect the result.

Although Afghanistan was specifically singled out, Bush also made clear that 'our war on terror begins with al-Qaida but it does not end there. It will not end until every terrorist group of global reach has been found, stopped and defeated.' Thus, September 11 marked a new American commitment to global involvement. Bush underlined that '[e]very nation in every region now has a decision to make: Either you are with us, or you are with the terrorists.' All countries in the world were asked to join in, but to the American audience he also said that this was to be a 'lengthy campaign, unlike any other we have ever seen'. Similar words were expressed by President Obama on September 10, 2014, when initiating a campaign against ISIS in Iraq and Syria.

Following the September 11, 2001 events, the global and shared fear of becoming a target of terrorism brought the EU, NATO and the other major powers on to the same side. Russia and China were supportive of action. A military build-up followed in Central Asia, in agreement with Russia. Naval units and military aircraft were brought into the Gulf region. Former Taliban-supporter Pakistan conveyed the American demands to the leadership in Kabul. The American president could act with unusual political consensus both domestically and internationally. On this score, his successor, Barack Obama, has pursued the same policies, adding the use of unmanned armed airplanes, drones, to the arsenal used to target particular individuals in places as divergent as Afghanistan, Pakistan, Yemen, Somalia and Mali.

The phenomenon of terrorism since the Cold War is different from such actions in earlier decades. Previously, hijacking of airplanes, taking of hostages and assassinations were ways for organizations to make themselves known, have their programmes published and, thus, in their own eyes, contribute to the advancement of their particular goals. Since the 1990s, this has not always been the case. No organizations took responsibility for bombings against US targets or the bombs in apartment buildings in Moscow. The lack of public explanation has made the actions more difficult to understand politically and the official interpretations made by the targeted governments have seldom been disputed. In this regard, the use by ISIS of the Internet represented a novel approach, clearly aimed at terrorising the opponents and recruiting new supporters.

The Security Council resolutions demonstrated a remarkable consensus against terrorism. The international message was clearer than had been the case a decade earlier. The 2001 war in Afghanistan resulted in the removal of the Taliban regime and the consensus on reconstruction of Afghanistan persisted. This remains true for the campaign against terrorism as well. New deeds, such as those in Bali (Indonesia) in 2002, Moscow and Baghdad in 2003, Madrid and Beslan (Russia) in 2004, London in 2005, and Mumbai (India) in 2008 or repeated suicide bombings in Afghanistan, Pakistan and Iraq have received the same world-wide condemnation. The mass executions in Iraq and Syria carried out by ISIS in 2014 served to reinforce this position. Following the military advances and video-taped beheadings of Westerners by ISIS in August 2014, international consensus emerged on action against the organization. An example was the UN Security Council resolution 2170.

Not all arguments were accepted, however. The Bush administration's attempts to link the regime of Saddam Hussein in Iraq to international terrorism, the danger of nuclear weapons proliferation and threats to US security were not generally understood. The UN Security Council was sharply divided and no authorization for a war on Iraq was issued. The war still took place in 2003, the regime was removed, to be followed by a protracted internal war and US-led efforts to create a more democratic system. This war complicated international relations and resulted in increasing divisions in America itself. The election of Barack Obama as US President in 2008 followed such sentiment. In August 2010 Obama declared an end to the US combat mission in Iraq, but instead emphasized the increasingly intensified war in Afghanistan. There was strong international support for this effort from the UN Security Council and from Western European and other countries. On May 2, 2011 President Obama announced that the USA had conducted an operation that killed Osama bin Laden in Pakistan, and added that this marked 'the most significant achievement to date' in the US effort to defeat al-Qaida. This confirmed that there was little explicit interest in finding solutions beyond the military battlefield.

Still, there seems to be consensus on how optimally to deal with terrorism. The use of the court system would seem the natural way. The court in The Hague for war crimes in former Yugoslavia issued indictments demanding that particular individuals be brought to the court. The international community had committed itself to act accordingly. That seemed the most logical procedure to follow. This was also the gist of the Security Council resolution on September 12, 2001, when it urged 'all States to work together urgently to bring to justice' the perpetrators of terrorism. Among the available options, the resort to legal procedures probably has the largest support. The use of sanctions targeting particular individuals, their personal resources and their economic basis was a novel development which became part of the counter-terrorism measures but also a means for bringing about change in war-torn societies. The UN found new ways of acting. Still, as of now, nobody accused of international terrorism has been brought to an international court. Even national jurisdiction has faced difficulties in dealing with terrorism in a legal and civilized way. There have been several court cases, notably in Indonesia, Spain and Great Britain. The US has not been at the forefront of this. Instead, the US-operated prison at Guantanamo Bay became a symbol of the lack of due process that is normally the hallmark of the rule of law. In spite of its ambition, the Obama administration had not been able to close these facilities by 2015.

Further Readings

Go to the *Understanding Conflict Resolution* web page at https://study.sagepub.com/wallensteen4e for free access to journal articles listed.

Deutsch, K.W. et al. 1957. *Political Community and the North Atlantic Area*. Princeton, NJ: Princeton University Press.
Karl W. Deutsch created the concept of a security community and built it on a series of comparable cases during a long historical period. The term has entered into political use. This work explains the original intensions and the distinctions that were made of different types of such communities.

Wallensteen, P. and Sollenberg, M. 1998. 'Armed Conflict and Regional Conflict Complexes, 1989–1997', *Journal of Peace Research*, 35: 593–606.
Building on early results of the Uppsala Conflict Data Program (UCDP) the two authors observed the connections between different conflicts, particularly with respect to regional settings. Thus, they coined the term 'regional conflict complexes'. In the book *Understanding Conflict Resolution*, the logical addition is also to discuss 'global conflict complexes', from the point of view of ending conflicts.

Buzan, B. and Waever, O. 2003. *Regions and Powers: The Structure of International Society*. Cambridge: Cambridge University Press.
In this comprehensive volume the two authors point to the importance of regions for understanding the operations of the international society. Security concerns create connections between societies, and thus they are interested in such 'regional security complexes'. It complements the previously mentioned UCDP-based article, but also contrasts it, in terms of methodology and emphasis.

9

INTERNATIONAL ORGANIZATIONS IN CONFLICT RESOLUTION

9.1 The Actors in Peace Processes

The UN is the primary international body for peace and security. It has many different roles in peace processes, which can be seen from its record in conflict resolution since the end of the Cold War. A fuller understanding of the United Nations also requires a look at its special legal standing and the concept of collective security. We then proceed to discuss how issues reach the UN agenda. This is the topic of Sections 9.2 through 9.4. Of late, also a host of other actors has emerged in conflict resolution. Some attention has been given to regional organizations. Thus, it is appropriate to discuss them and their relations to the UN. This we will do in Sections 9.5 and 9.6. The measures used by the various bodies will then be discussed in Chapter 10 (coercive responses) and Chapter 11 (peaceful responses).

9.2 The UN in Peace Processes

The UN is the central international organization for the maintenance of international peace and security. This is what the UN Charter establishes and it is partly, but not completely, confirmed by recent practice. The durable peace agreements that we have presented in Table 4.2 have a high degree of UN involvement. If we define that involvement as decisions pertaining to the particular conflict and its resolution made by the UN Security Council, the General Assembly and the Secretary-General, there is a UN contribution in a majority of all conflicts, at one stage or another. The variation among the three types of conflict is not striking. There might be somewhat more involvement in civil wars than in state formation conflicts, with the interstate conflicts between. However, it is also important to observe that there are peace processes which have taken place almost entirely outside the purview of the UN. To these belong the settlement between Ecuador and Peru, the agreements on Guinea-Bissau, several of the Sahel agreements, and the negotiations over Mindanao and Northern Ireland. Either way, it means that the UN and its leading organs for international security are involved, but also that the commitments vary. Furthermore, the UN is seldom the only outside actor dealing with a particular peace process.

Some conflicts have actually ended through a decision in the Security Council. This is rare, but it was the way the Iran–Iraq War was terminated. The parties accepted a resolution from the Council. The settlement over Namibia followed a similar form. In other circumstances, the office of the Secretary-General has been the forum for working out the agreement. This was the case with East Timor, where the parties met under UN auspices in New York and signed the final agreement with the Secretary-General as a witness.

In many situations the UN has been involved in the negotiations through Special Representatives. It has also meant that the Secretary-General has been highly engaged. In some such cases, the main forum for talk has been through the UN. This happened, for instance, in peace processes in El Salvador, Angola, Mozambique, Liberia, Central African Republic, Tajikistan, Western Sahara and Sudan. Through such means, the UN continues to be engaged in conflicts which have not been settled as of yet, notably Cyprus and Georgia.

There were also cases which can be described as failures for the UN. It was central to peacemaking in Rwanda in 1993–94. The UN was not able to achieve a cease-fire or the implementation of the peace agreement. It did not have the will or the resources to prevent the genocide. It provided important lessons, clearly stated in the report of the evaluation made by the Independent Inquiry set up by the Secretary-General some years later. In Bosnia-Herzegovina the UN led the efforts, together with the European countries. It was party to the failure to protect the 'safe areas' that had been identified by the Security Council. The fall of Srebrenica in July 1995 hurt the credibility of the UN peacekeeping operation. The initiative for peacemaking in this conflict was taken over by the United States. These two failures affected the standing of the UN in Western public opinion. It recovered through a thorough and open scrutiny of these experiences.

The perceived lack of determined action on the Darfur crisis in Sudan in the late 2000s drew similar criticism, but there was continuous presence of UN mediators. The Arab Spring has generated new challenges for the UN. On Syria, the Security Council has not been able to agree on mandatory decisions, for instance, on an arms embargo. It has, however, agreed to the mediators appointed by the Secretary-General. The first one was Kofi Annan in 2012, followed by Lakhdar Brahimi 2012–14 and since then Staffan de Mistura. These are experienced negotiators, but they have serious difficulties in moving the parties towards a solution. It goes back to the inability of the Security Council to support an agreed policy with effective measures.

The UN has been important in the implementation of many agreements. Finding their form in the middle of the 1950s, peacekeeping operations were changed after the Cold War. A new generation of more comprehensive peacekeeping operations was developed, including matters concerning elections, the return of refugees, educational components and human rights. The number and range of peacekeeping operations under UN auspices have been unprecedented. This has been of great value for making some agreements durable, notably in Mozambique and Cambodia, and for (re)building civilian governance in Kosovo, East Timor (Timor-Leste) and Liberia.

The UN has also authorized action, but left implementation to others. This was the case with the Gulf War, the primary example of peace enforcement. Security Council Resolution 678 of 1990 in essence gave the United States the right to use all necessary means to end the occupation of Kuwait. The war, furthermore, ended through a resolution in the Council, outlining the conditions on the losing side – Iraq – on such matters as compensation, border demarcation and weaponry. The implementation of this resolution led to further crises, continued sanctions and repeated air strikes during the following years. In the climate created by the events of September 11, 2001, the USA decided also to target Iraq. The activation of the UN mission for inspection of the military capabilities of Iraq (UNMOVIC) was, after a while, deemed inadequate by, in particular, the USA and the UK, who chose to still believe Iraq was developing weapons of mass destruction. Without the authorization of the UN, this coalition invaded Iraq in 2003. Following the removal of the regime in Baghdad, the UN was again asked to be involved in the reconstruction of the country. UN involvement, however, has remained limited. The fact that two permanent members acted in the war without the resort to the UN, of course, affected the standing of the organization, but also the credibility of the US-led actions.

Finally, the UN was on the sidelines of several peace processes, although it may have taken actions which were important for conflict dynamics. One case is South Africa. The international sanctions against the apartheid regime were among the few mandatory decisions taken by the Security Council during the Cold War. The negotiations that led to democratic elections in South Africa were held between the parties themselves, without the involvement of any international organization. Another case is the Israeli–Palestinian process, which largely was handled by the United States, following the breakthrough created by Norwegian diplomacy. Some time after the breakdown of negotiations in early 2001, a 'quartet' of the UN, the EU, Russia and the USA announced a 'road map' for peace, but no negotiations followed. A new start was attempted in 2007 and yet another in 2010. By 2014 this too was without results. In other words, major powers also may fail in their ambitions at brokering peace agreements.

This section has illustrated many of the ways in which the United Nations can be useful for peacemaking. Its roles are many. The UN may serve as a framework for action which is driven by other parties. It may also be an actor in itself, handling the settlement process but without losing sight of what member states may want (Weiss et al. 2013). It needs to be recalled, however, that the UN is a membership-directed organization and the members are all states. This strongly affects what it can do. Let us explore this further by analysing collective security through the UN (Section 9.3), agenda setting (Section 9.4), regional organizations (Section 9.5) and other international configurations (Section 9.6). The Secretary-General also has different roles and to these we shall return in Chapters 10 and 11.

9.3 Collective Security

The UN Charter

International collective security is the primary concern of only one organization, the United Nations. What the UN does is related to this framework, which thus requires some explanation. It normally works for the peaceful settlement of disputes, as stipulated in Chapter VI of the UN Charter. But it can also, by invoking Chapter VII, command the allegiance of the entire organization and its full membership. This is the quintessential meaning of collective security. It includes identifying a breach of international peace and security (Article 39), and then making decisions on measures to be taken by the members. These actions are for the Security Council to take on behalf of the entire organization. Through the Charter all members are obliged to carry out these measures. The Security Council, furthermore, has an extraordinarily powerful composition, as it is composed of the strongest military states. The power of the Council is vested in its position in the Charter and based on an underlying reality of power. This is what makes it unique, when compared to all other international organizations.

The only regional organization that is close to such a powerful position is the European Union and its Council of Ministers. With the ratification of the Lisbon Treaty in 2009, it may take on a larger role in peacemaking than has hitherto been the case (Johansson et al. 2010). Regional organizations are useful in conflict resolution, as we observed in Chapter 8. In addition to the EU, we referred to the OSCE, the AU and the OAS. However, none of them can legally define aggression, although they are increasingly active in conflicts within member states, as witnessed by AU sanctions against unconstitutional changes of government in Africa.

Decisions require the cooperation of all member states, meaning that there is a 'veto' for all. This is often a prerequisite for states to join. Thus, the organizations are not able to identify, publicly and with votes, one of their members as being at fault. The OSCE actually instituted a rule of 'Consensus Minus One' to prevent Yugoslavia from blocking the majority and preventing actions in the wars of the 1990s. Other organizations lack such procedures. Actions against aggression have been taken either against suspended members (OAS against Cuba) or against non-members (OAU on apartheid South Africa).

A unique task for the Security Council is to identify aggression. Article 39 gives three ways of categorizing a particular crisis situation under Chapter VII. It has to be an 'act of aggression', a 'breach of the peace' or a 'threat to the peace'. Mostly, the Council has refrained from using the label 'aggression', even if that is what it had in mind. Iraq's invasion of Kuwait in 1990 was not defined as an 'act of aggression'. The Council preferred a more diplomatic formulation: 'breach of the peace'. In practice, this made little difference, as the central decision was to invoke Article 39 (Security Council Resolution 660 of 1990). In September 2001, the Council decided that 'any act of terrorism' constitutes a threat to international peace and security (Resolution 1373, building on 1368), giving rise to a major counter-terrorism operation within the UN system.

A further enlargement of the UN agenda was outlined in the World Summit meeting of September 2005, when it accepted the notion of an international responsibility to protect exposed populations against genocide or ethnic cleansing, commonly known as R2P. This responsibility rests primarily with the sovereign government but, if it fails, the international community can and needs to act. The most dramatic applications of this to date are Resolution numbers 1970 and 1973 of 2011 on the situation in Libya, including an arms embargo and a no-fly zone. It also led to a counter-reaction preventing further application of this principle in other conflicts in the wake of the Arab Spring, notably the civil war in Syria.

Together, these measures may reduce the independence of individual states. Their only 'protection' as a UN member state, within the confines of the Charter, is that a permanent member can use its veto, or that they can muster the support of at least seven non-permanent Council members. This 'sixth veto' would prevent the Council from reaching the nine votes required for a decision. The major powers have accepted Chapter VII, as they themselves are protected through their own veto. The veto is criticized, but it is also important for smaller states. It provides a guarantee that the UN will not be used by one group of major powers against another. In this way, it makes it possible for neutral or non-aligned states to become members. This is a most important difference between the UN and the League of Nations, which could be used against major powers such as Japan, Italy and Germany. This is why major powers withdrew, or did not even join, as was the case for the United States. In the end it made the organization inoperative.

The armed conflict that the founders of the United Nations had in mind was an interstate conflict, where one state convincingly could be identified as an aggressor. The collectivity of states would then gather under UN guidance to force the aggressor to give up its aggression. In interstate conflict, this is largely a matter of returning to status quo ante bellum. In Chapter 5 we saw some examples of that (notably the Gulf War), but also some of the difficulties in arriving at such a shared judgement (for example, in the Iraq–Iran War). This notwithstanding, the UN has a particular function in interstate conflict, especially in those cases where none of the permanent members is directly involved. If a permanent member is one of the fighting parties, the UN will face a problem. It might mean that the UN will not be used at all (blocked by a veto) or that it involves itself on the side of this particular state (with the support of others on the Council). The first option is straightforward and the permanent member will act outside the UN framework, or possibly use some of the escape clauses that exist. Article 51 allows for the right of self-defence, for example, at least for a period of time. This is a clause that has been invoked by the USA in defending its actions against Iraq in March 2003. It may also resort to the use of a regional organization under Chapter VIII.

In the second option, where all permanent members are in support of action, it may be problematic for other members to determine if this is a strict application of UN procedures or a case of major power cooperation threatening the sovereignty of smaller states. It is a valid concern and raises the question of the representativity and composition of the Council. This argument has been used against Council action, for instance, by Iraq in the Kuwait crisis. In that case it received little sympathy internationally. The invasion of Kuwait was too flagrant and a potential precedent that made other states worried. Nevertheless, the UN Charter builds on the ability of major powers to cooperate. That may, at least in theory, result in policies that are negative for less powerful members or lead to neglect of issues that are important to them.

We have seen that the interstate conflict is not the most typical armed conflict. Instead, the record since the Cold War deals with civil wars and state formation issues even entangled in regional conflict complexes. Aggression is more difficult to define. Is it the rebels rising against repression who are to be deterred or the government that violated human rights? Are government and/or rebels receiving support from the outside and is that to be seen as aggression? Is the incumbent government merely defending the country's territorial integrity and political independence when it is attacking rebel positions in neighbouring countries? The aggression criterion becomes difficult to apply in a detached analysis. In the Security Council this may be compounded by the positions of member states and the possibility that members do not interpret facts in the same way.

In practice, the Council has defined situations in more general terms, such as 'threat to international peace and security'. Such formulations mean that the international repercussions of a particular conflict are the legal basis for action, notably, the flow of arms, the refugee situation, etc. In the debate, more stringent criteria have been proposed, such as 'genocide', 'mass violation of human rights' and 'ethnic cleansing'. These concepts cover situations with considerable international attention. They push members of the Council to take action, but also lead Council members to find ways to avoid action, when they do not want to act. The Genocide Convention contains strong stipulations for states to act against genocide. In the Rwanda genocide, the United States preferred officially to describe what was going on as 'acts of genocide' in order not to be forced to act. It was not alone among the permanent members in avoiding a description that would result in concrete measures. The mandate for the peacekeeping operation focused on restoring a cease-fire rather than preventing genocide, as observed in the Independent Inquiry that looked into the matter (1999).

There is a definite development in the internationally accepted collective security doctrine. It includes an enlargement of the meaning of security. The definition of the collectivity – whose security is to be protected – no longer includes only states and their survival; the fate of the populations of the states are also of international concern. Concepts such as human security have become important, as are common, cooperative, democratic and preventive security. The endorsement by the World Summit meeting in September 2005 of the principle of a responsibility to protect exposed populations (R2P) is a further expression of this. The understanding of what is problematic in a conflict has gradually shifted. It is not only a matter of bringing parties to cease-fire and negotiations, there is also an increasing commitment to reconciliation, peacebuilding, democracy, equal rights, gender equality and the protection of civilians.

UN Institutions

There are three bodies that may take actions in the advent of a serious conflict. They are concerned with conflict resolution and with the possibility of collective action, which may, in some instances, involve the use of violence: the Security Council, the General Assembly and the Secretary-General.

Some of the special features of the Security Council have already been noted. Among its 15 members, five are permanent, meaning that they have held this position since 1946, for 70 years, while ten are non-permanent members, elected by the General Assembly, for a period of two years. This imbalance in tenure in itself makes clear the difference between these two categories. It is further strengthened, of course, by the veto power given to the five permanent members. We have already noted that there is a hidden veto. If seven of the non-permanent members unite, they can block a decision. For this and other reasons, the permanent members will have to take into consideration the views of non-permanent states. This provides a measure of representativity of the decisions of the Council.

The activation of the Security Council since the end of the Cold War has pushed the more representative body of the UN, the General Assembly, into the background. When the Cold War was on, decisions in the General Assembly gained increasing stature. Its resolutions represented a broad spectrum of world opinion and contributed to some development in international legal thinking. An important decision was the Uniting for Peace Resolution in 1950. It meant that, if the Security Council were blocked from acting, this particular issue could be taken over by the General Assembly. This was a way of bypassing the veto of the Security Council. It was used during the 1950s. The decisions on the peacekeeping operations following the Suez Crisis in 1956 were taken in the General Assembly. In this case, Britain and France – the countries that had staged the intervention to wrest control over the Suez Canal from Egypt – prevented the Council from acting. Another example is the case of Afghanistan. The Security Council was blocked by a Soviet veto from acting on the Soviet invasion in late 1979. Instead, a resolution was passed in the General Assembly, giving the Secretary-General a mandate to take measures on the crisis.

However, reforming the institutions of the UN requires decisions through the General Assembly. The push for reforms of the UN during its 60th session (2005–06) made the Assembly more central than has been the case for a long time. It gave global attention to its President, Ambassador Jan Eliasson of Sweden. In 2012 he became the Deputy Secretary-General of the organization.

The Secretary-General, as the chief administrative officer of the Secretariat, has an important position. According to Article 99, the holder of the office can call to the attention of the Security Council any emerging threat to international peace and security. This is one of the ways in which the Secretariat works. Sometimes it may be necessary for the Secretary-General formally to invoke Article 99. In July 1960, Dag Hammarskjöld used this to have the Security Council meet on the crisis in the newly independent Congo. This was the first time Article 99 was used explicitly (Nicholas 1971: 179). Within a few days a peacekeeping operation was dispatched to the troubled country. It faced a complicated situation, bordering on what today is described as a state failure. One element was that the richest part, Katanga in the South, sought to secede from the state. This was something that the central government opposed, as did the African states, which all recently had acquired independence and might face similar challenges. It was one of the experiences that made it important for the OAU to establish in 1964 the principle that the colonial borders should not be changed. It became the task of the UN to find a negotiated solution to the attempted secession. In September 1961, the Secretary-General flew to meet the leader of the secession, Moise Tshombe. It was a unique action for a Secretary-General. Hammarskjöld's plane crashed on its way into landing at Ndola, in what is today Zambia (Urquhart 1994). The Congo conflict shows that the Secretary-General will have to build on the support of other states, whether in the General Assembly or in the Council. Hammarskjöld eventually met strong opposition from two permanent members, France and the Soviet Union, but had determined support from the emerging Third World and from the United States. The formal rights of the Charter have to be complemented with the ability to muster support among the member states.

Other Secretaries-General have also invoked Article 99, but seldom found themselves in a drama of such dimensions as Hammarskjöld. Kurt Waldheim did so at the outbreak of the war between Iraq and Iran in September 1980. Javier Pérez de Cuéllar used it in August 1989 to promote an ending to the civil war in Lebanon, something which set in motion a process leading to the peace agreement in 1990 in Taif, Saudi Arabia (Pérez de Cuéllar 1997: 57, 131). With these measures the Secretaries-General have sought to activate the Security Council. Some innovations have taken place. When Pérez de Cuéllar acted in the Lebanon crisis, it stemmed from dissatisfaction with the inability of the permanent members to take responsibility. Pérez de Cuéllar instituted a new form of cooperation among the permanent members. In January 1987 he initiated regular, informal meetings among the ambassadors of the five permanent members. Later, he noted that only with this initiative '45 years after the founding of the United Nations, did such cooperation become – tentatively, at first – a reality'. The first tangible result was the cease-fire resolution in the war between Iraq and Iran in August 1987 and the cease-fire in 1988 (Pérez de Cuéllar 1997: 152–74). The working arrangement has continued since then and is one factor behind the strong role of the Security Council today.

The three organs of the UN are interrelated in ways which actually support the viability of the United Nations. The organization may otherwise have collapsed. For instance, it is remarkable that the Soviet Union chose to return to the Security Council after the Council had voted in favour of a military operation in Korea in 1950, against an ally of the Soviet Union. If it had opted to stay outside the organization, the UN would have become a Western instrument against the Eastern bloc. This may be why the Soviet Union came back. It upheld the organization. Instead, the result was a deactivation of the Council, as the Soviet Union used its veto frequently. This made the Secretary-General and the General Assembly more important. The Uniting for Peace resolution was significant in an unexpected way, however, as it gave a chance for transferring international action to the General Assembly in the crucial Suez Crisis. The Council was prevented from action by Britain and France, not the Soviet Union. At this and other times, initiatives by

Secretaries-General may serve to make the organization responsive to the needs of member states. The roles of the three organs keep shifting, but together they contribute to make the UN relevant for international conflict resolution.

Following the Iraq War of 2003, UN Secretary-General Kofi Annan initiated a reform process that included the main organs of the UN. In December 2004, his High-Level Panel on Threats, Challenges and Changes presented 101 reform items. Many of these were dealt with at the World Summit in New York in September 2005. By January 2006, a new Peacebuilding Commission began to operate as a way of maintaining an international interest in post-conflict situations that earlier tended to relapse into war. It was an attempt to bring together development and security issues as equally significant matters in peacebuilding. Some years later the Mediation Support Unit was created to support the Secretariat's effort as a third party in ongoing armed conflicts. In recent years, however, the reform agenda has stalled.

9.4 The Security Council in Conflict Resolution

The role of the UN in conflict resolution changed during the 1990s. This can be seen most easily from the number of resolutions passed in the Security Council. Figure 9.1 shows the patterns since the Security Council began to operate (January 1946). It also displays the number of resolutions that were vetoed by a permanent member. In the first periods there was considerable activity, then for the early 1950s, at the 'coldest' periods of the Cold War, there were almost as many vetoes as there were resolutions. For the following three decades, a pattern developed where resolutions were passed, mostly as recommendations, that is, under Chapter VI of the UN Charter. The quantitative and qualitative shift came in 1990. It can be timed to the date: August 2, 1990. Upon Iraq's invasion of Kuwait, the Security Council met almost directly and arrived at a clear decision. The invasion was condemned and the Council demanded that the Iraqi forces leave immediately and without conditions. This action put the crisis firmly on the agenda of the Council. It also set a precedent. Many of the conflicts since the Cold War were brought to the Council for action. Thus, the activities of the Council increased dramatically, as can readily be seen in Figure 9.1. The Security Council has become a body that meets continuously and in so doing also makes important decisions. The UN now has a significant role in international affairs.

Figure 9.1 shows that the UN system was remarkably under-utilized during the Cold War. This is particularly obvious when comparing to Figure 2.1 (see p. 26) showing the armed conflicts in the same period. Important situations were not brought to the UN, such as the questions over countries and territories that were divided by the Cold War (Germany, Austria, Berlin, China, Vietnam and Korea). Conflicts inside each bloc were barred from entering the UN, for instance, the Soviet invasions of Hungary and Czechoslovakia. Thus, the major power conflagration meant that conflict management became a matter for the direct relations between the major powers. If they dealt with these conflicts at all, it was through bilateral arrangements. As these relationships were at the same time strained by nuclear weapons issues and armament decisions, and coloured by the ideological perspectives of the two sides, many conflicts were not handled in creative ways.

During the Cold War only one reunification was achieved through negotiated means, that of Austria in 1955. As might be expected, this took place during one of the first periods of *détente* between the East and West. It was as a result of such a *détente* period that other solutions were found, beginning in the middle of the 1980s. Mikhail Gorbachev's coming to power in the Soviet Union in 1985 made a significant difference, as mentioned in Section 8.3, but it was also important that his reform policy was received positively by the Western leadership at the time, particularly Ronald Reagan and Margaret Thatcher. The fear that the West would simply exploit a softening of the Soviet system turned out to be unwarranted. Such fears had triggered the Soviet invasions in Eastern Europe in the earlier periods. *Détente*, in other words, was the most important factor in bringing about the remarkable shift in the operation of the Security Council. It illustrates that the Council's continued role is dependent on the relationships between the major powers.

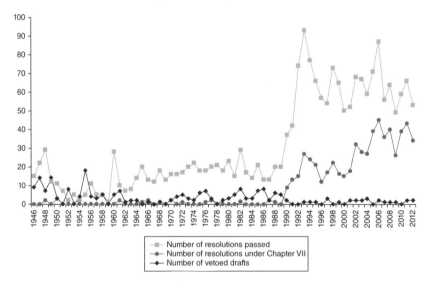

Figure 9.1 UN Security Council resolutions, 1946–2012 (number of resolutions passed, passed under Chapter VII and vetoed, absolute numbers)

The data on UN Security Council resolutions is compiled and used with permission by Dr. Patrik Johansson, Umeå University, from the UN Security Council website, www.un.org/en/sc/. For the definition of Chapter VII resolutions see P. Johansson, 'The Humdrum Use of Ultimate Authority: Defining and Analysing Chapter VII Resolutions', *Nordic Journal of International Law*, 78 (3) (2009): 309–42.

When the crisis of Kuwait erupted, there was an experience of cooperation among the major powers from previous crises. Gorbachev regarded the use of the UN as a way of extracting the Soviet Union from certain international commitments. It was used in ending the Soviet presence in Afghanistan. As a former US ambassador to the United Nations, the US president at the time, George H.W. Bush, was familiar with the UN. It was expedient for all sides to turn to the UN for this crisis, and the following ones.

The performance of the Security Council in the Gulf crisis built on the consensus among the major powers. China abstained from the most crucial vote in November 1990, but it did not act to undermine the decision. Thus, Security Council resolutions have been voted throughout the 1990s with the agreement of the five permanent members. There are only a few cases where a permanent member has abstained. The decision on Iraq in December 1999 on a new inspection scheme is unique in that three major powers abstained (China, France and Russia). The same powers, plus the non-permanent member at the time, Germany, united to resist the US and UK draft resolutions on Iraq in February and March 2003, this time joined by a considerable number of other Council members. The drafts were never put to a formal vote. In the Georgia crisis, however, a draft resolution was presented in 2009 and received a negative vote from Russia, thus limiting UN action in the conflict.

Unity is important. Opponents are likely to look for cracks in the Council membership. During the past decade some leaders have gained expertise in exploiting such disagreements. In his study of some UN missions and the activities of their opponents, the spoilers, Stedman finds major power unity to be essential in enhancing peace processes (Stedman 1997, 1998). Leaders in the Yugoslav, Iraqi and Syrian crises have understood how to use major power disagreements to their own advantage. Thus, the necessary compromising that takes place in the Security Council should be seen not only as a way of bridging intra-Council disagreements, but also as a way of making policies that can be implemented with the full support of the permanent members in the arena of conflict. Particularly in the aftermath of conflict, this is important so as to maintain international cooperation for reconstruction and post-war peacebuilding. The international reluctance to engage in Iraq after the interstate war of 2003 is indicative of this. It contrasts the ability of the Obama administration to build a coalition against ISIS, the Islamic movement that threatened Iraq and Syria in 2014. It includes Germany and France that both opposed the 2003 invasion.

In terms of UN politics, a united Security Council is likely to be most effective for international peace and security. At the same time, it makes other organs lose influence. The Secretary-General finds himself/herself in an entirely new situation. A pattern was set early in the post-Cold War period. The Secretary-General was not involved in the drafting of the key Council Resolution 678 (1990) in the Iraq–Kuwait Gulf crisis (Pérez de Cuéllar 1997: 249). During the first part of the 1990s, on several occasions the Secretary-General had a different preference from the Council and, in the end, had to yield. Kofi Annan was an assertive Secretary-General but faced the problematic US–UK intervention in Iraq in 2003, clearly taking place outside the Charter. His successor, Ban Ki-moon, has taken a low-key approach to the office, although he was in the lead in the crisis over Libya and Côte d'Ivoire in 2011. However, as the Security Council was completely blocked against taking mandatory action on the civil war in Syria it was difficult for the Secretary-General to move forward. Russia and China vetoed Western draft resolutions in 2011, 2012 and 2013. Thus, the UN role has been limited to humanitarian concerns and mediation efforts, but without the strong support of a united Security Council.

Agenda Setting

As we have just seen, the Security Council has been paramount among the UN organs since the end of the Cold War. We have also observed that many peace agreements have engaged peacemaking components of the UN. The world body, however, is not necessarily involved in all conflicts. There is a process of selection which sheds further light on how conflicts are handled in the present global system. This leads to the question of agenda setting. Which conflicts are more probable to come to UN attention?

With the more active role of the Security Council there is likely to be a closer correspondence between the world agenda and the UN agenda. In the Cold War, these agendas were clearly different, as few of the Cold War issues entered the UN system. Today, the concerns of the UN are also often of interests to the world as a whole. Furthermore, once an issue is under Council deliberation it will be of concern not only to Council members but also to all states. There is an agenda-setting function of the UN in general and of the Security Council in particular. When the Council defines a matter as a threat to international peace and security, all states have to be alert.

This issue can be approached be studying which comparable conflicts are on the agenda and which ones are not. Studying such attention in terms of Security Council resolutions shows that there are some distinct patterns (Wallensteen and Johansson 2014). The conflicts with the most resolutions, and thus international attention, can easily be identified and described by those who regularly followed the news media during the period. For the ten-year period 2004–13 UCDP listed 19 wars (that is, armed conflict with more than 1,000 battle-related deaths in a year). Those on the Council agenda include wars in Afghanistan, Iraq, Sudan, Somalia, several in the Central Africa region, and Syria. They no doubt draw high universal interest. They were largely located in Africa and in the Middle East. Complicating the pattern, however, some of the conflicts, which had the least attention, were also located in these regions. Seven wars were not on the agenda. Among the latter were protracted situations, notably the wars in Colombia, Kashmir, Chechnya, Uganda, Pakistan and Nigeria. The premise is that they all pass the same threshold of human suffering, and thus should be of concern to the international community and the UN. Even so, most of the seven probably received limited interest in foreign ministries or non-governmental organizations beyond the immediate group of concerned states and peoples.

This is a way of illustrating that there is a connection between the attention given by the Security Council and the understanding of which conflicts are important. It shows quite clearly that, if a conflict is on the Security Council agenda, it will receive global attention. Could it be, then, that those with little or no attention are also of minor importance to regional stability and, thus, are not seen as threats to international peace and security? The conflicts in Uganda, Sri Lanka and Chechnya did not give rise to Security Council resolutions. Some other conflicts in the same regions did, for example, in Central Africa and Central Asia. Several have resulted in large refugee movements within as well as across borders. Several have been connected with armed attacks outside the location of the conflict (kidnappings, murders, terrorism, assassinations, and interventions into neighbouring countries). This has obviously not been sufficient to bring all conflicts that meet these criteria to the Security Council agenda.

There is an important difference which relates to the basic topic of this book. In the cases that have attracted most attention, there have also been internationally driven peacemaking processes. In fact, most of them appear in the tables of peace agreements. Of the 12 wars in 2004–13 that were on the UN agenda, ten found themselves in an openly declared peace process at some time in the same ten-year period. There was information about attempted negotiations also in one of the remaining cases (Afghanistan). Contrasting this, four of the seven wars in the period saw no such contacts, most dramatically illustrated by the war in Sri Lanka. Thus, a reason for Security Council attention was to support peace processes.

This could possibly be generalized in the following way: conflicts that enter the Security Council agenda are likely to be those where there is international support for a solution. There is a selection effect. The Council acts when there is some prospect of peace and, obviously, becomes associated with such attempts. If a peace agreement is achieved, the Council attention would be expected to recede as a conflict enters an implementation phase. Crisis actions or peace process management are no longer required. If not, the issue will stay on the agenda and the UN will increasingly be seen to have failed. In fact, of course, it is the primary parties that have failed. Paradoxically, the onus for the continuation of the conflict often falls on the actor trying to end it, not on the parties pursuing the conflict. Even more remarkable is that armed conflicts which continue without being on the agenda are seldom seen as failures for the UN.

There is one more element that can be seen from the cases which have not come to the agenda in the same period. All seven wars that were off the Council's agenda were defined as internal matters by the governments concerned. International attention was not welcome, unless it meant support for the government. In the Cold War period references to Article 2.7 were often made by a major power that wanted to prevent opponents from interfering and creating international interest. In the post-Cold War period major powers may not necessarily play this role. For a conflict not to gain Council attention it was enough that it involved any other, comparatively powerful UN member. In the period, this was true of countries such as Russia, India, Sri Lanka, Colombia and Nigeria. Whether internationally supported or not, they had the ability to block others from interfering in these conflicts. Only one of these countries was a permanent member; the others were able to avoid such moves due to their regional or international stature.

At some juncture, major powers may positively seek to have conflicts of their particular interest brought to the agenda and not necessarily in conjunction with a peace process. The USA has been the main actor in three conflicts receiving the most attention: Iraq, Afghanistan and international terrorism (Wallensteen and Johansson 2014). Resorting to the UN has been a way to garner international support for its military actions, although this has led to compromises with other Council members. This, in fact, is why the onset of the Iraq War in 2003 was not on the agenda: the

USA, UK and their allies could not muster the same support that there was for actions on Afghanistan and international terrorism. Thus, major states can be powerful and generate attention, but they cannot always expect to command the organization.

The reverse is also conceivable, that weaker states get more attention. The cases with many resolutions concerned countries whose governments were weak or in transition (new, not established, or failing, as in Afghanistan, Sudan, Libya). The conclusion is that the Security Council is particularly motivated to act in a conflict when it is urgent to find a solution and when parties are willing to let that happen. Using the vocabulary of Zartman (1989), it means that the conflicts on the Security Council agenda are at moments more ripe for resolution than many others. Central to this is the role of the governments. They have to agree that such moments exist and accept international action. If they do not, the conflict is likely to continue. The question can legitimately be asked whether the Council is right in waiting to take up the issue. This would mean that the Council changes its role and is prepared to act more strongly for conflict prevention.

There are, however, some outliers that are interesting to observe as well. First, there were also peace processes outside the UN framework in this time period. In particular, the Colombian situation draws interest. The government and the FARC guerrillas initiated negotiations in 2012, but had a tailor-made setting involving Cuba and Norway as facilitators. Similarly, Pakistan has at times negotiated with Pakistan Taliban groups and Uganda has pursued its own talks with rebels in the country. There is no monopoly, of course, for the UN in peace processes. The question is if there is also a trend that more peacemaking is taking place without the purview of the global organization. The data so far are too limited to draw such a conclusion.

A second observation is that the UN has become involved in wars, but not as the traditional go-between. Instead it has taken a one-sided role and become a party to the conflicts. This is very much the case, of course, in Afghanistan where UN-authorized ISAF explicitly supports the Kabul government. Similarly, the invocation of the R2P doctrine in Libya, gradually but decisively made the UN line up with the forces against the incumbent Gaddafi regime. Thus, the UN was on the side of rebels, but without being aligned to any particular rebel group. The fear of a similar development in Syria made Russia and China veto resolutions that were too critical of the Assad regime. The UN role became limited to a more traditional one, but without the support of, say, an international arms embargo on all the warring parties. Again, it can be debated whether this is a trend. In several other recent situations the Council has sided with the government, notably in Mali and the Democratic Republic of Congo. There are also cases where it urged incumbent governments to step down, in view of election results, notably Côte d'Ivoire 2010–11. The application of strategies of counter-terrorism as well as R2P may gradually change the mission of the UN in armed conflicts. It goes without saying that such more intrusive mandates also require considerably more resources or cooperation with actors that have such resources.

Thus, we can see that the understanding of collective security is in a phase of refinement. Not all efforts at peaceful peacemaking are within the UN system, not all the means used by the UN are peaceful. In Chapters 10 and 11 this will be explored further.

World Regions

In Chapter 8, the significance of the regional dimension was emphasized. When observing the activities of the Security Council in this chapter we could point to some regional differences, but also suggest that the issues at hand may be more important for understanding UN action, notably the peace processes. Still, the regional dimension is worth closer observation. It is obvious that a high degree of conflicts in Africa and the Middle East reaches the Council's agenda. Many fewer conflicts in Asia and the Americas were brought to the UN, as exemplified by the conflicts in India, Pakistan and Colombia. Among the 12 wars in the period 2004–13 that drew some UN action, half were in Africa, and all wars in the Middle East were on the UN agenda. This variation deserves some reflection. There is as yet no Asia-wide organization for peace and security. The UN could logically be a possible alternative framework but it is still not being used. Asia, defined as the area east of the Indus, handles conflict in other ways. This region consists of countries with strong states, high consciousness about territorial integrity and entrenched notions of non-involvement in internal affairs. Its international security system is closer to the ones described by *Realpolitik* writers, than any other part of the world. India, Pakistan, Myanmar/Burma and the Philippines saw protracted armed conflicts, at times on the level of wars. All these governments were 'strong', as measured by the position of the military in the countries, or the popular bases of the regimes. Thus, they could repulse attempts to bring international organizations into 'their' conflicts.

Assuming that these patterns have a certain consistency, we might even suggest that the world presently has three geographically distinct systems for handling international conflict. This would be consonant with some of the observations made in Chapter 8. First, there is a *UN-focused regional security system* with a strong concentration on conflicts in Africa, Europe and the Middle East. Here the UN is highly involved and often enters quickly. Many of the conflicts have dealt with state formation issues or internal affairs involving issues of identity. This is also the area where much of the campaign against terrorism is taking place. In terms of economic relationships, migration, historical connections and conflict involvement, these three regions have unusually strong linkages. It is a remnant, most recently, of European colonization, but the relations go further back. A notable exception is conflicts where Russia is a major actor. The conflicts over Georgia in 2008 quickly disappeared from the UN agenda. In the Ukraine crisis in 2013–14, the UN Secretary-General attempted to carve out a role, but with little impact. The Council, however, reacted strongly to the downing of a Malaysian civilian aircraft over Ukraine territory in July 2014. Also OSCE and NATO wanted to participate, but negotiations were largely pursued directly between the parties. However, NATO saw an opportunity to reinforce its role as a collective defence organization against Russian expansionism. OSCE had a role in monitoring cease-fires.

Second, there is *the inter-American system* with few armed conflicts and, as we have seen before, incompatibilities which did not involve state formation questions. The interstate conflicts have not been many and mostly minor. Instead, internal issues relating to military rule, democratization, class struggle, left–right issues, land rights, drugs and, lately, the rights of indigenous people have been central. The regional agenda is markedly different. Furthermore, the OAS, as well as subcontinental initiatives, has been more important, as seen in Chapter 8. The use of extra-regional actors in conflict resolution has been limited. Again, there are strong connections. The role of the USA as the paramount actor serves to highlight the linkages, and the resentments this has created further strengthen the importance of the intra-hemispheric dynamic.

A third system is *the Asian 'non-system'*, consisting of the many countries of South Asia, Southeast Asia and East Asia. It is a set of relationships where each state is left on its own, to fend for itself. There is *Realpolitik* concern about arms development, nuclear weapons development, unsettled interstate conflicts, as well as internal issues, where involvement from the outside is strongly resented by the governments. At the same time, they are often prone to claim that these internal conflicts are instigated from the outside, attributing them to interstate conflicts (for example, the India–Pakistan–Kashmir connections, China–India–Tibet, Myanmar–Thailand–Karen). This non-system contains some subcontinental organizations. They are often not in a position to deal with conflicts of that particular region, as we saw in Section 8.2.

The Asian non-system is marked by the strong states which are eager to avoid international involvement and do not promote stronger regional bodies. The price is high, however, as few of the conflicts have moved to any form of settlement. Some of those that have found a peace agreement (Cambodia, East Timor, Aceh) have done so with international assistance. The UN had a large peacekeeping operation in Cambodia, there were international transitory arrangements for East Timor, and the EU was involved in the implementation of the Aceh agreement. International action can be of use to these actors. The notion of sovereignty is ingrained and reinforced by the views of regional major powers, making it difficult to introduce international action. Asia has robust states, considerable cultural, military and economic independence and modest regional integration.

This self-reliant attitude may be favourable for economic growth, but it does not seem to be conducive for the settlement of disputes. Only when seemingly solid states are weakened, for instance by state mismanagement (or the devastating tsunami of 2004), has international action been favoured. This is often late in a conflict process, and the tasks of peacebuilding become complex and costly, as witnessed both in Cambodia and East Timor. There are recent experiences in international contribution to peace, but they are *ad hoc*. A Nordic mission supervised the cease-fire arrangements on Sri Lanka that later lapsed into renewed war. A non-governmental initiative from the former President of Finland, Martti Ahtisaari, as well as the EU, played a role in the settlement over Aceh in Indonesia 2005. In the peace process in Mindanao in the Philippines, Malaysia has played a mediating role, and there is considerable international support for a successful conclusion.

The Permanent Members

What impact do the permanent members of the Security Council have on UN-led conflict resolution? There are contradictory arguments. First, the Council may concern itself primarily with conflicts in which the major powers are *not* involved at the outset. Permanent members may prefer to act on their own in conflicts in which they themselves are parties. The UN would, thus, be limited to conflicts which are not regarded as important to the interests of particular major states. Following this argument, we would expect the Security Council to take up conflicts that are peripheral from a *Realpolitik* perspective. However, the argument could be turned around. The UN may concentrate on *the* questions of the major powers, dealing with the dangers of world war, as presumably was intended at the inception of the organization. As the UN is a place where the major powers can meet, this would also be where they can sort out their disagreements. This would make the Security Council central to major power affairs, leaving out conflicts which are irrelevant to major power politics.

There are very few systematic studies of agenda setting from this perspective. There is much to indicate that the Council is likely to be particularly concerned with conflicts where *several* of the permanent members are involved. This was clearly the case when former Yugoslavia was at the top of the agenda. Also the situations of Iraq, Afghanistan and international terrorism involved the major powers from the beginning of the crises. The pattern does not fit all cases. In some, such as DRC, Mali, Sierra Leone or Liberia, only one of the major powers was historically involved (France, Britain and the USA, respectively), but mostly for economic or historical reasons, rather than strategic military concerns.

This actually means that the Council operates as a forum for major powers to sort out conflicts in which they are involved or even where they are pressured by the larger UN membership to get involved. This is in line with the original intentions of the UN and it may have become more true after the Cold War. However, these years have not seen any cases of a strategic confrontation directly between major powers. It could still be that such challenges are likely to be handled directly between the major powers, as was the case during the Cold War. Disputes over spies and border violations, for instance, have been handled by direct communication. The inability of the Council to agree on a common action on Iraq 2003 is testimony to this: the USA, UK and their allies chose to act outside the UN framework. Similarly, Russia did not wait for the Security Council to act in Georgia in August 2008 or in Crimea in March 2014. On the other hand, the fact that many conflicts of major power interest have been dealt with in the Security Council may have reduced the likelihood of them turning into direct major power confrontations. There has been an increasing expectation that all major conflicts should be brought to the UN. As we observed above, the events in the past few years may have affected this (the Arab Spring cases, the Ukrainian crisis).

There is a corollary to this conclusion. For effective action it is important for the major powers to work out a consistent policy. If the primary fighting parties learn to play the major powers against one another, they could expect to benefit from these disagreements. They may hope that the decisions would increasingly tilt the UN towards one or the other of the parties. The UN, therefore, instead of being the impartial arbiter, risks becoming just another actor in the conflict, applauded by some, opposed by others. Also on this score we have observed a shift where the permanent members sometimes agree that the UN should take a more partial position, in order to be a tool for universally agreed values (e.g., against terrorism and proliferation of weapons of mass destruction; for R2P).

The difficulty in handling disagreements among the strongest UN members creates a dilemma for the organization. On the one hand, disregarding the views of a permanent or otherwise important member may mean that this member will act to undermine the majority. There is much that such a member can do, given the resources available to a major actor. It may encourage an actor to resist the UN decision. It may send arms, for example, disregarding an arms embargo. It may choose more drastic means, by clandestine support of a particular party. From this point of view, it is preferable for the organization to have all important members as part of the consensus. On the other hand, it may result in decision delays and decision obscurity. As discussions take place during an ongoing armed conflict, much can change in a short period of time. The dilemma is between making quick decisions and consensual decisions. It is a difficult dilemma, as the 2003 Iraq War demonstrates. The proponents of military action were impatient with the pursued course of action, the UN inspection team (UNMOVIC). Instead of allowing time or accepting a consensus decision, they chose to move ahead, only later having to return to the organization. It led to a crisis, and made the Secretary-General initiate a broad reform process on the UN role in collective security. The World Summit meeting of September 2005, that has been mentioned above, agreed on significant reforms that also concerned UN principles of action. We have now alluded to the inability of the Council to act under Chapter VII in the Syrian civil war that has been going on since 2011. Whether this also will spark an urge for reform of the organization remains to be seen.

If there is no agreement but UN operations are in place, the situation becomes acute. The only solution may then be to withdraw, which is likely to make a situation even worse. That happened in the crisis in Rwanda in 1994, playing into the hands of the perpetrators of the genocide. This is an undesirable state of affairs for an international body. It is important to engage so that sufficient consensus develops and as long as there is a chance for coherent operative mandates. The UNMOVIC (led by Hans Blix) and IAEA (led by Mohamed ElBaradei) teams worked on such a mandate but they had to be cut short due to the military actions that were initiated against Iraq in March 2003. In 2013–14, it was remarkable to find that the international experts of OPCW (Organization for the Prohibition of Chemical Weapons) were able to operate in the midst of the Syrian civil war to bring out Syria's declared chemical weapons. It built on an agreement between Russia and the USA, demonstrating the reach of these two when working together. The UN resolution endorsing OPCW action in September 2013 did not impose conditions relating to the ending of the civil war. An opportunity to the end the war may have been missed.

The Council deliberations are not only a matter of bridging differences between democracies and other forms of governments. As most conflicts dealt with Europe, Africa and the Middle East, the countries interested were the European states and the United States. Only in some instances were Russia and China particularly involved. Among the democracies or democratizing major powers there were differences of interest and opinion. This has made them willing to bring up issues in the UN to find cooperative routes forward. It could also hamper the ability of the UN to act. Still, it suggests that they have some confidence in the organization.

What about the other two permanent members? Taking Soviet conflict involvement to the UN was part of Gorbachev's strategy of disengagement. An example is the Afghan conflict, where the UN was used to negotiate and observe the pullout of Soviet troops. By the early 1990s, this strategy had sharply reduced Soviet and Russian international interest and enlarged the UN agenda (Angola, Central America, Afghanistan). Russia limited its interest to a few situations close to, or within, its own borders (Chechnya, Caucasus and Central Asia), apart from the Yugoslav imbroglio. It watched critically EU and NATO enlargements into areas that had been part of the Soviet empire. It resulted in an interest in supporting pro-Russian regimes, for instance, in Ukraine. Russian President Putin's proposal for a Eurasian Union ran counter to the EU's idea of an Eastern Partnership. In 2013 Ukraine became a focal point for both projects, resulting in a clash that also divided the population in the country. Russia, however, was not interested in bringing the issue to the UN.

A conflict of high interest to China on the Security Council agenda has been the situation in Cambodia. This conflict became solvable following the normalization of relations between China and Vietnam in 1990–91 (Amer et al. 1996). The Paris Peace Treaty opened the route for a major UN operation. At the same time, China took part in the observer mission to Iraq and Kuwait. Many of the conflicts close to China, such as those over Korea, Taiwan and the maritime delimitations in East Asia, have not led to major armed conflicts in recent times. They have not been on the UN agenda, nor have they been handled in a regional framework. Lately, it has demonstrated a greater interest in participating in UN peace operations.

However, China has also seen increasing common interest with Russia, particularly on matters which have been defined as internal affairs. Together these two states blocked issues of Myanmar/Burma and Zimbabwe from entering the UN agenda in 2007 and 2008 (Wallensteen and Johansson 2014). They both, surprisingly, abstained on the crucial vote that led to Security Council Resolution 1973 on March 17, 2011, involving a no-fly zone over Libya. In the following draft resolutions on Syria, however, they returned to their sceptical position and together prevented the Council from Chapter VII decisions, relating to the internal conflict in Syria (although they agreed to the resolution on the elimination of chemical weapons, in September 2013).

The permanent members are crucial for the UN's ability to function in conflict resolution. Even though they sometimes hide behind the UN, as if it were an independent actor, they have to take the responsibility for which conflicts enter the agenda, how these conflicts are handled and how they ultimately leave the agenda. It is unlikely that any permanent member will ever get a decision exactly to its liking. Compromise is a necessity. Almost all resolutions passed under Chapter VII have been taken with the support of the three permanent Western members, and one or both of the other permanent members. No decision in the Security Council has ever been imposed on the leading member of the Western group, the United States. Furthermore, as most of the conflicts dealt with in the UN have concerned three regions of particular interest to the West, the resulting agenda has reflected the concerns of these three countries and their societies. We can take note of the fact that the Western European group among the UN member states elects two of the non-permanent seats. Furthermore, the East European seat is often allocated to countries in Central Europe with links to the West. Japan and South Korea have often held one of the Asian seats. Together, this demonstrates the strength of the Western, democratic and industrialized world in the Security Council. The agenda reflects this. It also fuels the interest in reforming the composition of the Council and in alternative fora for decisions on international peace and security. Let us thus proceed to a discussion on the regional organizations.

9.5 Regional Organizations in Conflict Resolution

In its Resolution 2167 of July 28, 2014, the Security Council identified 13 regional organizations with which it particularly wanted to cooperate. It also pointed to the UN Charter, and its Chapter VIII, as a way for such cooperation to materialize, largely as a complement to UN action. In a recent book on regional organizations, 31 such organizations were identified, all dealing to some degree with international peace and security issues (Wallensteen and Bjurner 2015, Appendix 2). It suggests that the definitions of 'regional' and 'international peace and security' vary substantially. All but one of the bodies mentioned by the Council are also on the longer list. The longer inventory, however, has two categories not mentioned in the UN resolution: three European organizations and ten trans-regional organizations. The former includes the European Union, the second bodies such as the Commonwealth, the Non-Aligned Movement, NATO, the Organization for Islamic Cooperation (OIC) and the Organization for Security and Cooperation in Europe (OSCE). All of these have played some role in armed conflicts. More recent crises may have strained the UN, but this is also true for many regional and trans-regional organizations.

Nevertheless, the data demonstrate important variations in the existence of regional and trans-regional networks that can be of use at the time of crisis. Regions with considerable numbers of organizations are Africa, South America and Europe; areas with a lack of such bodies are the Middle East and some parts of Asia. For none of the latter two regions is there a body that incorporates all the states of these geo-politically identified regions (i.e., Turkey and Israel are not parties to any organization for the Middle East; Asia does not have a body that brings together the entire continent of Asia; East Asia does not even have a subregional organization). The connections between such groupings and the ending of armed conflicts can be debated. Some may have arisen from the shared conflict experience (as is the case with Central American cooperation, as well as EU and OSCE). Some may be there for developmental purposes rather than security concerns, but still have an origin in a shared conflict (African organizations, where AU in particular has a background in Pan-Africanism and anti-colonialism). The trans-regional bodies may be rooted in similar experiences, where the commonwealth-type of organizations stem from colonial networks and the non-aligned movement from liberation struggles. NATO certainly was a result of the Cold War and a collective defence body, with varying functions since then, including as a provider of troops for UN-mandated operations.

This also leads us to ask what regional organizations can do that would not be possible for the UN to do equally well? We saw some of the limitations of regional frameworks in Section 8.3, above. Resolution 2167 talks about the regional organizations as useful complements to the United Nations, and also mentions some of their advantages. The Council lists matters such as knowledge about their particular region; possibility to contribute own resources, such as AU's African Standby Force; roles in the protection of civilians and in post-conflict peacebuilding; as well as an ability to act early. These, however, also appear to be roles that apply to the UN itself, if it had the resources that it requires.

The advantages are found in other matters, such as the proximity to the local situation; local networks that can be useful for peacemaking; a simpler and potentially quicker decision-making process than the UN; credible long-term commitments as the regionally based actors cannot leave their own region.

Some of these advantages can also be turned into disadvantages. Leading states in a regional organization may themselves be too heavily involved in the local situation and not be seen as impartial by governments or rebels. The networks may be outdated and not connect to new and revolutionary movements. The regional organization, in other words, may end up on one side of the conflict, and then, most likely, the one of status quo. The global or trans-regional organizations may instead appear more detached from local conditions and thus have more credibility. The fact that they do not necessarily stay for the long term may make their potential contribution more attractive. It is an opportunity to grasp while available.

Many of the regional organizations are dominated by particular member states. Often they are built around one or two states. Only those that encompass several major states can more convincingly claim to be more impartial, at least on this score. The EU Commission is interesting in this regard, as it has an exceptional control over EU resources and can act on its own. The member states have their power vested in the EU Council and it, then, has to build on the unity that can be achieved among the member states. The outcome, however, will not reflect the will of one particular state, but constitutes a shared decision, that is 'European' rather than German, French, British or some other national position. Several of the African sub-regional organizations can be seen as expressions of one dominant actor. The AU, however, would have similar qualities as the EU in this regard. The UN, of course, has an advantage in the strong role of the five member states, but also the drawbacks we discussed, in cases where the five do not agree.

The key problem is also mentioned in the UN resolution: the financial weakness of many of these organizations. In fact, there are very few international organizations that have a solid economic foundation. The EU with its vast resources is the exception. NATO is also comparatively affluent. Like all other intergovernmental bodies the UN has to build on the contributions of the member states. As states are not willing to yield some of its rights to taxation to international organizations, this is likely to be a persistent problem. It is not in the interest of the member states to provide the international organizations with such resources. One concern is that it might turn secretariats of the organization into autonomous centres of power.

Given all these constraints, there still seems to be a trend towards an increasing use of regional organizations for conflict resolution. The most promising form may actually be in cooperation between the UN and regional bodies. This has become a recent trend, often described as 'hybrid' arrangements, and lessons are now being learned.

For a country in conflict, the rise of regional organizations provides new alternatives for action and remedy. This is largely an advantage, even if it may lead to 'forum shopping': which body is likely to generate the 'best' outcome for a particular actor?

Most fundamental, however, is the legal framework on which peacemaking is based. The UN Charter and UN's accumulated experiences provide the most acceptable guide for this. Thus, Chapter VIII may constitute a platform also for regional bodies to work from, rather than developing their own mandates. If that were to be the case, conflict resolution may mean different things in different parts of the world. There is a need to deal with conflicts in a consistent way, and the UN framework is still the one that is the most widely agreed to and, hence, the most legitimate.

9.6 International Communities

Since the end of the Cold War, the concept of *the international community* has gained in use, without having a proper definition. We have used it throughout this book. The vagueness of the term makes it useful. But it also seems to have a particular content relating to the word 'community', which would then differentiate it from the existence of a mere 'system' with a number of autonomous actors.

Neither a 'community' nor a system needs to be based only on states. Also, non-state armed actors or rebel movements can be part of communities. The same goes for non-governmental organizations, or civil society organizations, that act as representatives of larger groups in society, but pursue action through non-violent means. Let us begin with those communities that focus on UN and UN conventions, which is often close to the notion of an 'international community', then proceed to 'systems' and relationships of power.

The International Community

The *international community* depicts a group of actors with some coherence, shared purpose of action, and moral standing. The international community is particularly concerned with matters of human rights, mass refugee movements, armed conflict and justice-based solutions to conflict. It does not have one identifiable institutional framework but refers to a network of actors. The international community includes actors in the leading Western countries and EU organs, but also international organizations (UN, UNHCR, UNHCHR), popularly based action groups and associations, media and religious societies. Furthermore, the concept extends beyond a confined

Western world: it is used, for example, by democracy-promoting groups in Asia. Thus, there is some common understanding of the international community. It is 'international' and it is also a 'community', as there are similar reactions to particular crises. It expresses widely shared democratic values. This community is important in setting the agenda for conflict resolution. This includes the activation of the United Nations, particularly its Secretary-General, thus, giving priority to negotiations, peace agreements and humanitarian action.

One problem with the international community may be its inability to maintain interest in one issue for an extended period of time. There is a volatility which allows attention to shift from one issue to another. What is urgent by necessity gets priority and will result in some action. Unfortunately, such action may be short-lived and unsustainable, particularly as new matters enter the agenda. Since the UN peacekeepers left Somalia in 1994, attention to this conflict in the international community has been minimal. Haiti was central in the mid-1990s, and again came into focus in 2004. Clearly, durable peace requires that institutions be left in place to follow the developments. This has been the argument in favour of the new UN Peacebuilding Commission that began its work in 2006. The devastating earthquake and the following cholera epidemic of Haiti in 2010 reinforced the importance of this, but also demonstrated that action had not come very far.

The Global System

The UN, along with its specialized agencies, is an institutional expression of the international community. However, the UN is not the domain of only one such label. It includes an even larger grouping than the international community. It is part of a *global system* that is also represented in the UN. This points to a wider and even more heterogeneous set of actors, not often forming a community. For many states, UN membership is a way to have their statehood confirmed, but they may not be willing to adhere to other implications of the Charter. Furthermore, this global system is comprised not only of states. There are state-like entities, popular movements, private corporations, armed non-state actors, and forceful individuals acting across state borders. The outer borders of the global system are not easy to depict. Almost any group which is able to act and has an impact on others is part of this system. The only shared value in the system is a desire to retain an element of independence so as to remain an actor. Some of the frustrations experienced in the international community have to do with this. In the Security Council, as well as in the General Assembly, there are actors who object to the basic values underlying the actions proposed by members of the international community. Stipulations of the UN Charter may be used to keep a particular conflict away from international concern, as examined earlier in this chapter, for example with reference to territorial integrity and political independence (Articles 2.4 and 2.7). This provides an inconsistency. As we have seen, some conflicts will be attended to, others will not, depending on the interest and ability of actors to block action.

The reasons go deeper than the wording of the Charter. It can be exemplified with Iran, but it applies to many other countries as well. The Islamic Republic of Iran would not accept international involvement for the Kurdish population, although such decisions were taken with respect to Kurds in neighbouring Iraq. It might undermine the authority of the government. Iran, however, would want to have Security Council measures protect its borders with Iraq and Afghanistan as this serves to maintain its integrity as an actor and a state. Actors are likely to make calculations of utility and act accordingly, even if it may appear opportunistic. At the same time, it means that Charter provisions cross cultural divides. They express a minimum of agreement in a global system of great diversity. The surprisingly uniform reaction to Iraq's invasion of Kuwait in 1990 indicated such common concerns among states, notably the preservation of territorial integrity. Similarly, there was a uniform condemnation of the terrorist acts on September 11, 2001. Initially there was also such a shared appreciation of the Arab Spring in January and February 2011, an agreement that gradually disintegrated, particularly with regard to the Syrian imbroglio, but again resurfaced on issues of chemical weapons, humanitarian action and the need for mediation. Some degree of consensus developed with respect to ISIS in 2014.

It could be said that the values of the UN are expressed in what the international community aims to achieve, rather than what the global system as a whole finds operative or even desirable. The Preamble to the Charter mentions fundamental human rights, dignity, equal rights, social progress, freedom and tolerance. The UN as an organization, however, has to act in the global system, not only within the international community. Thus, the UN can be caught between the concerns of the global system and the international community. Many violent clashes since the Cold War were fought along this divide. For example, the sympathetic reading given to popular-based claims for self-determination of national minorities in the international community clashes with the strong emphasis on state sovereignty, incumbent governments and territorial integrity as basic to the global system. This division cuts across states and regions. It makes it difficult to find common ground for peace. The UN is located on an uncomfortable dividing line.

Paradoxically, this particular location may also give the UN a special function as a conflict-solving body. UN representatives will have to talk to the rogue and shady characters who are real actors in real conflicts. These actors exert power and may be crucial for ending wars. Many of the peace agreements have included such encounters.

Democratic Communities

The UN may have a particular role as a gateway between the international community and the global system. That is not its only role, however. It can be of importance to any community, but in different ways. The idea has emerged of creating an entirely different framework that can more closely mirror a stronger value-based, democratic international community: *Pax Democratica*, a global association of democratic states. There is such an organization for Europe – the Council of Europe. It requires that states have functioning democratic institutions to attain membership. Since 2000 there is also a Community of Democracies, with its permanent secretariat in Warsaw, Poland, and with a large number of member states around the globe. Indeed, the European Union would also describe itself as a community of democracies. It has democracy as a membership criterion.

In Chapter 5, we observed that democracies rarely fight wars with each other, and in Chapters 6 and 7 the role of democracy for solutions to internal and state formation conflicts was discussed. Thus, democracy is an important factor in conflict resolution and prevention. It gives support for the idea of a specific community of democratic states. One may ask if a democratic international community would be needed to solve conflicts among the democracies. Most likely, the worst conflicts are to be found outside this group. It is also likely that there will be conflicts between members of this community and states outside it. This might make democratic states supporters for one side against another. To many, NATO's intervention to stop the armed conflict in Kosovo in 1999 was an expression of the ability of the democratic community to act. There are also fairly uniform ways in which democratic states react to particular crises, notably those in Syria or the challenge of al-Qaida successor ISIS. An idea is to create a caucus of democratic states *within* the UN system, rather than a democratic international association as its replacement or complement (Huntley 1998: 153–5). Clearly, this community will be more limited in numbers than either of the earlier two. It would be a novel constellation. The UN system, for instance, does not have special groups building on criteria other than power (Security Council members), geography (regional groupings) or development (the Group of 77 comprising most Third World nations).

The Security Community

There is another understanding of community, building on cooperation at regional or subregional levels. It includes even fewer states or actors, but with a distinct regional and sociological profile. It stems from the concept of a *security community*, developed by Karl W. Deutsch as a result of studies on peaceful interstate relations (see also Section 8.2). The notion has gained increasing saliency, with what Deutsch termed a pluralistic security community having particular relevance. It refers to situations of close cooperation, where states maintain their independence and where they do not expect to use violence among each other to solve mutual conflicts. This requires common values, mutual responsiveness and, possibly, common institutions. It is interesting to note, however, that institution building has not been seen as a necessary condition. Thus, the concept is applicable to areas where states remain independent, do not have the ambition of forming a union, but continue to cooperate and do not have recent experiences of mutual disputes turning into conflicts and wars (Adler and Barnett 1998; Deutsch et al. 1957).

The Nordic area exemplifies such an alternative, where some states joined NATO or the EU while others remained outside, but they still maintained a tradition of solving conflicts without violence. The European Union is an additional expression of this idea, although it is a much more centralized and institutionalized version. Either way, the examples show that in the concept of security community, the shared values apply to a more narrow group of societies and the values cut deeper into the social fabric than is the case of the international community. It applies primarily to neighbouring countries, constituting subregions in the global system. It is deeper, in the sense that there are shared experiences of dealing peacefully with conflict among the members, thus leading to shared values in conflict management. There are democratic values in the examples given, but they may be more autocratic, as has been the case when building the security community of Southeast Asia.

If developed solidly enough, there would be no reason for the outside world to follow conflicts in these areas at all. The security community would then be self-sustaining in the management of its own crises. As these communities often consist of smaller states, however, the principles of peaceful cooperation may not apply to all kinds of conflict. For instance, they are likely to have difficulties in deterring hostile action from strong neighbours outside the community. The members may also be reluctant to involve themselves in the internal affairs of others. The notion of a security community is very attractive. It suggests that attitudinal shifts inside countries will affect their relationship to the outer world. Countries in a security community could turn into actors on the international scene. Shared values are likely to result in common understandings of international affairs. The Nordic countries illustrate this. Their values place them as a central group in the international community, together with a set of other, like-minded states. In such a constellation we could find Australia, Canada, New Zealand, the Netherlands, but also today's Argentina, Brazil, Chile, Mexico and South Africa, and increasingly, the Philippines, Nigeria, and South Korea. They need international fora to act, and for many of these countries the UN, the EU or NATO are primary foci.

Major Power Constellations

There is another way by which a limited number of countries may cooperate, but without the term 'security community' being appropriate. They may be alliances or other forms of coordination, thus, we could call them 'constellations'. Throughout this book, we have seen the significance of major power relations for conflict patterns. When these relations are universalist, cooperation in the form of *major power concerts* prevails. In history, such periods have been identified and labelled, for example, the European concert of the early nineteenth century or periods of *détente* during the Cold War. It means that the powerful actors are incorporating the security concerns of the others into their own calculations of interest. The avoidance of major power war is an important element, but without fully excluding the possibility of resorting to armed conflict even among the majors. Thus, there may be a shared interest in security, but it does not extend as deeply as would be the case in a security community. We have noted that contentions among these actors historically have resulted in particularism and major war.

To some analysts, cooperative major power relations may still be the only way the world can be governed, although this is far from an ideal form of governance building on shared beliefs (Gilpin 2001: 402). It is an argument for vesting power with the permanent members of the Security Council and for developing the Group of 8 (G8) framework into consolidated cooperation among the leading economies of the world. The global financial crisis since 2008 has given a new role to the Group of 20 (G20), which originally was a meeting of finance ministers. As it incorporates a number of emerging economies, it pulls together countries with economic clout. To many, it is more attractive than the formation of a Group of 2 (G2), meaning the USA and China, as the largest economies. The Ukraine crisis in 2014, however, demonstrates the softness of such constellations: seven members of G8 decided not to invite Russia to the next meeting, thus reverting to a previous G7 format.

Unipolar Communities

An additional alternative constellation is one which is under the determined leadership of one powerful actor, what could be called 'unipolar' communities. By its strength, it makes other states fall in line. Its values are given prominence and radiated throughout the community. Today, this could be termed a community of *Pax Americana*. Clearly, only one country has the capacity to project force globally – the United States. After the end of the Cold War, European countries reduced their military expenditures and reallocated resources to matters which more immediately promoted the welfare of populations (unemployment support, educational investment, health and social services). There has been a peace dividend. As we have seen, the world has not remained peaceful. New challenges have required unprecedented international action, peacekeeping operations and even peace enforcement. For the time being, the United States is the only country that maintains a capacity to airlift troops to distant regions in a short period of time. Its fleets can provide bases for military actions in many parts of the world. It has ground forces that were used to invade Iraq in 2003. Its satellite systems give the United States more information than any actor for discovering troop movements, other military preparations and general intelligence. In 2010, the USA alone accounted for close to 42 per cent of world military expenditures, and by 2013 around 37 per cent. Corresponding figures for other militarily strong states were around 4–5 per cent (Russia) and 8–10 per cent (China) (based on SIPRI military expenditure database 2014). Such power calculations may initially have led the USA on a path of unilateralism, acting on its own or, as in Iraq, in a coalition of close allies, or in Afghanistan with the help of international organizations. It may also result in multilateralism and a realization of a need for cooperation. The record since the Cold War is mixed. Sometimes, the USA has acted in line with the international community as defined above; sometimes, it has pursued its own course. Increasingly, however, it seems to have realized the importance of international support for its actions. The Obama administration displayed a pattern of bringing together such coalitions, for instance, with respect to the conflicts around Libya in 2011, and on ISIS in 2014. However, in its fight against al-Qaida using, for example, drones and assassinations, it only consulted with the governments in question, if at all.

The United States is militarily unchallenged on a global scale. However, many of the wars since the Cold War have been highly local, and local opponents have found ways in which they can thwart action by powerful states. They are in an historical line of resistance movements fighting French and American forces in Vietnam, Soviet forces in Afghanistan, Russian troops in Chechnya and facing the USA in Iraq and Afghanistan. These struggles involved considerable casualties. Some led to political victories for the opponents. The US actions in October 1993 in Somalia aimed at capturing some of the collaborators of a Somali warlord. It resulted in the death of some US servicemen. The casualties among the Somalis included at least 500 killed (Bowden 1999: 333). Neither the American public nor the government was prepared for American casualties. This event changed the military intervention policy of the Clinton administration. It illustrated the potential military vulnerability of a strong power, whether acting alone or in concert with others. For the remainder of the decade, no American soldiers were put into ground battle operations.

The interventions that followed used air power. In 1995, this strategy achieved a retreat of Serb forces in Bosnia. The opportunity of weakened Serb positions created by the NATO bombardment was seized by Croat and Bosniak forces, which quickly pushed forward to conquer more territory. The USA created the conditions. The subsequent peacekeeping mission was done in a multilateral framework with NATO, the OSCE, the EU and the UN. In 1999, the air campaign influenced the Yugoslav leader Slobodan Milosevic to agree to a withdrawal from Kosovo. It was achieved through NATO, but the civil administration of Kosovo was turned over to the UN. All US administrations since the Gulf War used air raids against Iraq to achieve compliance with UN resolutions. In attempts to strike at international terrorism, US missiles hit installations in Afghanistan and a pharmaceutical plant in the Sudan in 1998 – again unilateral moves. Following September 11, 2001, the American public was more accepting of American casualties. Thus, US ground forces were deployed in Afghanistan, and an army of more than 150,000 soldiers invaded Iraq in 2003. The continued wars in Iraq and Afghanistan, however, have led to increased American battle deaths, and to an unease in the USA about the wars, their purposes, duration and ending.

The power of the US is extensive, but the results may not appear equally impressive. Years later, the agreements in Bosnia-Herzegovina and Kosovo remained fragile. The removal of Saddam Hussein in 2003 did not create a functioning state in Iraq, but led instead to a protracted war, continuing even as US forces began to leave the area in 2010. It even led to a return of an enlarged US military presence in 2014 to counter new threats. Years after the removal of the Taliban from power in Afghanistan, the new government remained brittle, the future uncertain and the return of the Taliban a possibility. Nevertheless, the ISAF forces left the country by the end of 2014. The killing of Osama bin Laden in May 2011 seems to have affected al-Qaida severely, but various other groupings subsequently emerged, several of them intent on conquering territory and establishing their preferred order locally, rather than fighting the US directly. To these non-state actors belong Boko Haram in Nigeria, al-Shabaab in Somalia, AQIM in Mali and ISIS in Syria and Iraq, to mention a few. In many ways these organizations constituted an international, Islam-based action community, a non-state armed challenge to the peacemaking communities. It is striking that there were almost no examples of these actors being involved in negotiations for settlements. The military arsenal of the United States remains the largest, but its contribution to peacemaking requires international consensus and credible local allies.

The political limits of US power not only stem from the military strategy used. The USA is a superpower, which often displays acute divisions among its policy-making circles on its role in world affairs. Traditionally, they have been about isolationism versus engagement. This is too simple a distinction. The internal debate is more complex, unpredictable and almost impulsive. There is a prominent role for media, NGOs and special interests, notably the large corporations, as well as for an entrenched military establishment in shaping US policy. The outcomes may in the end be more random than well planned and strategic.

This means that the most likely scenario for the future is not one of a community consciously developed by the United States for *Pax Americana*. Rather it is one of the United States avoiding having to act in isolation. This can be achieved through the United Nations, which gives other countries some influence on the course of action. It can also be done with international regional organizations that depend on the United States. It would constitute a network which may act outside the UN if necessary. There is a discernable trend in this direction, NATO being an example. NATO's enlargement (28 members by 2009) and its various affiliates have made NATO a comprehensive network for Europe and beyond. It is typical that the USA chose to hand over to NATO the air campaign against Libya in March 2011 and involved NATO members in military operations against ISIS in Iraq in 2014.

Emerging Communities?

There have also emerged state-based alternatives to the Western-dominated frameworks. The cooperation between Brazil, Russia, India, China and South Africa (BRICS) draws considerable attention. These countries have been regarded as emerging economies with considerable resources and influence in particular regions. In many votes in the UN, however, these countries have had very different positions (notably on the civil war in Syria). Whether this evolves into a strategically significant grouping – not just a meeting club or a joint development bank – needs to be observed.

Similarly, by January 1, 2015 the Eurasian Economic Union will come into force, consisting initially of Russia, Kazakhstan and Belarus. It is an economic project that has political overtones. Russia's ambition has several roots. One is a desire to regain an international standing and make up for the dissolution of the Soviet Union in 1991. Another is to develop an economic bloc that can prevent a further enlargement of the European Union. Thus, by 2013 Russia's plan ran counter to the EU's proposed

Eastern Partnership that initially also focused on Armenia, Azerbaijan, Belarus, Georgia, Moldova and Ukraine. The three latter planned to enter the agreement.

The crisis over Ukraine is instructive as it tells us that the formation of such communities also has its conflict dimension. The crisis began as the incumbent Ukrainian president decided in November 2013 not to sign the agreement with the EU. This led to protracted, pro-EU protests in Maidan Square in the capital Kiev, and in February the president left the country, without giving an explanation. In the unclear conditions that followed, and after less than legitimate procedures, the Crimean Peninsula was annexed into the Russian Federation in March 2014. Ukrainian elections took place and by June a new president was in place. After this, Ukraine entered the EU partnership. By that time, however, several Eastern provinces were under military control by pro-Russian separatists and serious battles took place. Thus, which community to join can be fraught with tension. Rarely, however, does it give rise to the drama that could be witnessed in Ukraine.

In this chapter, we have seen the types of international actors that appear in conflicts and in conflict resolution. It is now time to study the various measures, the instruments, that are being used. This is the topic of the following two chapters.

Further Readings

Go to the *Understanding Conflict Resolution* web page at https://study.sagepub.com/wallensteen4e for free access to journal articles listed.

On the United Nations

There is a considerable literature on the UN, but rarely is it as analytical as one would like. However, there are two books that are in a category of their own:

Weiss, T.G., Forsythe, D.P. Coate, R.A. and Pease K.K. 2014. *The United Nations and Changing World Politics,* Boulder, CO: Westview Press.
Now in its 7th edition this work is an indispensible and comprehensive introduction to the work of the UN with regard to security, human rights and development.

Axworthy, L. 2001. 'Human Security and Global Governance: Putting People First', *Global Governance,* 7 (1): 19–23.
In this article the former Canadian Minister for Foreign Affairs outlines the concept of human security. It was guiding Canadian approaches to the UN during the Liberal government and had an impact on UN affairs.

High Level Panel 2004. *A More Secure World: Our Shared Responsibility.* Report of the Secretary-General's High-level Panel on Threats, Challenges and Change, United Nations.

The high-level panel, appointed by Kofi Annan as UN Secretary-General, produced one of the most ambitious public reports to reform the UN system since the end of the Cold War. Its recommendations span many aspects of what is treated in Chapters 9–11 in *Understanding Conflict Resolution*, including Security Council reform.

On the Security Council

Einsiedel, S., Malone, D.M. and Stagno U.B. 2015. *The Security Council during the 21st Century*. Boulder, Co.: Lynne Rienner, 2015.

This is a sequel to a previous volume edited by David M. Malone in 2004, thus updating and further deepening the analysis of the work of the UN Security Council, as the most powerful of the UN organs engaged in peace and security matters.

Wallensteen, P. 1994. 'Representing the World: A Security Council for the 21st Century', *Security Dialogue*, 25: 63–75.

There has been a constant quest for reforms of the Security Council. Very little has happened, but there are ideas. In this article the author of *Understanding Conflict Resolution* outlines logical possibilities for making the Council more representative, without losing its efficiency.

Weiss, T.G. and Young, K.E. 2005. 'Compromise and Credibility: Security Council Reform?' *Security Dialogue*, 36 (2): 131–54.

In this article, the prolific UN observer Thomas G. Weiss and a colleague outline the possibilities and impossibilities of UN Security Council reform.

The UN Secretary-General

There are many good accounts of personal experiences in the UN. A valuable book giving the perspective from the top organ is the following:

Annan, Kofi and Nader Mousavizadeh 2012. *Interventions: A Life in War and Peace*. Penguin Books.

In this work the former Secretary-General Kofi Annan (at the helm of the UN 1997–2006) gives an account of his early days in Ghana, as well as his many years in various positions in the United Nations. It gives an eye-opening perspective of the organization from the inside.

On Regional Organizations

Compared to the extensive work on the UN there is less comparing regional organizations, their strengths and weaknesses with respect to peace and

(Continued)

(Continued)

security. Most recent is a collection of chapters dealing in particular with EU, OSCE, AU, ECOWAS and the League of Arab States:

Wallensteen, P. and Bjurner A. (eds) 2015. *Regional Organizations and Peacemaking. Challengers to the UN?* London: Routledge.

This book outlines the role regional organizations can play in peacemaking. Thus, its contributions are relevant also for the aspects developed in Chapters 10 and 11 of *Understanding Conflict Resolution*.

10
COERCION AND ENFORCEMENT

10.1 International Action and Peace Agreements

The expectation, by many parties, is that when an armed conflict enters the agenda of the UN or any other international organization there will be action. This is also a reason why some actors resist engaging international bodies. Since the end of the Cold War there has been an unprecedented set of actions by the United Nations, including sanctions, peacekeeping operations and peace enforcement. The extensive deliberations in the Council have to do with proposed, planned or ongoing actions. The same applies to other bodies, be they EU, NATO, AU or others. What the members can accept becomes the decision. A key problem is whether this is sufficient for dealing with a particular situation. This is a reason for the Security Council and other decision-making bodies to continuously review their actions. Thus, Chapters 10 and 11 deal with the instruments that can be used in international conflict resolution.

When thinking about possible measures, the distinction in the UN Charter between the coercive and mandatory action of Chapter VII and the peaceful and recommended action under Chapter VI is helpful. The former hopes to push the parties to a particular outcome that is specified by the organization, the latter hopes to persuade, or entice the parties to come to a decision of their own. We may also say that Chapter VII actions are part of managing crisis, whereas Chapter VI has a focus on pre- or post-crisis measures. Indeed, Chapter VII makes clear that the Council shall determine whether a particular situation constitutes a 'threat to the peace, breach of the peace or act of aggression' (Article 39) and then act accordingly. Chapter VI, however, states that the Council shall 'call upon' the parties to settle their disputes by a series of measures ranging from negotiations to the use of peaceful means of their own choice (Article 33). This is also the distinction applied here. Thus, Chapter 10 here deals with measures that relate to the provisions of Chapter VII of the UN Charter, while the following chapter takes up actions relating to Chapter VI.

This feature provides the UN with options in dealing with a crisis. Similar mandates are reflected also in other international organizations, notably the EU and AU, which can both mandate sanctions, but also have other, less coercive means at their disposal. However, only the UN Security Council can authorize the use of force with the support from international law. The Charter expects the permanent members to follow this as well. Still, we have seen in this book that this is not always the case.

A typical measure for the UN is the use of economic and other sanctions. These are mentioned in the Charter, and there has been a revitalization of this field. It is also an instrument used by other organizations, notably the EU and AU. A second major instrument is peacekeeping operations aiming to contribute to, implement and sustain a peace process. It is not mentioned in the Charter and is often said to be located between Chapters VI and VII (thus, termed 'Chapter 6 ½' measures). It was developed in the 1950s and has added new dimensions since 1989. A third measure is peace enforcement, a novel development. These tools are largely a matter of dissuasion, dissuading the parties from restarting armed conflict or from escalating it further. This is most clearly seen with respect to the peacekeeping operations that traditionally have been there to prevent the recurrence of fighting, and, thus, reduce tension. Sanctions are more complicated to define, as they do contain elements not only to contain but also to coerce the parties. The hardship from the sanctions is expected to get one or the other party to change conduct. It has also been observed that they are signalling the shared reactions of the international community (Giumelli 2011). Peace enforcement, finally, is, of course, particularly coercive. Originally conceived as protection of humanitarian deliveries, they have lately included mandates for the protection of civilians, with the use of force. As for actual and sustained combat, such missions have normally been handed to other bodies, notably NATO in Afghanistan. Thus, a UN military presence is more a matter of dissuading rather than compelling actors.

10.2 Sanctions

Sanctions are, today, used by a number of actors and for different purposes. Most sanctions are from the United States and relate to both political and economic motives that stem from US policy. Some of them are implementations of sanctions by the UN Security Council. Others are imposed without UN agreement in particular crises. The most typical case is the targeting with sanctions of different actors in the Syrian civil war. There is, however, nothing in the Charter to prevent countries or organizations to act on their own with this type of measures. Such unilateral (or sometime multilateral) actions outside the UN have been frequent throughout the organization's existence.

Also the European Union has a lengthy record of sanctions, or, as the term is, restrictive measures. EU motives often have to do with the promotion of democracy and human rights. Thus, specific EU sanctions have been directed against Zimbabwe and Myanmar/Burma, in order to promote a democratization process. As is the case with

US sanctions, these are often measures that were originally proposed as avenues for the UN. When the Security Council blocked action, they have been pursued by US, EU and other actors. A most remarkable case is the EU arms embargo on China, that has been in place since the massacre on the Tiananmen Square in Beijing 1989. The League of Arab States has pursued sanctions against Israel since its inception.

In terms of conflict resolution, the UN sanctions are most interesting. A sizeable proportion of all UN sanctions have been used for the support of peace processes. Thus, since 1990 the Security Council has decided on sanctions in 21 armed conflicts and for other reasons in five other situations, all under Chapter VII of the UN Charter (by July 2014), a total of 26 cases. During the Cold War there were only two cases, against South Africa and Rhodesia. The end of the Cold War resulted in a 'sanctions decade' (Cortright and Lopez 2000; Wallensteen and Staibano 2005). Sanctions on South Africa were introduced in 1977 and ended in 1994, following the country's first democratic elections. In the Rhodesian case, they were instituted in 1965, came under Chapter VII in 1966 and were lifted following the negotiated agreement ending the Rhodesian crisis, in December 1979. By July 2014 sanctions were in place against 13 member states, but targeting a great number of individuals from many more countries. Such targeted sanctions has been the typical approach for all recent sanctions from the UN, meaning that they target individuals, or particular goods (arms, diamonds) or services (visas, banks), and with fairly explicit demands of what the target needs to do (or not do) in order to have the measures removed. The rate of success, as well as the contribution to conflict resolution, is what we are interested in here.

In the nine cases where sanctions were ended, there was an element of success. In the case of Libya, sanctions were instituted in 1992, in connection with Libya's alleged involvement in two different aircraft bombings. One case came to be associated with the Scottish town of Lockerbie where the destroyed airplane hit the ground. The other case, which received much less attention, concerned a French plane exploded by a bomb while in the air over Africa. By 1999, after seven years, the Council determined that Libya had fulfilled UN demands. Two agents accused of planting the bomb in the Lockerbie case were handed over to a Scottish court, temporarily relocated to the Netherlands. One of them was convicted in early 2001. Later, Libya paid compensation to the families of the victims. In this case, the sanctions were the only coercive action used and they can, thus, be credited with having had an impact. In a controversial decision, the convicted person was released in 2009 on medical grounds and received a hero's welcome in Libya. In connection with the uprising that began in Libya in February 2011, new sanctions for a different purpose, the protection of citizens from the regime's violence, were imposed. In particular, the freezing of assets belonging to the Gaddafi family may have had an impact on the following civil war and the killing of Muammar Gaddafi in October 2011. It made it difficult for the regime to finance a consistent supply of weapons and munitions for loyal forces.

Another case where the impact of sanctions may have been in the direction desired by the initiators concerned former Yugoslavia. An arms embargo was instituted against all states of former Yugoslavia in 1991, and specific sanctions were imposed on the successor-state, the Federal Republic of Yugoslavia (Serbia and Montenegro), in 1992. These measures were removed in 1996 following implementation of the Dayton peace accords. In this case, the effects of the sanctions were interwoven with the effects of the war. Still, it is likely that the sanctions played an instrumental role, making, in the end, some parties more eager to conclude agreements and establish some degree of 'normal' conditions for their international relations.

The impact of sanctions on Côte d'Ivoire may have been along the same line. There was an agreement, there were elections, but the incumbent refused to step down, thus encountering international isolation, including sanctions. It may have made it difficult for him to get the supplies needed in order to maintain power. After a short war in 2011, he was captured and soon thereafter transferred to the ICC in The Hague.

In another case of terminated sanctions, the measures on Haiti were instituted in an unusual on-off pattern. They were imposed in June 1993, suspended in August, only to be reinstituted in October 1993, and then terminated in October 1994, when the previously ousted, democratically elected government had been returned to power. The economic effects in Haiti seem to have been devastating, but the military regime, which took power in a coup in 1991, refused to comply. It was not until it faced an invasion from an overwhelming American force that the regime finally yielded. The immediate military threat was decisive.

In the cases of the civil war in Angola and the war on the Horn of Africa, the role of sanctions can be debated. In Angola, the war ended as a result of the killing of Jonas Savimbi, the leader of UNITA, the armed opposition. The sanctions impacted on the economy of UNITA, but more important was that the change in leadership now made it possible for UNITA to abide by the previous agreements with the government.

In the case of sanctions on Eritrea and Ethiopia, they were instituted to prevent a return to fighting and to support peace efforts. The peace agreement was signed in 2000 and the sanctions expired in 2001, thus claiming some impact on ending the war. As we have seen in Chapter 5, Ethiopia did not implement the agreed measures, but the Council chose not to reintroduce the sanctions. Eritrea, however, was exposed to new sanctions in 2009 due to its involvement in the Somalia conflict and in a conflict with neighbouring Djibouti.

The sanctions on Liberia and Sierra Leone have also been terminated, but were kept long after the war had ended and the main warlords were gone, as a way of pressuring the governments to make required changes. In the post-war situation the UN sanctions were used for peacebuilding purposes.

The results in these cases are mixed. In several instances, the conflictual conditions remained or even worsened (Iraq, Rwanda, Somalia, Sudan) but efforts of peacemaking may have been strengthened in others (Democratic Republic of Congo, Côte d'Ivoire, Liberia, Sierra Leone). In the case of the 2005 Lebanon sanctions, the aim was to support the investigation into the assassination of former Prime Minister Rafik Hariri, and thus was not directly related to an ongoing armed conflict (but potentially helped to prevent a new one).

There is, thus, some success in sanctions, but there is also considerable concern. Expectations are higher. This has led to a need for the more precise targeting of the sanctions. The sanctions of the 1990s were criticized as they affected an entire population of a state. In this way, they could serve to undermine the chances of opponents to become stronger against the government. It could be observed that the targeted government improved its standing, partly by branding the opponents as 'unpatriotic' or as 'foreign agents'. A national crisis means that a government can assume extraordinary powers.

A seminal case is the comprehensive sanctions operation against Iraq in the 1990s, which was vigorously debated because of its humanitarian consequences. The UN and the Security Council tried to smooth the effects on the general population through an oil-for-food arrangement. Iraq was entitled to sell oil under UN control, and to use the proceeds to buy food. It improved the situation for the population, but it also tilted the internal balance of power in favour of the regime of Saddam Hussein, who could control the proceeds. After the US-led invasion in 2003, the sanctions were instead targeted on particular individuals associated with that regime, while the rest of the economy became entirely unrestricted. Documents found in the Iraqi ministries exposed a number of persons, companies and countries that benefited unduly from the sanctions regime. This scandal was investigated by several independent commissions.

These examples further strengthened the need for more targeted sanctions as well as closer monitoring of their implementation. Such moves were visible earlier, for example, in the case of Angola, where an oil embargo was specifically instituted against UNITA in 1993. Another example is the sanction regime against Rwanda. Arms trade with the post-genocide government of Rwanda was allowed but sanctions were imposed on opposition forces. Thus, the Council attempted to shift the strength of the forces inside countries so as to disfavour a particular party. Sometimes this has been stated explicitly, as in the case of UNITA in Angola, other times this follows by implication.

In October 1999, sanctions were also introduced against Afghanistan, directed against the internationally unrecognized Taliban regime. This was done because of the Taliban's unwillingness to take action against terrorism and, in particular, because it had not turned over Osama bin Laden to 'appropriate authorities in a country where he will be arrested and effectively brought to justice' (Security Council Resolution 1267 of 1999). Following the September 11, 2001 attacks on the USA, there was increased support for stronger measures (Security Council Resolution 1368 of 2001). After the war that deposed the Taliban regime, the sanctions remained in place, targeting specific individuals, wherever they were on the globe. These sanctions became part of the global struggle against terrorism and listing new persons or organizations turned into a major concern for these sanctions regimes.

Sanctions are obvious demonstrations of the intentions of the Security Council and thus of the international community. Targeting particular actors makes them more precise, but also provides opportunities for evasion by the actors, using go-betweens, family or clan members, even strengthening the determination of the ruling clique to keep itself in power. In an imperfect world, it remains, after all, an action with some impact, and it is non-violent at that. In the context of peace negotiations, the lifting of sanctions becomes an additional bargaining chip for which the senders, the outside world, may be able to extract additional concessions. Thus, originally conceived as punishment, in the later phase their ending can be turned into potential rewards. This assumes that the goals of the sanctions are clear and that, as part of a deal, it is possible for the negotiators to ensure that the sanctions actually will be lifted (Doxey 1996: 119–21).

It also presumes that sanctions are properly implemented. By making sanctions more targeted, the demands on government bureaucracies increase. Now they have to identify commodities going to or stemming from a particular country. It is also required that specific individuals are prohibited from entering a country. Their bank accounts have to be frozen and they are prevented from trading in particular commodities. The sanctions reform process has resulted in a number of reports aimed at improving the use of sanctions, but also enhancing national capacity to carry them out. A result is to demonstrate that sanctions are not necessarily always useful. Furthermore, as individuals are listed in the Council decisions, there were significant human rights aspects to consider (Cameron 2005; Wallensteen et al. 2003). In 2009, the Council finally decided to institute a more transparent system for the listing and delisting procedure. A special focal point for such matters was created, giving a possibility for those listed to appeal.

Among the sanctions in armed conflicts, peace agreements were signed, or reactivated, and became durable in 12. The sanctions literature has been more concerned with success and failure of sanctions from the point of view of the initiator, the sender (Wallensteen 2011b). Their role in a peace process requires a more detailed analysis.

The threat of not lifting sanctions was used to push recalcitrant parties in several negotiations, for example, Rhodesia and former Yugoslavia. It means that the lifting of sanctions was part of the peace negotiations, either directly as an element in the negotiations or indirectly as a promise to the parties if they agreed. The sanctions clearly contributed to the negotiated outcome in South Africa in 1994. Their impact was a burden on the apartheid government and worked in combination with pressure from below. Writings on the earlier Liberia peace agreements do not credit the sanctions regime for the outcome (Alao et al. 1999). However, President Charles Taylor had to leave the country in 2003 as his regime was running out of resources to fight insurgents. Afterwards the sanctions, combined with peacekeeping, helped to lay the ground for the implementation of the peace agreement and the presidential elections in 2005. In the cases of Angola and Sierra Leone, sanctions could not help to maintain the agreements, but with additional developments (the death of leaders, the presence of international peacekeeping) they may have served to return the states to peaceful conditions. Similarly, the peace processes in the Côte d'Ivoire and the Democratic Republic of Congo may have had support from the sanctions, as they reduced the strength of potential spoilers. The contributions of targeted sanctions to peace settlements are difficult to assess, but this overview suggests that they may constitute a significant element in a broader international strategy to deal with ongoing violence. Combining targeted sanctions with peacekeeping might be particularly important.

In addition, regional organizations have also been engaged in the use of sanctions, most recently exemplified by the European Union and the African Union. Of course, mandatory sanctions imposed by the Security Council have to be implemented by the members of the EU and AU. In addition, these organizations are also free to operate their own sanctions regimes. In many of the EU cases the ambition has been the promotion of democracy and human rights – that is a somewhat different agenda from the UN institutions. This means that the EU has mandated sanctions in a wider set of cases. It had imposed sanctions on Zaire (presently named Democratic Republic of Congo) well before the civil war that led to the downfall of President Mobutu. It also decided on repeated sanctions on Myanmar (Burma) and Zimbabwe, situations which both had been blocked from the UN agenda (Eriksson 2007, 2010a, 2010b; Portela 2010; Giumelli 2011, 2013). Many of these sanctions have been intended to support a democratic opposition, and at times there were real openings for negotiations and freer elections. They may, thus, have helped to highlight these situations ('signalling', Guimelli 2011) and possibly dissuaded the regimes from repressive actions (at least for a time).

The EU sanctions on Russian individuals and corporations have emerged from the Ukrainian crisis in 2014. The measures have included travel bans and the freezing of financial assets. Also equipment for oil and gas drilling has been affected. EU sanctions have targeted oligarchs, political and military leadership as well as particular individuals in Eastern Ukraine and Crimea. The EU sanctions in March 2014 underlined the illegality of the incorporation of Crimea into Russia. The US has imposed similar sanctions. Interestingly, Russia responded in August 2014 by banning certain food imports from the EU. A new set of EU sanctions in September 2014 aimed at accelerating the implementation of the agreed cease-fire agreements in the East of the country. They sought to stop fighting and promote dialogue.

The African Union has also its own sanctions regimes with a particular focus on constitutionality. Thus, the AU has objected to unconstitutional regime changes and imposed sanctions in several cases, notably Togo, Mauretania, Guinea and Madagascar (Eriksson 2010b), some of which also have involved armed conflicts (Côte d'Ivoire). As the economic integration among African countries is limited the impact of the sanctions is also likely to be more political, or in line with targeted sanctions, affecting particular individuals. These sanctions have not only been intended to achieve a return to the constitutional order but also prevent other potential coups.

Sanctions obviously have a role in peace processes, as a way to push parties towards negotiations, or, in a way, becoming a reward by lifting them following an agreement. There is evidence that sanctions can be useful in this regard.

10.3 Peacekeeping Operations

In his study of six major peacekeeping operations, Paul F. Diehl concludes on the role of peacekeeping in conflict resolution: 'What is abundantly clear is that they are not very successful.' The record was clearly better with respect to limiting armed conflict. 'Peacekeeping operations may be best suited for use *after* some measure of conflict resolution, rather than the traditional preresolution deployment' (Diehl 1993: 105–6). Diehl's study concerns the original type of peacekeeping operations. However, it points to an important element. Peacekeeping operations are basically thought of as measures to be instituted after a peace agreement. They are there to implement what has been agreed. They have an impartial role after a devastating war when the conflicting parties are not likely to be able to cooperate easily among themselves.

The peacekeeping record since 1989 is impressive. The number of new peacekeeping operations, renamed peace operations, using the definition given by the UN, closely mirrors the curve of resolutions passed in the Security Council. A total of 69 peacekeeping missions were mandated by the United Nations from 1948 to 2014. Fifteen were initiated prior to 1989. Thus, three-quarters of all operations belong to the post-Cold War period. Fifteen were ongoing by 2014. Interestingly, non-UN actors initiated even more peace missions, defined in the same way as the UN. There were 67 such operations for the 1948–2005 period. The mandate, duration and size of all these operations vary considerably. It is not surprising to find that most UN peace operations were in the three regions which are typical UN areas of operation: Africa, Europe and the Middle East. Non-UN action often meant more regional activities, but the patterns are not sharply different (Heldt and Wallensteen 2006). As could be expected, most of the operations were associated with ongoing or recently terminated major armed conflicts. An interesting exception was UNPREDEP, the preventive deployment in Macedonia, which became an independent operation in 1995 and was closed down in 1999 (Pellnäs 1997). There was no armed conflict going on in Macedonia and the UN mission was meant to prevent the spread of wars from former Yugoslavia. It served to consolidate the newly independent country that was exposed to pressure from Greece (which resisted the right of the new state to call itself Macedonia) and dissent from a sizeable Albanian population. Such preventive measures need a separate discussion (see Chapter 11.1).

Concentrating on the UN operations, their contribution can be discussed in the terms suggested by Diehl. Do they contribute to a reduction in actual conflict behaviour and lead to conflict resolution? That they have a quick impact in the reduction of armed conflict and that they serve to pacify their immediate area of operation is beyond doubt. There is strong evidence that points to their ability to reduce civilian killing and preventing, for instance, genocide (Melander 2009b). Thus, the continued resort to peacekeeping operations can be understood. It makes logical sense to inject a non-partial force in a society ripped apart by conflict. Thus, peacekeeping can help defuse situations and give space for negotiations, which is also in accordance with the prevalent peacekeeping theories.

However, this effect may not only be to the credit of the operation as such. There may, in fact, be a prior accord among the parties. The presence of UN forces makes possible the implementation of what has been agreed. Among the operations that have been terminated, it can be asked whether violence returned to the same parties after the ending of the mission. These would then be the most obvious cases of failure, whereas operations where this did not take place would appear to be associated with a genuine change in the relationships among the contending parties.

Among all the terminated missions in actual conflict situations since the end of the Cold War, the same conflict continued in only three cases (Angola, Rwanda and Somalia). In some cases, notably Haiti, the Central African Republic and Timor-Leste, peacekeepers had to return several years later. In Angola, a peace agreement was implemented, no less than twice, but the war ended only after a leadership change. In Rwanda, the peace agreement of 1993 was never put into practice and, in Somalia, it was not possible to get credible commitments from the warring factions and thus, the UN mission was withdrawn by 1995.

There are also cases where the mandates and resources of the peacekeeping operation have been assessed to be insufficient. As a consequence, other actors have intervened from the outside. US and NATO actions in the Bosnian War in 1995 are often credited with the ending of this conflict through the Dayton Agreement later the same year, rather than the simultaneously ongoing UN operations. Such interventions may not always result in peace accords, however. In Somalia the UN mission was supplemented with a US-directed and ill-fated peace enforcement operation in 1993. It led to the withdrawal of the American forces and undermined the UN operation. It also made the USA reluctant to get into the ensuing crisis in Rwanda less than six months later. Thus, UN deployments in Rwanda could not carry out the assistance they were supposed to provide to the Rwandan peace process. One failed intervention actually resulted in two failed peace processes.

These missions could be seen as failures in contributing to a peace process. It is a failure rate that is unacceptable in view of the suffering involved. The blame for violence, of course, has to rest primarily with the parties themselves. It is not likely that the wars would have stopped without the UN presence. The record shows that the wars continued after the UN had departed. These UN missions can be seen as lost opportunities for the parties as well as a failure for the UN strategy for conflict resolution. It is not the full picture, however.

In a large number of cases, operations were terminated without further conflict among the same parties. Most of these are associated with durable peace agreements that have been identified in Chapters 5, 6 and 7. This must be seen as a more acceptable outcome than expected. This means that the record for UN peacekeeping in contributing to actually ending armed conflicts is remarkable. The conclusion can be phrased as follows: If there were peaceful conditions when the UN left, it is likely that the peace arrangement was going to be sustained; if, however, the UN left under conditions that were turbulent, its departure was not likely to restore peace to the situation.

Most of the situations have been missions to maintain peace in typical civil wars. Among the terminated operations in the post-Cold War era, only four (Namibia, East Slavonia in Croatia, Georgia, and East Timor/Timor-Leste) dealt with state formation issues. Among the continuing operations, several were in state formation conflicts (Western Sahara and Kosovo). Some of the longest-serving missions were initiated before 1989 and they are in this category as well (notably UNTSO for the Palestinian situation, and UNMOGIP for the Kashmir conflict between India and Pakistan). It shows what has been illustrated before, that state formation conflicts are difficult for any international organization to deal with. States have often resisted such engagement; movements for independence have demanded it. These are conflicts on the threshold between internal and international relations. They have an ambiguity which makes them difficult to handle. As they make up half of all conflicts, this underlines the necessity of coming to grips with them.

Most peacekeeping operations, as well as the uses of sanctions, treat conflicts in a basic, almost bilateral way. As has been demonstrated in Chapter 8, conflicts may sometimes be part of a regional or global conflict complex, requiring broader approaches. Such measures have rarely been tried. Among the terminated peace-keeping operations, ONUCA for Central America had a regional mandate. So has the oldest ongoing peacekeeping operation, UNTSO, for truce in the Middle East. More typically, conflicts have been conceptually isolated from one another. This is a way to achieve a manageable mandate and a broader consensus. More recently there have been moves in this direction. Thus, peacekeeping operations in Côte d'Ivoire could connect to the parallel mission in Liberia. In 2014 the stabilization mission in Mali, MINUSMA, could as well draw on these operations, what was termed inter-mission cooperation. In this case, the challenges to Mali were also seen as a regional challenge. This development may ultimately lead to UN-sponsored regional peace processes.

What we note is that there is a distinctly positive contribution to conflict resolution associated with UN peacekeeping. This, in a sense, qualifies the conclusions suggested by Diehl (1993) for cases during the Cold War. Conditions have changed. In particular, the contributions of peacekeeping are now associated with the cooperative relations in the Security Council.

This has made constructive work possible. It is logical that it would be connected with finding agreements among warring factions. The UN peacekeeping operations are working together with other measures undertaken by major powers. The importance of the Council is that it synchronizes the efforts of interested major powers, generates international support for the missions and, thus, brings out a coherent message to the targeted group.

10.4 Peace Enforcement

The UN Charter does not exclude the use of force to deal with a breach of the peace. On the contrary, Chapter VII outlines a procedure for that. It also notes the possibility of members of the Council acting on their own, but under the consent of the Council. It means that wars are supposed to be brought to a halt through direct and overwhelming military intervention under the auspices of multilateral organs. It is a rare event. There are two examples of military actions that have been outside direct UN control, but based on UN decisions: Korea in 1950 and the Gulf War in 1991. In both cases, the operations were firmly controlled by the USA. In both cases, the situation was seen as one of repelling aggression. The decision on Korea was taken under peculiar conditions. At the time of the North Korean attack, the Soviet Union was boycotting the work of the Security Council. This was due to the fact that the majority refused to allow the government of the People's Republic of China to take China's seat in the Security Council. Thus, the majority consisted of the United States and its allies. The decision to send UN forces to fight the North Koreans was done under circumstances that cannot be regarded as a precedent.

The second situation is more interesting as it involved a wilful agreement of the members of the Council to take concerted action against Iraq. The processes of the Charter were used. In one sense, it was a textbook case of the UN dealing with aggression. It also showed the limits of UN influence. Following Iraq's invasion of Kuwait, the Security Council instituted a series of gradually escalating measures, resulting, on November 29, 1990, in an ultimatum to Iraq. This is found in Security Council Resolution 678. At the same time, there were different negotiation initiatives and compromise solutions put forward. The parallel build-up of forces around Iraq made negotiations less credible. It became increasingly clear that the military option was preferred by the American side and was expected also on the Iraqi side. When the Council's conditions were not met, an extensive air campaign was initiated, followed by a short ground operation, all under US command. By the end of February 1991, the Iraqi forces had been driven out from Kuwait's territory. Security Council Resolution 687 laid out the conditions for Iraq's defeat.

The central formulation in Resolution 678 was the granting of the use of 'all necessary means' to the countries cooperating with Kuwait. All military actions were taken by these countries. The UN regained a role through the Special Commission for the monitoring of Iraq's implementation of Resolution 687, UNSCOM. This was a UN operation, but not peacekeeping. Its mandate was to supervise the conditions laid down in the resolution terminating the war. It had no precedent. The obstructions of Iraq in carrying out the required dismantling of weapons of mass destruction, as well as its capacity to construct and deliver such weapons, led to repeated crises, sanctions and air raids against Iraq.

The formulation 'all necessary means' in the mandate for the Gulf War was repeated in some other conflicts. In the conflict in former Yugoslavia it was used for the protection of humanitarian deliveries. The same was true for the UN commitment to protect six designated 'safe areas'. Necessary means, however, in the form of equipment and troops, were never extended to the UN peacekeepers on the ground. It resulted in the tragedies of Srebrenica, Gorazde and Zepa in 1995. These towns were all 'protected' by the Security Council, but could not be defended by the peacekeepers entrusted with the task. They were easily overrun by Serb forces. It led to a further loss of credibility for UN peacekeeping. An air campaign, under the command of NATO, was launched against the Bosnian Serb positions, shifting the military balance and creating conditions for negotiations and a peace agreement (Holbrooke 1999).

In the Somalia operation, the formulation of 'all necessary measures' was used, but in this case the target was the Somali faction believed to be responsible for armed attacks on UN peacekeepers in 1993 (Security Council Resolution 827 in 1993). This led the USA to deploy a special force in Somalia, resulting in military operations against the warlord defined as most responsible for preventing a peace arrangement. The battle between US forces and Somalis resulted in the deaths of more than 100 peacekeepers, including 36 Americans (Lyons and Samatar 1995: 60). The UN operation was terminated shortly thereafter.

However, the war in Afghanistan in 2001, the aim of which was the removal of the Taliban regime and the bases of al-Qaida operations, was not authorized in this way. The Council resolution of September 28, 2001, reaffirmed the inherent right of self-defence at the same time as it identified terrorism as a threat to international peace and security (Security Council Resolution 1373). Thus, the US war in Afghanistan was seen as a matter of self-defence against the groups that orchestrated the attacks on the USA on September 11, 2001. This war took place with unusually strong international support. The international security assistance force (ISAF) created in December 2001 to support the new government was not a UN peacekeeping operation, although authorized by the UN, but was under NATO command, and it remained in place until the end of 2014.

Many recent UN missions are allowed to use force for the aim of protecting civilians, also with formulations on the use of 'all necessary means'. This is true for the missions in DRC since 2010 (the UN Stabilization Mission in the Democratic Republic of Congo, MONUSCO); the UN Mission in Mali since 2013 (MINSUMA, the UN Multidimensional Integrated Stabilization Mission in Mali), and the Central African Republic (MINUSCA, the United Nations Multidimensional Integrated Stabilization Mission in the Central African Republic) beginning in 2014. Their actual forcefulness would depend on the type of troops that were supplied. For several of these missions, French forces constituted the operational arm of the international ambitions.

There are also experiences of peace enforcement outside the framework of the UN. The USA and the UK have bombed Iraq repeatedly. In December 1998, the two escalated the continued disputes over UN inspectors into an intensive bombing campaign, on their own initiative, without achieving the desired change. By early 2001 a new UN body, UNMOVIC, had still not been able to carry out its inspection mandate in Iraq. However, in November 2002, facing increased US military deployments, Iraq agreed to accept UNMOVIC and IAEA inspections to determine the issues of its possible access to weapons of mass destruction. Reports to the Council in January and February 2003 did not satisfy the USA, the UK and other allies, who continued to claim that there were Iraqi weapons programmes, actually or potentially. Without the authorization of the Council, they intervened to remove the regime in March and the USA proclaimed major military combat to be over by May 2003. However, the war continued in different forms, giving Iraq little chance of peaceful reconstruction, except in the Kurdish-dominated areas. Official US investigators concluded in early 2004 that Iraq possessed no weapons of mass destruction or the capacity to produce them. By that time, the rationale for the war had turned into the construction of a democracy and the elections of 2005 were seen as a first achievement of this. However, the war escalated, only to change by 2007 when agreements were made with particular Iraqi groups, notably tribal leaders from the Sunni communities. In August 2010, President Obama proclaimed that the USA had met its responsibility and officially ended its combat role, although US troops remained in the country, for the purpose of training the Iraqi army.

In Kosovo in 1999, the United States chose, together with the United Kingdom, to act entirely outside the UN framework, in a NATO-led air campaign against targets in Kosovo as well as in the rest of Yugoslavia. This was designed to gain Yugoslavia's acceptance of peace conditions laid out by the United States. It was an attempt to prevent the ongoing violence in Kosovo from turning into another protracted Balkan conflict. It also was meant to prevent further expulsion of Kosovo Albanians. The war lasted for more than two months, leading to a vast exodus of Albanians into neighbouring countries and considerable destruction in Serbia as well as in Kosovo. It resulted in the acquiescence of the Yugoslav government, in June 1999 and to a NATO-led force, KFOR, stationed in the province. The Kosovo Albanians could return and an international regime was created for Kosovo, although it remained technically a part of Serbia. The Serbs remaining in the province could stay under international protection. Many, however, chose to leave. As we have seen, Kosovo continued to be under international administration until its declaration of independence in 2008. By 2014 it was recognized by about half of all states in the world. Using arguments explicitly referring to the Kosovo situation, Russia acted militarily and without UN authorization in South Ossetia in 2008, repelling an attack from Georgian forces to retake the area that formally belonged to Georgia. The armed conflict was a military disaster for Georgia. Immediately following this, South Ossetia declared itself independent. Abkhazia, another Russian-controlled area in Georgia, did the same. Only a few countries, notably Russia, have recognized these entities as sovereign states.

These cases of peace enforcement point to a different route for international action from the earlier ones assumed under the UN Charter. The success rate is mixed. In one way it has meant an enlargement of available options. In another way it has led to actions that are of questionable legitimacy. The actions in the Gulf War, Bosnia-Herzegovina, Somalia and Haiti were all agreed within the UN framework and, thus, were internationally legitimate. The Afghanistan War of 2001 was defined as a matter of self-defence under Article 51 of the Charter. The actions in Iraq, Kosovo and Georgia require more elaborate arguments to be compatible with the letter of the law. The use of force is normally legitimate only through a decision in the Security Council. In the case of Iraq, it has been argued that earlier resolutions bestowed that right to the United States, the United Kingdom and their allies. However, a new Council resolution had been agreed only in November 2002 on another course of action, first using the inspections. The other possibility is that these actions also constituted self-defence, according to Article 51. Iraq's future capacity of nuclear and other weapons would then be such a threat that it would have to be eliminated. However, it would require a prior establishment of such a threat, where the inspections would provide the evidence. On Kosovo, it might be possible to argue that NATO was acting in self-defence on behalf of the Albanian population that was driven out from their homes in Kosovo. As they could not defend themselves, NATO undertook that task. A third possible argument is to appeal to an emergency. The situation in Kosovo was extreme and military actions were the last resort after negotiations had failed. Such an argument would be difficult in the case of Iraq, however, as oppressive conditions had remained for a long period of time without any international action.

To this could be added a fourth argument, that humanitarian concerns now are as legitimate as others for intervention in another country, even against the will of an internationally recognized government. This would be in line with the actions to protect the Kurdish populations that were fleeing from the onslaught of Iraqi forces in March 1991. In its Resolution 688 (1991), the Security Council authorized such assistance. In the parallel situation of Kosovo in 1999, it was thought that the Council was not likely to agree to such actions. Vetoes by Russia and China were expected. Instead of going along the route suggested with the Uniting for Peace resolution, the Western countries chose to use NATO. A chance to find unquestionable legitimacy was lost. The actions were not in accordance with the letter of the Charter, but may have been in accordance with the spirit of humanitarian priorities. The World Summit in 2005 agreed that such principles, the responsibility to protect exposed populations (R2P), could be used in cases where a government does not meet its international obligations to its own population.

In the Georgian cases, Russia used self-defence arguments, claiming that many of the inhabitants in South Ossetia were Russian citizens who needed protection. It did not take the matter to the UN. The following declarations of independence, furthermore, contradicted Russia's position when denying Kosovo the same right.

This means that the no-fly zone instituted by the UN over Libya in March 2011 was the first international use of force built on R2P. Upholding the zone required precise bombings of military assets used by the Gaddafi regime to attack opposition strongholds throughout the country. The leadership of the bombing campaign was handed to NATO.

In addition to the operations led by UN or leading powers, we need also to mention recent missions by regional organizations. There is one, in particular, that deserves attention: the African Union's force that was set up in 2007 for Somalia with UN Security Council endorsement, and remains in operation (AMISOM, Fahlén 2015). It is a force that supports the constitutionally elected government, and finds itself in battles with the al-Shabaab movement. This movement has been defined as terrorist and is the target of repeated US attacks. Military forces from neighbouring countries have been supportive of AMISOM and constitute important parts of the mission. However, by the end of 2014 it did not appear that the solution of Somalia's problem had come closer. The country continued to be the location of one of the most protracted wars since the Cold War.

The UN-authorized peace enforcement operations accomplished the immediate goals in the Gulf War and Bosnia-Herzegovina. It failed in Somalia. Several of these conflicts still have not been removed from the agenda. Iraq continues to be a problem for the Security Council, the United States and the region. The workings of the Dayton Agreement are cumbersome and require revision, but that has not taken place.

Some cases are in a grey zone. For Kosovo, there is hope for a qualitatively improved peace following the declaration of independence. Haiti, which saw the threat of an international intervention in 1994, was off the list of armed conflicts for a period, only to return in 2004. The future of the two new Russian dependencies, created by Russia's unilateral military operations in the Caucasus, is uncertain, as international recognition is unlikely. The record of success for multilateral and unilateral peace enforcement in contributing to durable peacemaking is limited. It may be an instrument that handles a particular crisis, but lasting peace obviously requires very different measures.

In this chapter, we have seen the importance of the UN in many peace processes. At times, there has been cooperation with regional organizations. At other moments, responsibility has been given to regional organizations. There are strengths and there are limits. For decision-making that promotes conflict resolution, there are many alternative measures, ranging from sanctions to peace enforcement. On the whole, these options relate to different phases of a peace process. Sanctions may be useful for keeping actors interested in negotiations, peacekeeping may more be a matter of implementation of an agreement, while international peace enforcement measures may in fact be what needs to be done to protect civilians when armed conflicts have not ceased. However, in cases where the measures aim at compelling actors, they seem more often to be done by a major power or a coalition, whether sanctioned by an international organization or not.

Further Readings

Go to the *Understanding Conflict Resolution* web page at https://study.sagepub.com/ wallensteen4e for free access to journal articles listed.

Sanctions

The use of economic and targeted sanctions has given rise to considerable debate and reforms within international organizations. Mostly this has dealt with the UN and the EU:

Eriksson, M. 2010. *Targeting Peace, Understanding UN and EU Targeted Sanctions* Farnham, UK: Ashgate.
Eriksson deals both with UN and EU targeted sanctions, the type of sanctions that have entirely replaced the earlier comprehensive approaches.

Wallensteen, P. and Grusell, H. 2012. 'Targeting the Right Targets? The UN Use of Individual Sanctions', *Global Governance*, 18 (2): 207–230.
In this work, the UN application of sanctions on individuals is analysed. It uncovers in some detail the various ways in which targeted individuals react to this type of pressure.

Peacekeeping

Melander, E. 2009. 'Selected to go where murderers lurk? The preventive effect of peacekeeping on mass killings of civilians', *Conflict Management and Peace Sciences*, 26 (4): 389–406.

As is the case with sanctions, also peacekeeping has been much debated with respect to its actual impact in local situations. Melander studies the impact on the security of civilians, taking into account that peacekeepers often go to the most difficult cases.

11

PREVENTION AND PEACEBUILDING

11.1 Tools for Pacific Settlement

Chapter 10 included a look at the measures used by the international community in dealing with the challenges of armed conflicts and promoting conflict resolution. They draw on the UN Charter, Chapter VII. As we have seen, many of them reflect a need to act quickly and deal with immediate crises. Thus, sanctions, peacekeeping and peace enforcement come to mind. However, there are also matters that can be done before and after crisis that is of significance. This would mean tools aimed at conflict prevention and peacebuilding. Also these measures can be of a direct and immediate nature as well as long-term structural changes. This is what we find in the Charter's Chapter VI, titled Pacific Settlement of Dispute. In all, eight measures are mentioned. We will single out some of them, even adding measures that are not explicitly mentioned but fit within the opening article, Article 33.

11.2 Early Action and Conflict Prevention

As we have seen, the winding down and ending of the Cold War resulted in an increase of armed conflicts. Thus it is natural that the world became interested in actions to reduce the number and intensity of armed conflicts by finding solutions at an early stage. These ambitions can be described as conflict prevention. The idea is simple. By observing early warning signs, developing agendas for early action, summoning support, implementing particular measures and sustaining collective action, the chances of reducing suffering increase. The world would be spared more disasters.

The purpose is clear, but in order to clarify this line of thought we need to distinguish between structural and direct forms of conflict prevention. The direct prevention approach comes into play when there are actors, incompatibilities and action, but where violence is still not the dominant expression of the problem. Structural prevention, however, deals with the underling issue and aims at solving problems before they have even entered the political arena as disputes. It is a matter of long-term economic, social and military development. It is close to peacebuilding, and we return to this under that heading (Section 11.5).

Direct prevention aims to reduce or eliminate violence in a conflict, not necessarily to eliminate the conflict as such. It includes constructive actions taken by third parties to avoid the likely threat, use or diffusion of armed force by parties in a political dispute. This is referred to as preventive action or preventive diplomacy. A broad spectrum of actions is customarily included, even military measures (Cahill 1996; Carnegie Commission 1997; Lund 1996; Malone and Hampson 2001; Stedman 1995; Wallensteen 1998). As can be seen from this list of references, the debate was intense on this in the 1990s, while contributions have been more limited since then. The ambition has remained on the political agenda, however, and there are also now data to approach these questions giving us more basis for plausible strategies (Öberg et al. 2009; Melander et al. 2009; Croicu et al. 2013). For instance, UCDP records more than 2,800 third-party mediation attempts in internal armed conflicts in Africa in the period 1993–2007 (Croicu et al. 2013: 10). The results demonstrate that both the UN and a colonial hegemon, in this case France, do have an impact on reducing the intensity of armed conflict. Their ways of impact is different, however.

Preventive actions are not actions undertaken by the parties themselves to scale down a conflict, but rather by third parties. This is not normally the perspective held by the primary parties themselves. It is more likely that each regards itself as 'well-intended'. Their actions are taken in order to bring the conflict to a speedy ending, to their own advantage, no doubt. There were comparable concepts in use during the Cold War. They often communicated a party-based perspective. To many, prevention was synonymous with pre-emptive actions by one side before the other side could launch its attack. Prevention was connected to imminent crisis. However, there were attempts at a third-party position as well, not the least associated with the UN Secretary-General Dag Hammarskjöld, who reportedly coined the term preventive diplomacy. This has been even more pronounced after the Cold War. Preventive diplomacy is now seen as coming from the outside, building on goals such as those expressed in the international community. It serves to reduce tension in a conflict and move the parties towards a negotiated solution. To be effective, it has to be credible by not benefiting one or the other of the fighting parties. Thus, the community to which the actors belong becomes important.

Lately, 'preventive war' has acquired prominence in US strategic doctrine. This is a return to the unilateral concepts of the Cold War era, but focuses today on potential terrorist threats, primarily to the United States itself. Thus, it is an outgrowth of the September 11 events and has led to a debate on, for example, the notion of self-defence, as that is the argument for unilateral 'preventive' action. Clearly, the UN Charter allows for self-defence in face of an imminent threat. However, the US use of the concept to defend its war on Iraq in 2003 was much wider, and the arguments were not accepted by the UN Security Council. In September 2014 the United States again acted in Iraq from a self-defence perspective, following the shocking executions of American journalists by the ISIS movement. In legal terms, however, the US air campaign took place on the invitation of the Iraqi government. In 2003, the US and its allies acted outside the Charter when invading and deposing the government. US air strikes against ISIS in Syria, however, would be a different matter. Syria is a sovereign state; the US does not have the permission of the Assad regime and has not been authorized by the UN to act. The idea of military prevention, in other words, depends on a strong case of self-defence and UN agreement. In many such situations, the self-defence arguments build on consecutive steps that are far from the imminent threats that customarily is referred to.

The preventive actions dealt with in this book are those carried out by third parties and emphasize the use of non-military means. The idea is to prevent war, rather than using war to prevent further war.

Examples of Conflict Prevention

The efficiency of preventive actions is difficult to ascertain. How do we know that there was an imminent threat? If there is no crisis, do we know that one was likely? It is easier to establish that preventive actions have failed than to show that they have succeeded. However, history is full of examples of crises that many expected would become serious. The Cuban Missile Crisis is but one case. There are also historical records of the successful management of tension among major powers in previous centuries (Schroeder 2006). Sometimes these have involved third parties; oftentimes the actors have controlled actions among themselves. In fact, it is likely that great powers are reluctant to have other states involved in their conflicts as third parties.

There are also examples of preventive action since the Cold War. In chronicles of events, it is possible to find disputes that were regarded as having a potential for violent escalation. Observers and policy-makers may agree on this. The examples of conflict prevention cases often include more interstate conflicts than we would expect from the fact that the armed conflicts of this decade have largely been internal. There have been close to 20 such crises since 1989, most of them well documented in international media and scholarly work. A typical example is the conflict between former Yugoslavia and Macedonia in the early 1990s, when the UN positioned a peacekeeping operation on the border. A number of cases have also been brought to the International Court of Justice or found neighbouring countries as mediators. Most recently, this was the case for the 2011 conflict between Thailand and Cambodia, with an ICJ decision pending. The 2011 separation of South Sudan from Sudan left a number of border issues unsolved. Neighbours and regional organizations have been involved in the search for solution. There was an arbitration court that delivered its award in 2009 for one of the areas, Abyei. This has been followed up by a minor UN peacekeeping mission and considerable diplomacy. A key question has become the definition of who is a resident in the area, where many are nomadic and traditionally move across the territory. A positive reading of this is that there are instruments in place to handle such conflicts. The examples show that such measures are used, perhaps even more often than can be expected, although not always bringing about a lasting solution. A negative reading is that interstate conflicts receive more attention and, as a consequence, will see more international preventive action than internal conflicts.

Either way, this suggests that interstate conflicts can be handled and that this often has been regarded as the expected outcome. The inter-Sudan case demonstrates that this is not always the case, particularly if there is a longer and repetitive history of conflict. For instance, there were severe tensions between Russia and Ukraine over the division of the Black Sea fleet early in the 1990s. Similarly, the same countries had repeated confrontations over natural gas prices in 2006–09. These issues were solved between the parties with minimal outside involvement. However, the conflicts that arouse in 2013, which included Ukraine's accession to the EU Eastern Partnership, rather than the Russian-led Eurasian Economic Union, resulted in a confrontation where potential intermediaries became parties to the conflict (notably the EU). By September 2014 this conflict had resulted in a new government in Kiev but also a dismemberment of the country. Armed conflicts were waged in Ukraine's eastern provinces while Crimea in the south had been annexed by Russia. The repeated conflict experience seems to strongly have coloured relations, and led to actions that further deepened the crisis. In addition, it could be that the expectation that interstate conflicts can be defused is more applicable to conflicts which do not directly involve the major powers as they add larger, strategic perspectives. Thus, interstate conflicts continue to constitute dangerous elements in global conflict patterns.

Let us turn to the internal conflicts. There is likely to be a larger number of them with serious crises than is normally observed. They might have been handled by local actors and thus only reported about locally (if at all). Authoritarian governments are not likely to allow much attention to such conflicts either. Still, some cases can be identified. In the protracted crisis in Zimbabwe, which politically began with the elections in 2002, international action focused on democratization as a possible way to avoid a future civil war. Another case concerned the rights of the Albanian population in Macedonia in 2001, where a peace agreement could be concluded before the level of violence had escalated (Väyrynen 2004).

Similarly, we might expect an under-reporting for state formation conflicts. In this case, however, there might be groups outside the country which could document what has happened. Some state formation conflicts are also part of regional conflict complexes and, thus, are often more likely to draw outside attention.

Among conflicts contained through preventive measures, the state formation conflict over Palestine has probably received the most attention. In fact, the Oslo peace process saw a series of crises and crisis management efforts. Often, outside parties have been able to undo some of the tension. One situation was sparked by Palestinian President Yassir Arafat's threat to declare independence when the Oslo process formally expired on May 4, 1999. It would be a unilateral action, not based on an agreement with Israel. The threat had credibility and led to a series of diplomatic and political actions. Chief among these were the summit negotiations in October 1998. The international engagement to prevent an imminent crisis was impressive and, in effect, successful. No immediate crisis followed; instead, a new Israeli government with a strong commitment to peace came into office. However, this also demonstrates the concern: it may be possible to prevent one crisis, but what about the next one?

Clearly, the next crisis did not work out in a similar way. The second Intifada that began in late September 2000 resulted in summit diplomacy. It involved some of the same actors as in the efforts less than two years earlier. This time, the UN and the EU were also drawn in. Again, a sizeable part of the international community acted to prevent the events from escalating and spreading. These efforts did not succeed equally well, neither bringing peace negotiations to an end nor reducing violence. Possibly, it served to keep international attention on the issue. It is not easy to see why efforts worked in 1998 but not in 2000. The same means were tried, but important elements of trust and confidence had evaporated. Not until 2007 was a governmental attempt made to restart the dialogue followed by one more try in 2010 and then again in 2013–14. In these latter situations, the threat of a unilateral Palestinian declaration of statehood may again have spurred the international community into action, although in the 2010s formulated as a demand to become the 194th member of the United Nations. However, none of these peaceful threats let to negotiations that also resulted in a lasting agreement. Neither was there a return to armed conflict, however, at least not between the Palestinian Authority controlling the West Bank, and Israel.

Additional shortcomings in conflict prevention can be seen in the case of Gaza, where the unilateral Israeli withdrawal in 2005 has been followed by a decade of repeated confrontations, rather than openings for peace. First, there was one between the two Palestinian organizations Fatah and Hamas (2007) resulting in Hamas taking control over the area. Then, this was followed by repetitive military confrontations with Israel, most recently during seven weeks in 2014. The deaths on the Palestinian side can be counted in the thousands, the impact on Israel being less deadly, but devastating from the point of view of making peace. In all instances, international action was intensive to prevent further escalation. In 2012, the Egyptian government under Mohammad Morsi and the Muslim Brotherhood, functioned as a broker, in 2014 the military regime under Abdel Fattah el-Sisi had the same role (although it at the same time was responsible for brutal repression of Egyptian Muslim organizations). The preventive actions were too late to stop the confrontations, but they may still have served to end it earlier than otherwise would be the case and, in all likelihood, reduce regional repercussions. The Uppsala Conflict Data demonstrates that few conflicts have seen as much preventive action as the various manifestations of the Israeli-Palestinian complex (Melander et al. 2009). It may have served to avoid escalation. This is conflict prevention, but the hope that it would also lead to sustained negotiations for peace has not borne out.

It has been suggested that preventive actions need to go beyond the diplomatic efforts that often are in the centre: a form of peacekeeping that could be termed preventive deployment. This means stationing third-party troops between the parties before shooting has started. Such efforts have been part of crisis control, not only in the case of the UN preventive deployment in Macedonia in 1993–99 (UNPREDEP). Another mission was in the Central African Republic 1998–2000

(MINURCA). A special development was the European force under Italian command that was deployed in Albania for some months in 1997 (ALBA). Also, the regional organization, Southern Africa Development Council (SADC), stationed troops in Lesotho in 1998. To set up such operations in a short time indicates a strong commitment and concern about developments. A very special deployment was the EU-led, UN-mandated ARTEMIS mission that was placed in Bunia, in the Ituri region of the Democratic Republic of Congo in September 2003 to deal with the violence among ethnic groups in the area. In these cases, tension was reduced.

In other instances, peacekeepers were already in place when the crisis occurred. This was the case in the 2000 crisis over armed Albanian incursions from Kosovo into southern Serbia. The NATO-led KFOR mission was stationed on one side of this divide. As a result of negotiations, Serb police forces were allowed again to enter the demilitarized zone on the other side of the lines to reduce the danger of escalation. In this case as well as in the one in Macedonia, where the international force also had an impact, conflicts were brewing in areas of considerable international involvement already. The swift actions taken suggested that the international community was unwilling to let the conflict linger. At least militarily, these crises were defused. Similarly, there were peace operations in place in several of the interstate conflicts. These may have contributed to keep tension within limits (Korea, Cyprus and Kashmir). These examples of preventive deployment suggest their utility, but underlines that further steps to conflict resolution do not come automatically. Many preventive actions may, in fact, serve to freeze a status quo, and with that also threaten a return of the conflict.

Predicting Escalation

Many of the disputes just mentioned were well known to decision-makers and analysts. They concerned unsettled borders, minorities with majorities on the other side of a border, claims on islands and historical tensions. Largely, these conflicts were 'frozen' in an uneasy state of affairs. To predict that such conflicts are prone to escalation is not difficult. To specify more exactly the time and conditions when acute danger will arise is less simple.

It is particularly difficult to predict which internal conflicts are likely to escalate into severe violence at what time and what type of international preventive action they may require. For instance, it is difficult to determine if actions of a particular government towards its opposition will 'work' without leading to a severe crisis internally. The government may feel confident as it takes actions, but it may make a serious error. It will not be easier for outsiders to predict what will happen. Also, a government may fall more quickly than anticipated because the opposition turns out to be better prepared than expected. The fall of Yugoslav leader Slobodan Milosevic in October 2000 was unexpected, as he himself had called the election. At a crucial moment, it turned out that he no longer had the support of the armed forces. The unarmed opposition could take over and Milosevic had to resign. Was this a crisis which was prevented from escalating, for instance by the sanctions imposed? Or was it a crisis that was not likely to escalate, as the police and military remained neutral?

The same question can be asked of the democratizing Orange Revolution in Ukraine in late 2004, where the actions of the EU High Representative Javier Solana could be interpreted as a successful contribution both to democracy and to the prevention of violence. Others, however, saw these preventive actions as a way of forcing a premature compromise on a non-violent revolution (Cloos 2005; Maksymenko 2005). In the Ukraine crisis of 2013, the EU approach was different. The non-violent protests that followed on the Maidan Square in Kiev when the government withdrew from signing the Eastern Partnership agreement with the EU, saw active support from the EU, notably in the form of visits by EU representatives. The EU was no longer a third party, and, thus, there may have been no credible actor that could defuse the crisis. Few may have predicted, however, that it would result in the military actions taken by Russia during 2014. Conflicts have their own dynamics. Although actors may make their calculations, the resulting actions may lead to unanticipated reactions.

Similarly, during the Arab Spring, Western countries pressed Egypt's president Hosni Mubarak to resign in February 2011, clearly in the hope of preventing a violent turn of events. Later, the same countries acted to impress on the elected president, Mohammad Morsi, the importance of a compromise in view of the large protests in June 2013. Morsi, however, refused to back down and a predictable military coup followed, on July 3, 2013. The new regime turned out to be more repressive than any Western leader may have foreseen.

Thus, even if it may be possible to predict the outcome of particular crisis, the parties themselves may not see developments in a similar light. They may stick to what is 'right' according to the constitution, perhaps even thinking of their role in history, no matter what outcome. Conflict prevention, in other words, may not be the priority of either side, and thus, the role of third parties diminishes accordingly.

It is likely that most government crises do not result in violence and thus do not warrant international concern. Sometimes deals are made between opponents and governments. The existence of legal structures and democratic forces may be a necessary condition for non-violent change. The fear of intervening when matters are changing through their own dynamics makes international actors reluctant to act. They may even be afraid to stimulate counter-actions that prevent desirable change. There is a danger that international measures will increase tension. When the options are unattractive, the outside will tend to postpone action. But the longer the international community waits to act, the more difficult it will be to intervene at all. As a consequence, for the outside world, the balance will often tilt in favour of taking no action.

These arguments apply even more stringently to state formation conflicts. They threaten the break-up of states. Most external states are reluctant to encourage such prospects. The Palestinian question is special in its international support. It is more typical that the local governments actively and often successfully prevent international approaches to challenging groups. From the incumbent government's perspective, for outsiders to establish relations with such groups is equal to accepting their claims. For the opposition, the reverse is of true. Early action would be vindication of the 'justice' of the struggle and may further its chances of victory. Thus, we would expect early action from the international community in state formation conflicts to be rare, at least on the open and diplomatic levels. Even if there is an expectation of violence, the interstate system often prefers not to take up the issues.

The Palestinian case had been high on the world agenda for more than half a century and is quite exceptional. Its regional repercussions are well known. Other issues which have drawn attention, such as Tibet in China, Aceh in Indonesia, Corsica in France, Samis in Scandinavia, or Native Americans in the United States, have rarely been the focus of international governmental organizations. However, some situations have been handled on an international level and at an early stage. The OSCE has taken a particular role in European disputes and has been more active than, for instance, the UN. This has been achieved through the office of the High Commissioner on National Minorities. The relatively low-key approach taken may have been highly effective in defusing tension (Kemp 2001). However, when matters become really serious and arrive at a high political level, this office may find it difficult to take a role. This was evident in the creeping Russian invasion of Crimea in March 2014, when the office should have had a role in protecting the interests of minorities in the peninsula, for instance the Tatars.

Prevention departs from an assumption that the parties actually do not want disputes to escalate. They have a preference for finding a solution and the international community can contribute by rewarding that option. We have already seen examples of where this may not be true. There are also other challenges, for instance, where parties do their utmost to hide their plans. There are some cases that illustrate this. The initiation of large-scale hostilities includes considerable planning and is not made by spontaneous action at the whim of a leader. Thus, interstate armed conflicts sometimes escalate on purpose. Egypt and Syria planned carefully and their attack in October 1973 against Israel aimed at surprising the other side. Information was not available, weapons deliveries were not stepped up but spread over time, troop movements were credibly described as manoeuvres. The initiation of the war was, from that point of view, a success. It was purposefully done so as to avoid preemptive action by the adversary or by the major powers. Iraq's occupation of Kuwait on August 2, 1990 had similar features. Clearly, neither the Kuwaiti leadership nor the major powers anticipated this move, although the concentration of Iraqi troops around Kuwait was observed and should have been a warning signal.

The actions by the USA and its allies against Iraq in 2003, however, were entirely in the open, as this was a way to pressure its regime. It left some space for preventive action. The hope that the UN weapons inspectors would be able to conclude their work was one element in possibly delaying a war, or even making it unnecessary. The delaying tactics, however, seem only to have increased the determination, primarily of the US, to act decisively and early.

Surprise situations are also found in internal conflicts. The coup in Romania in 1989 against the Communist Party leader Ceauşescu came as a surprise, although the tensions had been rising in the country days before. Coup leaders challenging an incumbent government will always have to build on their ability to surprise and, thus, they will camouflage moves that might constitute early warnings. The same is true for the government side, which has its intelligence network in operation and would like to have information as early as possible in order to be able to pre-empt threatening moves. The timing of action will depend on how suspicious the leaders are. It is not uncommon that authoritarian governments claim to have foiled a coup attempt and arrested culprits. Sometimes there is evidence. Whether it would withstand independent court review is another matter. These accusations are seldom put to trial.

Also, state formation conflicts can have such coup-like patterns, either from the side of the challengers or from the government. Many successful rebellions start with complete military failures, as shown by the Easter uprising in Dublin in 1916. The survivors became heroes for the Irish nationalists, but the action did not lead to the victorious ending that the originators had hoped for. It became a starting point, nevertheless, of an armed and political process that gave independence to the Irish Republic in 1922, albeit at the price of dividing the island in two.

The delicacy of early detection means that direct conflict prevention has to be conceived in a different way. It is not there to compete with intelligence planning of the contending sides. The lessons for prevention and early warning are different. Sometimes it may be possible to warn the primary parties of impending events. It is often more certain to point to conditions that enhance the likelihood of violent actions, and ask for remedial measures. This points to situations of human rights violations, lack of democracy and need for transparency. These are matters which have implications for internal and state formation conflicts as well as interstate conflicts. Global human rights monitoring is already an established activity and it is useful also from the prevention perspective.

However, in authoritarian societies, violations of human rights are routine. They are even important for regime survival and the violations may give few clues as to whether a civil war or an interstate conflict is about to break out at a particular time. When repression increases, does it mean tensions in society increase and the escalation of conflict is more likely? Is it instead when repression decreases, and societies open up and more becomes known that the likelihood of conflict increases? Is it more important to identify which groups are targeted by repression and which leaders are harassed? Such questions need to be used in the analysis of particular societies. Too general indicators may imply different things, depending on economic conditions, political situations and other local circumstances.

The issue of direct conflict prevention faces particular challenges. We have seen that there is a record of early action, particularly for interstate conflicts. There are considerable difficulties for conflict prevention in internal affairs and state formation conflicts. Observing human rights violations, ethnic discrimination, lack of access to institutions and other political measures are useful early indicators of possible conflicts. International organizations are giving more attention to preventive work, notably the United Nations, the OECD and the World Bank. The World Summit in 2005 also emphasized the significance of preventive actions. The difficulties notwithstanding, the idea of prevention is a chief lesson from the conflict experiences of the post-Cold War period.

This can be seen in the work of some non-governmental actors. To these belong The Carter Center, International Alert, Conciliation Resources, Search for Common Ground and the International Crisis Group, among others, including university departments. They have taken different approaches. Some concentrate on early warnings; others try to bring parties together, using variants of the problem-solving workshops; still others provide analyses of rising tensions. Many of these activities have been instrumental in bringing about cease-fires or laying the groundwork for peace agreements. Often, non-governmental activities have a broader purpose than simply preventing a particular crisis from erupting into violence. The aim is to contribute to long-term constructive relations between a broad set of actors who are divided by a particular conflict. To influence government policy is but one aspect of the activities. Dialogue, confidence-building and identifying common interests are as important as finding immediate prevention measures.

There are two additional matters to keep in mind. The first is that it is difficult to know whether it actually was the preventive action that worked and not some other factor. It could even be that the parties would say – afterwards – that the threats of escalation or diffusion were never that serious. This is difficult to establish and only an educated guess is possible. Conflict dynamics may be analysed and compared to cases with similar characteristics. We can establish that all major armed conflicts continuing today were relatively minor and insignificant once upon a time. This makes it likely that at least some of the conflicts mentioned here would have escalated if no preventive actions had been taken. Some systematic studies are emerging, however, particularly focusing on what actions might be more conducive for prevention. In 67 ethnic conflicts since 1990, it was established that contacts between the parties had a particular effect in reducing the likelihood of escalation (Öberg et al. 2009). A new database on preventive measures in minor, intra-state armed conflicts 1993–2004 has been published at the Uppsala Conflict Data Program (www.ucdp.uu.se) and is developed further.

The second issue is the question of the ethics of direct conflict prevention. Effective preventive actions are probably agreeable to most. They achieve a reduction in tension that is beneficial to the different sides. But there is a danger that outside actions will be to the advantage of one or the other side in the conflict. It could be that they help to consolidate a situation which in the long run is unsound and necessary changes are prevented, as well as unnecessary violence. This basic normative issue should be part of the discourse on direct conflict prevention. It may, at times, be unethical to intervene too early if this will inhibit a positive long-term development. At the same time, it could be unethical not to act early, when there is a danger of innocent people being victimized. The ethics of intervention and non-intervention are fundamental. There has to be an ethical answer before action is taken.

11.3 Third Parties and Mediation

Since the end of the Cold War, third parties have been involved in conflict resolution as a normal state of affairs. It is increasingly difficult for countries to refuse access for the outside community into particular conflicts. However, it is still common that countries decline offers of using the good offices of international secretariats, other governments or even non-government organizations. Thus, Russia has not been prepared to invite outsiders to assist in settling the conflict in Chechnya. Similarly, the protracted conflict over Afghanistan has not given rise to international mediation, although some secrete channels may have existed at times. In the civil war in Syria, however, the present mediator is the third one, suggesting both a need for mediation and an inability of the parties even to agree on an agenda for conflict resolution.

The United Nations Secretary-General is a resource of global significance. The Secretary-General has appointed a number of Special and Personal Representatives for particular issues or conflicts (Peck 2004). This is done with consent from the parties. A new development is the pressure from non-governmental actors. During the crisis over East Timor in September 1999, the Secretary-General received thousands of messages calling for action. In this conflict, the Secretary-General served as a mediator, being instrumental in forging the referendum agreement of May 1999. Thus, the outside world can have an impact on the actions taken. The UN Secretary-General may have a more uncontested status as a third party than any other of the UN collective security institutions. The World Summit in 2005 suggested that this capacity should be further strengthened, and later the Mediation Support Unit was created in the Secretariat. Also, a new development is that countries interested in the promotion of conflict resolution have begun to appoint their own envoys for conflicts of particular interest. There are groups of 'Friends of the Secretary-General' for different conflicts. On the initiative of Finland and Turkey, the General Assembly has accepted a series of resolutions on the importance for mediation. This means that the options for the primary parties interested in finding a solution are widening. There are competent persons to turn to. Whether a conflict is settled or not no longer depends on the availability of mediation possibilities. The early literature on third parties assumed that such parties would be strategic for turning a conflict from war to peace. The post-Cold War experiences suggest that this is no longer a crucial variable. Parties are increasingly aware of the possibilities of settling their conflict. The decisions are now even more strongly connected to their interest in a settlement. The excuses for not engaging in a peace process are increasingly limited.

In many cases of peace agreements, there is a record of mediation in the process leading to a settlement. Often the parties express their satisfaction with such efforts. Unfortunately, there is also a record of such efforts in conflicts that were not solved. It suffices here to mention the conflicts in Angola and Somalia, which drew considerable efforts during the 1990s, Sri Lanka during the early 2000s, the many efforts with respect to Sudan and, most recently, the Syrian tragedy.

Increasingly, mediation has been seen as a process, where a third party enters, acts, coordinates and leaves the scene. This process has been studied with respect to one mediator involved in third-party activity during a 30-year period, Ambassador Jan Eliasson (Svensson and Wallensteen 2010). Other efforts have also been investigated. Here we single out two issues of particular importance for a third party. The first has to do with the appointment and mandate of the mediator, the second with the approach taken by the third party in dealing with the primary and secondary parties. These issues can be seen in two highly publicized experiences: Bosnia-Herzegovina and Northern Ireland. Both found a settlement in the 1990s, and years later remained in a volatile phase of implementation. Both had considerable international attention. Only one was on the UN agenda.

Entering a Conflict

The question of the appointment of a third party is central, as it will determine the mandate and the parties' perception of the mediator. The traditional form is a mediator chosen, for instance, by the UN Security Council or the UN Secretary-General. This is a procedure which ensures the impartiality of the mediator, if the Council or the Secretary-General is viewed as impartial. As we have seen earlier, this is not necessarily true for the Council, but is more often the case for the Secretary-General. It is important that the candidacy of the third party, if appointed by the UN, is accepted or not actively opposed by the warring parties. They need to have had a chance to express their opinion on the selection. It does not make sense, of course, for a world organization to appoint a person for mediation if there is no interest among the parties to talk to this particular individual. The UN appointment procedure gives the parties influence on the decision.

The parties may, if they are in direct contact with one another, agree on an appointment without involving the UN or any others. Direct contacts can result in secret negotiations (as exemplified by the Oslo Channel in 1993) or open ones (as was the case in the Northern Ireland talks). In principle, nothing prevents the parties from making an arrangement of their own.

It can be a complicated procedure, as in the case of Northern Ireland (Mitchell 1999a: 26–7, 48–50). The Northern Ireland independent commission was to have three international chairpersons, drawn so that one was selected jointly by the two governments which initiated the negotiations (Britain and Ireland). They chose former US Senator George Mitchell. Following this, each side chose one person. Similar procedures have been applied in other conflicts. It gives the opposing sides a stake in the process. In this case, it meant that the real contenders, the Northern Ireland parties, had little say on the selection. However, they were not left out. In a remarkable procedure, they were to agree to the international chairpersons taking the presidency in the plenary sessions of the negotiation forum. Thus, all parties involved in the peace process convened and debated this issue for two days. Meanwhile the selected persons were waiting in an adjacent office. When they finally could enter the room, a British officer was sitting in the chair in which George Mitchell, as the leader, was to sit. He was not leaving until Mitchell was about to sit down. The explanation was that, in this way, the opponents could not take the seat, physically preventing the negotiations from starting and, thus, having to be expelled by force! The chairpersons faced an uphill struggle to gain the confidence of these parties. The opposition was directed not at the leadership as such, but at the idea of negotiations. They were the spoilers, who were participating in the process to prevent it from succeeding and, later, when this was not possible, left the forum and tried to wreck the process from the outside.

In other instances, the mediator is appointed by an outside party, with or without consultation. The United States has acted in a number of conflicts. The actors may have been the President, the Secretary of State or high-ranking officials of the administration. They are often seen as 'mediators' and, indeed, perform some of the same functions. In the strictest sense of the word, they often are not third parties. Their appointment is made by American authorities. Ambassador Holbrooke is often described as a mediator in the conflicts in Southeast Europe. In fact, he was the US Assistant Secretary of State for European Affairs when he dealt with Bosnia-Herzegovina, undeniably the most difficult and acute issue of his area of assignment. It may well have been understood from the beginning that this was his role. Nevertheless, he entered into a conflict in a role which is different from the one Mitchell had in Northern Ireland. He could rely on the official support and resources of the United States.

The USA might appear to be a normal third party, but this is not the case. It often has its own interest in the outcomes. It will benefit from the settlement of the conflict, but it also has its own agenda. It may give priority to issues which other parties may not. It may be prepared to exert pressure on some parties, but not on others. There is also the possibility that the USA may resort to military power. This has meant that the United Nations, for instance, has used relatively few American officials as Special Representatives for mediation. The problem of bias can also affect the United Nations, as the Security Council may have its own view on how a particular conflict should be solved. We have seen that this happened during the Iran–Iraq War (Chapter 5). The Security Council was negative to the Islamic government of Iran. Thus, Iran's government preferred to relate to the Secretary-General. The Secretary-General appointed his own special representative. This position was held by the Swedish statesman, Olof Palme, until his assassination in 1986. He was later replaced by a Swedish diplomat, Jan Eliasson (Svensson and Wallensteen 2010). The solution that finally brought an end to the war was made under the auspices of the UN Secretary-General, building eventually on a more balanced position taken by the Security Council. Similar experiences have also been noted for the post-Cold War period. There were efforts by Secretary-General Kofi Annan to defuse some of the crises with Iraq over the UNSCOM inspections. These repeatedly led to threats against Iraq, particularly from the United States. The Secretary-General made a special agreement with the Iraqi leader, Saddam Hussein, in February 1998. This prevented an escalation of that particular crisis while maintaining the inspections. Unfortunately, the relationship between UNSCOM and the Iraqi government resulted in a new crisis later the same year and inspections ceased. From the Iraqi perspective, UNSCOM was not seen as balanced, although Iraq apparently was willing to deal directly with the Secretary-General. In 2003, the situation was reversed, when Iraq was willing to work with UNMOVIC (having replaced UNSCOM), while the USA and its allies did not want to rely on this process. Thus, no space was left for third-party action.

Much experience suggests that the parties to a conflict primarily want a mediator who is impartial to their position. It means that the mediator correctly appreciates their interests and properly transfers information and evaluations between the sides. It does not, however, require an entirely neutral position. Bias can sometimes be useful (Svensson 2009). The fact that a mediator is close to one side can satisfy the other, as it hopes this will bring more pressure on that particular side.

Approaches to Mediation

The possibility of issuing credible threats are one of the 'cards' that is uniquely available to the USA in the post-Cold War period. The distinction between mediators with much power – 'muscle' – and those with little or no physical power is important. Senator Mitchell, when chairing the negotiations on Northern Ireland, had no such power. Some of the negotiating parties in the talks had access to sympathetic violent groups. Britain, furthermore, had its forces as well as its legal preponderance, as it were, controlling the sovereignty of Northern Ireland. Mitchell could rely on the parties with a strong interest in making an agreement, but the use of force was beyond his realm. If for no other reason, he was not part of a chain of command. Furthermore, the parties had agreed to a cease-fire, reducing the pressure of violence on the negotiations.

Ambassador Holbrooke could act with the certitude of official US support. He was implementing, as well as influencing, US policy. From this position he could, for instance, support some parties to use force in order to facilitate the negotiations. In the autumn of 1995, Croat and Bosniak forces were encouraged to take as much land as possible, only with the warning of not creating large refugee flows. The preconditions of the negotiations that were to convene at the Air Force base in Dayton, Ohio, were that they would arrive at a 49–51 formula of territorial division. The Serbs would have 49 per cent of Bosnia's territory, and the Croat-Bosniak Federation the rest. As the Serbs held more territory than this, it was important to achieve a territorial division on the ground. The losses of territory by the Bosnian Serbs in September and October 1995 reduced their share to the stipulated 49 per cent. This was the result of a US air campaign that allowed Federation forces to conquer more land (Holbrooke 1999: 160, 166, 199). There was a definite bias in American policy. For instance, the US side was reluctant to put pressure on the Bosniak leadership. This was the country whose independence the USA was protecting. At a crucial juncture in the Dayton peace talks, when the American negotiating team felt that some pressure would be needed also on the Bosniak side, the White House National Security staff reportedly balked and prevented any such action (Holbrooke 1999: 301).

The experiences from these two negotiations are interesting, as they suggest two distinct forms of mediation. As both negotiators were Americans, there was no cultural distinction between the two, although their class background and careers were different. It was the format for the talks that differed. One was done without power, the other one with power. Let us look more closely at the two.

The first approach had to work with persuasion, developing confidence with the parties, finding intelligent propositions and, thus, attempting to transcend some of the difficulties. It was deal-making, but not only that. It appears as a genuine search for common agreement. It would, inevitably, take time. Reaching the Good Friday Agreement in 1998 took two years. The question is whether this would also make the agreement stick. It is interesting, however, that when the implementation reached an impasse on the way forward for demilitarization a year later, the leaders of Britain and Ireland tried hard to reach an agreement but without success. Senator Mitchell was called in again for a review. It took 11 weeks of painstaking talks in seclusion before the parties finally found a way out of this stalemate. Thus, by the end of November 1999, the agreement's first provisions on self-rule could begin to be implemented. Clearly, it had been a time-consuming task. It may have the advantage, however, of making the parties themselves take control over the process (Mitchell 1999b). A remarkable achievement was noted in May 2007 when Ian

Paisley, leader of the Democratic Unionist Party, became First Minister in a Northern Ireland government with Sinn Fein leader Martin McGuinness as Deputy First Minister. The return to war seemed increasingly unlikely.

The second approach requires considerable ingenuity as well. Parties will not subscribe to an arrangement which they fear. However, the use of the threat of force changes the dynamic, particularly when, as was the case in the Bosnia-Herzegovina crisis, the force used by the outside was targeting one side only. There was a clear basis on which the outside power, the United States, made its evaluation of the outcome. It had a preference. It may be one that was shared internationally, but nevertheless it shifted the talks from searching for common positions to finding positions that were compatible with this basic premise. The talks in Dayton lasted for three weeks. It was, in the words of Holbrooke, 'the Big Bang approach to negotiations: lock everyone up until they reach agreement' (Holbrooke 1999: 232). It achieved a permanent cease-fire and a constitution for the Republic of Bosnia-Herzegovina. To implement the agreement a NATO-led force was placed in the country, as was an international police force and an internationally appointed High Representative for civilian affairs. The implementation required close surveillance and these institutions were still in place 20 years later.

The results were remarkable in both circumstances. The agreements were detailed, concrete and gave directions for implementation. Clearly, the strong international presence differentiated the Dayton Agreement from the Northern Ireland one. This reflects more the differences in the issues that had to be solved, the ferocity of the wars and the magnitude of state-building tasks that lay ahead. It can be asked, however, whether the result in the first process is such that the parties are prepared to take more responsibility for implementation than in the second case. The sharing of power by two parties that were seen as each other's extremes is a mark of this, taking place eight years after the original agreement. Has the second approach resulted in an agreement that is heavily dependent on a sustained international interest? The international development has been scaled down but still remains crucial. The constitution that was part of the peace agreement is increasingly challenged but to change it is difficult.

If the first approach had been used in the Bosnia-Herzegovina case, it might have meant that Dayton would only result in a cease-fire agreement, after which the parties were to start to negotiate among themselves. A momentum for settlement would have been lost and the difficulties of keeping the state of Bosnia-Herzegovina together would have been apparent. In the autumn of 1995 there may not have been many viable alternatives to the process selected. A process of the first type requires a somewhat better chance of meaningful dialogue. At the same time, a solution is still needed to provide for a smooth-functioning daily life. The parties may easily walk out as they are not forced into the arrangements. A process of the second type requires considerable and constant pressure, in the end exhausting the participants. It is an expensive approach and the chance of failure is high. Even if the parties cannot walk out, they can procrastinate and obstruct. For both processes, the benefit from success may still be considerable and change their priorities for the future.

The evaluation of the two approaches is important. It is a general question of interest to many types of conflict. Both agreements have remained in place and there has been no outbreak of war. But the quality of the peace can be questioned.

The opportunities for economic growth and development are greater in Northern Ireland. Bosnia remains aid-dependent.

We have seen that conflicts increasingly have been brought to international attention. They become issues for the UN, for human rights and conflict resolution organizations, for those fearing genocide, as well as for compatriots spread around the world. A global economy creates global connections for local conflicts. Thus, issues of prevention and mediation are central concerns for the different new communities that are emerging.

11.4 Arms Control and Disarmament

A cease-fire remains an integral part of peace agreements. It relates to the physical security of the inhabitants. We have discussed the security dilemmas in Chapters 5, 6 and 7, and they have to do with this matter. However, the presence of arms and the accumulation of new weaponry are also likely to be signs of possible tension in the future, whether near or long term. Assessments of future distributions of power often point to military expenditure, new weaponry and new military doctrines as indicators. Matters of armaments relate both to the ending of particular conflicts and to the possible rise of new tensions and wars. Thus, arms control and disarmament belongs to the agenda of conflict resolution, and point to an inventory of possible actions that can consolidate peace as well as prevent conflicts.

With respect to conflict resolution and peace processes it has often been debated whether a cease-fire should come early or late in the process of negotiations. In some instances, a small number of determined soldiers with limited military equipment can block the progress of peace talks which may be favoured by the majority on each side. Thus, early demilitarization is in the interest of both sides. In the negotiation framework, however, parties may prefer to have a military option available, and thus even use disarmament as an instrument for achieving concessions in other fields. The logic is such that 'If you give us A, we may be willing to make disarmament move B.' However, following an agreement, the parties may all see that it is unlikely that it will be maintained if new fears are generated by the accumulating armaments. Demilitarization thus has been a necessary element to reduce fears after the peace. This is also the idea with the notion of the acronym of DDR: disarmament, demobilization and reintegration. The issues of ex-combatants have caught attention (Gleichmann et al. 2004; Humphreys and Weinstein 2005; Themnér 2013). Military and police need to be reformed, whether countries are coming out of conflicts or authoritarian conditions, giving rise to programmes on security sector (or system) reform (SSR). This is not only a matter of disarming the former warriors, it is also one of disbanding military formations, including informal networks, and achieving the reintegration of the war veterans into civilian pursuits (Themnér 2013). Interestingly, Joshi and Darby (2013) find that if disarmament precedes elections, implementation of a peace agreement is likely to be less violent.

Also in interstate relations, actors tend to be highly concerned about the armaments of the others. It is part of the *Realpolitik* thinking and the security dilemma: armament imbalances, even created for defensive reasons, may inject fear on the other side of a contentious border, thus initiating a series of actions that may result in war. This is particularly true, of course, for nuclear weapons. Thus, the full range of disarmament, arms control and transarmament measures are part of the agenda of policies that deal with direct conflict prevention, but also relate to the structural causes of conflict. Thus, the issue of disarmaments moves us in the direction of structural conflict prevention.

There are various measures in place to reduce access to armaments. The Land Mines Convention of 1997 was an important achievement to curtail production of one such weapon with particular effects for civilians. In many conflicts, light arms have been readily available and put to use. This remains an urgent issue. An important concern is how to strengthen arms embargoes (Fruchart et al. 2007). In 2013, the long-awaited Arms Trade Treaty was concluded, making it easier to identify illicit arms trade, and thus control international arms flows. The treaty requires the ratification by 50 signatories in order to enter into force. By September 2014, only five more ratifications were needed and thus the Treaty was expected to go into force by the end of the year. Several major arms producers had not signed, however, notably China, Russia, India, Pakistan, Israel and Iran. Some had signed but not ratified (USA and Brazil, for instance) whereas most EU-members, including three large arms producers, and Japan had taken all the steps needed.

For the major power relations there are implemented measures, for instance, on conventional weapons in Europe and on confidence-building measures. The Anti-Ballistic Missiles (ABM) Treaty of 1972 aimed at preventing an arms race in the field of anti-ballistic defence between the USA and the Soviet Union. It served to reduce fears in East–West relations. The idea of creating a system of missile defence, as implemented by the United States in the early 2000s, had unsettling effects and the programme was scaled back. This applies particularly to the relations between the USA and Russia, and to some extent also China. The treaty on the reduction of strategic nuclear weapons signed in Prague 2010 is also an important measure for tension reduction. However, progress beyond this has been difficult. The Ukraine crisis led in 2014 to the idea of NATO bases closer to Russia, thus, keeping tension high in Europe.

Another important measure of general conflict prevention is the Non-Proliferation Treaty of 1968. The treaty created an international instrument against the proliferation of nuclear weapons. Thus, sinister prognoses made at the time did not materialize. The treaty has a basic flaw in the distinction made between states that have and those that do not have nuclear weapons. Some of the known or new nuclear weapons states are countries that have not signed the treaty (Israel, India, Pakistan). Some states may attempt to develop nuclear capacities clandestinely, threaten to or formally opt out of the treaty (Libya and Iraq prior to 2003, Iran, North Korea). Nevertheless, the Non-Proliferation Treaty has managed to prevent developments that definitely would have made the planet more unsafe. Similarly, the comprehensive nuclear weapons test ban aims at preventing the development of new nuclear weapons. These are examples of structural prevention. They reduce the risks of escalation and decrease the likelihood of disputes occurring as a result of miscalculation.

The crisis over Ukraine in 2014, however, raised important concerns about the value of major power guarantees. Ukraine, following the dissolution of the Soviet Union, became a nuclear weapons state. In the Budapest Memorandum of December 1994, USA, UK and Russia reaffirmed their commitment to respect the independence and sovereignty of Ukraine and its 'existing borders'. They also stated that their weapons would not be used against Ukraine except in self-defence. The principles of the UN and OSCE were explicitly referred to. In the crisis 20 years later, however, the Ukrainian territory of Crimea was annexed into the Russian Federation in a questionable process of swift military action, a hasty referendum and quick constitutional changes in the Russian Federation allowing the incorporation of Crimea as two new federal units. By using unmarked equipment and unidentified troops this was supposed to appear as a Crimean process. If brought to the International Court of Justice the legality of these events could be judged, including whether this was a violation of the Budapest Memorandum. Similar arguments, furthermore, could be applied to the developments in eastern provinces of Ukraine. A serious implication of this goes beyond the sovereignty of Ukraine: it makes it less likely that explicit nuclear weapons states such as India, Pakistan and North Korea, de facto states (notably Israel), or aspiring ones (that is Iran), would be satisfied with the type of security guarantees given to Ukraine for going ahead with nuclear disarmament and entering the Non-Proliferation Treaty. In this way, the Ukrainian crisis has made matters of arms control and disarmament more difficult. In addition, it also sparked a renewed urge for increased military expenditures in neighbouring countries in general and in Western Europe in particular.

The Chemical Weapons Convention aims at the elimination of an entire class of weapons, chemical weapons, and has been in force since 1997. OPCW, the Organisation on the Prohibition of Chemical Weapons, has this mandate and gained prominence in 2013 when it was awarded the Nobel Peace Prize. This followed on the agreement between Russia, Syria and the United States after a documented used of chemical weapons in the Syrian civil war in August 2013. The United States threatened to attack Syria, unless it gave up its chemical weapons. In a remarkably quick sequence of diplomatic moves, Syria agreed to enter the convention and a process of elimination was initiated. Within a year it was announced that Syria, in fact, had given up its entire, declared inventory of chemical weapons. Although questions may remain, it was a major achievement, suggesting that also other categories of weapons could possibly be abolished in similar ways and with similar international agreement. It did not, however, lead to an end of the war in Syria.

11.5 Peacebuilding Strategies

Peace agreements, such as those we have studied here, aim at creating conditions for lasting peace. Thus it is part of the ambition to develop strategies of peacebuilding. Elements in this have to do with the construction of peace agreements apart from dealing with the central incompatibility that we dealt with in Chapters 5, 6 and 7. It also has to do with other matters resulting from the war, as well as how they relate to significant international norms (notably the issue of territorial integrity), the role of transparency and democratic institutions, and even with the state structures themselves. Let us here illustrate this based on the experience of partial and comprehensive peace agreements in the post-Cold War period. They constitute the agreed document to which the parties will have to relate. Obviously, such agreements will also have to be revised as conditions change.

Research into these issues is still fairly limited, although the world has such a vast experience in peacemaking. There is a resource dealing with one set of agreements, the comprehensive peace agreements, which can be seen as attempts to solve a host of the issues that the most significant parties find important to deal with. The Peace Accords Matrix at the Kroc Institute, University of Notre Dame, is a resource for the analysis of these agreements and for their long-term impact (Joshi and Darby 2013).

The study into the causes of conflict can yield some insights into broader changes that are required for reducing the danger of new wars. This is consonant with the idea of a structural approach to conflict prevention, peacebuilding and strategic peacebuilding (Lederach 1997; Wallensteen 2001, 2010). It means taking a long-term perspective. Conflicts develop from grievances experienced in a society, actions are based on deliberate considerations of gains, and conflicts escalate to levels where they may become violent, as we have seen in Chapter 3. Such a structural approach would have to involve measures to influence this chain so as to allow for legitimate change without the need for violence. It becomes a broad programme and the results are not too easily observable in the course of a particular conflict. The measure of success is seen in an analysis of a conflict over a longer period of time. It would be, for instance, where formerly conflictual interstate relations are no longer tense, once conflict-ridden societies are integrated, and previously divided societies have found ways to cooperate. It is a matter of arriving at a peace which is not just a matter of absence of war, but the presence of societal qualities. In short this is *quality peace*: 'to provide the post-conflict conditions that make the inhabitants of a society secure in life and dignity now and for the foreseeable future' (Wallensteen 2015). In short, we are looking for results where historical conflicts are turned into non-conflict or even cooperation.

This is a broad agenda. The peace agreements since the Cold War give some clues to the possibilities. Most of them aim at converting conflictual relations. Many of them are still too fresh to suggest safely that such shifts have taken place. The institutions put in place through the peace agreements include measures that might also be useful for other situations. Chapters 5, 6 and 7 give ideas for a structural conflict prevention programme. Conclusions can also be drawn from studies of the causes of war and the causes of internal war. It gives a role for development cooperation, but also economic planning, political engineering and popular movements for change. In addition to the disarmament issue that we dealt with in 11.4 there are the questions of the lingering effects of the war, removing the most contentious issues, the construction of new institutions and state structures.

Undoing the Effects of War

Peace agreements, particularly those that failed, illustrate the fears and concerns that parties have when they try to end one war in which they are not the victors. A peace accord, of course, will have implications for future relations. In order to avoid the phenomenon of a repetition of war, the war effects have to be undone. Studies suggest that the length of a situation without war is related to a reduction in the likelihood of new internal war (Collier and Hoeffler 2000; Vasquez 2012). This means that peace processes need support in the early phase of implementation to have a chance of success. This might be a way to break historical cycles of violence. We have illustrated such cycles with the Franco-German relations. There are also the more recent experiences of repetitions of war, for instance, Iran–Iraq, Israeli–Arab relations and India–Pakistan. Cycles have also been reported from internal wars, such as between Hutus and Tutsis in Central Africa, or Serbs and Albanians in the Balkans, around the Taliban in Afghanistan (which may be an element in long-standing tensions between Pashtuns and other groups), Sunni, Shiites and Kurds in Iraq, or between ethnic groups in the Sudans, Chad, and Sahel states.

There are ways in which such cycles can be broken. The return of refugees is an important and concrete aspect. Forceful evictions are not easily forgotten. People in refugee camps are in conditions that daily remind them of their fate and who is responsible. Most peace agreements allow for the return of refugees, but in some cases, ethnic cleansing has been the objective of one or several parties. It is possible that the question of the return of refugees is particularly difficult in state formation conflicts. The advance in approaches to war crimes is another important achievement. It serves to make a distinction between those more responsible than others, and thus can reduce stereotyping between the parties. A more difficult, but urgent field of inquiry concerns reconciliation and peacebuilding. Different approaches have been developed, notably government-sanctioned truth commissions (Brounéus 2003; Hayner 2011). The issue of amnesty for war crimes can be seen as setting peace versus justice and decency. Some studies suggest that agreements with amnesty are more durable (Wallensteen et al. 2012). Such findings contribute to a discussion on the difficult trade-off considerations that peacemaking entails. It also leads to new ideas for possible solutions, notably on sequencing of measures (security first, other issues later, for instance) or levels (some issues are for the national level, others for the regional or global level). Similar discussions can be waged on the victims. Issues of compensation are important in peace agreements, but they seem often to be left without implementation (Joshi and Darby 2013). It suggests the importance of creating institutions that attend to such matters. Again this may have to be developed on different levels of society (national, regional, global). Undoing such effects of the war appears logically to be of a high priority; in the real world, power holders may make other assessments. There is, as a matter of fact, a need for a *Peace Watch* function: an independent organization that can scrutinize the implementation of agreements and strike alarm when matters are left without consideration or measures are taken contrary to the stipulations of an agreement.

Tackling the Territorial Issues

We have also seen that territorial issues remain pertinent, both for interstate conflicts and state formation conflicts. Grievances over the borders themselves or problems experienced by groups divided by borders are causes of conflict. At the same time, the strict rules in the UN Charter, the AU (OAU) and the OSCE may for a long time have served to prevent parties from raising demands for border changes. There is a normative framework against territorial change by violent means. It is remarkable, for instance, that the demands for border revisions in Europe have been few after 1945 compared to the situation before 1939. The record of forced changes is also limited. Thus, as a preventive measure, the norms enshrined in these international institutions may have been successful. Even in the dissolution of states in the early 1990s, there was an attempt to follow previously drawn lines, albeit internal ones, to reduce the pain of border revisions. There remain in the world a great number of dormant border disputes that very well could have surfaced without these norms and their support by the overwhelming majority of the members of the global system.

Nevertheless, there are cases where territory is an element of conflict. The puzzle for a structural approach is to find ways in which present borders can be maintained, but be made less 'hard' so as to remedy popular grievances. The security of some identity groups rests on the possibility of having access across borders (Albanians, Armenians, Kurds, Serbs, Somalis, for instance). However, softer borders can create new problems. It may result in unwanted movements across the same borders (drug trade, prostitution, human trafficking, organized crime).

A preventive approach may require a regional framework where common interests, such as sharing of water, may serve as an impetus for softening the impact of borders. Using geographical features, cooperative ventures can be found to ameliorate grievances of the local population and worries of governments. In a regional framework, it may even be possible to give one country a say in what occurs on the other side of the border.

This can be a guarantee for minorities, but also for the governments as relations become more transparent. Such arrangements may be attractive for Central Africa, Kurdish-populated areas in the Middle East and Albanian-populated areas in Southeast Europe. If this is coupled with a government renouncing territorial demands, a reasonable trade-off is made. Some peace accords have such arrangements. For instance, the Belfast agreement includes a deal between Great Britain, Northern Ireland and the Republic of Ireland, thus cutting across the borders.

The world was strongly reminded of the importance of these issues when Russia administered the breaking away of Crimea from Ukraine in a quick sequence of events in March 2014. There had been little mentioning of this territory as a grievance in the various disputes between Ukraine and Russia since the dissolution of the Soviet Union in 1991. The turmoil that followed the regime change in Ukraine in February 2014 created an opportunity for Russia's action. The integrity of Ukraine was threatened, the central government was fully engaged in getting itself organized and the Western world tried to find ways to support the more democratic regime. There was no military capacity that could outpower Russia on the Crimean Peninsula. There were also incentives for Russia to militarily secure its naval base in Sevastopol, particularly if the rest of Ukraine was moving closer to NATO. Thus, Russia organized an unprecedented and largely non-lethal take-over and annexation of the area. It was opportunistic and also contrary to a consistent emphasis in Soviet and Russian policy since the end of the Cold War: to be a champion for territorial integrity and state sovereignty.

At the same time, a parallel development took place as an outgrowth of the civil wars in Syria and Iraq. A group declared itself as an Islamic State and announced a caliphate on an undefined territory that seemed to include at least Syria and Iraq. ISIS made some spectacular territorial gains during 2014, took control over some major cities in both these states, instituted a brutal regime that negated human rights and at the same time challenged the existing borders. Indeed, as ISIS controlled both sides of the Syrian-Iraqi border it dismantled the border controls and began to institute its vision.

The consequences of these actions remain to be seen. Russia's action has encountered numerous sanctions measures from the EU, US and other Western states. Certainly, this aims at preventing further Russian incursions into Ukraine or elsewhere. It also sends a message to other states that may contemplate similar moves. However, the opposite signal is also there: 'if Russia can do this (and seemingly get away with it), so can we'. The same applies to the challenge from ISIS, and it soon involved the United States as a military actor in the conflict. None of the actors left any space for negotiations or proper identification of what the local population may have asked for. For different reasons and with different consequences, an important norm was violated in practice at about the same time. It may make it difficult to resurrect its credibility. A tenet in the post-1945 order has been challenged, potentially affecting many conflict resolution efforts.

If there is a need for a Peace Watch, as suggested in the previous section, there may also be a need for an independent monitoring of dormant ('frozen'), active and potential territorial disputes. This would provide the world with a resource for pre-conflict action, as an element in peacebuilding.

Developing Democratic Institutions

Democracy has emerged as a factor of significance for all conflicts in the conflict trichotomy. Democratic states rarely fight wars with other democracies, democratic institutions have been used as ways of solving civil wars, and state formation conflicts often have had an origin in the lack of access to authority. Thus, a structural approach would include the support of emerging and fragile democratic institutions. It is closely tied to the promotion of human rights, but is not necessarily the same. There are more countries that have signed the convention on human rights than are democratic. From a conflict prevention perspective, the essence is not a strict electoral process, issues of representation or other constitutional matters. Rather, the key is in institutions that are unbiased and offer the opportunity of having a decision corrected. This is what we have defined as the rule of law. The legal institutions, of course, reflect political decisions, as law is a political matter, but such institutions have a longer duration than political leadership. Laws are maintained even if governments change. The independence of the juridical and administrative institutions is important for predictability and transparency. To be durable, laws have to reflect a degree of consensus in society, meaning that broader governments are preferable when institutions for conflict resolution are created. This is the reason why constitutional changes require wider support than ordinary political decisions.

Democracy, however, is more than institutions. It is a form of governance building on shared values. The viable democracy is one which has the ability to use the conflict resolution forms introduced in Chapter 3 and applied, for instance, in internal conflicts in Chapter 6. It requires that the public at large, as well as various special interest groups, be in agreement on the rules of the society. It builds on an attitude where the democratic machinery is important in itself and worth the protection of the population. This requires a vibrant civil society, the development of which is also part of a structural approach.

It appears that the single most effective way in which democracy can lose its legitimacy is from corruption. The internal security dilemma may stimulate kleptocracy, particularly under authoritarian regimes. Democracy would remove some of these dynamics. However, in any social system whose leadership is mostly concerned with its own enrichment, state institutions are affected. Even a democracy may turn into a kleptocracy that generates new conflict. Ukraine is a recent illustration of this, where the ousted leadership used its power for personal enrichment. It remains to be seen if the new leaders perform better. The new societies that followed from the Arab Spring demonstrate many different courses of action, ranging from the reasonably functioning Tunisia to the dramatic swings experience in Egypt to the collapse of central institutions in Libya. Charges of corruption have been important in all these cases. Whether the problem really has been tackled by any of the new power holders can be questioned.

Still, there is much that speaks in favour of democratic principles as important for long-term conflict resolution. There has to be an ethically and politically viable trade-off between support of democratic institutions and the actual desires of a given population to have them. There is likely to be, in most societies, groups that embrace concepts of human rights, democracy and the peaceful settlement of disputes. There are others who will view such matters from an opportunistic perspective, and still others who regard them as threatening. Normally, democratic institutions have to build on local conditions. The experiences of democracy-building in Japan and Germany following the Second World War are not typical, even though the strong international presence in Bosnia-Herzegovina and Kosovo may have a corresponding impact. Timor-Leste (East Timor) and Liberia seem now to be on paths towards democracy. Research points to the importance of inclusivity and to constitutions that enhance broad participation, e.g. proportional representation, parliamentary systems (Joshi 2013). At the same time there seems to be common agreement that any democratic system is connected to local beliefs, concerns and issues. Otherwise, it may later come to be regarded as something introduced by international institutions or external forces for reasons other than the genuine concern of the local society.

Finding New State Structures

The state is central in our deliberations, and it is likely to remain so. We find the state at the same time to be an actor in conflict and a disputed resource. It gives rise to hope for protection for some and fear of repression for others. This is particularly pronounced in countries with many identity groups. Thus, there is a need to consider alternatives in state-making.

A federal solution may effectively deal with state formation issues within a democratic framework. Many of the large federal states that exist today – the United States, the Federal Republic of Germany and the Russian Federation – were only partly designed to handle such conflicts. Switzerland remains the classical example, but it grew as a federation from below. The different cantons got together to form the state. As we have seen, India made a conscious effort to redraw its internal borders in the 1950s. The record from these five cases is not entirely convincing. The US Civil War of the 1860s is the most devastating war in the country's history. The Russian Federation is young and has faced severe problems, not least with two consecutive wars in Chechnya and an increasingly more dominant centre. India is the more interesting example. Although it has faced several internal state formation conflicts, they are not directly related to the federal structure created in the 1950s. The reforms sought to meet the fears of a bid for secession by the Tamil population in the South and that has not happened. The conflict in Punjab was severe, however, and was not handled in a similarly peaceful way. Switzerland went through a process of dividing one of the cantons in order to alleviate fears of one part of the population.

Federation has been applied in some peace agreements, as we have seen in Chapter 7. Bosnia-Herzegovina is a federal state. Federalism is suggested as a solution to many conflicts. More recently it has been proposed by Russia as a fitting form for Ukraine, a rather unprecedented approach, which immediately made the idea suspect in Ukraine. Iraq has been organized accordingly, but it may have enhanced conflict rather than the reverse. Following the upheavals in 2007–08 Kenya adopted a federal constitution. The idea is, that federalism works as conflict preventive measures. In a recent study it was found that such federal arrangement might function as long as the military resources are not dispersed. In cases where the constituent units control their own forces, however, conflicts may escalate quicker and become more brutal, if they do break out (Regan and Wallensteen 2013).

It is possible that the very limited state concept that has been applied throughout the twentieth century needs reconsideration. It has assumed a fairly centralized political unit, which carries out uniform policy within the territory to which it has legal access. Thus, all parts of the state are treated in an equal way. However, we have noted that many states do have interesting constitutional variations: Puerto Rico in the United States, the Channel Islands in the United Kingdom, the Åland Islands in Finland, Zanzibar in Tanzania. Spain has different layers of self-rule for its mainland regions. There is a clash between the uniformity required by existing state structures and the diversity of the populations of these states. Inside the same state, conditions are likely to vary economically, culturally and politically. Thus, there is a need to produce models for alternative state structures. A case in point is finding a solution to the Palestinian conflict. It may require out-of-the-box thinking (Mossberg 2010). Such alternatives will have to find ways of forming governance, protection and welfare for the inhabitants against criminality and other unwanted interference, while meeting the needs for diversity and ease of international connection. These demands are high but not unreasonable. A state has to earn the allegiance of its inhabitants and, thus, it has to be able to respond to such demands.

This chapter has demonstrated some of the possibilities for peaceful and long-term action for conflict resolution. It has focused on measures available to international organizations and states. Certainly, the inventory is much larger, particularly if the creativity of civil society organizations is added. Thus, Chapters 10 and 11 hope to stimulate thinking as well as action. Our final chapter tries to assess the situation for peaceful conflict resolution in the middle of the 2010s.

Further Readings

Go to the *Understanding Conflict Resolution* web page at https://study.sagepub.com/wallensteen4e for free access to journal articles listed.

Prevention

Conflict Prevention has been on the agenda of the international discussions since the early 1990s:

Carnegie Commission 1997. *Preventing Deadly Conflict: Final Report*. Carnegie Commission on Preventing Deadly Conflict, Washington, DC.
This was a remarkable project initiated by a private foundation to raise the issue of early action for conflict prevention. It had a strong impact on the debate and on actual behavior, particularly in the United Nations.

Lund, M.S. 1996. *Preventing Violent Conflicts: A Strategy for Preventive Diplomacy*. Washington, DC: United States Institute of Peace Press.
Michael Lund's book reflected the international reactions to the crises in Bosnia and Rwanda in the first half of the 1990s. Many of the 'tools' described have remained on the agenda of international actors.

Öberg, M., Möller, F. and Wallensteen, P. 2009. 'Early Conflict Prevention in Ethnic Crises, 1990–98: A New Dataset', *Conflict Management and Peace Science*, 26 (1): 67–91.
This is one of the few, systematic studies trying to ascertain whether early action actually works in preventing conflicts from escalating. It generated unexpected results.

Mediation

Svensson, I. 2009. 'Who Brings Which Peace? Neutral versus Biased Mediation and Institutional Arrangements in Civil Wars', *Journal of Conflict Resolution*, 53 (3): 446–69.
A central tenet in mediation is the importance of being unbiased and impartial. Svensson's study questions this. This article has drawn considerable attention in the literature on mediation research.

Svensson, I. and Wallensteen, P. 2010. *The Go-Between: Jan Eliasson and the Styles of Mediation*. Washington, DC: United States Institute of Peace Press.
This work attempts a different approach. It 'follows' one mediator, Swedish diplomat Jan Eliasson, in six different mediation situations taking place within three decades. It opens up for a close look at mediation in practice, but also how mediation has evolved from inter-state relations to complex regional and multi-dimensional concerns.

Peacebuilding

After the Cold War the issues of peacebuilding became a major concern. Whether it really worked or not draws a considerable discussion. A central work in this was:
Paris, R. 2004. *At War's End: Building Peace after Civil Conflict*, Cambridge, MA: Cambridge University Press.

The discussion was far-reaching, however, and has still not ended. It has distinguished liberal peacebuilding from other approaches, even including 'strategic' peacebuilding. See, for instance:
Philpot, D. and Powers, G.F. 2010. (eds), *Strategies of Peace*, Oxford University Press.

A further contribution, based on empirical work on post-war conditions within as well as between states is this work, arguing in favour of the notion of 'quality peace', replacing 'positive' peace as well as peacebuilding:
Wallensteen, P. 2015. *Toward Quality Peace: Peacebuilding, Victory and World Order*, Oxford University Press.

The work on peacebuilding is also relevant for thinking about the options in a peace process. In this work, Swedish diplomat Mathias Mossberg suggests a new type of state structure as a solution for the Palestinian issue:
Mossberg, M. 2010. 'One Land, Two States? Parallel States and an Example of 'Out of the Box' Thinking on Israel/Palestine', *Journal of Palestinian Studies*, 39 (2): 40–45.

12

CONFLICT RESOLUTION IN THE 2010s

12.1 Need for Reflection

By the mid-2010s, the ambitions of peaceful conflict resolution appeared to be challenged from many simultaneous developments. There were concerns about the future of peace. Was the world going deeper into a period of particularism, with increasing major power tensions and local conflicts? It is important for students of international conflict resolution to reflect on these challenges. What do 'we' know from academic work and practical experiences? Do they require new types of study or innovative practice? There is more knowledge but there may also be developments that reduce general interest in the peaceful settlement of disputes.

We know that the world historically has seen swings between particularist and universalist international relations. The dangers of the 2010s make it important to reflect on these patterns. There is much as stake and there is much to be lost if global efforts cannot focus on matters of significance for the survival of the planet. This chapter serves to initiate some reflections on this from a planetary perspective. Is the world now and in the coming years particularly turbulent? Is there a peace fatigue? Are the important new paradigms of gender equality and R2P creating new conflicts? What is the impact of fragmentation, corruption, religious revival and major power rivalry on the ability to solve conflicts in durable ways? What may this entail for our planet? The questions are many, the answers fewer. But it is important to begin an inquiry into these challenges: this is the only way to find answers, solutions and eventually a practice that can lead the planet in a constructive direction.

12.2 A New Turbulence?

In 1990, American international relations scholar James Rosenau published *Turbulence in World Politics*, trying to make sense of the upheavals that followed after the Cold War. The book's cover was aptly illustrated with one picture from Berlin in November 1989 ('the fall of the wall') as well as one from Beijing in June the same year (Tiananmen Square). This contradictory image of the world still holds 25 years later. The turbulence following the Arab Spring has set in motion dynamics in the Middle East and Northern Africa that quickly draw Europe and USA into the flow of events. These dynamics, furthermore, appeared to include challenges to established notions of territorial integrity, national sovereignty, protection of civilians and of national heritage, as well as a backlash against gender equality and due processes.

Parallel to this, developments were unfolding centred on Russia's relations, particularly to its neighbouring states, which also inevitably and quickly involved the European Union and the USA. All this was largely unpredicted and, thus, the term 'turbulence' appeared fitting.

However, there were also other trends. China and East Asia saw – at the same time – unprecedented growth; almost no active armed conflicts; and an amassment of wealth unimaginable 25 years earlier. And indeed, similar developments were reported from South Asia and Africa. Poverty was declining, health conditions were improving. All this should, for the long term, contribute to a reduction in the start of armed conflicts and wars. This is what a team of researchers also predict for the period until 2050 (Hegre et al. 2013). Others were inclined to see less of such changes (Kissinger 2014). However, the revolutionary changes Rosenau was concerned about resulted in globalization, democratization and concerted efforts for conflict resolution.

12.3 Peace Fatigue or Learning Peace?

There are fewer peace agreements in the past years compared to the peace process enthusiasm that marked the 1990s. The number of new peacekeeping operations declined from 18 and 15 in the two first five-years periods after the end of the Cold war, to 7 in each of the following periods and 5 in the last one, 2009–13. If we relate the data of peacekeeping operations to the number of armed conflicts, as presented in Table 4.1 (see p. 74), the ratio goes down from 0.19 and 0.21 in the two first periods to 0.125 in the following two to a mere 0.09 in the most recent period. Differently put: statistically, the ratio goes from one peacekeeping operation for every fifth conflict to one in every tenth conflict. Similarly, we can calculate the trend in peace agreements that we presented in Chapter 4: there is a remarkable drop of new peace agreements for the most recent period. For each five-year period since 1989 the number of peace agreements have ranged between 40 and 50, but the most recent one which saw 54 armed conflicts had only a dozen peace agreements.

This is not a full measure of an international commitment to peacemaking. The frequency of UN Security Council decisions has not declined, as we observed in Chapter 9. Also, regional organizations have become more active. Still, we may ask if the peacemaking impact has become more limited. The total number of armed conflicts has not decreased. There was, instead, a whole set of new ones, particularly after the Arab Spring, as observed throughout this book. These were challenges that initially made other governments hesitant to act, and later, seem to have made them more inclined to act with military means. It is most clearly observable in US actions, focusing on withdrawal of major forces for much of the period, but increasingly acting with technological means (drones, targeted assassinations, air campaigns). There were remarkably few US-brokered peace agreements in the latest five-year period. This is turn may relate to the increasingly divergent policies of the US and Russia, particularly over Syria (since 2011) and Ukraine (since 2013). The two appeared increasingly to act on their own, without prior consultation with each other, particularly on some civil war issues. A common observation in this book is that reasonable cooperation between the major powers is a necessary condition for sustained peace processes.

But there is also another way of reading these statistics: it could mean an improvement in the quality of peacemaking. The processes that started to bear fruit in the mid-2010s were all protracted as they dealt with conflicts that had lingered for a considerable period of time. Clearly, peace accords have become longer documents; deal with more problems; and do so in more detail. They also have to face the challenge of turning into legally valid documents, not only staying as the political framework that was typical for earlier agreements (Bell 2008). Many imply constitutional changes. The process in the Philippines demonstrated the significance of legal considerations, as the Supreme Court in 2008 overturned a previous agreement. All this means that the agreements may become more thorough and, thus, have a more lasting quality. The study of peace agreement implementation testifies to some of these observations (Joshi and Darby 2013). Thus, it might be a healthy sign that the agreements are fewer, if it means that the resulting accords have emerged from a more focused, deliberative process. The peace process in Colombia since 2012 is clearly of this type. This suggests that learning has taking place and that there is a professionalization of peacemaking. The picture is, of course, not complete. There are still documents that have been hastily composed in order to solve acute crises, thus largely cementing status quo, rather than taking up issues of importance of long-term peace processes. The many cease-fire agreements in Ukraine during 2014 have all the traits of such improvised arrangements.

12.4 New Paradigms, Necessary Conflicts?

Two particularly strong new paradigms have emerged and are likely to have an impact for the future: gender equality and responsibility to protect (R2P). Both provide lenses through which conflicts can be seen and solutions considered. As is often the case with novelties, they also give rise to dispute and conflict.

Gender issues have gained particular strength following the formative Security Council Resolution 1325 of October 2000. It outlined criteria for measuring advancement of women's participation in peace processes. The idea was to move the discussion from a focus of women as victims to one of women as actors. At the same time, of course, the issue of victimhood remained, and a series of later Council resolutions dealt with issues of sexual violence in conflict. However, it is important not to lose track of the ambitions of Resolution 1325 and continue to consider the role of women in peace processes. A landmark experience was the way the peace agreement over Liberia in 2003 came about. Women's organizations were in the forefront of pushing the negotiators to find an end to 14 years of war. The 2005 election in Liberia also made Ellen Johnson Sirleaf the first elected woman president in Africa. The Nobel Peace Prize in 2011 to three women (including President Johnson Sirleaf) constituted additional confirmation on the importance of women in peace processes. It demonstrated also an increasing international awareness of the particular security threats to women during and after war. Research had shown the importance for peacekeeping operations to attend to this properly (Olsson 2009).

Gender equality involves the relationship between men and women. It is not merely a matter of improving women's condition; it is also a matter of changing the role of men in the direction of equality (Tickner 1993). There is now a body of literature that statistically demonstrates the connection between gender equality and the reduction in civil and interstate wars (Caprioli 2005; Melander 2005). This, consequently, is an agenda item in peacebuilding after war and in the construction of societies that are not to relapse into war. However, only a few of the comprehensive peace agreements from the 1989–2007 period have attended to these matters. It affects the quality of the agreements and also their chance of success (Joshi and Darby 2013).

For women's movements, gender equality is of course central. It has a central position among the values shared in the international community that we identified in Chapter 9. For other groups it is seen as a 'Western' concern, not an element of globally shared human rights. Instead it is a threat to traditional ways of organizing society. Thus, many of the armed groups that have gained strength in the wake of the Arab Spring have particularly targeted women, from school children to professionally active women. It has turned into a brutal backlash. There are now groups with such agendas in armed conflicts, from Afghanistan to Mali. They often act in the name of Islam, but with purposes and methods that most adherents to Islam find entirely unacceptable. This means that gender equality is not only a matter of women being victims or actors, but of structure and power in society as a whole. For many of these groups, furthermore, questioning the role of men, discussing issues of homosexuality and transgender and other matters relevant in this context, is foreign. There is little hope for dialogue under such conditions. Pertinent questions then become if such groups and societies provide space for non-violent change, whether that space can be enlarged, and how it can be encouraged from within society as well as from outside. It suggests that there are limits to compromise and that programme of peaceful social change also is part of conflict resolution. Ultimately, it has to do with the ability to build societies that are non-discriminatory, tolerant and meet the conditions of durable peace.

The second normative novelty is the doctrine of R2P that was specified in the World Summit Outcome in 2005, and thus accepted by all the member states of the UN. It is a way of reacting to humanitarian crisis afflicting large civilian populations and emerging from war, genocide and mass violations of human rights. The doctrine gives the primary responsibility to the states themselves. It is only when a state is not able to pursue this that the international community takes over the role of protecting the civilian population. It has most clearly been used in the case of Libya in 2011, something we have mentioned throughout this book. We have also noted that the application of the principles with the use of sanctions and a no-fly zone initially met Security Council approval. However, when the no-fly zone not only meant the bombing of Libyan assets that could be used to threaten the monitoring missions, but also targeted other Libyan military resources, some countries saw this as intervention to overthrow a government. The agreed goal of civilian protection was, according to Russia, China and other countries, transformed into 'regime change' in a sovereign country. It meant that they were not willing to grant similar authorization in the case of the civil war in Syria. Certainly, humanitarian efforts were encouraged, but in a more traditional way. No binding Council resolution could deal with the political conditions in the country, if it meant the use of sanctions or other measures against the incumbent regime. Remarkably, a set of other decisions was agreed upon, including the elimination of Syrian chemical weapons and on the importance of mediation. That reflects the peculiarities that could be observed also with the Cold War: agreements were possible in some areas, but not in those that actually had to do with the disagreements.

Also with respect to this new development, conflict resolution efforts ran into situations where the possibilities of reasonable pressure to further diplomatic solutions were blocked. Mediators were forced to find ways around such impasses. They could hope to work out agreements on some issues that might set dynamics in motion favouring a solution of the major issues. It is not a matter of waiting for the ripe moment, but contributing to conditions that may generate such opportunities.

We can observe that two significant normative developments in the past decades have encountered opposition in some cases. It should be recalled, however, that this was not a uniform development. The idea of civilian protection has been used in a number of other situations, particularly in cases on the African continent. It has been with the explicit support of governments. As is the case with gender equality, these are two constructive notions that meet resistance only under particular circumstances. It largely happens when the new norms affect traditional distributions of power. From a conflict resolution perspective, such resistance has to be overcome if a high quality peace is to emerge.

12.5 Towards Fragmentation or Concentration?

There are two forms of fragmentation that affects conflict resolution. The first is the increasing number of recognized states and the other is the rising number of non-state actors in armed conflicts.

With respect to state separation, there are presently 193 states with seats in the United Nations, and a dozen state entities that aspire to get universal recognition. Some of them may eventually become members of the UN, although it requires the consent of the permanent members of the Security Council. Two states with most recognition but still without UN seats are Palestine and Kosovo. In both these cases there are objections from one or several permanent members. As these two cases illustrate, there is often a connection between fragmentation and conflict. Many, but not all, states emerge from armed conflicts. It is important to recall that there are highly peaceful state separations, using agreed procedures, as exemplified with the 1993 division of Czechoslovakia. Most of today's newer states have emerged from colonial empires without war. Still, the creation of new states affects the issue of conflict resolution, not only in the way we discussed in Chapters 5 and 7 but also for the distribution of power in the world as a whole.

It is possible to suggest a remarkable paradox: the more smaller states, the more powerful the remaining majors. The UN system has more members than ever, but the Security Council is now more powerful than ever. To get something done in the system requires the cooperation of the few big ones. The work of coordinating a number of smaller states may even exhaust their ability to confront the bigger one. Thus, while many small entities may feel more independent when they have their own states, their actual impact on international affairs may be smaller than if they were part of a larger constellation. They may still make this choice, of course, and possibly feel more secure. No UN member state has disappeared through the occupation of another member. That was the message of the Gulf War in 1990 when the UN defended the independence of the UN member state Kuwait. But the messages have been more mixed since then, as neither Kosovo nor Ukraine had the support of the UN in their time of crisis. Instead the EU and NATO acted.

Clearly, the trend since the end of the Second World War has been towards increasing state fragmentation. There is little to suggest a reverse trend. It is more likely that the world will see ten more states in the coming decade than ten fewer. In fact, global democratization may further the process, as state separation may be achieved through referenda and organized dissolution. The list not only includes Scotland and Catalonia, but also Bougainville and Greenland, all operating in a democratic framework. The contribution of conflict resolution is to find peaceful ways in which questioned state structures can be dissolved while maintaining close and constructive cross-border connections.

The second problem of fragmentation has to do with the proliferation of non-state actors or rebel groups. During the Cold War, the parties in civil war were often brought together in various fronts. This was done from the point of view of the funders (mostly the West or the Soviet Union, in some cases China or Middle Eastern countries). They preferred it that way. It, so to say, replicated the Cold War polarization. Also, many of the rebel leaders may have seen the utility of coordination against the central government. Fragmented opposition movements may yield less influence against a determined and centralized government. This also meant that peace agreements could be worked out and be sustained (Nicaragua, Mozambique, El Salvador, Guatemala, all testify to this).

After the Cold War, however, the emergence of a multitude of actors has constituted a major problem for conflict termination and conflict resolution. The number of groups involved in the various peace processes in the Democratic Republic of

Congo could be counted to 40 or 50, the Darfur negotiations at times threatened to involve some 20 armed parties. The number of actors in the Syrian civil war is difficult to estimate. Some have very local agendas; others have national or international ambitions. Thus, actual warring parties may be in three digits. This is a remarkable change during the past twenty-five years. Its sources can be debated. The availability of small arms and smuggling networks; a proliferation of funders who preferred to support 'their' ideological, religious or ethnic brethrens; mobilization of recruits and supporters along identity lines; neighbours with their own agendas; and major powers with specific preferences; these may all be factors contributing to this fragmentation.

It is a challenge to peace processes as it will be more significant to determine, for instance: (a) if some actors are more powerful than others, and thus constitute the 'real' parties; (b) if negotiations should only concentrate on such actors or be fully inclusive; (c) on a reasonable balance between such armed actors and a civil society that may have more appeal to the general public, but does not have access to weaponry. There is also an ethical issue: should the peace process reward those groups that equip themselves with weapons, no matter what their support is in the community or what values they espouse? These are questions that affect all the stages of conflict resolution from the inception of negotiations to the final implementation of what has been agreed. Thus, the challenge of non-state actors as well as to the increasing number of states requires considerable thinking.

12.6 A Choice between Kleptocracy and Theocracy?

Throughout this book there have been references to corruption as a gigantic problem that is difficult to pin down. There is little data to use and there are few studies linking the issue of corruption to the onset, pursuit and ending of armed conflicts. There are anecdotes, no doubt, as well as case studies of particular states or political figures that have been brought to trial. There is considerable attention to this when describing the demise of states (e.g., the fall of Rome; Macmullan 1988) as well as the importance of this for trust, or lack thereof, in contemporary societies (Rothstein and Uslander 2005; Rothstein 2011). The Quality of Government Institute at Göteborg University in Sweden is a leading research milieu. The topic has drawn fewer studies with regard to armed conflict. Those that exist do not necessarily find close correlations, at least when oil wealth is introduced and can be used as a way of preventing conflict (Fjelde 2011). Building on this, Hegre and Nygård (2014) demonstrate that 'good informal governance' may be more optimal in reducing armed conflict in the long run, meaning democracy and economic growth, together with informal processes of governance.

The issue of governance is one important aspect of corruption: it will exclude some from power, possibly buy-off others, and thus a corrupt society can sustain itself for considerable periods of time. It may be a way of postponing conflict. It is definitely not a way of solving it. It is also clear, judging from history, that corruption constitutes a strong argument for revolution. In the most recent experiences of popular revolts, such as those associated with the Arab Spring and the changes in Ukraine, accusations of corruption figured prominently. Public displays of the former leaders' extravagances served to legitimize the revolts (examples are the pictures of the palaces of the departed leaders in Tunisia, where the Arab Spring originated in 2011, and in Ukraine in 2014).

Corruption is also a matter of moral decay, and thus feeds into the appeal of morally righteous movements. This has been a feature in the upheavals of the Middle East, going back to the Iranian Revolution of 1979. Turning to religion was, by many, seen as a return to traditional values of right and wrong, virtue and decency. This may have been part of the reasons for the rise of the Muslim Brotherhood in Egypt, when elections were called in 2011. Many of the warring parties in Syria and Iraq have also appealed to such values. In reality, however, there is little to show that the resulting regimes of theocracy would, in the long run, be less corrupt than others. Iran encountered repeated counter-movements on this score, most strongly in 2009 when protests were violently suppressed, but could also be seen reflected in the outcome of the elections in 2013. The solution to corruption may thus not rest in religion as such but in the creation of a 'new game' where there is a credible expectation and actual experience of non-corrupt behaviour from the top down. Singapore has been cited as an example (Persson et al. 2013). Thus, anti-corruption measures in peace agreements or in peacebuilding following a war are likely to work only if coupled with significant changes in policies and composition. Peace agreements that include, for instance, power-sharing, may, from this perspective, be too conservative. This is a further challenge to conflict resolution practise.

12.7 Traditional Politics or Planetary Contract?

These reflections are but a few that can be made, when considering the challenges of the 2010s. They build on the upheavals following from the seemingly promising developments with the early Arab Spring. There was an expectation that the international withdrawal from the war scenes of Afghanistan and Iraq, the winding down of the threats from al-Qaida, and the hope for economic recovery would also result in renewed chances for conflict resolution and peacebuilding. Other challenges that seemed to be more important, notably those of climate change and global inequalities, could then step forward and be faced with more determination. These issues are still on the agenda, but large-scale wars in volatile regions and in neighbourhoods of major powers always take precedence. This is what has been seen in the past few years and is likely to be the agenda for coming years.

For the media, citizens and decision-makers, it appears as 'conflict overload'. There are many issues that demand equally much attention at the same time. In the perspective of conflict resolution that includes not only the Middle East or Russia's neighbours but also persistent conflicts in Africa, migration across North–South divides in Europe, North America, Australia or Asia. It seemed difficult to develop shared understandings of these matters, and thus also to develop common policies or even common priorities. And in the meantime, there were also reactions, for instance, within Europe or the USA of nationalist and reductionist policies that emphasized simple solutions, often focusing on immigrant groups. From a global perspective it was as if too few political leaders had to deal with too many and seemingly unrelated concerns at the same time. Thus, traditional political responses again came forth, associated with terms such as *Geopolitik* and *Realpolitik*. However, the world is no longer the same.

The peace agreements since 1989 illustrate that there is a profound new world order. It was not constructed deliberately after a major war, as has often been the case throughout history (Holsti 1991; Kegley and Raymond 1999). Instead, it has grown out of the unprecedented ending of a major power confrontation, the Cold War. It is an arrangement that developed in a piecemeal and pragmatic way. The peace agreements are one indication of this, the efforts at direct conflict prevention another, and ambitions at structural change for conflict prevention a third. In a remarkable way, it could be seen as a planetary dialogue where actors involved in the peace processes also participated in shaping an order, through the practical application of the many principles associated with the international community. Also in this sense it has been a universalist experience, not a creation by one particular state.

Through the 25 years since the end of the Cold War it has become apparent that the United States is not the only power or even the 'omni-power' that can direct all other actors in the global system. International action is modified by other states, be they the permanent members of the Security Council, members of the EU or important regional actors. An increasingly powerful China is gaining a greater say. Even local actors with limited resources have an impact on US policy. It is still true that no outside actor can force an international agenda on the United States. But, remarkable as it may be, the US is still not able to set the global agenda to its liking. The Obama administration wanted to give priority to Asia in general, and East Asia in particular. This had to do both with economic and political developments. As a long-term strategy this seems reasonable, but continuous upheavals in other parts of the world almost mechanically pulled the US back to an agenda of acute crisis management. Brutality against locals and Westerners was transmitted instantly through media and demanded reaction. Collapsing states and local power considerations made it imperative for the US to remain engaged where it may have wanted not to be and where it may not be able to prevail.

The traditional politics of the Cold War would have made it possible for the two superpowers to connect and work out deals. That was the essence of the periods of détente, but they were arrived at through the frightening experience of confrontation in other periods. The post-Cold War setting does not work in the same way. First of all, the relations between the leading nuclear powers were, by 2014, one of constrained rivalry. Russia's actions in Ukraine made it less of a partner and more of a competitor or even adversary. That was the case of its support for the Assad regime in Syria. The cooperation in the Group of 8, the G8, that Russia long had expired to be part of, was unilaterally terminated by the West, returning to the previous Western-dominated format of the G7. It was a type of action that confirmed Russia's suspicion that it would not become an equal party to the West. In effect, Russia's world perspective was increasingly one of regional *Geopolitik* and emphasis on Russia's interest and being critical to EU and US policies of humanitarian concern, human rights and global counter-terrorism. And even that was subject to domestic constraints, with an increasing inward orientation of the Western public.

Tea Party movements, nationalist parties, regional separatism and immigration issues seemed increasingly to determine the Western perspective also on international issues. Thus, there were strong elements of particularism that ultimately also would reduce interest in cumbersome processes of conflict resolution.

Predictions are notoriously difficult, and many events since the end of the Cold War point in unexpected directions. Initially, there were more conflicts in Europe than anticipated and also new forms of involvement by the North in the South. Global terrorism was not predicted. The Arab Spring was a hopeful change that turned into a regional nightmare. Although this book is based on an analysis of close to 150 armed conflicts in the past decades, it cannot suggest which conflicts will dominate the concerns a decade from now. Surprises are part of the picture. For bad, sometimes also for good. But conflicts also invite discussion. The local issues are affected by the global developments. It also works the other way around. Seemingly local actors can still draw in major powers. Finding solutions involves an unstructured conversation from which may eventually emerge a planetary understanding of how conflicts should be regulated and on what principles it should be based.

The peace agreements that have provided material for this book give insights into strategies for solving conflicts and preventing violence tomorrow and in the future. Some simple concepts, such as those introduced here, may be helpful in making important distinctions. They are meant to guide analysis and suggest policy. They will need continuous processing. Their use in the real world will provide feedback. The conditions of the new world will affect their uses and consequences. No analysis of the chances for peace is made without an interaction between analysis and reality. In that interaction, both the analysis and the reality may change. This is relevant in whatever conditions the world finds itself. The task is the same: to move the world towards less conflict, less suffering and more human cooperation, democracy and justice. The beauty of the planet deserves just that.

Further Readings

Go to the *Understanding Conflict Resolution* web page at https://study.sagepub.com/wallensteen4e for free access to journal articles listed.

Not many researchers attempt to do predictions for the future, with respect to the field of peace and security. A remarkable attempt, however, is one which projects the amount of civil armed conflicts for the coming forty years. It thus constitutes an interesting point of departure for an empirically based discussion:

Hegre, H., Karlsen, J., Nygård, H.M., Strand, H. and Urdal, H. 2013. 'Predicting Armed Conflict, 2011–2050,' *International Studies Quarterly*, 57 (2): 250–270.

(Continued)

(Continued)

It contrasts more traditional Realpolitik thinking about the future, as evidenced in a recent best-seller:
Kissinger, H. 2014. *World Order*, Penguin Press.

New conceptual contributions are rare, particularly from political actors. Thus, a small article by UN Secretary-General Kofi Annan deserves attention:
Annan, K.A. 1999. 'Two Concepts of Sovereignty', *The Economist*, September 18, pp. 49–50.

Many of these ideas were refined in reports that followed, one of which had a direct impact on reforming the UN. It has already been referred to but still deserves mention here as well, as it brought the issue of Responsibility to Protect firmly to the policy level:
High-Level Panel 2004. *A More Secure World: Our Shared Responsibility*. Report of the Secretary-General's High-Level Panel on Threats, Challenges and Change. New York and Geneva: United Nations.

REFERENCES

Adetula, Victor 2015. 'African Conflicts, Development and Regional Organizations in the Post-Cold War International System', *Current African Affairs*, Uppsala, Sweden: Nordic Africa Institute (forthcoming).

Adler, Emanuel and Michael Barnett (eds) 1998. *Security Communities*. Cambridge: Cambridge University Press.

Alao, Abiodun, John Mackinlay and Funmi Olonisakin 1999. *Peacekeepers, Politicians and Warlords: The Liberian Peace Process*. Tokyo: UN University Press.

Amer, Ramses, Johan Saravanamuttu and Peter Wallensteen 1996. *The Cambodian Conflict 1979–1991: From Intervention to Resolution*. Penang and Uppsala: Department of Peace and Conflict Research, Uppsala University.

Anderson, B. 1991. *Imagined Communities: Reflections on the Origin and Spread of Nationalism*. London: Verso.

Annan, K.A. 1999. 'Two Concepts of Sovereignty', *The Economist*, September 18, pp. 49–50.

Annan, Kofi and Nader Mousavizadeh 2012. *Interventions: A Life in War and Peace*. New York and London: Penguin Books.

Arnson, Cynthia J. (ed.) 1999. *Comparative Peace Processes in Latin America*. Washington, DC: Woodrow Wilson Center Press, and Stanford, CA: Stanford University Press.

Axelrod, Robert 1984. *The Evolution of Cooperation*. New York: Basic Books.

Axworthy, L. 2001. 'Human Security and Global Governance: Putting People First', *Global Governance*, 7 (1): 19–23.

Azar, Edward E. and John W. Burton (eds) 1986. *International Conflict Resolution: Theory and Practice*. Boulder, CO: Lynne Rienner.

Backer, David, Paul Huth and Jonathan Wilkenfeld 2014. *Peace and Conflict 2014*. Herndon, VA: Paradigm Publishers.

Bednar, Jenna 2009. *The Robust Federation: Principles of Design*. Cambridge, MA: Cambridge University Press.

Bell, Christine 2008. *On the Law of Peace: Peace Agreements and* Lex Pacificatoria. Oxford: Oxford University Press.

Bell-Fialkoff, Andrew 1996. *Ethnic Cleansing*. New York: St Martin's Press.

Bercovitch, Jacob (ed.) 1996. *Resolving International Conflicts: The Theory and Practice of Mediation*. Boulder, CO: Lynne Rienner.

REFERENCES

Berdal, M. and D.M. Malone 2000. *Greed and Grievance: Economic Agendas in Civil Wars*. Boulder, CO: Lynne Rienner.

Bilder, Richard B. 1997. 'Adjudication: International Arbitral Tribunals and Courts', in I. William Zartman and J. Lewis Rasmussen (eds), *Peacemaking in International Conflict: Methods and Techniques*. Washington, DC: United States Institute of Peace Press. pp. 155–89.

Blake, Gerald 1999. 'Is the Time Ripe for a Voluntary Register of Boundary Status with the United Nations?', in Julie Dahlitz (ed.), *Peaceful Resolution of Major International Disputes*. New York and Geneva: United Nations. pp. 145–67.

Bowden, Mark 1999. *Black Hawk Down: A Story of Modern War*. New York: Simon & Schuster.

Brecher, Michael 1993, 2010. *Crises in World Politics: Theory and Reality*. New York: Pergamon Press.

Broome, Benjamin J. 1997. 'Designing a Collective Approach to Peace: Interactive Design and Problem-Solving Workshops with Greek-Cypriot and Turkish-Cypriot Communities in Cyprus', *International Negotiation*, 2: 381–407.

Brounéus, Karen 2003. *Reconciliation: Theory and Practice for Development Cooperation*. A report for the Swedish International Development Cooperation Agency, Stockholm.

Brounéus, Karen 2008. *Rethinking Reconciliation: Concepts, Methods and an Empirical Study*. Uppsala: Department of Peace and Conflict Research, Uppsala University.

Burton, John W. 1987. *Resolving Deep-Rooted Conflict: A Handbook*. Lanham, MD: University Press of America.

Burton, John. W. 1990. *Conflict: Resolution and Provention*. London: Macmillan.

Burton, John W. 1996. *Conflict Resolution: Its Language and Processes*. Lanham, MD, and London: Scarecrow Press.

Buzan, Barry 1991. *People, States and Fear* (2nd edn). Boulder, CO: Lynne Rienner.

Buzan, Barry and Ole Waever 2003. *Regions and Powers: The Structure of International Society*. Cambridge: Cambridge University Press.

Cahill, Kevin M. (ed.) 1996. *Preventive Diplomacy: Stopping Wars before They Start*. New York: Basic Books.

Cameron, Iain 2005. 'Protecting Legal Rights: On the (In)security of Targeted Sanctions', in Peter Wallensteen and Carina Staibano (eds), *International Sanctions: Between Words and Wars in the Global System*. London: Routledge/Frank Cass. pp. 181–206.

Cañas, Antonio and Héctor Dada 1999. 'Political Transition and Institutionalization in El Salvador', in Cynthia J. Arnson (ed.), *Comparative Peace Processes in Latin America*. Washington, DC: Woodrow Wilson Center Press, and Stanford, CA: Stanford University Press. pp. 69–95.

Caprioli, M. 2005. 'Primed for Violence: The Role of Gender Inequality in Predicting Internal War', *International Studies Quarterly*, 49: 161–78.

Carment, David 1993. 'The International Dimensions of Ethnic Conflict: Concepts, Indicators and Theory', *Journal of Peace Research*, 30: 137–50.

Carnegie Commission on Preventing Deadly Conflict 1997. *Preventing Deadly Conflict: Final Report*. Washington, DC: Carnegie Commission on Preventing Deadly Conflict.

REFERENCES

Carter, Jimmy 1992. *Keeping Faith: Memoirs of a President.* New York: Bantam Books.

Case, William 2001. 'Malaysia's Resilient Pseudodemocracy', *Journal of Democracy*, 12 (1): 43–57.

Chan, Steven and Moisés Venancio, with Chris Alden and Sam Barnes 1998. *War and Peace in Mozambique.* London: Macmillan.

Cloos, Jim 2005. 'Conflict Prevention as an Instrument in the EU's Security Box', in Anders Mellbourn (ed.), *Development, Security and Conflict Prevention.* Brussels: Madariaga Foundation, Bank of Sweden Tercentenary Foundation and Gidlunds. pp. 14–23.

Cohen, Saul B. 1999. 'The Geopolitics of an Evolving World System: From Conflict to Accommodation', in Paul F. Diehl (ed.), *A Road Map to War: Territorial Dimensions of International Conflict.* Nashville, TN, and London: Vanderbilt University Press. pp. 271–98.

Collier, Paul and Anke Hoeffler 2000. *Greed and Grievance in Civil War.* Washington, DC: World Bank. Mimeo.

Collier, Paul, V.L. Elliott, Håvard Hegre, Anke Hoeffler, Marta Reynal-Querol and Nicholas Sambanis 2003. *Breaking the Conflict Trap: Civil War and Development Policy.* Washington, DC: World Bank.

Corell, Hans 1999. 'The Feasibility of Implementing The Hague/St. Petersburg Centennial Recommendations under the UN System', in Julie Dahlitz (ed.), *Peaceful Resolution of Major International Disputes.* New York and Geneva: United Nations. pp. 31–48.

Cornell, S.E. 2002. 'Autonomy as a Source of Conflict: Caucasian Conflicts in Theoretical Perspective', *World Politics*, 54 (2): 245–76.

Cortright, David and George Lopez 2000. *The Sanctions Decade: Assessing UN Strategies in the 1990s.* Boulder, CO: International Peace Academy and Lynne Rienner.

Coser, Lewis A. 1956. *The Functions of Social Conflict.* New York: Free Press.

Coser, Lewis A. 1967. *Continuities in the Study of Social Conflict.* New York: Free Press.

Croicu, Mihai, Erik Melander, Marcus Nilsson and Peter Wallensteen 2013. Mediation and Violence: Searching for Third-Party Intervention that Matters. Paper for the 48th Annual Convention of the International Studies Association, San Francisco, CA, April 2013. Download: http://www.pcr.uu.se/digitalAssets/279/279399_1mediation-and-violence.pdf

Daalder, I.H. and M.B.G. Froman 1999. 'Dayton's Incomplete Peace', *Foreign Affairs*, 78 (6): 106–13.

Davies, James C. (ed.) 1971. *When Men Rebel and Why.* New York: Free Press.

Deeb, Mary Jane and Marius Deeb 1995. 'Internal Negotiations in a Centralist Conflict: Lebanon', in I. William Zartman (ed.), *Elusive Peace: Negotiating an End to Civil Wars.* Washington, DC: Brookings Institution. pp. 125–46.

Desch, Michael C. 1999. *Civilian Control of the Military: The Changing Security Environment.* Baltimore, MD, and London: Johns Hopkins University Press.

Deutsch, Karl W., Sidney A. Burrell, Robert A. Kann and Maurice Lee, Jr. 1957. *Political Community and the North Atlantic Area.* Princeton, NJ: Princeton University Press.

Diamond, L.J. 2005. 'Lessons from Iraq', *Journal of Democracy*, 16 (1): 9–23.

REFERENCES

Diehl, Paul 1983. 'Arms Races and Escalation: A Closer Look', *Journal of Peace Research*, 20 (3): 205–12.

Diehl, Paul F. 1993. *International Peacekeeping*. Baltimore, MD, and London: Johns Hopkins University Press.

Diehl, Paul F. (ed.) 1999. *A Road Map to War: Territorial Dimensions of International Conflict*. Nashville, TN, and London: Vanderbilt University Press.

Dixon, Jeffrey 2009. 'What Causes Civil Wars? Integrating Quantitative Research Findings', *International Studies Review*, 11 (4): 707–35.

Dollard, J., L.W. Doob, N.E. Miller, O.H. Mowrer and R.R. Sears 1939. *Frustration and Aggression*. New Haven, CT: Yale University Press.

Doob, Leonard W. (ed.) 1970. *Resolving Conflict in Africa: The Fermeda Workshop*. New Haven, CT: Yale University Press.

Doxey, Margaret P. 1996. *International Sanctions in Contemporary Perspective* (2nd edn). London: Macmillan, and New York: St Martin's Press.

Duchacek, Ivo D. 1977. 'Antagonistic Cooperation: Territorial and Ethnic Communities', *Publius*, 7: 145–60.

Duffield, Mark 1998. 'Post-Modern Conflict: Warlords, Post-Adjustment States and Private Protection', *Civil Wars*, 1: 65–102.

Eck, Kristine 2005. *A Beginner's Guide to Conflict Data: Finding and Using the Right Dataset*. UCDP Papers No. 1, Uppsala: Uppsala Conflict Data Program. Download: www.ucdp.uu.se.

Einaudi, Luigi R. 1999. 'The Ecuador–Peru Peace Process', in Chester A. Crocker, Fen Osler Hampson and Pamela Aall (eds), *Herding Cats: Multiparty Mediation in a Complex World*. Washington, DC: United States Institute of Peace Press. pp. 407–29.

Einsiedel, Sebastian, David M. Malone and B. Stagno Ugarte 2015. *The Security Council during the 21st Century*. Boulder, CO: Lynne Rienner.

Ekstrand, Eric Einar 1944. *Jorden runt på trettio år* (*Around the World in Thirty Years*). Stockholm: Norstedts.

Eriksson, Mikael 2007. *Targeting the Leadership of Zimbabwe: A Path to Democracy and Normalization?* Uppsala: Department of Peace and Conflict Research, Uppsala University.

Eriksson, Mikael 2010a. *Supporting Democracy in Africa: African Union's Use of Targeted Sanctions to Deal with Unconstitutional Changes of Government*. Stockholm: FOI (Swedish Defence Research Agency).

Eriksson, Mikael 2010b. *Targeting Peace: Understanding UN and EU Targeted Sanctions*. Farnham: Ashgate.

Etzioni, Amitai 1967. 'The Kennedy Experiment', *Western Political Quarterly*, 20: 361–80.

Fahlén, Marika 2015. 'The Africa Union Mission in Somalia: Towards a New Vision of Peacekeeping?', in Peter Wallensteen and Anders Bjurner, *Regional Organizations and Peacemaking: Challengers to the UN?* London: Routledge. pp. 179–93.

Fearon, James D. and David D. Laitin 2003. 'Ethnicity, Insurgency, and Civil War', *American Political Science Review*, 97 (1): 75–90.

Fisher, Roger and William Ury 1981. *Getting to Yes*. Boston, MA: Houghton Mifflin.

Fisher, Ronald J. 1983. 'Third Party Consultation as a Method of Intergroup Conflict Resolution: A Review of Studies', *Journal of Conflict Resolution*, 27 (2): 301–34.

Fisher, Ronald J. 1997. *Interactive Conflict Resolution*. Syracuse, NY: Syracuse University Press.

Fjelde, Hanne 2009. 'Buying Peace? Oil Wealth, Corruption and Civil War, 1985–99', *Journal of Peace Research*, 49 (2): 199–218.

Forsberg, Erika, A. Duursma and L. Grant 2012. *Theoretical and Empirical Considerations in the Study of Ethnicity and Conflict*. Uppsala: Uppsala University, UCDP Paper No. 8. Download: www.pcr.uu.se/digitalAssets/66/66310_1paper8.pdf

Fox, Mary-Jane 1999. 'Somalia Divided: The African Cerberus (Considerations of Political Culture)', *Civil War*, 2: 1–34.

Frances, David J. 2013. *The Regional Impact of the Armed Conflict and French Intervention in Mali*. Norwegian Resource Center for Peacebuilding. Download: www.peacebuilding. no/var/ezflow_site/storage/original/application/f18726c3338e39049bd 4d554d4a22c36.pdf

Fruchart, Damien, Paul Holtom, Siemon T. Wezeman, Daniel Strandow and Peter Wallensteen 2007. *United Nations Arms Embargoes: Their Impact on Arms Flows and Target Behaviour*. Uppsala: Stockholm International Peace Research Institute (SIPRI) and Special Program on International Targeted Sanctions (SPITS) Department of Peace and Conflict Research, Uppsala University. 58 pp.

Fry, Douglas P. and Kaj Björkqvist 1997. *Cultural Variation in Conflict Resolution: Alternatives to Violence*. Mahwah, NJ: Lawrence Erlbaum.

Galtung, Johan 1965. 'Institutionalized Conflict Resolution', *Journal of Peace Research*, 2 (4): 348–97.

Galtung, Johan 1969a. 'Conflict as a Way of Life', in J. Galtung, *Essays in Peace Research* (Vol. 3). Copenhagen: Ejler. pp. 484–507.

Galtung, J. 1969b. 'Violence, Peace and Peace Research', *Journal of Peace Research*, 6 (3): 167–91.

Galtung, Johan 1996. *Peace by Peaceful Means: Peace and Conflict, Development and Civilization*. London: Sage.

Gantzel, Klaus Jürgen and Jörg Meyer-Stamer (eds) 1986. *Die Kriege nach dem Zweiten Weltkrieg bis 1984: Daten und Analysen* (*The Wars since the Second World War to 1984: Data and Analysis*). Munich: Weltforum Verlag.

Gantzel, Klaus Jürgen and Torsten Schwinghammer 2000. *Warfare Since the Second World War*. New Brunswick, NJ, and London: Transaction Publishers.

Geller, Daniel S. and J. David Singer 1998. *Nations at War: A Scientific Study of International Conflict*. Cambridge: Cambridge University Press.

Gibler, Douglas M. 2012. *The Territorial Peace: Borders, State Development and International Conflict*. Cambridge, MA: Cambridge University Press.

Gilpin, Robert 2001. *Global Political Economy*. Princeton, NJ: Princeton University Press.

Giumelli, Francesco 2011. *Coercing, Constraining and Signalling: Explaining UN and EU Sanctions after the Cold War*. Colchester: ECPR (European Consortium for Political Research) Press, University of Essex.

Giumelli, Francesco 2013. *The Success of Sanctions: Lessons Learned from the EU Experience*. Farnham, UK: Ashgate.

Glaser, Charles L. 1997. 'Why NATO is Still Best: Future Security Arrangements for Europe', in Paul F. Diehl (ed.), *The Politics of Global Governance: International Organizations in an Interdependent World*. Boulder, CO: Lynne Rienner. pp. 121–58.

REFERENCES

Gleditsch, N.P., S. Pinker, B.A. Thayer, J.S. Levy and W.R. Thompson 2013. 'The Forum: The Decline of War', *International Studies Review*, 15: 396–419.

Gleichmann, Colin, Michael Odenwald, Kees Steenken and Adrian Wilkinson 2004. *Disarmament, Demobilisation and Reintegration*. Stockholm: Swedish National Defence College.

Goldstein, Erik 1992. *Wars and Peace Treaties*. London: Routledge.

Greig, Michael J. and Patrick M. Regan 2008. 'When Do They Say Yes? An Analysis of the Willingness to Offer and Accept Mediation in Civil Wars', *International Studies Quarterly*, 52: 759–81.

Gurr, Ted R. 1970. *Why Men Rebel*. Princeton, NJ: Princeton University Press.

Gurr, Ted R. 1993. *Minorities at Risk*. Washington, DC: United States Institute of Peace Press.

Gurr, Ted R. 2000a. *Peoples Versus States: Minorities at Risk in the New Century*. Washington, DC: United States Institute of Peace Press.

Gurr, Ted. R. 2000b. 'Ethnic Warfare on the Wane', *Foreign Affairs*, 79 (3): 52–64.

Hampson, Fen Osler 1996. *Nurturing Peace: Why Peace Settlements Succeed or Fail*. Washington, DC: United States Institute of Peace Press.

Harbom, Lotta and Peter Wallensteen, 2005. 'Armed Conflict and Its International Dimensions, 1946–2004', *Journal of Peace Research*, 42 (5): 623–35.

Harbom, L., Högbladh, S. and Wallensteen, P. 2006. 'Armed Conflict and Peace Agreements', *Journal of Peace Research*, 43 (5): 617–31.

Hauge, Wenche and Tanja Ellingsen 1998. 'Beyond Environmental Scarcity: Causal Pathways to Conflict', *Journal of Peace Research*, 35 (3): 299–317.

Hayner, Priscilla B. 2011. *Unspeakable Truths: Transitional Justice and Truth Commissions* (2nd edn). New York: Routledge.

Hegre, Håvard and Håvard Mokleiv Nygård 2014. 'Governance and Conflict Relapse', *Journal of Conflict Resolution*. February 28. Online version.

Hegre, Håvard, Joakim Karlsen, Håvard Mokleiv Nygård, Håvard Strand and Henrik Urdal 2013. 'Predicting Armed Conflict, 2011–2050', *International Studies Quarterly*, 57 (2): 250–70.

Heldt, Birger 1996. *Public Dissatisfaction and the Conflict Behavior of States: A Theory Reconstruction with an Empirical Application*. Uppsala: Department of Peace and Conflict Research, Uppsala University.

Heldt, Birger and Peter Wallensteen 2006. *Peacekeeping Operations: Global Patterns of Intervention and Success, 1948–2004* (2nd edn). Stockholm: Folke Bernadotte Academy.

Hellquist, Elin 2014. *Regional Organizations and Sanctions against Members: Explaining the Different Trajectories of the African Union, the League of Arab States and the Association of Southeast Asian Nations*, KFG Working Paper Series, No. 59, January, Kolleg-Forschergruppe (KFG) 'The Transformative Power of Europe'. Berlin: Freie Universität Berlin.

Henderson, John and Greg Watson (eds) 2005. *Securing a Peaceful Pacific*. Christchurch: Canterbury University Press.

Herz, John H. 1950. 'Idealist Internationalism and the Security Dilemma', *World Politics*, 2: 157–80.

High-Level Panel 2004. *A More Secure World: Our Shared Responsibility*. Report of the Secretary-General's High-Level Panel on Threats, Challenges and Change. New York and Geneva: United Nations.

REFERENCES

Högbladh, Stina 2006. 'Finding a Peace that Will Last – Examining Peace Processes and Peace Agreements', Paper Presented at the Annual ISA Convention, San Diego, CA, March.

Höglund, Kristine, 2008. *Peace Negotiations in the Shadow of Violence*. Leiden: Martinus Nijhoff.

Höglund, K. and M. Söderberg Kovacs 2010. 'Beyond the Absence of War: The Diversity of Peace in Post-Settlement Societies', *Review of International Studies*, 36 (2): 367–90.

Höglund, Kristine and Magnus Öberg (eds) 2011. *Understanding Peace Research*. London: Routledge.

Holbrooke, Richard 1999. *To End a War*. New York: Modern Library.

Holsti, Kalevi J. 1991. *Peace and War: Armed Conflicts and International Order, 1648–1989*. Cambridge: Cambridge University Press.

Human Security Report 2005: War and Peace in the 21st Century. New York: Human Security Centre, University of British Columbia Press and Oxford University Press.

Humphreys, Macartan and Jeremy Weinstein 2005. 'Disentangling the Determinants of Successful Demobilization and Reintegration', Paper Presented at the 101st Meeting of the American Political Science Association, Washington, DC, August 31–September 3.

Huntington, Samuel P. 1996. *The Clash of Civilizations and the Remaking of World Order*. New York: Simon & Schuster.

Huntley, James Robert 1998. *Pax Democratica: A Strategy for the 21st Century*. New York: St Martin's Press.

Independent Inquiry into the Actions of the United Nations during the 1994 Genocide in Rwanda, chaired by Ingvar Carlsson, United Nations, December 1999.

International Center for Transitional Justice 2005. *Annual Report 2003–04*. Available at: www.ictj.org.

Jarstad, Anna 2001. *Changing the Game: Consociational Theory and Ethnic Quotas in Cyprus and New Zealand*. Uppsala: Department of Peace and Conflict Research, Uppsala University.

Johansson, P. 2009. 'The Humdrum Use of Ultimate Authority: Defining and Analysing Chapter VII Resolutions', *Nordic Journal of International Law*, 78 (3): 309–42.

Johansson, Emma, Joakim Kreutz, Peter Wallensteen, Christian Altpeter, Sara Lindberg, Mathilda Lindgren and Ausra Padskocimaite 2010. *A New Start for EU Peacemaking? Past Record and Future Potential*. Uppsala Conflict Data Program, Report No. 7. Uppsala University.

Johnson, James Turner 1999. *Morality and Contemporary Warfare*. New Haven, CT: Yale University Press.

Joshi, Madhav 2013. 'Inclusive Institutions and Stability of Transition toward Democracy in Post-Civil War States', *Democratization*, 20 (4): 743–70.

Joshi, Madhav and John Darby 2013. 'Introducing the Peace Accords Matrix (PAM): A Database of Comprehensive Peace Agreements and Their Implementation, 1989–2007', *Peacebuilding*, 1 (2): 256–74.

Journal of Peace Research 1964. 'An Editorial', *Journal of Peace Research*, 1 (1): 1–4.

Jung, Dietrich, Klaus Schlichte and Jens Siegelberg 1996. 'Ongoing Wars and Their Explanation', in Luc van de Goor, Kumar Rupesinghe and Paul Sciarone (eds),

REFERENCES

Between Development and Destruction: An Enquiry into the Causes of Conflict in Post-Colonial States. London: Macmillan, and New York: St Martin's Press. pp. 50–63.

Kacowicz, Arie M. 1994. *Peaceful Territorial Change*. Columbia, SC: University of South Carolina Press.

Kaldor, M. 2006. *New and Old Wars* (2nd edn). Cambridge: Polity Press.

Kant, I. 1795. *Perpetual Peace: A Philosophical Sketch*.

Kaufman, Stuart 1996. 'An "International" Theory of Ethnic War', *Review of International Studies*, 22: 149–71.

Kaufmann, Chaim D. 1996. 'Possible and Impossible Solutions to Ethnic Civil Wars', *International Security*, 20 (4): 136–75.

Kegley, Jr., Charles W. and Gregory A. Raymond 1999. *How Nations Make Peace*. New York: St Martin's Press and Worth.

Kelman, Herbert C. 2008. 'Evaluating the Contributions of Interactive Problem Solving to the Resolution of Ethnonational Conflicts', *Peace and Conflict*, 14: 29–60.

Kelman, Herbert C. and S.P. Cohen 1976. 'The Problem-Solving Workshop: A Socialpsychological Contribution to the Resolution of International Conflicts', *Journal of Peace Research*, 13 (2): 79–90.

Kemp, Walter (ed.) 2001. *Quiet Diplomacy in Action: The OSCE High Commissioner on National Minorities*. The Hague: Kluwer.

Kinzer, Stephen 1999. 'Kurds Sense a Shift toward Peace after 15-Year War', *The New York Times*, 27 November.

Kissinger, Henry 2014. *World Order*. New York: Penguin Press.

Kolodziej, Ed 1998. 'The Regionalization of International Security', in Roger E. Kanet (ed.), *Resolving Regional Conflicts*. Urbana, IL: University of Illinois Press. pp. 11–42.

Kotkin, Joel 1992. *Tribes: How Race, Religion and Identity Determine Success in the New Global Economy*. New York: Random House.

Kotliar, Vladimir S. 1999. 'The Elements of a "Model Negotiation" for the Settlement of Major Border Disputes between States', in Julie Dahlitz (ed.), *Peaceful Resolution of Major International Disputes*. New York and Geneva: United Nations. pp. 127–40.

Kreutz, Joakim 2010. 'How and When Armed Conflicts End: Introducing the UCDP Conflict Termination Dataset', *Journal of Peace Research*, 47 (2): 243–50.

Kriesberg, Louis 1992. *International Conflict Resolution*. New Haven, CT: Yale University Press.

Kriesberg, Louis 1997. 'The Development of the Conflict Resolution Field', in I. William Zartman and J. Lewis Rasmussen (eds), *Peacemaking in International Conflict: Methods and Techniques*. Washington, DC: United States Institute of Peace Press. pp. 51–77.

Lacina, Bethany and Nils Petter Gleditsch 2005. 'Monitoring Trends in Global Combat: A New Dataset of Battle Deaths', *European Journal of Population*, 21 (2–3): 145–66.

Lacina, Bethany, Nils Petter Gleditsch and Bruce Russett 2006. 'The Declining Risk of Death in Battle', *International Studies Quarterly*, 50 (3): 673–80.

Lederach, John Paul 1997. *Building Peace: Sustainable Reconciliation in Divided Societies*. Washington, DC: United States Institute of Peace Press.

REFERENCES

LeVine, Mark and Mathias Mossberg (eds) 2014. *One Land, Two States: Israel and Palestine as Parallel States*. Oakland, CA: University of California Press.

Levy, Jack 1983. *War in the Modern Great Power System, 1495–1975*. Lexington, KY: University of Kentucky Press.

Licklider, Roy 1995. 'The Consequences of Negotiated Settlements in Civil Wars, 1945–93', *American Political Science Review*, 89 (3): 681–90.

Lijphart, Arend 1975. *The Politics of Accommodation: Pluralism and Democracy in the Netherlands* (2nd edn). Berkeley, CA: University of California Press.

Lijphart, Arend 1984. *Democracies*. New Haven, CT: Yale University Press.

Luard, Evan 1986. *War in the International Society*. London: IB Tauris.

Lund, Michael S. 1996. *Preventing Violent Conflicts: A Strategy for Preventive Diplomacy*. Washington, DC: United States Institute of Peace Press.

Lyons, Terrence and Ahmed I. Samatar (eds) 1995. *Somalia: State Collapse, Multilateral Intervention and Strategies for Political Reconstruction*. Washington, DC: Brookings Institution.

Machiavelli, N. 1532. *The Prince*.

Macmullan, Ramsay 1988. *Corruption and the Decline of Rome*. New Haven, CT: Yale University Press.

Maksymenko, Serhiy 2005. 'European Neighbourhood Policy and Post-Orange Revolution Ukraine', in Anders Mellbourn (ed.), *Development, Security and Conflict Prevention*. Brussels: Madariaga Foundation, Bank of Sweden Tercentenary Foundation and Gidlunds.

Malone, David and Fen Osler Hampson (eds) 2001. *From Reaction to Conflict Prevention: Opportunities for the UN System*. New York: International Peace Academy.

Mason, T. David and Patrick J. Fett 1996. 'How Civil Wars End: A Rational Choice Approach', *Journal of Conflict Resolution*, 40: 546–68.

Melander, Erik 1999. *Anarchy Within: The Security Dilemma between Ethnic Groups in Emerging Anarchy*. Uppsala: Department of Peace and Conflict Research, Uppsala University.

Melander, Erik 2005. 'Gender Equality and Intrastate Armed Conflict', *International Studies Quarterly*, 49 (4): 695–714.

Melander, Erik 2009a. 'Justice or Peace? A Statistical Study of the Relationship between Amnestied and Durable Peace'. Working Paper, Lund University, Download: http://www4.lu.se/upload/LUPDF/Samhallsvetenskap/Just_and_Durable_Peace/Workingpaper4.pdf

Melander, E. 2009b. 'Selected to Go Where Murderers Lurk? The Preventive Effect of Peacekeeping on Mass Killings of Civilians', *Conflict Management and Peace Sciences*, 26 (4): 389–406.

Melander, Erik, Frida Möller and Magnus Öberg 2009. 'Managing Intrastate Low-Intensity Armed Conflict 1993–2004: A New Dataset', *International Interactions*, 35 (1): 58–85.

Merrills, J.G. 1999. 'International Boundary Disputes in Theory and Practice: Precedents Established', in Julie Dahlitz (ed.), *Peaceful Resolution of Major International Disputes*. New York and Geneva: United Nations. pp. 95–112.

REFERENCES

Mitchell, Christopher R. 1981. *The Structure of International Conflict*. New York: St Martin's Press.

Mitchell, Christopher and Michael Banks 1996. *Handbook of Conflict Resolution: The Analytical Problem-Solving Approach*. London: Pinter.

Mitchell, George J. 1999a. *Making Peace*. New York: Alfred Knopf.

Mitchell, George J. 1999b. 'Rebuilding the Path to Peace in Northern Ireland', *The New York Times*, November 20.

More, T. 1516. *Utopia*.

Morton, Jeffrey S. and Harvey Starr 2001. 'Uncertainty, Change, and War: Power Fluctuations and War in the Modern Elite Power System', *Journal of Peace Research*, 38: 49–66.

Mossberg, Mathias 2010. 'One Land, Two States? Parallel States and an Example of "Out of the Box" Thinking on Israel/Palestine', *Journal of Palestinian Studies,* 39 (2): 40–5.

Newman, Edward and Karl DeRouen, Jr. (eds) 2014. *Routledge Handbook of Civil Wars*. New York and London: Routledge.

Nicholas, H.G. 1971. *The United Nations as a Political Institution* (4th edn). London: Oxford University Press.

Nilsson, Desirée 2008. 'Partial Peace: Rebel Groups Inside and Outside of Civil War Settlements', *Journal of Peace Research,* 45: 479–95.

Nincic, Miroslav 1985. *How Wars Might Spread to Europe*. Stockholm International Peace Research Institute. London: Taylor & Francis.

Nordquist, Kjell-Åke 1992. *Peace after War*. Uppsala: Department of Peace and Conflict Research, Uppsala University.

Nordquist, Kjell-Åke 1998. 'Autonomy as a Conflict-Solving Mechanism – An Overview', in Markku Suksi (ed.), *Autonomy: Applications and Implications*. Amsterdam: Kluwer. pp. 59–77.

Öberg, Magnus, Frida Möller and Peter Wallensteen 2009. 'Early Conflict Prevention in Ethnic Crises, 1990–98: A New Dataset', *Conflict Management and Peace Science*, 26 (1): 67–91.

Ohlson, Thomas 1998. *Power Politics and Peace Policies: Intra-State Conflict Resolution in Southern Africa*. Uppsala: Department of Peace and Conflict Research, Uppsala University.

Ohlson, Thomas (ed.) 2011. *From Intra-State War to Durable Peace: Conflict and Its Resolution in Africa after the Cold War*. Dordrecht: Republic of Letters Publishing.

Olson, Jr., Mancur 1971. 'Rapid Growth as a Destabilizing Force', in James C. Davies (ed.), *When Men Rebel and Why*. New York: Free Press. pp. 215–27.

Olsson, Louise 2009. *Gender Equality and United Nations Peace Operations in Timor-Leste*. Leiden: Brill Publishers.

Osgood, Charles 1962. *An Alternative to War or Surrender*. Urbana, IL: University of Illinois Press.

Owen, David 1995. *Balkan Odyssey*. New York: Harcourt Brace & Co.

Peck, Connie 2004. 'Special Representatives of the Secretary-General,' in David Malone (ed.), *The UN Security Council: From the Cold War to the 21st Century*. Boulder, CO, and London: Lynne Rienner. pp. 325–39.

Pellnäs, Bo 1997. 'UN Preventive Deployment in the Former Yugoslav Republic of Macedonia', in Peter Wallensteen (ed.), *International Intervention: New Norms in the*

Post-Cold War Era? Uppsala: Department of Peace and Conflict Research, Uppsala University. pp. 107–14.

Pérez de Cuéllar, Javier 1997. *Pilgrimage for Peace: A Secretary-General's Memoir.* New York: St Martin's Press.

Persson, Anna, Bo Rothestein and Jan Teorell 2013. 'Why Anticorruption Reforms Fail: Systemic Corruption as a Collective Action Problem', *Governance,* 26 (3): 449–71.

Pettersson, Thérése 2010. 'Non-State Conflict 1989–2008: Global and Regional Patterns', in Thérése Pettersson and Lotta Themnér (eds), *States in Armed Conflict 2009.* Uppsala: Department of Peace and Conflict Research, Uppsala University. pp. 183–285.

Pettersson, Thérése and Lotta Themnér (eds) 2010. *States in Armed Conflict 2009.* Uppsala: Department of Peace and Conflict Research, Uppsala University.

Philpott, Daniel and Gerard F. Powers (eds) 2010. *Strategies of Peace.* Oxford: Oxford University Press,

Pillar, Paul R. 1983. *Negotiating Peace: War Termination as a Bargaining Process.* Princeton, NJ: Princeton University Press.

Pinker, S. 2011. *The Better Angels of Our Nature.* New York: Viking.

Portela, Clara 2010. *European Union Sanctions and Foreign Policy: When and Why Do They Work?* London: Routledge.

Pruitt, Dean G. and Jeffrey Z. Rubin 1986. *Social Conflict: Escalation, Stalemate and Settlement.* New York: Random House.

Prunier, Gérard 1995. *The Rwanda Crisis: History of a Genocide.* New York: Columbia University Press.

Putnam, Robert D. 1993. *Making Democracy Work: Civic Traditions in Modern Italy.* Princeton, NJ: Princeton University Press.

Rapoport, Anatol 1960. *Fights, Games and Debates.* Ann Arbor, MI: University of Michigan Press.

Regan, Patrick M. 2014. 'Bringing Peace Back in: Presidential Address to the Peace Science Society, 2013', *Conflict Management and Peace Science,* 31 (4): 345–56.

Regan, Patrick and Peter Wallensteen 2013. 'Federal Institutions, Declarations of Independence and Civil War', *Civil Wars,* 15 (3): 261–80.

Reno, William 1998. *Warlord Politics and African States.* Boulder, CO: Lynne Rienner.

Rosenau, James N. 1990. *Turbulence in World Politics: A Theory of Change and Continuity.* Princeton, NJ: Princeton University Press.

Rothstein, Bo 2011. *The Quality of Government. Corruption, Social Trust and Inequality in International Perspective.* Chicago, IL: University of Chicago Press.

Rothstein, Bo and Eric M. Uslander, 2005. 'All for All: Equality, Corruption and Social Trust', *World Politics* 58 (1): 41–72.

Rouhana, Nadim A. 1995. 'The Dynamics of Joint Thinking between Adversaries in International Conflict: Phases of the Continuing Problem-solving Workshop', *Political Psychology,* 16 (2): 321–45.

Russett, Bruce M. 1993. *Grasping the Democratic Peace.* Princeton, NJ: Princeton University Press.

Russett, Bruce M. (ed.) 1997. *The Once and Future Security Council.* London: Macmillan.

Russett, Bruce M. and John R. Oneal 2001. *Triangulating Peace: Democracy, Interdependence, and International Organizations.* New York: W.W. Norton.

REFERENCES

Safire, William 1999. 'The Skillful Envoy', *The New York Times*, November 8.

Sarkees, Meridith Reid and Frank Whelon Wayman 2010. *Resort to War 1816–2007*. Washington, DC: CQ Press.

Schaeffer, Robert 1990. *Warpaths: The Politics of Partition*. New York: Hill & Wang.

Schahczenski, Jeffery 1991. 'Explaining Relative Peace: Major Power Order, 1816–1976', *Journal of Peace Research*, 28: 295–309.

Schelling, Thomas 1960. *The Strategy of Conflict*. Cambridge, MA: Harvard University Press.

Schroeder, Paul W. 2006. 'The Life and Death of a Long Peace, 1763–1914', in Raimo Väyrynen (ed.), *The Waning of Major War: Theories and Debates*. London: Routledge. pp. 33–63.

Sharp, Gene 1973. *The Politics of Nonviolent Action*. Boston, MA: Port Sargent.

Shaw, Malcolm N. 1999. 'Peaceful Resolution of "Political Disputes": The Desirable Parameters of ICJ Jurisdiction', in Julie Dahlitz (ed.), *Peaceful Resolution of Major International Disputes*. New York and Geneva: United Nations. pp. 49–75.

Singer, J.D. 1972. 'The Correlates of War Project', *World Politics*, 24: 243–70.

Singer, J. David 1991. 'Peace in the Global System: Displacement, Interregnum or Transformation', in Charles W. Kegely, Jr. (ed.), *The Long Postwar Peace: Contending Explanations and Projections*. New York: Harper Collins. pp. 56–84.

Sisk, Timothy D. 1996. *Power Sharing and International Mediation in Ethnic Conflicts*. Washington, DC: United States Institute of Peace Press.

Small, Melvin and J. David Singer 1982. *Resort to Arms*. Beverly Hills, CA: Sage.

Snow, Donald M. 1996. *Uncivil Wars: International Security and the New Internal Conflicts*. Boulder, CO, and London: Lynne Rienner.

Sollenberg, Margareta and Lars van Dassen 1998. 'The Intervention that Never Was: Crises, Politics, and the Refugees in Eastern Zaire', in Peter Wallensteen (ed.), *Preventing Violent Conflicts: Past Record and Future Challenges*. Uppsala: Department of Peace and Conflict Research Uppsala University. pp. 139–52.

Sorokin, Pitirim A. 1937. *Social and Cultural Dynamics* (Vol. 3). New York: American Book Company.

Southall, Roger, Neo Simuntanyi and John Daniel 2005. 'Former Presidents in African Politics', in Roger Southall and Henning Melber (eds), *Legacies of Power: Leadership Change and Former Presidents in African Politics*. Uppsala: Nordic Africa Institute. pp. 1–25.

Spalding, Rose J. 1999. 'From Low-Intensity War to Low-Intensity Peace: The Nicaraguan Peace Process', in Cynthia J. Arnson (ed.), *Comparative Peace Processes in Latin America*. Washington, DC: Woodrow Wilson Center Press, and Stanford, CA: Stanford University Press. pp. 31–64.

Starr, Harvey and G. Dale Thomas 2005. 'The Nature of Borders and Conflict: Revisiting Hypotheses on Territory and War', *International Studies Quarterly*, 49 (1): 123–39.

Staub, Ervin 1989. *The Roots of Evil: The Origins of Genocide and Other Group Violence*. New York: Cambridge University Press.

Stedman, Stephen John 1991. *Peacemaking in Civil War: International Mediation in Zimbabwe 1974–80*. Boulder, CO: Lynne Rienner.

Stedman, Stephen John 1995. 'Alchemy for a New World Order: Overselling "Preventive Diplomacy"', *Foreign Affairs*, 73 (3): 14–20.

REFERENCES

Stedman, Stephen John 1997. 'Spoiler Problems in Peace Processes', *International Security*, 22 (2): 5–53.

Stedman, Stephen John 1998. 'Conflict Prevention as Strategic Interaction: The Spoiler Problem and the Case of Rwanda', in Peter Wallensteen (ed.), *Preventing Violent Conflicts: Past Record and Future Challenges*. Uppsala: Department of Peace and Conflict Research, Uppsala University. pp. 67–86.

Stedman, Stephen John, Donald Rothchild and Elizabeth M. Cousens (eds) 2002. *Ending Civil Wars: The Implementation of Peace Agreements*. Boulder, CO: Lynne Rienner.

Stockholm International Peace Research Institute (SIPRI), *Yearbook* (selected years). Oxford and Stockholm: Oxford University Press.

Strandow, Daniel 2006. *Sanctions and Civil War: Targeted Measures for Conflict Resolution*. Uppsala: Special Program on International Targeted Sanctions (SPITS), Department of Peace and Conflict Research, Uppsala University.

Su Wei 1999. 'Confidence Building and Efficient Methods for Border Dispute Resolution', in Julie Dahlitz (ed.), *Peaceful Resolution of Major International Disputes*. New York and Geneva: United Nations. pp. 113–25.

Svensson, Isak 2009. 'Who Brings Which Peace? Neutral versus Biased Mediation and Institutional Arrangements in Civil Wars', *Journal of Conflict Resolution*, 53 (3): 446–69.

Svensson, Isak and Peter Wallensteen 2010. *The Go-Between: Jan Eliasson and the Styles of Mediation*. Washington, DC: United States Institute of Peace Press.

Themnér, Anders 2013. 'A Leap of Faith: When and How Ex-Combatants Resort to Violence', *Security Studies*, 22 (2): 295–329.

Themnér, Lotta and Peter Wallensteen 2014. 'Armed Conflicts, 1946–2012', *Journal of Peace Research,* 51 (4): 541–54.

Thibaut, John W. and Harold H. Kelley 1959. *The Social Psychology of Groups*. New York: John Wiley & Sons.

Tickner, A. 1993. *Gender in International Relations*. New York: Columbia University Press.

Tickner, A. 1997. 'You Just Don't Understand: Troubled Engagements between Feminists and IR Theorists', *International Studies Quarterly*, 41 (4): 611–32.

Tillema, Herbert 1989. 'Foreign Overt Military Intervention in the Nuclear Age', *Journal of Peace Research*, 26: 179–95.

Tilly, Charles 1990. *Coercion, Capital and European States AD 990–1990*. Cambridge, MA: Blackwell.

Tyler, Tom R. 2000. 'Social Justice: Outcome and Procedure', *International Journal of Psychology*, 35 (2): 117–25.

Urquhart, Brian 1994. *Hammarskjold*. London and New York: W.W. Norton.

Vasquez, John 1993. *The War Puzzle*. Cambridge and New York: Cambridge University Press.

Vasquez, John 1995. 'Why Do Neighbors Fight? Proximity, Interaction and Territoriality', *Journal of Peace Research*, 32: 277–93.

Vasquez, John A. (ed.) 2012. *What Do We Know about War?* (2nd edn). Lanham, MD: Rowman and Littlefield Publishers.

REFERENCES

Väyrynen, Raimo 2004. 'The Challenge of Preventive Action: The Case of Macedonia', in Anders Mellbourn (ed.), *Developing a Culture of Conflict Prevention*. Brussels: Madariaga Foundation, Bank of Sweden Tercentenary Foundation and Gidlunds. pp. 91–100.

Wallace, Michael 1979. 'Arms Races and Escalation: Some New Evidence', *Journal of Conflict Resolution*, 23: 3–16.

Wallensteen, Peter 1981. 'Incompatibility, Confrontation and War: Four Models and Three Historical Systems, 1816–1976', *Journal of Peace Research*, 18: 57–90.

Wallensteen, Peter 1984. 'Universalism vs Particularism: On the Limits of Major Power Order', *Journal of Peace Research*, 21: 243–57.

Wallensteen, Peter 1994a. *Från krig till fred: Om konfliktlösning i det global systemet* (*From War to Peace: On Conflict Resolution in the Global System*). Stockholm: Almqvist & Wiksell.

Wallensteen, Peter 1994b. 'Representing the World: A Security Council for the 21st Century', *Security Dialogue*, 25 (1): 63–75.

Wallensteen, Peter 2001. 'Reassessing Cases: Direct versus Structural Prevention', in David Malone and Fen Osler Hampson (eds), *From Reaction to Conflict Prevention: Opportunities for the UN System*. New York: International Peace Academy. pp. 213–28.

Wallensteen, Peter 2010. 'Strategic Peacebuilding: Concepts and Challenges', in Daniel Philpott and Gerard F. Powers (eds), *Strategies of Peace*. Oxford: Oxford University Press. pp. 45–64.

Wallensteen, Peter 2011a. 'The Origins of Contemporary Peace Research', in Kristine Höglund and Magnus Öberg (eds), *Understanding Peace Research*. London: Routledge. pp. 14–32.

Wallensteen, Peter 2011b. *Peace Research: Theory and Practice*. London: Routledge.

Wallensteen, Peter 2015. *Toward Quality Peace: Peacebuilding, Victory and World Order*. Oxford: Oxford University Press (forthcoming).

Wallensteen, Peter (ed.) 1998. *Preventing Violent Conflicts: Past Record and Future Challenges*. Uppsala: Department of Peace and Conflict Research, Uppsala University.

Wallensteen, Peter and Helena Grusell 2012. 'Targeting the Right Targets? The UN Use of Individual Sanctions', *Global Governance*, 18 (2): 207–30.

Wallensteen, Peter and Patrik Johansson 2014. 'The United Nations Security Council in State-Based Armed Conflicts', *SIPRI Yearbook 2014*. Oxford: Oxford University Press. pp. 56–69.

Wallensteen, Peter and Margareta Sollenberg 1998. 'Armed Conflict and Regional Conflict Complexes, 1989–1997', *Journal of Peace Research*, 35 (5): 593–606.

Wallensteen, Peter and Anders Bjurner (eds) 2015. *Regional Organizations and Peacemaking: Challengers to the UN?* London: Routledge.

Wallensteen, Peter and Carina Staibano (eds) 2005. *International Sanctions: Between Words and Wars in the Global System*. London: Routledge/Frank Cass.

Wallensteen, Peter, Erik Melander and Stina Högbladh 2012. 'Peace Agreements, Justice and Durable Peace', in Karin Aggestam and Annika Björkdahl (eds), *Rethinking Peacebuilding: The Quest for Just Peace in the Middle East and the Western Balkans*. London: Routledge. pp. 125–39.

REFERENCES

Wallensteen, Peter, Erik Melander and Frida Möller 2011. 'Preventing Genocide: The International Response', in Mark Anstey, Paul Meerts and I. William Zartman (eds), *The Slippery Slope to Genocide: Reducing Identity Conflicts and Preventing Mass Murder*. Oxford: Oxford University Press.

Wallensteen, Peter, Carina Staibano and Mikael Eriksson 2003. *Making Targeted Sanctions Effective: Guidelines for the Implementation of UN Policy Options*. Uppsala: Department of Peace and Conflict Research, Uppsala University.

Walter, B.F. 2004. 'Does Conflict Beget Conflict? Explaining Recurring Civil War', *Journal of Peace Research*, 41 (3): 371–88.

Waltz, Kenneth N. 1959. *Man, the State and War*. New York: Columbia University Press.

Waltz, Kenneth N. 1979. *Theory of International Politics*. Reading, MA: Addison-Wesley.

Wantechekon, Leonard 1999. *Why do Resource-Rich Countries have Authoritarian Governments?* New Haven, CT: Department of Political Science, Yale University. Mimeo.

Weart, Spencer R. 1998. *Never at War: Why Democracies Will Not Fight One Another*. New Haven, CO: Yale University Press.

Weber, Max 1964. *The Theory of Social and Economic Organization*. New York: Free Press.

Weiss, T.G. 2005. 'Compromise and Credibility: Security Council Reform?' *Security Dialogue*, 36 (2): 131–54.

Weiss, Thomas G., David Forsythe and Roger A. Coate 2013. *The United Nations and Changing World Politics* (7th edn). Boulder, CO: Westview Press.

Whitfield, Teresa 1999. 'The Role of the United Nations in El Salvador and Guatemala: A Preliminary Comparison', in Cynthia J. Arnson (ed.), *Comparative Peace Processes in Latin America*. Washington, DC: Woodrow Wilson Center Press, and Stanford, CA: Stanford University Press. pp. 257–90.

Wiberg, Håkan 1976/1990. *Konfliktteori och fredsforskning* (*Conflict Theory and Peace Research*) (2nd edn, 1990). Stockholm: Esselte Studium.

Woodworth, John A. 1999. 'Dispute Resolution in Bilateral Arms Control: The INF Experience', in Julie Dahlitz (ed.), *Peaceful Resolution of Major International Disputes*. New York and Geneva: United Nations. pp. 181–201.

World Summit Outcome 2005. United Nations General Assembly, September 15.

Wriggins, Howard 1995. 'Sri Lanka: Negotiations in a Secessionist Conflict', in I. William Zartman (ed.), *Elusive Peace: Negotiating an End to Civil Wars*. Washington, DC: Brookings Institution. pp. 35–58.

Wright, Quincy 1942/1965. *A Study of War* (2nd edn, 1965). Chicago, IL, and London: University of Chicago Press.

Zartman, I. William 1989. *Ripe for Resolution: Conflict and Intervention in Africa* (updated edn). New York and Oxford: Oxford University Press.

Zartman, I. William and Maureen R. Berman 1982. *The Practical Negotiator*. New Haven, CT, and London: Yale University Press.

Zartman, I. William and Alvaro de Soto 2010. *Timing Mediation Initiatives*. Washington, DC: United States of Peace Press and Johns Hopkins University, 51 pp.

REFERENCES

Zartman, I. William (ed.) 1995a. *Elusive Peace: Negotiating an End to Civil Wars*. Washington, DC: Brookings Institution.

Zartman, I. William (ed.) 1995b. *Collapsed States: The Disintegration and Restoration of Legitimate Authority*. Boulder, CO: Lynne Rienner.

Zartman, I. William and J. Lewis Rasmussen (eds) 1997. *Peacemaking in International Conflict: Methods and Techniques*. Washington, DC: United States Institute of Peace Press.

Websites

AKUF (Working Group on the Causes of War), University of Hamburg: www.sozialwiss.uni-hamburg.de/publish/Ipw/Akuf/

CIDCM (Center for International Development and Conflict Management), University of Maryland: www.cidcm.umd.edu

Correlates of War Project: www.correlatesofwar.org

Targeted Sanctions: www.smartsanctions.se

Uppsala Conflict Data Program: www.ucdp.uu.se

INDEX

THE WORLD BANK

Research Observer

Volume 21 • Number 1 • Spring 2006

Subscriptions

A subscription to *The World Bank Research Observer* (ISSN 0257-3032) comprises 2 issues. Prices include postage; for subscribers outside the Americas, issues are sent air freight.

Annual Subscription Rate (Volume 21, 2 issues, 2006)

Academic libraries

Print edition and site-wide online access: US$115/£73/€110

Print edition only: US$109/£69/€104

Site-wide online access only: US$104/£66/€99

Corporate

Print edition and site-wide online access: US$172/£109/€164

Print edition only: US$164/£104/€156

Site-wide online access only: US$155/£98/€147

Personal

Print edition and individual online access: US$41/£29/€44

Please note: £ Sterling rates apply in the UK, € in Europe, US$ elsewhere.

Readers with mailing addresses in non-OECD countries and in socialist economies in transition are eligible to receive complimentary subscriptions on request by writing to the UK address below.

There may be other subscription rates available; for a complete listing, please visit www.wbro.oxfordjournals.org/subscriptions.

Full prepayment in the correct currency is required for all orders. Orders are regarded as firm, and payments are not refundable. Subscriptions are accepted and entered on a complete volume basis. Claims cannot be considered more than four months after publication or date of order, whichever is later. All subscriptions in Canada are subject to GST. Subscriptions in the EU may be subject to European VAT. If registered, please supply details to avoid unnecessary charges. For subscriptions that include online versions, a proportion of the subscription price may be subject to UK VAT. Personal rates are applicable only when a subscription is for individual use and are not available if delivery is made to a corporate address.

Back issues: The current year and two previous years' issues are available from Oxford University Press. Previous volumes can be obtained from the Periodicals Service Company, 11 Main Street, Germantown, NY 12526, USA. E-mail: psc@periodicals.com. Tel: (518) 537-4700. Fax: (518) 537-5899.

Contact information: Journals Customer Service Department, Oxford University Press, Great Clarendon Street, Oxford OX2 6DP, UK. E-mail: jnls.cust.serv@oxfordjournals.org. Tel: +44 (0)1865 353907. Fax: +44 (0)1865 353485. **In the Americas, please contact:** Journals Customer Service Department, Oxford University Press, 2001 Evans Road, Cary, NC 27513, USA. E-mail: jnlorders@oxfordjournals.org. Tel: (800) 852-7323 (toll-free in USA/Canada) or (919) 677-0977. Fax: (919) 677-1714. **In Japan, please contact:** Journals Customer Service Department, Oxford University Press, 1-1-17-5F, Mukogaoka, Bunkyo-ku, Tokyo, 113-0023, Japan. E-mail: okudaoup@po.iijnet.or.jp. Tel: (03) 3813 1461. Fax: (03) 3818 1522.

Postal information: *The World Bank Research Observer* (ISSN 0257-3032) is published by Oxford University Press for the International Bank for Reconstruction and Development/THE WORLD BANK. Send address changes to *The World Bank Research Observer*, Journals Customer Service Department, Oxford University Press, 2001 Evans Road, Cary, NC 27513-2009. Communications regarding original articles and editorial management should be addressed to The Editor, *The World Bank Research Observer*, The World Bank, 1818 H Street, NW, Washington, D.C. 20433, USA.

Permissions: For information on how to request permissions to reproduce articles or information from this journal, please visit www.oxfordjournals.org/jnls/permissions.

Advertising: Inquiries about advertising should be sent to Helen Pearson, Oxford Journals Advertising, PO Box 347, Abingdon OX14 1GJ, UK. E-mail: helen@oxfordads.com. Tel: +44 (0)1235 201904. Fax: +44 (0)8704 296864.

Disclaimer: Statements of fact and opinion in the articles in *The World Bank Research Observer* are those of the respective authors and contributors and not of the International Bank for Reconstruction and Development/THE WORLD BANK or Oxford University Press. Neither Oxford University Press nor the International Bank for Reconstruction and Development/THE WORLD BANK make any representation, express or implied, in respect of the accuracy of the material in this journal and cannot accept any legal responsibility or liability for any errors or omissions that may be made. The reader should make her or his own evaluation as to the appropriateness or otherwise of any experimental technique described.

Paper used: *The World Bank Research Observer* is printed on acid-free paper that meets the minimum requirements of ANSI Standard Z39.48-1984 (Permanence of Paper).

Indexing and abstracting: *The World Bank Research Observer* is indexed and/or abstracted by ABI/INFORM, CAB *Abstracts, Current Contents/Social and Behavioral Sciences, Journal of Economic Literature/EconLit, PAIS International, RePEc (Research in Economic Papers), Social Services Citation Index*, and *Wilson Business Abstracts*.

Copyright © The International Bank for Reconstruction and Development/THE WORLD BANK

All rights reserved; no part of this publication may be reproduced, stored in a retrieval system, or transmitted in any form or by any means, electronic, mechanical, photocopying, recording, or otherwise without prior written permission of the publisher or a license permitting restricted copying issued in the UK by the Copyright Licensing Agency Ltd, 90 Tottenham Court Road, London W1P 9HE, or in the USA by the Copyright Clearance Center, 222 Rosewood Drive, Danvers, MA 01923.